# Navies
## of the
## Napoleonic Era

*Uniform with this book*
Armies of the Napoleonic Era *by Otto von Pivka*

# Navies
# of the
# Napoleonic Era

**Otto von Pivka**

**David & Charles**
Newton Abbot   London

**Hippocrene Books Inc**
New York

This edition first published in 1980
in Great Britain by
David & Charles (Publishers) Ltd   Newton Abbot   Devon
and in the United States of America by
Hippocrene Books Inc   171 Madison Avenue
New York   N.Y. 10016

ISBN 0-7153-7767-1 (Great Britain)
ISBN 0-88254-505-1 (United States)
Library of Congress Catalog Card Number 80-80652

Printed in Great Britain
by Biddles Limited, Guildford, Surrey

# Contents

# Acknowledgements

A book of this type is bound to be more or less a team effort, spanning as it does so many different states and aspects of a turbulent historic period.

I am very grateful to all those who have given assistance in the form of data or advice and these include the naval attachés of Denmark, Holland, Italy, Portugal and Sweden; the directors and staffs of the following naval museums: National Maritime Museum, London; Marinmuseet, Karlskrona, Sweden; Museu de Marinha, Lisbon and the Turkish Naval Museum, Besiktas, Istanbul. Many contemporary sources have been used and inevitably there is some discrepancy between them.

I am, as all too often, greatly indebted to the staff of the Ministry of Defence Library in Whitehall, particularly Mr Andrews, Mr Potts and Miss Glover.

Finally, good friends have also been of great assistance; I express my thanks to Fred Feather for his invaluable help with the Russian and Turkish sections, to Mike Cox and to Miss Beryl Leman of Ashfield-cum-Thorpe for provision of excellent data for many of the maps in the book. It is my sincere hope that even old sea dogs may glean the odd fact or two of interest from this, necessarily compact book which it has been great fun to write.

Otto von Pivka
Ashfield-cum-Thorpe 1979

# Introduction

The aim of this book is to give the reader a concise, readily understandable account of the navies of the period 1792–1815, of the ships they sailed and of their achievements.

All too often in the past accounts have been produced of land warfare alone or of naval warfare also in isolation. History is never so tidy a study that such extractions can be made; naval and military affairs impinge upon one another and are both inextricably bound up with social, economic and political events. Any attempt to study one of these in isolation must produce only part answers. For this reason the writer has tried to illustrate the major interactions between political, military and naval affairs although lack of space has meant that selectivity and brevity have necessarily limited what can be presented.

An effort has also been made to explain some of the naval terms and techniques used so that a layman can understand much more of the atmosphere of the events portrayed.

One facet of naval battles of this era – the age of sail – which may not be readily apparent, is the extremely slow and cumbersome manner in which engagements often developed. There was no dashing cavalry charge to cut across the 'field of battle', no steam-driven destroyers creaming their wakes towards the enemy's capital ships. This was the period of the graceful, slow-motion battle, often fought in faint winds, sometimes in dead calm where opposing ships would lie like dogs for hours in full view of one another, totally unable to manoeuvre.

Some major battles were fought with both sides anchored (the Nile) while in others, in becalmed situations, ships would launch their long boats and tow the mighty three-deckers laboriously into a suitable combat position.

The weather could, and often did, frustrate carefully woven battle plans with its violence as well as with its placidity, a sudden storm could scatter opposing fleets making them common refugees in search of safety – or it could, as after Trafalgar, rob the victor of his prizes or wreak more destruction than opposing cannon ever could.

Some fleets, constantly at sea for years like the British, lost far more ships to the weather than they did to the enemy.

Researching for this book has been a fascinating experience; it is hoped that the reader will find it not only informative but interesting as well.

# Part One
# The Ships and the Men

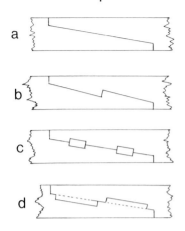

**1**

a

b

c

d

**2**

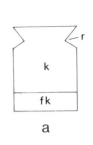

d

r

k

fk

a

r

k

fk

b

**3**

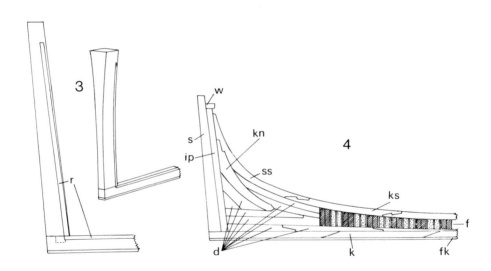

r

w

s

ip

kn

ss

**4**

ks

f

d

k

fk

Ship construction
1. Scarphs (plan view of keel in each case)
   a – plain, b – hooked, c – tabled with coaks, d – tabled without coaks
2. Cross sections of keel and false keel (a – forward and amidships, b – stern)
   d – deadwood, fk – false keel, k – keel, r – rabbet
3. Sternpost and after end of keel
   r – rabbet
4. Sternpost with deadwood (side view)
   d – deadwood, f – main frames (hatched) and filling frames (dotted), fk – false keel,
   ip – inner post, k – keel, kn – knee of sternpost, ks – keelson, s – sternpost,
   ss – sternson, w – wing transom (end view)

# Construction of Ships of the Period

Long before any work commenced at the shipyard, the most suitable timber, oak and elm, had to be planted, grown in the right manner, selected, cut and seasoned and again selected. Certain trees were deliberately deformed so that they grew in a curve; these timbers were of great value as we shall see later. Seasoning could take from two to three years and a mature tree might require sixty years to develop so the shipbuilding industry of the nineteenth century was a long-term, deliberate and fairly inflexible operation. Care was taken to maintain forests of the right trees, and Britain, not being able to grow all the oak and elm she needed, imported large quantities from the Baltic states who were also a vital source of coal tar, hemp and oakum.

When the shipbuilding industries of several European nations were working at full tilt (as from 1792–1814) other woods were examined to see if they would be suitable for shipbuilding and could ease the bottleneck on oak and elm supplies. Maple wood was tried but eventually rejected and the Spanish *Santissima-Trinidad* – one of the largest ships of the era – was built of cedar wood. Many British frigates and sloops were built of fir and seem to have functioned well enough.

Shipbuilding took place, logically enough, on waterways which would be capable of conveying the completed ship to her fitting-out berth. Most ships were built on slipways, angled down towards the water's edge so that, when finished, the ship would slide into the water of her own accord. This was the cheapest method but another system was by use of the dry dock whereby a dock would be pumped dry, the ship built in it and then the water allowed to enter slowly and float the new ship. After this, the gates of the dock would be opened and the ship towed out. Most slipway-built ships were launched bows first as this was the blunt end of the craft and would most quickly bring the ship to a halt by resistance of the water after it had slid down the slipway. On narrow waterways smaller craft might be built and launched broadside to the water.

The building slipway was prepared with a series of massive timber blocks placed about 1.5m apart; the gradient was about 1:12 or 8%. The top of each block was faced with straight-grained oak, the grain running down the slope, and each block was about 1.5m tall so as to permit men to work underneath the ship. Along the blocks was laid the keel, made up of various lengths of English elm – a wood which stands up well to constant immersion in salt water. The different pieces of the keel were joined by scarphs of which there were various types but all scarphs in the keel were in the vertical plane. A description of the building of a first rate British ship in the late nineteenth century follows.

## The Keel

This type of ship of the British navy had a keel of about 53.2m (175ft) in which were to be no more than seven separate sections (thus each was 7.6m). Each scarph was at least 1.5m long to ensure maximum possible strength and before being bolted together with eight 3.1cm diameter bolts, the inner faces were lined with tarred flannel. Prior to the keel sections being bolted together a 'rabbet' or horizontal groove was cut out along each upper side to form a bed for the lowest or 'garboard' strake of the outside planking. The finished keel was 53.3cm square in the centre of the ship and while its height remained constant throughout, it tapered in width to 40.6cm at the sternpost and 45.7cm at the stem.

The keel was now 'faired' or straightened along its length and then secured to the underlying blocks with metal spikes or 'tree nails' (large round wooden pegs) to prevent subsequent lateral movement.

## The Stern

The next operation was to set in the sternpost, preferably made from a single piece of oak 9.1m long and 66cm square at the top. At the bottom it was as wide as the keel but 91.4cm along the fore and aft axis. It was jointed to the keel by a mortice and tenon to one-third of the keel depth and stood with a slight rake aft (it leaned backwards) but was vertical when viewed from along the keel axis. A rabbet was cut in both forward edges to take the rear planking. An 'inner post' was then 'fayed' on to the forefront of the sternpost. Faying meant ensuring that the two surfaces were in contact over their whole areas, and the inner post was jointed to the keel as for the sternpost, the two posts were fixed together with tree nails or bolts.

For the greater part of the midships section, a ship was roughly square in cross section; towards stem and stern, however, the vessel tapered away so as to present less resistance to the water through which she moved. As the existing keel was flat and thin, it had to be extended vertically at stem and stern to allow strong joints to be made with the ribs or 'frames' which would be fixed to the keel at acute vertical angles in the bow and stern sections. This extension was achieved by means of 'deadwood' and there was a lot more of it at the stern than at the bows.

In the stern, the more elongated shape that could be achieved, the less drag there would be as the ship passed through the water and this was termed the 'run' of a ship. The finer the run (more elongated shape) the less drag and the quicker a ship would answer the helm.

Deadwood was built up of several horizontal pieces of oak, the lowest fayed and bolted to the keel and being of the same width as the keel (less one width of planking on each side). Where deadwood came into contact with the sternpost it was either bolted or tenoned into it. The deadwood tapered from the stern down towards the midships and was wider at the top than at the keel.

## The Stem

Due to the very bluff shape of ships' bows at this period, there was not the need for nearly as much deadwood here as at the stern. The stem was curved and thus had to be made of several pieces of oak, as wide as the keel, scarphed together, raked forward and jointed to the keel by the 'boxing'. It tapered in towards the top. Over the boxing, on the inside curve of the stem was the 'apron' – a sort of second stem, also formed of several pieces of oak. The scarphs of apron and stem did not coincide; they 'gave shift' to one another – like successive layers of brickwork. The rear sides of the stem were rabbeted to accommodate the outer planking. Projecting forward from the stem were added the 'gripe' (at keel level and designed as an extension of the keel to help a ship sail to windward) and the 'knee of the head' which was a survival from the days when fighting ships had rams at the prow. The knee of the head supported the 'beak head', which gave a false impression of fineness to the bluff bows, and the beak head culminated in the ship's figurehead. The beak head was pierced with several holes to take

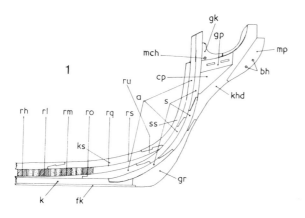

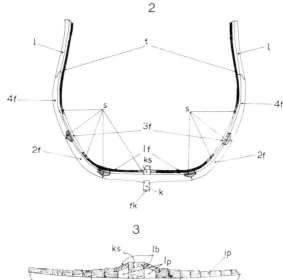

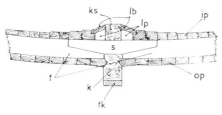

**1** Side view of stem
   a – apron, bh – bobstay holes, cp – chock piece, fk – false keel, gk – gammoning
   knee and extension piece, gp – gammon piece, gr – gripe, k – keel, khd – knee of
   the head, ks – keelson, mch – mainstay collar hole, mp – main piece, rh – rib h,
   rl – rib l, rm – rib m, ro – rib o, rq – rib q, rs – rib s, ru –rib u, s – stem,
   ss – stemson
**2** A main frame or rib
   1f – 1st futtock, 2f – 2nd futtock, 3f – 3rd futtock, 4f – 4th futtock, fk – false keel,
   k – keel, ks – keelson, l – lengthening piece, s – angular scarph chocks, t – toptimber
**3** Section through keel and limbers
   f – frame or rib, fk – false keel, ip – inner planking, k – keel, ks – keelson,
   lb – limber boards, lp – limber passages, op – outer planking, s – angular
   scarph chock

15

the heavy rope, or 'gammoning', which lashed the bowsprit into place and to take the bobstays which gave the bowsprit lateral stability.

To either side of the stem were the 'knightheads' between which the bowsprit would later lie; they were bored through at the top to take the mainstay collar.

## The Outer Frames or Ribs

On a ship of this size, each midships frame was in the approximate shape of a huge 'U' about 15.2m high and of the same width. For greatest strength, it was desirable that the grain of the oak should follow the curves as closely as possible and it was at the lower, sharpest, corners that specially grown 'compass timber' was most valuable as it was grown curved and did not have to be bent into shape or constructed of several separate pieces.

Each frame was built of two slices, the scarphs on the one giving shift to those of its fellow. They were constructed according to huge templates and placed at right angles to the keel at intervals of 84cm for a first rate ship.

The dividing line between fore and aft of a ship was known as the 'dead flat' and those frames extending forwards were labelled sequentially A, B, C etc while those extending to the rear were numbered 1, 2, 3 etc towards the stern. The dead flat was located at a variable point slightly forward of the mainmast.

Each frame was built up from the keel outwards in pieces named sequentially as follows: First half frame – floor, 2nd futtock, 4th futtock and lengthening piece; Second half frame – 1st futtock, 3rd futtock, top timber.

The floor consisted of one piece of timber (oak), the centrepoint of which was jointed to the top of the keel. The outer ends of the floors were slightly higher than the centres. The 1st and 2nd futtocks were usually of compass timber, the 1st futtock was jointed into the keel by a central 'chock' and the two half frames were bolted together.

Each frame was built, according to light wooden patterns prepared in the moulding loft, on a platform beside the ship and hoisted into position when completed. At this point they were 'horned' or set at right angles to the keel and shored into position. All such frames at right angles were termed 'square frames'. Towards stem and stern the frames were increasingly inclined away from the midships section at their outer ends and were called 'cant frames'. There were about a dozen cant frames at each end of the ship and they started at about the foremast and mizzenmast joints.

When all square frames had been set up, stout timbers, called 'ribbands' (or harpins at the cant frames) were nailed along their outer edges at various heights. These ribbands had been specially shaped in the moulding loft to the ship's plans and were used firstly to give the frames lateral rigidity during building and secondly to show up any errors in conformity of any individual frame.

The outer surface of each frame was bevelled off towards stem or stern so that the outer planking would easily be fayed onto it.

At the bows, where cant frames were no longer of practical use owing to the acute angle at which they would have to be set to the keel, 'hawse pieces' – vertical timbers parallel to and flanking the knightheads – were used instead. The hawse holes were cut through these timbers.

At the stern the cant frames had no floors, were fixed directly onto the deadwood and ran up to the 'wing transom', this was a lateral timber set horizontally about 90cm below the top of the sternpost and resting on the top of the inner sternpost. It was a vital timber, selected with great care and made from a single piece of oak 10.7m long, 38cm thick and 69cm wide at the centrepoint, this point being about 15cm higher than the extremities and projecting about 18cm more to the rear than the ends. It was horned with great care and was the foundation for the entire 'counter' or stern erection. Each outer end was about 53cm wide. The aftermost cant frames were called 'fashion pieces' and extended from the deadwood up to the extremities of the wing transom to which they were fayed and bolted. The transom was further secured to the other cant frames by two powerful 'knees' (sharply angled timbers) 5.5m long along the insides of the frames, 2.3m long the forward edge of the transom.

The gaps between sternpost and fashion pieces were filled in with six or so horizontal 'filling transoms' below and parallel with the wing transom, each fixed to the sternpost at their centres and to the fashion pieces at their extremities. Below the bottom filling transom were two small triangular gaps, one each side of the sternpost. These were filled with vertical timbers extending to the deadwood and termed 'filling pieces'. Between each frame in a ship 'filling frames' would be inserted in order to minimise the enclosed air spaces within the lower hull and to give greater buoyancy.

The framing of the ship was now completed and a series of locking devices were next added to ensure subsequent rigidity; the first was the 'keelson', laid along the top of the keel, made of six pieces of elm 51cm square scarphed together, with each scarph being 1.75m long and in the horizontal plane (as opposed to the vertical plane scarphs employed on the keel). It was bolted to the keel with 5cm diameter copper bolts and connected by scarphs to the 'sternson' (which ran up the inside of the inner sternpost) and to the 'stemson' (which ran up the inside of the apron).

An inside skin of planking was now attached to the ribs and at the higher levels gaps (for ventilating the enclosed air spaces deep in the floor and thus preventing rotting timbers) would be left of about 10cm between certain planks. Inside this inner planking another set of inner frames or 'riders' was inserted to give greater strength. As with the outer frames, the riders were made up of floors, futtocks, etc.

On either side of the keelson the inner planking was arranged to form a gutter or 'limber passage' so that bilge water – which inevitably seeped through between the outer planks – could run into a central well at the foot of the bilge pump which was located amidships. The limber passages were covered by the 'limber boards' which could be easily removed for cleaning purposes.

'Deck hooks' were now inserted at stem and stern, inside the inner planking. These were of compass timber and laid athwartships at levels coinciding with the bottom of the deck planking to be inserted later. Other hooks also built into the ship and not designed to support decks were called 'breast hooks'. In the bows the deck hooks were extended along the ship's sides by 'ekers' – pieces of timber lying along the inside of the inner planking. 'Deck clamps' were now added; they were horizontal strakes of timber, a little below the level of each deck and were designed to support the lateral 'deck beams'.

These deck beams traversed the ship and were made of two or three lengths of timber joined by long scarphs. Their outer ends rested on the deck clamps and they were supported along their lengths by two or more strong pillars. All deck beams were convex when viewed from fore and aft, with a central point higher than the outer ends. On the gundeck this 'rounding up' was about 15cm, the middle deck 17.5cm and on the upper deck 20cm. This aided the ship to shed water.

To strengthen the ship, each beam was supported by 'knees' (right-angled pieces of timber, later reinforced with iron). The 'lodging knee' was placed in the fore or aft direction in the angle between deck beam and the side, the 'hanging knee' was placed vertically beneath the beam end and the side. Usually each beam had only one lodging knee at each end but at vulnerable points (athwart the masts) they would have two, one each towards stem and stern. Athwart, and to the fore of the mainmast, one or two 'beam arms' would be inserted. These were extra beams lying in the same horizontal planes as the deck beams and extended in a very broad 'V' shape (when viewed from above) across the ship, reaching to about the halfway point between the two external deck beam ends.

'Carlings' (short timbers) were inserted in a fore and aft direction between the deck beams; there were about four lines of these along the ship and these were jointed into lateral 'ledges' (thinner pieces of timber).

This completed the skeleton of the ship and if time was not pressing (as in war), it was customary to leave the ship to weather and settle for about two years before putting on the outside planking and the decks.

## The Outer Planking and the False Keel

After the seasoning was over, the ribbands were removed and the outer planking applied. Until late in the nineteenth century this planking was horizontal but it was discovered that diagonal planking lent extra strength, so this was introduced. On top of the wing transom was built the 'counter' extending upwards and out to the rear; on top of the counter were constructed three tiers of windows leading into the quarter deck, upper deck and middle deck (from top to bottom).

The lower masts would be stepped into the ship prior to launching; these massive pieces were formed of dozens of carefully interlocked lengths of timber and were set into great blocks of timber at keelson level.

To the rear of the sternpost was fastened the rudder, fixed by means of several heavy iron hinges. Movement of the ship's wheel was translated by a system of chains and gears to lateral motion on a chain loop running from side to side of the ship usually at the rear of the middle deck. To this chain was fixed a horizontal lever connected to the top of the rudder. In rough weather it would often require four or six men to control the ship's wheel to give the desired direction.

When the ship was practically ready to be launched, the oak caps on the tops of the blocks of timber supporting the keel were removed one by one and a 'false keel' of elm, about 15cm thick, was nailed on under the keel proper. It is not known why this operation was not carried out as the first step in the building process instead of being practically the last. The false keel fulfilled three aims: first, it extended the keel and gave the vessel improved properties for sailing into the wind; second, it protected the real keel from damage if the ship ran aground; and third, it could be ripped off relatively easily if the ship ran aground and this could make it easier to refloat the vessel.

The ship would now be ballasted, usually with pig iron, to give her greater stability in the water and could be launched and towed off to be 'fitted out'. Fitting out consisted of adding topmasts, yards, rigging, guns, stores and supplies and this process could also take months before a new ship was

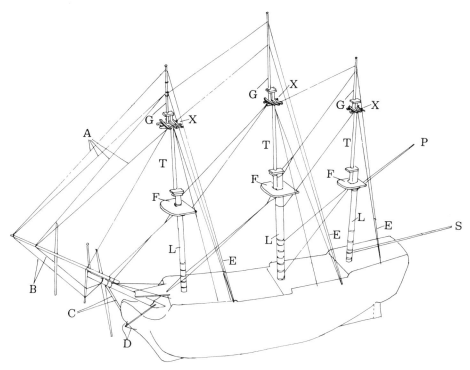

Diagram of standing rigging of 1st rate British ship (not to scale; no shrouds shown)

A – jib stays
B – bowsprit guys
C – bobstays
D – bumpkin guys
E – back stays
F – fighting tops

G – topgallant masts
L – lower masts
T – topmasts
X – crosstrees
P – spanker gaff
S – spanker boom

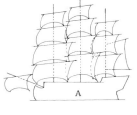

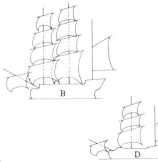

Diagrammatic representation of main sail characteristics of various types of ship
(not to scale; no studding sails or staysails shown)

A – ship of the line or frigate
B – barque
C – brig or aviso

D – schooner
E – cutter
F – ketch

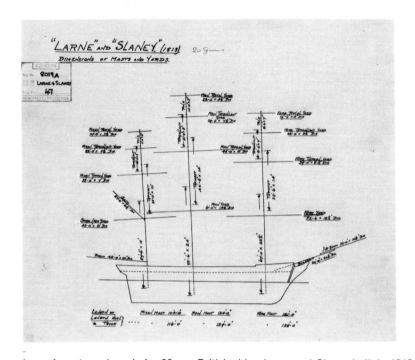

Dimensions of masts and yards for 20-gun British ships *Larne* and *Slaney* built in 1813
(*National Maritime Museum*)
Bowsprit – 8.84m × 57.2cm diameter (29ft × 22½in)
Jib boom – 10.06m × 26.7cm diameter (33ft × 10½in)
Foremast – 36.88m overall length (121ft); 39.01m keel to truck (tip) (128ft)
   Lower foremast –19.51m × 57.2cm diameter (64ft × 22½in)
   Fore topmast – 12.04m × 35.6cm diameter (39ft 6in × 14in)
   Topgallant – 5.64m × 17.8cm diameter (18ft 6in × 7in)
   Pole – 3.81m × 17.8cm diameter (12ft 6in × 7in)
Foremast yards
   Main – 16.00m × 31.8cm diameter (52ft 6in × 12½in)
   Topsail – 11.89m × 21.6cm diameter (39ft × 8½in)
   Topgallant – 7.93m × 16.5cm diameter (26ft × 6½in)
   Royal – 5.94m × 10.2cm diameter (19ft 6in × 4in)
Mainmast – overall length 40.84m (134ft); from keel to truck 42.7m (139ft)
   Lower mainmast – 22.10m × 61cm diameter (72ft 6in × 24in)
   Topmast – 13.56m × 35.6cm diameter (44ft 6in × 14in)
   Topgallant – 6.40m × 20.3cm diameter (21ft × 8in)
   Pole – 4.27m × 20.3cm diameter (14ft × 8in)
Mainmast yards
   Main – 18.59m ×36.8cm diameter (61ft × 14½in)
   Topsail – 13.72m × 25.4cm diameter (45ft × 10in)
   Topgallant – 8.99m × 19.1cm diameter (29ft 6in × 7½in)
   Royal – 6.71m × 11.4cm diameter (22ft × 4½in)
Mizzenmast – overall length 31.7m (104ft); from keel to truck 35.36m (116ft)
   Lower mizzzenmast –17.53m ×45.72cm diameter (57ft 6in ×18in)
   Topmast – 10.06m × 25.4cm diameter (33ft × 10in)
   Topgallant – 4.88m × 15.24cm diameter (16ft × 6in)
   Pole – 3.35m × 15.24cm diameter (11ft × 6in)
Mizzenmast yards
   Cross jack – 13.11m × 25.4cm diameter (43ft × 10in)
   Topsail – 10.06m × 17.78cm diameter (33ft × 7in)
   Topgallant – 6.71m × 13.97cm diameter (22ft × 5½in)
   Royal – 4.27m × 8.89cm diameter (14ft × 3½in)
   Gaff – 8.84m × 16.51cm diameter (29ft × 6½in)
   Boom – 12.8m × 25.4cm diameter (42ft × 10in)

actually ready to be joined by her crew and taken out on her maiden voyage to be 'worked up' into an efficient ship of the line.

When a ship was in service, seaweed, barnacles and other parasites would attach themselves to her wooden bottom and, with increasing growth, cause reduced speed. Periodically the ship would have to be beached and the bottom scraped clean or she would become too slow to manoeuvre. In the 1790s the British began to cover the underwater section of the ships' hulls with copper plate which much retarded the growth of the seaweed and barnacles. This process was of course extremely expensive but resulted in ships which were faster for longer periods and required less maintenance. It gave rise to the expression 'copper-bottomed' as being synonymous with excellence.

# Life at Sea

**Discipline**

Regardless of which navy of this era is taken for close examination, the conditions of life on board a warship were extremely similar.

Much is heard of the terrible brutality, almost sadism, of the British naval code of discipline with its inhuman floggings or beatings for trivial offences and the all too frequent use of the death penalty. The same criticism has also been levelled at the British army of the period; some regiments even had their suffering under the lash eternalised in nicknames – the Northamptonshire Regiment was known as 'The Steelbacks' from the stoicism with which the men endured their endless floggings. To put this brutality in the armed services in perspective, it should be realised that the civilian population of Britain, and many other countries, lived in an age when human life was cheap and when theft, poaching and many other offences were punishable by death or transportation to the colonies for long periods. Life in the late eighteenth century was a brutalising affair and order was enforced in the then appropriate manner. The disciplinary codes of the armed forces of other European nations were no less harsh in many instances than that of the British but there was to be an exception; a turning point and this was the post-revolutionary French army and navy. Under the new disciplinary code drawn up when the old royalist regime was swept away, physical abuse was formally abolished as a punishment and was replaced with varying degrees of arrest. The visible symptom of this change was that French officers and NCOs abandoned the canes which had for centuries formed part of the symbolism of their office and been instruments of discipline.

So we have a system where servicemen generally were subject to a code of discipline which was only marginally worse than the contemporary criminal law although of course there were some captains who were far harsher in their allocation of punishment than others; but even the much-maligned Captain Bligh of the *Bounty* was reckoned by his fellow officers not to be exceptionally severe with his men.

**Daily Routine**

Apart from divisions of rank, the ship's company was split into two other main sections – the 'idlers' on one hand and the main body on the other. Idlers were the technical specialists and artificers – painters, coopers, butchers and the barber among them. These men worked by day but did not stand watch like the rest of the ship's company at night. The main body of the men were divided into two watches, 'port' and 'starboard', who worked and rested turn and turn about, manning the ship and adjusting (trimming) the sails according to wind and weather. The men who went aloft for the hazardous task of reefing or letting out the topgallant and royal sails were specially selected for this hazardous task and their dexterity could earn a ship the reputation of being smartest in the fleet by the speed with which canvas could be set.

On a fighting ship the bulk of the space was allocated to the guns and associated equipment as first priority, human beings had to squeeze in around these essentials as best they could. The men were accommodated on the gundecks and lived in 'messes' of eight men each who ate around a table slung from the rafters between the guns. The table was kept lashed up out

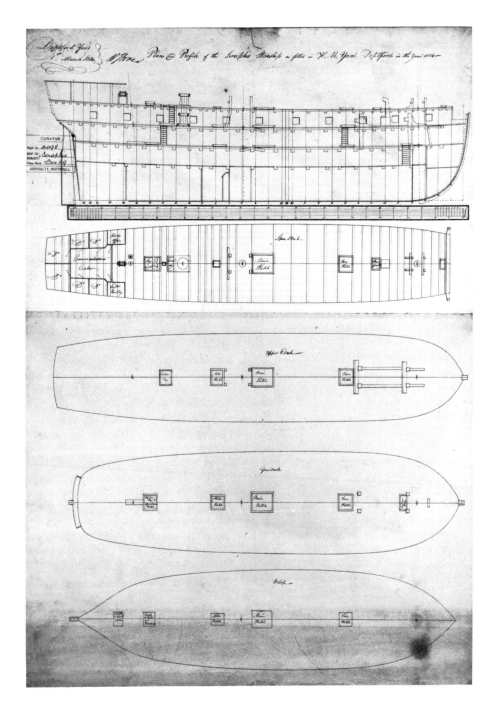

Plan and profile of the storeship *Seraphis* as fitted in HM Deptford Yard in 1814.
This fleet auxiliary, fitted to carry 22 guns, was devoted mainly to cargo carrying; the
rearmost hatch on the orlop deck is labelled 'spirit room' (*National Maritime Museum*)

of the way when not in use. They slept in canvas hammocks slung from the beams when in use, and tightly rolled up and lashed into a 'sausage' and tied around the vertical supports along the gundecks when the men were on duty.

The marines were kept separate from the sailors and always acted as the enforcers of the captain's orders on discipline.

Officers lived in the rear of the ship, in much better conditions than those of the men but still very cramped when compared to conditions ashore. The captain enjoyed the best accommodation of course and was frequently accompanied by his wife.

## Rations

The problem of keeping food fresh for long periods had not really been well solved at this stage and the rations on board ship were generally terrible, sometimes revolting. They consisted mainly of salt meat, pease pudding, rancid butter, dubious cheese, the legendary ship's biscuit (always infested with weevils), water (which ranged from brackish to foul) and a liberal ration of alcohol – beer and rum – which must have been one of the few things which made life bearable. The ration of beer was a gallon per man per day; rum was issued at a gill per man per day. It was not until the 1970s that the Royal Navy finally stopped issuing every man with his free daily ration of rum – some customs die hard! Scurvy was the common disease which affected men deprived of vegetables and other vitamin-bearing foods for long periods and the British had long since taken the precaution of issuing lime juice (rich in vitamin C) to their warships which gave rise to the nickname 'Limeys' applied to the British by the Americans. Fresh vegetables were of course taken aboard ship whenever possible but with navies cruising for long periods on blockade duty like the British, these were soon eaten and resupply was often impossible.

Officers were of course insulated from the harsher side of the seamen's diet because they could afford to bring on board their own private supplies of food and wine.

One method of improving food at sea was the practice of taking cows, pigs, sheep and chickens on board to be slaughtered later in the voyage as required. These animals were kept in the manger at the forward end of the gundeck.

It was the poor diet, coupled with very long periods of duty at sea, low pay, harsh discipline and the fact that many sailors were cheated out of their pay and prize money which led to the mutinies in the Royal Navy in 1797. These were suppressed but conditions of service did change slightly for the better as a result.

## Action at Sea

Clearing the ships for action was a process, carried out at great speed (and lasting only some five or six minutes on an efficient ship) by which the daily domestic clutter of a ship was re-organised so that an enemy could be engaged efficiently.

All the hammocks were brought up on deck and stowed in the netting and canvas cages on top of the bulwarks where they gave protection against hostile small arms fire to the men on deck. If guns were situated in or were to be fought from the wardroom, all furniture there, specially designed to fold up, was stowed away and the guns brought in (if not already there).

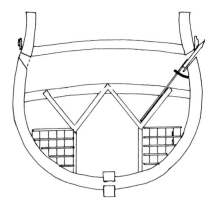 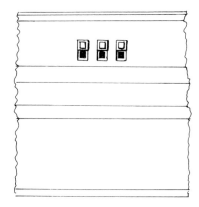

Possible arrangement for firing rockets broadside from a vessel; note iron sparkguard under rocket warhead

On deck the royal, topgallant and coursing sails were reefed and boarding nets were slung up all around the ship to prevent hostile boarders swinging over from the enemy rigging. The rope cradles of the yards would be reinforced with chains to prevent them crashing down on the gun crews if the usual ropes holding them were to be cut by shot, and all decks would be soaked with water and strewn with sand. This hindered the outbreak of fire and helped the barefooted men keep a grip on the pitching, rolling deck.

### The Guns

Naval guns were essentially just the same as those used in land warfare except that they were generally of heavier calibre and their carriages were not designed to move far or fast. Each gun was held in position by a complex system of ropes and pulleys to stop it rolling about and causing damage in heavy weather. The guns fired through gunports which were normally kept shut to prevent ingress of sea water. One British ship is recorded as not having been able to use the guns on her lower deck during action in a storm because the ports were so low that the ship was in danger of being sunk if they were kept open.

To bring a gun into action the port had first to be opened and held up with a rope and pulley. The cartridge was then loaded and rammed home, the pan around the touch hole filled with gunpowder and the gun 'run out' by means of being moved up to the gunport with the pulleys and held there if needed until the piece was fired.

Each gun barrel was held by a very strong cable secured to the bulkhead at the sides of the gunport at both ends and looped through a large ring at the breech end of the barrel. It was this cable which took up the recoil when the gun was fired. To fire the gun most navies of the period used the 'slow match' – a slow-burning fuse – as in land artillery. This had the disadvantage of being a naked spark and should it be overset by motion of the ship or by effects of enemy shot, it could fall into nearby gunpowder and cause fire or explosion.

The British navy had introduced a newer, safer system in about 1790 by mounting a flintlock onto each gun barrel just by the touch hole. When the gun was loaded, the pan of the flintlock could be filled with powder, closed

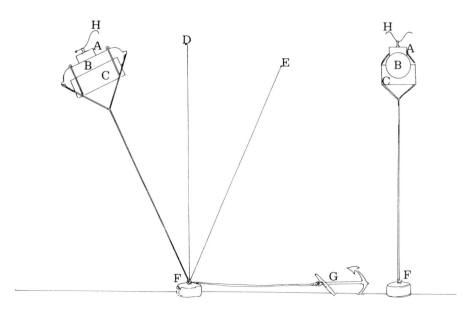

Fulton's torpedo in the static role

and cocked. By pulling a lanyard the flint would strike the steel pan cover, knocking it open and sending a spark into the powder, igniting it and causing it to burn into the touch hole to ignite the main charge.

The gun would shoot backwards with the recoil, would then be pulled fully back, swabbed out and reloaded. The use of flexible ramrods made of stiff cable enabled the rate of fire to be increased.

Ammunition was kept deep in the ship in the magazine and cartridges were taken to the guns by the 'powder monkeys' – the ship's boys.

## Medical Care

As in contemporary civilian practice, the naval medicine of the Napoleonic wars was often horrific when compared with modern methods. Ships were veritable hotbeds of corruption and disease with rats living and dying in the lower decks, hundreds of men cramped into insanitary, dank, gloomy, badly ventilated wooden caves and existing on food which was frequently only just short of poisonous itself.

The forecastle was usually the sick bay and the casualties from disease in the world's fleets at this time often exceeded those caused by enemy action. The same was true of the armies of the period.

During a battle the surgeon would set up to ply his trade in the cockpit, deep in the ship's bowels where his skill was all too often limited to the speed with which he could saw off a shattered limb (without anaesthetics) and sew up the stump and not cause the unfortunate patient so much post-operational shock that he would die of a wound which today would probably be considered minor.

26

# Naval Tactics 1792

It was considered best at that time to attack an enemy fleet in line ahead from the windward side, the approach being made at an angle to the course of the enemy vessels thus exposing the attackers to the raking fire from the opposing broadsides. There was no conscious attempt to overwhelm or cut out part of the enemy force; this was to come later, as did the operation of breaking through the enemy line.

Naval ships had by now developed into fairly efficient mobile artillery batteries carrying guns throwing shot of up to 42lb in weight and able to cruise for weeks on end without calling at a port to replenish. Special projectiles had been developed for sea warfare; red-hot shot had been adopted from land warfare so that enemy vessels could be set afire and several types of special shot had been invented to tear away rigging and spars to disable an opponent. These projectiles were designed to fit a normal cannon, like round shot, but when fired they expanded into two halves held together by chain or rods or developed into a grapnel hook configuration so that maximum damage could be caused to ropes, shrouds, stays and sails.

The most effective range for naval guns was about 500 paces (approximately 400yds), but the mobile nature of the gun platform (the ship) pitching and rolling in the swell added a hazard which the land artillery did not have to cope with. Round shot would bounce off the sea if it struck at the right angle and speed; it was British policy to aim for the hull of an enemy vessel while the French tended to fire into an opponent's rigging with the aim of disabling her as quickly as possible. The British tactic led to heavy casualties on the other vessel and usually resulted in them overpowering the enemy guns, thus bringing the fight to a bloody decision.

It was not the French habit to engage in a battle at sea unless it would bring some tangible result apart from the possible destruction of the enemy ships. The British on the other hand regarded destruction of a hostile vessel an end in itself and could be relied upon to attack any enemy seen if they possibly could, providing always that there was a faint chance of success. The heaviest weight of fire could be brought to bear by a ship of the line firing her entire broadside at a target directly on her beam – on either side. A ship had very little firepower either directly ahead or astern and if a ship was struck by a broadside from another, either through the stem or stern, she was termed to be 'raked' by the shot and this was most damaging as the shot could penetrate bow or stern walls and travel the length of the ship wreaking havoc as it went.

A sea battle could only be truly decisive if the beaten party could be sunk or brought into the power of the victor. The fruits of victory could be snatched away by a storm or poor visibility or by the inability of the victor to move to secure the enemy prizes. This meant that it was often necessary to invade the enemy ship – to board her – with one's own sailors and marines and fight down the enemy crew. Indeed it was often the case that naval engagements were carried out at such close range that sharpshooters with muskets, positioned in the rigging of one ship, could bring effective fire to bear on the enemy crew.

In 1804 the Briton, John Clerk (not a seaman but one who had analysed naval history) published an *Essay on Naval Tactics* in which he discounted the conventional windward attack (with no attempt being made to pierce the enemy line) as being scarcely capable of bringing about a decision due to the shattering effects of enfilading fire from the enemy (in broadside-on position). Clerk suggested a concentration of part of the attacking ships in overwhelming force against the enemy rearguard while the other part held the enemy main body in check (this assumes that the enemy was sailing before the wind). This would cause the enemy van and main body to turn and tack back to their threatened rearguard, a manoeuvre which in days of sail could easily lead to confusion in the line of battle. As abandoning their rearguard would be unthinkable, even the careful French would be forced to fight if confronted with these tactics. It is amazing how closely Clerk's theory coincided with Nelson's practice in 1805 at Trafalgar.

# The Balance of Naval Forces
# from the Outbreak of War in 1792

In the following table a fairly accurate idea can be gained of the numerical strengths of the leading navies at this time. The nations are arranged in descending order of magnitude according to the numbers of ships of the line which they possessed. It will be noticed that the United States is not included – Congress had not yet realised the importance to their nation of a strong navy. Austria too is missing although, as will be seen, she was to be given the chance more than once to become a naval power, but bungled them due to lack of imagination. Prussia too had decided to remain a land power and had no real navy to speak of.

On the other hand, nations appear in the table which have since vanished from the political map of the world, such as Venice and the Kingdom of the Two Sicilies (Naples). While the former was in decline after an illustrious naval past, Naples was a second or third rate power which was to be absorbed into Italy in the mid-nineteenth century.

Numbers alone, of course, tell less than half the story; many of the ships shown overleaf were not in seaworthy condition at the outbreak of hostilities, some were 'mothballed', as many modern American and British ships are today, and this was certainly the case with the British navy then. Other ships, however, were out of commission and in a nearly derelict state and their associated naval dockyards were similarly run down.

Let us now examine each of the listed navies in the light of three other factors as well as their numerical strengths.

The other considerations which affected (and affect) the efficiency of a navy are the political direction of the country – whether the government understands the strengths and weaknesses of its navy and how best to use that navy as a tool of its policy; the crews of the ships – were they efficient and practised seamen with energetic, trustworthy commanders; and the dockyards – were they well-stocked and able to respond to the demands made upon them by the floating units.

## Britain

Apart from having the strongest fleet, Britain's warships were in good condition, even those temporarily out of commission. In spite of the fact that almost half the crews of British warships in these wars were pressed men, they formed efficient sailing and fighting crews and were lucky enough to have excellent commanders.

A high degree of mutual trust existed between officers and men as was witnessed by the many bold operations undertaken in face of extreme odds. The British naval dockyards were well staffed and stocked and gave excellent service to the ships. Another important factor in naval warfare was the ability of ships' crews to carry out damage control during battle and repairs to storm damage at all times – often the difference between saving and losing a ship; here the British were skilful and resourceful.

Given that Britain possessed a first class naval machine, she also had a government which well understood how best to use it to further national interests.

## TABLE OF RELATIVE NAVAL STRENGTHS IN 1790

| | Ships of the line | Guns | Frigates | Guns | Sloops | Total vessels | Total guns | Total crew |
|---|---|---|---|---|---|---|---|---|
| Britain | 195 | 100-50 | 210 | 44-32 | 256 | 661 | 12000 | 100000 |
| France | 81 | 118-64 | 69 | 50-40 | 141 | 291 | 14000 | 78000 |
| Spain | 72 | 112-58 | 41 | ? | 109 | 222 | 10000 | 50000 |
| Russia | 67 | 110-66 | 36 | 44-28 | 700 | 803 | 9000 | 21000 |
| Holland | 44 | 74-56 | 43 | 40-24 | 100 | 187 | 2300 | 15000 |
| Denmark | 38 | 90-50 | 20 | 42-20 | 60 schebecks | 118 | 3000 | 12000 |
| Turkey | 30 | 74-50 | 50 | 50-10 | 100 galliots | 180 | 3000 | 50000 |
| Sweden | 27 | 74-50 | 12 | 38-20 | 40 galleys | 79 | 3000 | 13000 |
| Venice | 20 | 88-16 | 10 | ? | 58 | 88 | 1000 | 14000 |
| Portugal | 10 | 80-58 | 14 | 44-30 | 29 | 53 | 1500 | 1000(sic) |
| Naples* | 10 | 74-50 | 10 | ? | 12 | 32 | 1000 | 5000 |
| Totals | 594 | | 515 | | 1605 | 2714 | 59800 | 359000 |

This table from page 48 of *Torpedo War and Submarine Explosions* by Robert Fulton (New York 1810) merely gives total numbers of vessels and does not consider the condition of such vessels (in service, out of commission, hulk, derelict, etc). When compared with other much more detailed sources, it proves to be difficult to relate to any given date.

* Kingdom of the Two Sicilies.

## France

The French navy was sadly deficient on most counts. Their government scarcely understood the best use of sea power and repeatedly squandered what little serviceable resources they had on irrelevant expeditions. Many of the ships were in poor condition in 1792 and the British blockade kept them inactive and their neglected dockyards short of vital supplies. What little resources were available were frequently wasted by administrative inefficiency while the inexperienced crews often caused more damage to their own ships by bad seamanship than they suffered at enemy hands. French ships were longer and slimmer than their British foes and thus sailed better, but gunnery was poor and discipline so chaotic in the fervour of revolutionary egalitarianism that this advantage was completely cancelled out.

## Spain

If the condition of the French navy was poor, that of the Spanish navy was verging on the terrible. Still an active colonial power, corruption in the upper echelons of Spanish society and government had reduced her armed forces to the status of paper tigers. Dockyards were derelict, ships neglected, crew morale low due to the injustices of a promotion system where money completely outweighed seniority or merit. The government was too torpid to use their fleet properly and after Trafalgar they had little to fight with.

## Russia

Throughout her history Russia had been predominantly a land power even though Peter the Great had started her along the road towards the sea and had moved his capital from Moscow to St Petersburg on the shores of the Gulf of Finland in order to emphasise the importance he placed on the navy.

It was not until after the Second World War that Russia finally realised that to be an effective world power she had to develop a fleet which could enforce her policies in all corners of the globe. This development has caused consternation in London, Washington and Peking.

During the period 1792–1815 the Russian government's attention was almost totally absorbed by a series of life-and-death struggles in Europe and her navy, operating from land-locked seas and from ports which were mostly ice-bound for much of the year, was not permitted to stride boldly on the world's stage. When it did, as in the battle of Lemnos in 1807, it demonstrated sound seamanship and gunnery and good command.

Many senior Russian naval officers were in fact British or had been trained in Britain and this leavening of high professional skill helped greatly. The Russian dockyards seem to have been well stocked and efficient. Like Sweden, Russia had developed special shallow-draught vessels to operate in the Baltic.

## Holland

Holland had a long and successful naval history by 1792 and a small but highly competent fleet, with supporting dockyards, in good condition and crewed by excellent seamen and commanders. The Dutch government knew the value of sea power and had fought the British on many previous occasions. In 1797 however, the navy of the Batavian Republic (as Holland was then called) was dealt some shattering blows from which it never fully recovered. After being tied to France's apron strings in 1795 the political direction of naval affairs suffered and by 1815 the Dutch fleet was relatively insignificant and had been forced into years of idleness by the British blockade.

31

**Denmark**

The Danish navy of 1792 was small but in good heart and fairly good condition. The main naval base in Copenhagen was well stocked, at least until 1807 when Britain looted it.

Denmark was too small a state to exercise great influence on international affairs but although little political direction was evident in the handling of naval matters, the quality of the officers and men was so high that during 1801–07 and in the 'Gunboat War' of the subsequent seven years, the small Danish navy was to perform extremely well.

**Turkey**

By 1792 the Ottoman Empire was in an advanced state of decay with practically no political direction of any consequence evident in naval affairs. Turkey was essentially a land power even though she possessed a vital strategic position and many good natural harbours. Ship design was not as good as in most European countries and naval tactics were almost non-existent. The Turkish navy seems to have been relegated to one domestic role – that of guarding the Dardanelles. Following their defeat by the Russians at the battle of Lemnos in 1807, little was heard of the Turkish navy.

**Sweden**

Sweden was a nation in the difficult process of declining to a second- or third-rate power in 1792. Her monarch exercised a decidedly negative influence on the fortunes of his armed forces and this bred lack of confidence and mistrust at all levels in the heirarchy. Due to the shallow, confined nature of the Baltic the Swedes had developed two fleets; a conventional high seas force and a 'shallows fleet' of galleys and other craft, novel in construction but impractical in operation and scarcely capable of co-operation with the conventional ships of the high seas fleet. Financial stringencies caused shortages in Swedish dockyards and the loss of Finland to Russia in 1809 (together with almost all the shallows fleet) severely hampered Swedish naval operations in the following years. Indeed the Swedish navy was practically never seen outside the Baltic.

**Venice**

Venice was another declining power at the outbreak of war; her ship design and construction were no longer of the best, finances were short, political direction lacking and morale in the fleet was low. In 1797 France and Austria divided the ancient republic up between them, most of the fleet was destroyed and the remainder split up between the predators.

**Portugal**

Portugal had a long colonial history to look back on in 1792 but had allowed her navy to fall into disuse. As with the Portuguese army at this time, neglect and the symptoms of lack of finance and political interest were apparent. Close contact with the British navy and the seconding of British officers to serve with the Portuguese navy brought about considerable improvements and a Portuguese squadron operated well with the Royal Navy in the Mediterranean at the turn of the century. Dockyard facilities were limited however and the French occupation of 1808 left them destitute. With the seat of Portuguese government (and with it most of the fleet) transferred to Brazil from 1807–14, their navy was involved in no great events for the rest of the period.

## Naples

Naples (or more correctly, the Kingdom of the Two Sicilies) was a minor power, which, however, occupied a strategically important position across the centre of the Mediterranean.

Although lacking in domestic political initiative, the Sicilian monarch gladly followed Britain's lead and his small and relatively efficient navy participated in some important operations as part of an allied task force.

The main naval base at Naples suffered much disruption at the turn of the century as French-inspired republicans took it over and some of the Neapolitan fleet was left in enemy hands in 1806 when the mainland was taken to become the Kingdom of Naples. The Neapolitans were competent sailors although political intrigue detracted from the efficiency of the officers.

If one were to look forward to 1815 and reshuffle the table of relative naval strengths to reflect the status of the fleets at that time, it would probably look like this: Britain had maintained her position of supremacy and increased her lead at the expense of her enemies; Russia, with much of her fleet refurbished by Britain, was probably in second place but was not to remain there for long; France lay third, her navy in a parlous state in every respect but soon to recover, partially at least; the Netherlands navy had been similarly dragged down but was later to recover; the Spanish navy must be considered to have slipped from third to about fifth place, while the Danish navy, although still seventh in the table had become far less effective than in 1792. Turkey and Sweden too had retained their relative positions but had diminished greatly in potential, while Portugal had overtaken Naples, mainly because of the heavy losses incurred by the latter state. The United States of America was by now rising sharply as a naval power and was qualitatively excellent if numerically limited. Austria had come in at the bottom of the league table but was never to achieve the status at sea which she enjoyed on land.

# Part Two
# The Engagements

# The War of the First Coalition 1792-7

2 January 1793: first act of hostility; batteries at the entrance of Brest harbour fire on HM brig *Childers* (*National Maritime Museum*)

Revolutionary France stood alone against Britain, the Netherlands, Spain, the Italian kingdoms, Austria and Russia. She raised her armies by the 'levée en masse' and, inspired with a unifying national spirit, these amateurs soon learned to stand up to the small professional armies of their adversaries and beat some of them quite convincingly. At sea, however, the lack of serviceable ships and trained crews could not so easily be overcome. Added to these external foes was the fact that some parts of France remained actively loyalist and a civil war had to be fought as well as a conventional, external conflict. In mid-August 1793, Admiral Lord Hood with 21 ships of the line, captured the French main naval base at Toulon without firing a shot as the royalist inhabitants welcomed his aid for their cause. He was then joined by 17 Spanish ships of the line and found himself in possession of 17 serviceable French ships of the line in Toulon, 12 more unserviceable, 24 frigates and some other vessels. At one swoop Britain had undisputed mastery of the Mediterranean and possession of about a third of the enemy fleet as well as one of their major bases. Britain at once applied her ruthless blockade of enemy harbours and the control of all shipping of whatever flag, tactics which had proved themselves in the past and which were to be so effective against France now.

To add to French discomfort their Brest fleet, under Admiral Morard de Galles, mutinied off the Vendée (a royalist stronghold) and had to be withdrawn to Brest, thus permitting undisputed resupply of the royalists by France's enemies.

During late 1793 British naval strength at sea increased rapidly to reach 24 ships of the line in the Channel Fleet (Lord Howe), 24 in the Mediterranean (Lord Hood), 12 in the West Indies and 24 in reserve.

The allies in Toulon now had 17,000 troops from 5 nations there and the French beseigers had 15,000 troops but made little progress until a certain artillery officer, Napoleon Bonaparte, took a hand in events and things began to move in their favour.

The British ships with Lord Hood in August 1793 were *Victory, Britannia* (100s); *Windsor Castle, Princess Royal, St George* (98s); *Alcide, Terrible, Egmont, Robust, Courageux, Bedford, Berwick, Captain, Fortitude, Leviathan, Colossus, Illustrious* (74s); *Agamemnon, Ardent, Diadem, Intrepid* (64s). There were also some 7 frigates and 10 corvettes.

The French ships in Toulon harbour which were ready to put to sea included *Commerce de Marseille** (120); *Tonnant* (80); *Apollon, Centaure, Commerce de Bordeaux, Destin, Duguay-Trouin, Entreprenent, Généreaux, Héros, Heureux, Lys, Orion, Patriote, Pompée*, Scipion*, Themistocle* (74s). Those ships marked * were subsequently added to the Royal Navy. There were also several frigates and corvettes. Ships refitting or under repair were *Dauphin Royal* (120); *Couronne, Languedoc, Triumphent* (80s); *Puissant*, Suffisant, Alcide, Censeur, Conquérant, Dictateur, Guerrier, Mercure, Trajan, Souverain* (74s) with a further 74 under construction. One 36-gun frigate was refitting, two more and two 32-gunners were awaiting repair, as were two corvettes, and two 40-gun frigates were under construction. Apart from these 58 vessels, a further 17 were cruising in the Mediterranean (one 74, three 40s, two 38s, five 36s, two 28s and four corvettes).

On 14 September 1793, Lord Hood sent the four least-serviceable French 74s (*Entreprenent, Orion, Trajan* and *Patriote*) out of Toulon, after having removed all their guns except two 8pdrs each, to loyal French ports with such French seaman who wished to serve the republic – a magnanimous gesture indeed!

Two Neapolitan 74s (*Tancrédi* and *Guiscardo*) joined the Anglo-Spanish force in Toulon on 28 September with 2,000 troops, and 350 Sardinian troops were also brought in aboard *Colossus* (74). On 5 October a third Neapolitan 74 (*Samnita*) arrived with 2,000 more of their troops and a further 900 came on in November. Allied land forces (after deducting casualties) now numbered 1,542 French royalists, 1,583 Piedmontese, 4,832 Neapolitans, 6,840 Spaniards and 2,114 British; a total of 16,902.

When the decision was taken to evacuate Toulon due to the worsening of the landward situation, great haste was caused and the destruction of the enemy vessels was mishandled. At his own request Captain Sir William Sydney Smith was entrusted on 18 December with preparing the French ships in Toulon harbour for destruction, for which duty he had a tender, three British and three Spanish gunboats. A fireship, *Vulcan*, was anchored across the line of warships with double-shotted cannon to cause maximum damage and she and the other demolition trains were ignited at 10pm. The Spaniards had set fire to the French frigate *Iris*, which was loaded with several thousand barrels of gunpowder and the resulting explosion caused widespread confusion during which the Spanish withdrew. *Héros* and *Themistocles* were burnt, another powder-laden frigate exploded and the British demolition party pulled away, having lost one boat blown up by the *Iris.*

The French Republican general Fréron extracted a terrible revenge on the luckless citizens of Toulon who were not able to be evacuated with the

18 December 1793: defence of Toulon by allies against French Republicans
(*National Maritime Museum*)

allied fleet (about 15,000 were taken off); he bragged that 'every day since our arrival we have cut off 200 heads' and it seems that about 6,000 men, women and children were murdered by the vengeful republicans. Such is the character of any civil war.

Of the French vessels at Toulon, three 80-gunners, fourteen 74s, two 40s, five 32s, two 20s and one 16-gunner were destroyed; one 120, two 74s (Clowes gives three); two 40s *Arethuse* (later *Undaunted*) and *Perle* (*Amethyst*); three 32s *Topaze, Aurore* and *Lutine*; two 26s *Poulette* and *Belette*, one 24; three 20s (Clowes shows only the *Moselle*) and one 14-gunner (not shown by Clowes) were taken by the British; one 32 *Alceste* (Sardinian), one 20 *Embroye* (Neapolitan) and one 18 *Petite Aurore* (Spanish) were taken by the allies and the rest (two 120s, four 80s, twenty-one 74s, four 40s, nine 32s, two 26s, one 24, seven 20s, two 18s, one 16 and one 14) were left to fall into French hands.

Whatever the factors which led to this extraordinary event, blame for allowing most of the Toulon fleet to fall back into enemy control intact cannot be thrust upon Sir Sidney Smith who merely tried to do as best he could at the eleventh hour and in the face of active resistance from republican sympathisers. Real blame must lie with Lord Hood who was in command before the final débâcle and who should have had these matters attended to long before December.

The balance of naval power in the Mediterranean moved considerably in France's favour and British loss of control there in 1795 can be directly attributed to this failure to destroy the enemy fleet.

Harvests in France in 1793 had been bad and this natural problem had been aggravated by the upheavals of the revolution. Consequently food had to be bought from overseas and the French had secured large stocks of grain in America. This was to be brought back to France by a convoy of 125 merchantmen and the Brest fleet under Rear Admiral Villaret-Joyeuse, with 25 ships of the line, was ordered to go and escort the convoy back to France. Villaret-Joyeuse left Brest in mid-May 1794 with the *Montagne* (120) as his flagship. On board was a deputy of the Convention to ensure correct political actions.

The British knew of these measures and at the end of April 1794 had sent Lord Howe from Portsmouth with 34 ships of the line and 15 frigates to stop the convoy. Howe detached Admiral Montagu with 8 ships of the line to escort a British convoy of 150 sail, destined for the Americas and the West and East Indies, to Cape Finisterre where 6 of the warships were then to scout mid-Biscay for the French prey.

Howe with the main body went to Brest, found the French fleet still at anchor and sailed westwards. On 19 May he returned to Brest to find that the French had gone so he at once sailed west again. On 21 May he encountered a French convoy of 16 ships and captured 10 of them which he burnt as he did not wish to weaken his manpower before a battle by detaching prize crews. On 28 May he met Villaret-Joyeuse 400 sea miles west of Ushant; both fleets consisted of 26 ships of the line.

The French fleet consisted of *Montagne* (120); *Terrible, Révolutionnaire* and *Républicain* (100s); *Indomptable, Jacobin, Juste* and *Scipion* (80s); *Achille, America, Conception, Entreprenant, Eole, Gasparin, Jemmappes, Impétueux, Montagnard, Mont Blanc, Mucius, Neptune, Northumberland, Patriote, Pelletier, Tourville, Tyrannicide* and *Vengeur* (74s).

The British had *Queen Charlotte, Royal George* and *Royal Sovereign* (100s); *Barfleur, Impregnable, Queen* and *Glory* (98s); *Gibraltar* and *Caesar* (80s); *Bellerophon, Montagu, Tremendous, Valiant, Ramillies, Audacious, Brunswick, Alfred, Defence, Leviathan, Majestic, Invincible, Orion, Russel, Marlborough, Thunderer* and *Culloden* (74s). The frigates were *Phaëton* and *Latona* (38s); *Niger, Southampton, Venus* and *Aquilon* (32s); *Pegasus* (28) and the hospital ship *Charon*. There were also two fireships *Comet* and *Incendiary*, a sloop *Kingfisher* and two cutters *Rattler* and *Ranger*.

Howe formed his fleet into two parallel battle lines with a 'light division' of his four fastest 74s between them and the French. By 2.30pm it looked as if the French were going to break off contact and Howe signalled 'general chase' and by 6.20pm fire was opened on the rearmost Frenchman – *Révolutionnaire* – by *Bellerophon, Marlborough, Russel* and *Thunderer*. By 10pm the *Révolutionnaire* was very badly battered and it is claimed that she struck her colours having by then about 400 killed and wounded but no British ship was close enough and in a fit enough state to board and take possession and so she limped away to rejoin the French fleet. The *Audacious* had suffered most in the combat of the British ships involved but only in the rigging, masts and yards, her casualties being 3 killed and 19 wounded (3 died later). Next morning the *Audacious*, alone, was chased by 3 French ships but fought them off and slipped away to safety in the bad visibility. *Révolutionnaire* was towed back to Rochefort by the French *Audacieux* which came on to the scene of the action after battle was joined.

Dawn of 29 May found both main fleets about six miles apart, the French on the weather bow of the British. At about 8am the British opened fire on the French rear, and their van tacked about to help the threatened ships. At 10am broadsides were exchanged, *Royal George, Valiant, Russel, Queen* and *Caesar* achieving hits on the leading French ship *Montagnard*. Two hours later Lord Howe signalled his fleet to tack in succession in order to pass

40

through the enemy line but, due to the gunsmoke, the signal was not seen by all and only partially obeyed. *Caesar* was unable to tack, *Queen* too damaged to do so, *Russel* and *Valiant* did not succeed either, *Royal George* was the first ship to obey and the *Invincible* followed but they could only catch the last 2 French ships, *Tyrannicide* and *Indomptable*. At 1.30pm Lord Howe, seeing that his signals were ineffective, determined to 'lead by example' and caused *Queen Charlotte* to cut the French line between their sixth and seventh ships from the rear (astern of *Eole*). *Bellerophon* and *Leviathan* followed, the former passing through ahead of *Terrible*. The *Orion* passed between *Tyrannicide* and *Indomptable* and was followed by *Barfleur*. Villaret-Joyeuse now tacked in his turn to save his rearward ships and *Queen Charlotte* was now too unmanageable to take effective action to prevent this. By 5pm all firing ceased, there never having been a general engagement of the entire fleets. The sea was rough and made manoeuvring difficult. Damage to the British ships was quickly repaired—total casualties 67 killed and 128 wounded.

## The Glorious First of June 1794

At 8.30am on 1 June both fleets still lay in sight of one another, sailing west with the wind south by west. On both sides, some vessels had left the area of battle, others had joined. There were now 25 British ships facing 26 French. Howe steered towards the enemy and in 90 minutes was close enough to open fire. His orders were for each ship in his line to seek out its corresponding French vessel, to close, and if possible to break the line and continue to fight from the lee side. The leading British ship *Caesar* turned too soon (at a range of 1,500 feet from the enemy) and remained out of the battle. General engagement began at 9.30am. Only about a quarter of the British ships actually broke through the French line. *Queen Charlotte*

The Glorious First of June 1794: HMS *Brunswick* battering *Vengeur*; to her port side is *L'Achille,* having struck her colours to *Brunswick* (*National Maritime Museum*)

41

slipped through behind *Montagne* and engaged her from the stern and lee side, causing the Frenchman 300 casualties with her raking-fire, and on the other side *Queen Charlotte* battered the *Jacobin* which had tried to avoid being raked over her bows. The *Montagne*, her lee side gunports shut, was unable to fire a shot in return during this dreadful battering from *Queen Charlotte* until about 10.10am when she set her main topmast staysail and pulled ahead of her tormentor.

*Brunswick*, the last British ship, collided with *Vengeur*, also a 74, went alongside and held the French ship close with her anchor, and opened a three-hour fight. *Brunswick* had her gunports open and was thus clear for action but *Vengeur* had only opened the gunports on the side originally threatened so that when *Brunswick* closed on the lee side, *Vengeur* could not use her guns. The British, using flexible ramrods made of stiff cable, could load and fire in this close position and by depressing and elevating the guns could hit upper and lower decks as well as that directly opposite the gun decks. Eventually the ships broke apart in the heavy seas whereupon *Brunswick* again enfiladed *Vengeur* and raked her anew. Eventually *Vengeur* sank – by then a dismasted wreck. The British saved almost 400 of her 756 crew of whom 250 were by then dead or wounded.

Lord Howe signalled general chase at 10.13am when the French began to pull away and proceeded to engage the *Juste* (80). The French towed 5 of their dismasted ships with them and at 11.30am the main action was over. They had 13 more or less dismasted ships, *Trente-un-Mai*, *Tyrannicide*, *Terrible*, *Républicain*, *Scipion**, *Mucius**, *Jemmappes**, *Achille**, *America**, *Juste**, *Northumberland**, *Sans-Pareil**, and *Impetueux**. (Those ships marked * lost all three main masts.) *Achille* had previously struck to *Brunswick* but slipped away again and rehoisted her colours. The British had 11 ships more or less dismasted: *Impregnable*, *Royal Sovereign*, *Orion*, *Glory*, *Queen Charlotte*, *Bellerophon*, *Brunswick*, *Royal George*, *Queen*, *Defence* and *Marlborough* (all three lower masts had been lost by these last two ships).

The British now moved to secure 6 French ships – *Sans-Pareil*, *Juste*, *America*, *Impétueux*, *Northumberland* and *Achille*. British casualties were 290 killed and 858 wounded; the French admitted 3,000 dead and wounded and in addition 4,524 (including 690 dead and 580 wounded) were aboard the 6 captured ships making their total loss 7,524. Lord Howe's fleet remained 'on the battlefield' until 3 June securing prizes and carrying out essential repairs; he then sailed to Spithead.

The French grain convoy reached port safely so Villaret-Joyeuse had achieved his aim but at very heavy cost in ships and in valuable, trained officers and men.

Howe's tactics – breaking the enemy line at all possible points simultaneously, giving enfilading fire on passing through the line and then continuing the fight from the lee side – had not been perfectly achieved but even with the limited number of British ships which did carry out the plan, the success was impressive. The old disadvantage of naval tactics when fighting a battle in line ahead remained, however, in that the attacking rearguard only came into action very late in the contest and often played no part at all in the battle. Howe's double column did help to reduce this delay.

In September 1794, Howe cruised over the Bay of Biscay with 29 British and 5 Portuguese ships of the line but found neither merchant prey nor naval opponents. Meanwhile a French division of 5 ships of the line took a British convoy from its 2 escorts after a hard fight.

On 24 December 1794, Villaret-Joyeuse was ordered to leave Brest with

The Glorious First of June 1794: prizes *Juste* and *America* (*National Maritime Museum*)

The Glorious First of June 1794: Lord Howe (*National Martime Museum*)

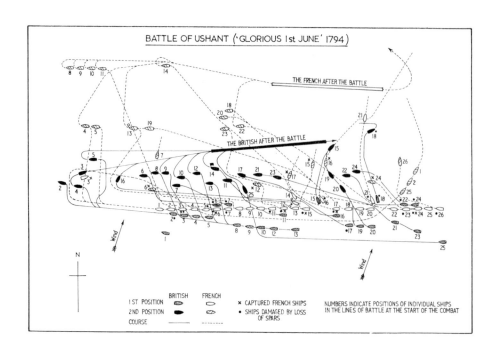

BATTLE OF USHANT ('GLORIOUS 1st JUNE' 1794)

The Glorious First of June 1794: defence at close of action (*National Maritime Museum*)

35 ships of the line to escort 6 ships of the line to Toulon. A heavy storm in early January 1795 capsized 3 of these ships and 2 more had to be beached. It was not until 2 February 1795 that the last of the Brest ships returned to base.

## The Mediterranean 1794

Corsica rose in revolt against France in 1793 and the Royal Navy under Hood were quickly on the scene, capturing the various frigates and corvettes in the harbours and landing troops.

Hood captured the town of San Fiorenzo on 19 February and negotiated with the rebel leader, General Paoli, to secure the whole island as a base for his fleet. He then blockaded the port of Bastia for seven weeks after which the 3,000 strong garrison surrendered. Captain Nelson with 1,250 sailors and marines had operated on the landward side of the town. It was at this time that Nelson lost the sight of his right eye when sand was thrown into it from a cannonball which struck nearby. Calvi fell in mid-August 1794 and Britain retained control of the island until 1796 when France reclaimed it. For two years it was a valuable source of timber and seamen for the Royal Navy.

In June 1794 Rear-Admiral Comte Martin took the Toulon fleet to sea with the *Sans-Culottes* (120) as his flagship. He was soon sighted by Lord Hood's fleet and ran into Golfe Juan near Cannes and took up a strong defensive position. He was bottled up here for five months before he could dodge back to Toulon when a gale had blown the British away for a day or two.

Late in 1794 France overran the Netherlands and set up the Batavian Republic organised on French republican lines. The Dutch fleet passed into French control having been captured (frozen in the ice) by cavalry and artillery, and Britain at once extended her blockade to cover all Batavian ports.

## The West Indies 1794–1800

Vice-Admiral Sir John Jervis with *Boyne* (98), *Vengeance* and *Irresistable* (74s), *Asia* and *Veteran* (64s) and several frigates and sloops arrived off Martinique on 5 February 1794. On board he had Lieutenant-General Sir George Grey with 7,000 troops. By the middle of March he had taken the whole island and Guadaloupe was also captured on 20 March. The French reacted vigorously however, and landed 1,400 troops on Guadaloupe on 3 June and by the end of 1794 they had wrested the island back from British control.

Tobago fell to the British in April 1794 as did St Lucia, but the latter was recaptured by the French in the summer of 1795. During that year several French frigates and private vessels were very successful in raiding British commerce (coffee and sugar) from the West Indies and were operating boldly in the mouth of the Channel.

On the island of Haiti the negroes rose in revolt and set up their own black republic.

At the end of April 1796 Rear-Admiral Sir Hugh Christian, with 8 ships of the line and 16,000 troops under General Abercromby retook St Lucia and other Caribbean islands as well as small Batavian colonies in South America.

In February 1797 Rear-Admiral M. Harvey captured Trinidad from Spain as well as a ship of the line that was there, *San Damaso* (74). Four other

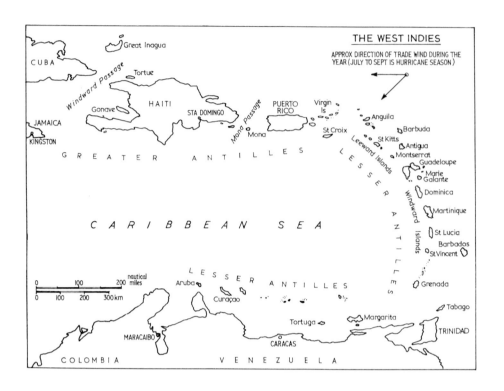

2 December 1794: HM packet *Antelope* beating off the French privateer *Atalante* in the West Indies (*National Maritime Museum*)

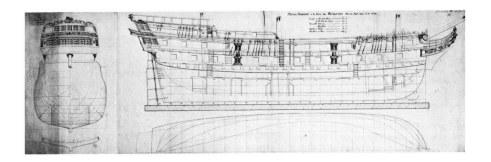

Profile and rear view of the *Prince Frederic* (64) previously called *Revolutie* – a Dutch
ship taken at the Cape of Good Hope on 17 August 1796 (*National Maritime Museum*)
   Length of gundeck – 108.74m (356ft 9in)
   Length of keel – 100.38m (329ft 4in)
   Beam – 12.88m (42ft 3in)
   Depth in hold – 11.06m (36ft 3½in)
   Tonnage – 3319.5 tonnes (3.267tons 1½cwts)

vessels were burnt by the Spaniards to prevent their capture, *San Vincente*
(80); *Arrogante, Gallardo* (74s) and *Santa Cecilia* (34). A raid on Puerto Rico
however failed to secure it for Britain.

## The East Indies

On 16 February 1796 Rear-Admiral Peter Rainer arrived off the Batavian
island colony of Amboyna in the Moluccas with a small squadron and three
troop transports and took possession of the place. On 8 March they landed
on Banda Neira and took the town after a short struggle in which they were
supported by the frigate *Orpheus.*

## The Cape of Good Hope

A small Batavian expedition sailed in February 1796 to recapture Cape
Colony from the British but landed in Saldanha Bay near Cape Town, only to
surrender to Vice-Admiral Sir Keith Elphinstone on 17 August 1796. The
ships captured were *Dordrecht* (64) Schout bij nacht Lucas; *Revolutie* (64)
Kapitein Reinbende; *Tromp* (54) Kapitein Luitenant Valkenburg; *Castor*
(44) Kapitein Clarisse; *Brave* (44) Kapitein Luitenant Soetemans; *Sirene* (26)
Kapitein Luitenant De Cerf; *Bellona* (24) Kapitein Luitenant De Falk; *Havik*
(18) Luitenant Bezemer; *Vrouw Maria* (16) Luitenant Barbier.

## The Mediterranean 1795

The Toulon fleet was now ordered to prepare for the recapture of Corsica
from the British; although having 12,000 crewmen available, only 3,000 of
these had any naval experience and the state of repair and readiness of the
vessels left much to be desired. Martin put to sea with 15 of the line and 12
frigates and other vessels, leaving the troop transports and 18,000 men in
harbour. His flagship was the *Sans-Culottes.* He came upon the dismasted
British ship *Berwick* (74) and captured her and then ran into the British
Mediterranean fleet of 13 British and 1 Neapolitan ships of the line under
Vice-Admiral Hotham coming from Leghorn to intercept him. For three
days the fleets lay close by one another but the wind was too light for them
to come to grips. In this period the poor level of French seamanship became

13 March 1795: *Agamemnon* engages *Ça Ira* off Genoa (*National Maritime Museum*)

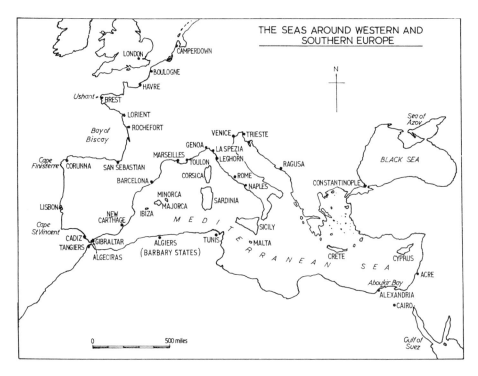

evident when *Mercure* (74) lost her main topmast and *Ça-Ira* (80) and *Victoire* (80) collided, *Ça-Ira* lost her topmast and she and *Mercure* left the fleet. Two days later the British gained a light wind and attacked *Censeur* (74) and *Ça-Ira*, who both struck their colours after a fight. Martin took the rest of his fleet back to Toulon and Hotham did not pursue him.

Captain Horatio Nelson on *Agamemnon* distinguished himself. Losses were 74 dead and 284 wounded for the British and 400 dead and wounded for the French plus the captured crews of the 2 ships. The projected French invasion of Corsica was abandoned. The Royal Naval *Illustrious* (74) was wrecked near Avenza after the action.

In April 1795 Admiral Renaudin arrived in Toulon with 6 ships of the line from Brest and the French now had 20 serviceable men of war against only 13 British ships of the line in that theatre. There now followed a period in which the Admiralty in Whitehall exercised direct control on their various fleets, leaving local commanders practically no opportunity for initiative. The stringent blockade of French ports suffered and Royal Naval forces were sent instead on unrewarding expeditions.

**Action off Ile de Groix, 23 June 1795**
Admiral Lord Bridport with 14 of the line came up with 12 French ships of the line under Admiral Villaret-Joyeuse from Brest. In a brief action the French ships *Tigre*, *Alexandre* and *Formidable* were captured after having lost 700 dead and wounded. Had Lord Bridport been more aggressive, it is likely that his victory would have been greater, but the French were allowed to slip into Lorient at high water.

On 21 June 1795, Vice-Admiral Hotham sent Commodore Nelson with 5 ships to Vado on the Italian Riviera to support the Austrians operating along the coast against the French there, but little was achieved as the French were far too strong on land for their opponents, so Nelson, too weak at sea, returned to the fleet. On 13 July Hotham with 23 ships of the line met Rear-Admiral Martin off the Hyères Islands (near Toulon) with 17 ships of the line. In a fierce but brief action the French *Alcide* (74) struck her colours but then caught fire and blew up. Hotham's lack of vigour prevented a greater victory. In the same month Nelson took Elba.

Vice-Admiral Hotham handed over command of the Royal Navy Mediterranean Fleet to Admiral Sir John Jervis on 1 November 1795 and a new spirit was breathed into British operations.

# The Change of Balance of Naval Power in the Mediterranean 1796

The First Coalition collapsed when Prussia and Spain signed peace with France at Bâsle on 22 July 1795 and Spain became France's ally on 19 August 1796 by the Treaty of Ildefonso. With some of her continental foes no longer active, France concentrated against Austria in northern Italy and soon achieved successes which caused the Austrians to withdraw eastwards and allowed ports like Leghorn and Genoa to fall under French influence, thus robbing the Royal Navy of base facilities in the northern Mediterranean. Added to this the French fleet in Toulon was becoming so bold, thanks to Admiral Hotham's lack of activity and energy in trying to destroy them, that most of the British fleet was tied down to hold the French in check instead of being able to operate freely.

In March 1796, Napoleon assumed command of the Army of Italy and began at once to rush against the Austro–Sardinian forces opposing him.

15 July 1796: HMS *Glatton*, commanded by Captain Henry Trollope, after defeating a squadron of French vessels seen sailing off on the right (*National Maritime Museum*)

On 9 April he was at Savoy where he forced Sardinia to sign a separate peace on 15 May 1796 and to surrender Nice and Savoy to France. The Austrians, now alone, were pushed away from the coast and their communications with the British fleet were cut. Napoleon pushed on to Milan; the King of Sicily signed an armistice with him on 16 October and the minor northern Italian principalities were soon cowed into submission.

These events on land, coupled with the growing threat from the Toulon fleet, caused the British admiralty to order the evacuation of Corsica and Elba. On 27 June 1796 Britain had evacuated Leghorn at the approach of the French army and Napoleon was able now to use the port to mount his invasion of Corsica.

At the end of August 1796, when Spain had declared war on Britain, there had been a British squadron under Mann stationed off Cadiz to observe the Spanish fleet; this was later withdrawn by Sir John Jervis and ordered to join him; it arrived at his location with supplies exhausted and was at once sent back to Gibraltar to replenish.

The Spanish fleet of 19 of the line and 10 frigates, commanded by Admiral Don Juan de Langara, left Cadiz and, passing through the Straits of Gibraltar, captured 2 British merchantmen from a small convoy making for Gibraltar itself. On 1 October 1796, Langara picked up 7 more ships of the line at Cartagena and sailed on to Toulon, reaching it on 26 October where he joined 12 French ships of the line and 7 frigates making a total of 38 ships of the line and 17 frigates, heavily outnumbering Sir John Jervis who then had only 14 ships of the line to hand. Mann's squadron from Cadiz had been chased by Langara near Gibraltar and had sailed home to Britain where Mann was relieved of his command. The French invasion of Corsica was commanded by General Gentile, himself a Corsican; the advance guard

50

sailed from Leghorn on 14 feluccas and other small craft and landed on Corsica on 19 October. Had the Royal Navy been in firm control of the sea, this venture would never have been attempted. The British garrison was evacuated on board *Captain* and *Egmont* (74s) commanded by Commodore Nelson on 2 November; these ships, together with 12 merchant vessels, joined Sir John Jervis who took the whole force – 16 of the line and some frigates, back to Gibraltar where they anchored on 11 December. The Mediterranean had thus been wrested from the control of the Royal Navy in 1796, not by means of naval battles but by the use of diplomacy and the effects of adverse developments in land warfare along the northern shores of that sea, coupled with the resurgence of the Toulon fleet. The French navy, beaten repeatedly at sea, had control of the Mediterranean handed to it on a plate by her army's successes in northern Italy.

Early in December 1796, Sir John Jervis sent Nelson back into the Mediterranean to evacuate the British garrison from Elba; this was done and Nelson was back in Gibraltar before mid-February 1797.

Admiral Villeneuve with 5 ships of the line left Toulon with the Spanish fleet of Admiral Langara, 26 ships of the line, on 1 December 1796; the Spaniards returned to Cartagena while Villeneuve passed through the Straits of Gibraltar on 10 December in an east-south-easterly gale and took his ships, *Formidable* (80); *Jean-Jacques, Jammappes, Mont Blanc* and *Tyrannicide* (74s), to Brest.

## The Attempted Invasion of Ireland, December 1796

Aware of the anti-British sentiment in Ireland, the French resolved to increase their enemy's domestic troubles by supporting the potential rebels with their own troops. The fleet in Brest, under Vice-Admiral Villaret-Joyeuse together with 20,000 troops under General Hoche, who had just 'pacified' the Vendean royalists, were ordered to prepare for the undertaking. In all 17 ships of the line, 13 frigates, some smaller warships and 20 transports were available, but the condition of many of the ships and the poor state of crew-training were such that Villaret-Joyeuse was strongly against the venture; he was thus replaced by Vice-Admiral Morard de Galles. As the transports were wholly taken up by horses, artillery and supplies, the troops were carried aboard the warships, 600 being put on each ship of the line and 250 on each frigate. With such an increased loading of 'landlubbers' aboard, the French naval commanders were even more anxious than usual to avoid a sea battle. Brest was blockaded by 15 Royal Naval ships of the line under Admiral Colpoys but, although warned of the impending exit of the French fleet by the frigate *Indefatigable* under Captain Pellew, Colpoys allowed the entire convoy to slip past him on 16 December. Luckily for the British, a rising easterly storm on the same night scattered the French ships and Morard de Galles with his chief of staff, Rear-Admiral Bruix, and General Hoche were all aboard the frigate *Fraternité*, and together with 12 other ships were separated from the main body. The effects of the bad weather were magnified by poor French seamanship and confused French signalling by gunfire; the *Séduisant* (74) had run on the rocks and was firing distress guns at the same time as the *Fraternité* was signalling a change of channel and the British frigate *Indefatigable* was firing rockets and broadsides in a successful attempt to add to the chaos. Rear-Admiral Bouvet, second-in-command of the fleet, gathered 35 ships after the storm and sailed on for Cape Clear off Bantry Bay which was the intended landing place.

Morard de Galles and Hoche on board *Fraternité* were at this point being chased into the Atlantic by a British ship of the line and had to jettison some guns in order to escape.

At Bantry Bay all except the French commanders and 2 ships of the line were now present but, in the teeth of the prevailing easterlies and with heavy snow showers to contend with, the unpractised crews were unable to tack efficiently enough to get into the bay to the chosen landing place. Two frigates, *Impatient* (44) and *Surveillante* (36), were wrecked and Bruix stood away to the west leaving only General Grouchy with 6 of the line and 2 frigates in the mouth of the bay.

The invasion of Ireland fell quietly to pieces of its own accord and the expedition slunk back to Brest on 1 January 1797 after having waited off Bantry Bay for a week. On the return trip the *Révolution* was rescuing men from the sinking *Scévola* (44) when the two commanders at last appeared, only to be told that the expedition had dispersed. They were so harried by the British on their way back to France that they had to run for Rochefort and the frigate *Tartu* and some transports, *Tortue*, *Ville de Lorient*, *Suffren*, *Atalante* and *Allègre*, were captured. The French commanders reached Rochefort on 13 January 1797.

## The Battle of Cape St Vincent, 14 February 1797

The projected invasion of Ireland remained firmly in French designs for 1797 despite the disgraceful performance of the Brest fleet the previous December. General Hoche devised another plan to mount the invasion, this time with the extensively refitted Brest fleet in conjunction with the Batavian and Spanish fleets.

To this end Admiral Don José de Cordova was to bring the Spanish fleet from Cartagena to Brest via Cadiz; on 12 February he set sail with 27 ships of the line and 12 frigates with his flag on board the four-deck *Santissima-Trinidad* (130). They were sighted as they passed through the Straits of Gibraltar however and the British frigate *Minèrve* (with Commodore Nelson aboard) hurried north west to carry this vital news to Admiral Sir John Jervis who was off Cadiz with the Mediterranean fleet of 15 ships of the line and the two fleets sighted one another at about 8.30am on 14 February; the conditions were calm and foggy with a slight westerly breeze, with the British to the north of the Spanish.

At 11am the British could see that the Spanish main body, 19 ships of the line, with the wind on the starboard quarter, were striving to join up with a lee division of 6 of the line who were close-hauled on the same tack, also trying to close the dangerous gap. Jervis formed his ships into line of battle ahead and astern of his flagship, *Victory*, and steered to the south west, keeping the 6 detached enemy ships on his lee (port) bow. At 11.30am the leading vessels opened up long-range fire but not before 3 Spanish ships had succeeded in crossing from the main body to join the endangered lee division. The British line penetrated the gap between the two Spanish divisions and at 12.08pm the leading British vessel, *Culloden*, with Troubridge aboard, having passed the sternmost Spanish weather ship, tacked and steered north northwest. At the same time the Spanish lee division also went about and stood towards the head of the British line apparently hoping to cut it ahead of *Victory*. It became a test of nerves; *Victory* held her course and the Spaniard tacked close under her lee and was well raked with broadside as she did so. As she bore away in confusion, she was followed by 6 of the other ships but *Oriente* bravely remained on the larboard (port) tack, passed along

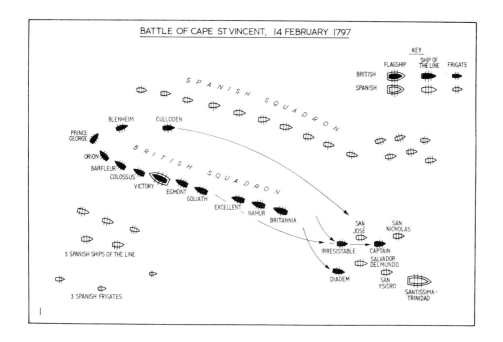

BATTLE OF CAPE ST VINCENT, 14 FEBRUARY 1797

the British line and rejoined the main body of the Spanish fleet.

At 1pm the leading ships of the Spanish main body bore up in a last effort to reach their detached fellows to leeward. The British fleet was now in a 'V' shape with the Spaniards outside either upper extremity and there was a real chance that the enemy would unite before the *Culloden* could come far enough to the north to block the path. Seeing this danger, Nelson (now aboard *Captain* and third from the rear of the British line) at once bore round to port, passed between *Diadem* and *Excellent*, the rearmost ship, and made off on an almost westerly course, veering gradually to north-north-west to come athwart the bows of the sixth Spanish ship from the rear of their main body at 1.30pm. He was engaging *Santissima-Trinidad* when *Culloden* came up at that time. At 2.26pm *Excellent* (Captain Collingwood) opened fire on *Salvador del Mundo* as she passed her bow, then engaged the *San Ysidro* until 2.53pm when that latter ship struck her colours. *Excellent* passed on to engage the *San Nicolas* (80) which had been fighting with *Captain*; *San Nicolas*, hauling in to avoid *Excellent*, collided with *San José* whose mizzen mast had been shot away. *Captain* ran alongside the stern quarter of *San Nicolas*, Nelson boarded her with sailors, marines and some of the 69th Foot who were aboard his ship and in a few minutes the *San Nicolas* struck. The 3 ships were now locked together by their rigging and Nelson gave orders to continue the boarding process through to *San José* but that ship too struck before the boarding parties actually reached her.

*Santissima-Trinidad* was now engaged by *Orion* and *Irresistable* when *Excellent* also moved in on her; she struck her colours but at 4pm 11 other Spanish ships came to her rescue and the British had to pull away. Sir John Jervis now gave orders for the frigates to take the prizes in tow and for the ships of the fleet to form close line ahead behind *Victory*. By 5pm firing had ceased and the British had captured the *San José, Salvador del Mundo* (112s), *San Nicolas* (80) and *San Ysidro* (74), 10 other Spanish ships were badly damaged and their losses were 5,000 dead, wounded and captured. British

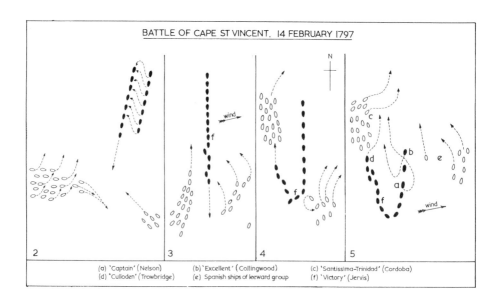

| | | |
|---|---|---|
| (a) 'Captain' (Nelson) | (b) 'Excellent' (Collingwood) | (c) 'Santissima-Trinidad' (Cordoba) |
| (d) 'Culloden' (Trowbridge) | (e) Spanish ships of leeward group | (f) 'Victory' (Jervis) |

losses were 73 killed and 227 wounded; 5 British ships were badly damaged but only one lost a spar – *Captain* whose fore topmast had been shot away.

The British ships engaged and their casualties were as follows: *Culloden* (74) Capt T. Troubridge – 10 killed, 47 wounded; *Blenheim* (98) Capt T. L. Frederic – 12 and 49; *Prince George* (98) Rear-Admiral W. Parker, Capt J. Irwin – 8 and 7; *Orion* (74) Capt Sir James Saumarez – 9 wounded; *Colossus* (74) Capt G. Murray – 5 wounded; *Irresistable* (74) Capt G. Martin – 5 and 14; *Victory* (100) Admiral Sir John Jervis KB, Capts R. Calder and G. Grey – 1 and 5; *Egmont* (74) Capt G. Sutton – nil; *Goliath* (74) Capt Sir C. H. Knowles, Bart – 8 wounded; *Barfleur* (98) Vice-Admiral Hon William Waldegrave, Capt J. R. Dacres – 7 wounded; *Britannia* (100) Vice-Admiral Charles Thompson, Capt T. Foley – 1 wounded (69th Foot); *Namur* (90) Capt J. H. Whitshed – 2 and 5; *Captain* (74) Commodore H. Nelson, Capt R. W. Miller – 24 killed, 56 wounded; *Diadem* (64) Capt G. H. Towry – 2 wounded (11th Foot); *Excellent* (74) Capt C. Collingwood – 11 and 12.

Jervis' boldness, and the supreme mutual confidence shown to exist between the British commander and his crews had plucked a useful victory from a numerically superior enemy. A vital result of this conflict was that the Spanish fleet withdrew into Cadiz and was at once blockaded there by Sir John Jervis; the planned union with the French at Brest was thus frustrated and a large-scale French invasion of Ireland averted. The blockade of Cadiz was maintained until mid-1799.

## The Channel Mutinies 1797

In May 1797 the Royal Navy at the Nore and Sheerness was badly disrupted by several mutinies in protest at the appalling conditions aboard ship. The mutineers blockaded the Thames but retained respect for their officers and even saluted the King's birthday! The army was called in to help suppress the mutinous crews and they set up artillery batteries on the banks of the Thames opposite the affected ships; loyal vessels (including some Russian ships) were anchored around those of the mutineers but no offensive action was taken and in mid June, the mutineers surrendered.

Trials and executions of the ringleaders dragged on into the autumn of

1798 but the main danger to the fleet was over. Admiral Sir John Jervis dealt with the mutinies in his ships with vigour but the high regard in which he was held by the men was not diminished by this firm disciplinary action.

Although of a minor nature when compared with the troubles suffered by the French navy, the British mutinies caused disruption to the blockade of the enemy coasts and one frigate, *Hermione* (32), was actually taken into La Guaira by her mutinous crew after her commander, Captain Hugh Pigot, had been killed. The Royal Marines were of great value in maintaining and restoring discipline in the fleet.

## The Action at Tenerife, 24/25 July 1797

In early July Sir John Jervis detached from his fleet blockading Cadiz 3 ships of the line; *Theseus, Culloden, Zealous* (74s); 3 frigates, *Sea Horse* (38), *Emerald* (36), *Terpsichore* (32), a cutter *Fox* and a mortar boat under Rear-Admiral Nelson to attack the harbour of Santa Cruz on Tenerife in the Spanish Canary Islands to try to capture a silver galleon there. The Spanish garrison numbered about 3,000 men; Nelson arrived off Santa Cruz on 15 July and made preparations for a landing but this was delayed by adverse weather until 9pm on 22 July. The landing party attacked the heights north of the bay but found them too strong and re-embarked without loss. On 24 July the *Leander* (50) joined the British force and at 11pm that night another landing was made with 700 men under Nelson's command. The weather was rough and the Spanish detected the attackers just off the mole at 1.30am on 25 July and opened fire with 30 artillery pieces on the *Fox*, damaging her so badly that she sank with a loss of 97 men. Nelson was hit in the right elbow and had to be evacuated. The landing was carried out and 6 captured guns were spiked; another British party of 340 men entered the town after having lost all their boats in the surf while landing. Being confronted at dawn by 8,000 Spaniards and 100 French soldiers, they capitulated and were permitted to return to their ships in Spanish boats after having been treated to biscuits and wine by the enemy who also offered to allow the British to buy provisions ashore if they wished. The expedition withdrew without achieving its aim; Nelson had his arm amputated and the total losses were 102 drowned, 45 killed, 5 missing and 105 wounded. Nelson required a long recuperation in England before he was fit for service again.

## The Battle of Camperdown (Kamperduin), 11 October 1797

In accordance with the French plan to invade Ireland, the Batavian fleet under Vice-Admiral de Winter left the Texel to join up with the Brest fleet. The British blockading force under Admiral Duncan, had left station in order to refit in Great Yarmouth, leaving a small squadron under Captain Trollope to watch the Batavians. Trollope at once sent the cutter *Active* back to alert the main British force on 9 October, and Duncan immediately put to sea, went to the Texel but found only 22 Batavian merchantmen there. He sailed south and sighted the enemy near the Dutch coast off Kamperduin (north of Haarlem) at 7am on 11 October.

The Batavian fleet consisted of 26 ships of varying size, the exact details of which can be seen in Appendix 2, and de Winter's flagship was the *Vrijheid* (74). He formed two lines ahead, both sailing north-north-east in the light north-north-westerly breeze, with the heavier ships towards the British, the 9 lighter ships towards the coast.

The British strained to attack but were so scattered that at 11am Duncan came onto the starboard tack to allow the rearmost ships to catch up, but

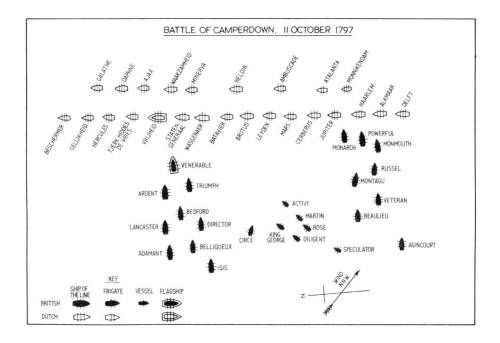

BATTLE OF CAMPERDOWN, 11 OCTOBER 1797

seeing that the enemy were making inshore he set the signals 'each ship to engage her opponent – to bear up – the van to attack the enemy rear'. The British formation resembled coincidentally, that adopted intentionally by Nelson at Trafalgar eight years later – two roughly equal parallel lines heading to pierce the enemy line in the centre and the rear.

Duncan now set the signal to pass through the enemy line and engage from the lee side and then 'close action'. At about 12.30pm Vice-Admiral Onslow on *Monarch* (74) cut the enemy line astern of *Jupiter* (74) 3 ships from the Batavian rear and came up to engage her from the lee side. *Powerful* (74) engaged the Batavian *Haarlem* (68) from the weather side and *Monmouth* (64) and *Russel* (74) took up the fight with *Alkmaar* (56) and *Delft* (54), the rearmost Batavian vessels.

The northernmost British column, headed by *Venerable* (74) with Duncan aboard, broke the Batavian line astern of *Staten-Generaal* at about 12.45pm; *Triumph* (74) closed with *Wassenaer* (64). By now *Vrijheid* (74) was engaged by *Ardent* (64) on one side and *Venerable* on the other, and by the *Bedford* (74) from ahead. The Batavian *Hercules* (64) caught fire in the poop and fell out of the line, striking her colours shortly after putting out the fire as she had jettisoned most of her powder in fear of the fire reaching the magazine.

*Venerable* was now so badly damaged as to have to leave the fighting line; *Triumph* (74) forced *Wassenaer* to strike and then moved up to join in the battering of the *Vrijheid*, by now dismasted. This gallant Batavian ship was fought to a wreck by 4 strong opponents before she struck her colours which signalled the end of the action.

The British were in possession of the following prizes: *Vrijheid* (74); *Jupiter* (72); *Tjerk Hiddes de Vries, Gelijkheid, Haarlem* (68s); *Hercules, Wassenaer* (64s); *Alkmaar* (56); *Delft* (54); *Monnikedam* (44); and *Galathe* (18). The *Delft* sank on 14 October and the *Monnikedam* was beached off West Kapelle. The Batavians lost 540 killed and 620 wounded as well as those captured in the prizes.

56

The battle was so hard fought that the British were in no state to chase the remnants of the enemy fleet in the shallow coastal waters. British losses were: 203 killed and 622 wounded; their ships engaged and their casualties were as follows: *Venerable* (74) Admiral A. Duncan, Capt W. G. Fairfax – 15 killed, 62 wounded; *Monarch* (74) Vice-Admiral R. Onslow, Capt E. O'Brien – 36 and 100; *Russel* (74) Capt H. Trollope – 7 wounded; *Montagu* (74) Capt John Knight – 3 and 5; *Bedford* (74) Capt Sir T. Byard – 30 and 41; *Powerful* (74) Capt W. O. B. Drury – 10 and 78; *Triumph* (74) Capt W. Essington – 29 and 55; *Belliqueux* (64) Capt J. Inglis – 25 and 78; *Agincourt* (64) Capt J. Williamson – nil; *Lancaster* (64) Capt J. Wells – 3 and 18; *Ardent* (64) Capt R. R. Burgess – 41 and 107; *Veteran* (64) Capt G. Gregory – 4 and 21; *Director* (64) Capt W. Bligh – 7 wounded; *Monmouth* (64) Capt J. Walker – 5 and 22; *Isis* (50) Capt W. Mitchell – 2 and 21; *Adamant* (50) Capt W. Hotham – nil.

Unlike the French and Spanish fleets, the Batavians directed their gunfire into their opponents' hulls and at the end of this action the British ships appeared almost undamaged in their masts, spars and rigging.

Captain Williamson of *Agincourt* was tried by court martial for not closing with the enemy in accordance with Duncan's signals and was sentenced to be placed at the bottom of the list of post captains and to be rendered incapable of serving again in the navy. The charge was brought by the indignation of Captain Thomas Hopper, Royal Marines, who was serving on the *Agincourt* and was so mortified at the failure of his captain to come to grips with the enemy that he exclaimed loudly: 'This is the second time that I have seen the British flag disgraced by the cowardice of my captain!'

The French General Hoche's grand plans for the invasion of Ireland had thus been dealt two great blows by the battles of Cape St Vincent and Camperdown and the Spanish and Batavian fleets had been neutralised.

## Political Developments in 1797

On land the British fortunes were not nearly so favoured as at sea however. On 17 October 1797 France forced Austria to sign the Peace of Campo Formio (and the German states to agree to the Congress of Rastatt) whereby Austria received Venice, Istria and Dalmatia, but surrendered to France Milan, the Austrian Netherlands (Belgium) and the Holy Roman Imperial possessions on the left bank of the River Rhine, including the city of Mainz. France also took Corfu and the Ionian Islands. These events left Britain once more as France's only active enemy.

Admiral Brueys with the Toulon fleet was enabled by the absence of the Royal Navy in the Mediterranean to sail into the Adriatic and seize the neutral Republic of Venice, which was divided between Austria and the Cisalpine Republic at the Peace of Campo Formio, and subsequently to carry off the four best Venetian ships of the line. The remainder of the extensive Venetian fleet was destroyed or damaged prior to being left to the Austrians at Napoleon's express command.

# The War of the Second Coalition 1798-1802

## Napoleon's Egyptian Expedition 1798

Deprived of any chance of gaining control of the seas around Britain by the naval defeats of 1797, France postponed any further plans to invade Ireland and that restless genius, General Napoleon Bonaparte, sought now to strike at Britain's colonial empire by a drive on India via Egypt, Syria and Persia. He convinced the Directory of the merits of his plans and was ordered to proceed. This course of action became feasible by the British naval evacuation of the Mediterranean and by the pacification of France's continental foes in 1797. An extensive programme of shipbuilding and refurbishing of the French naval dockyards began and in February 1798 naval vessels and transports were concentrated in Toulon and other southern ports together with an army of 36,000 men. Naval stores, equipment and ammunition were still in short supply however, and the French navy still lacked self-confidence. Operational security had been excellent and the British had no idea of the real scope or aims of the French in Toulon. The British, secure now that the invasion of Ireland was less imminent, felt able to venture again into the Mediterranean and on 10 April 1798, sent Nelson, now recovered from his Tenerife wound, to Lord St Vincent (as Sir John Jervis was titled after his elevation to the peerage following his victory) off Cadiz with orders that he should give Nelson 3 ships of the line to enable him to observe Toulon. On 17 May Nelson captured a French frigate but was able to glean little intelligence of the activity in Toulon and in other French riviera ports.

The Toulon force was now joined by other ships from Marseilles and Napoleon arrived to take command; Vice-Admiral Brueys was in charge of the naval vessels. Lord St Vincent, meanwhile, had been reinforced off Cadiz by 8 ships of the line and had been instructed to send 12 into the Mediterranean to bolster up Nelson's small squadron. This he did, under the command of Captain T. Troubridge in the *Culloden*.

On 19 May Napoleon's expedition left Toulon and the other smaller French harbours, and joined up at sea. The fleet consisted of 13 ships of the line, 8 frigates, 2 ex-Venetian 64s, 6 frigates *en flute* (ie with many of their guns removed or stored in the hold so that the deck space might be used for other purposes), and various other ships totalling 72 men-of-war and 400 transports. The naval crews numbered 10,000 men—about 1,700 less than establishment figure for the ships involved. The fleet went first to Genoa, undetected by Nelson who had been blown off station by a gale and was repairing his ships, picked up more transports there and sailed down the east coast of Corsica and reached Malta in early June. This island, governed by the Knights of St John, was neutral and refused to permit the French fleet to enter Valletta to replenish their water supply. Napoleon promptly invaded the island, the Knights capitulated and most of them went into exile. The French garrisoned Malta, intending to hold it as a naval base to secure their lines of communication from France to Egypt. Two ships of the line and 4 other vessels were taken in Malta's harbours.

During this voyage Napoleon organised the frigates into a light reconnaissance force operating ahead and to the flank of the main body of the fleet as light cavalry did for a land army; this was the first instance of this being done in the French navy.

17 June 1798: the British fleet in the Bay of Naples before the Battle of the Nile
(*National Maritime Museum*)

Leaving a garrison of 4,000 men in Malta, Napoleon sailed for Egypt on 19 June, still completely undetected by the Royal Navy. On 1 July, the French fleet anchored off Alexandria, having received news the day before that Nelson was now hot on their heels.

Troops were hurriedly disembarked that night and Alexandria was stormed and occupied within a few days. Although the transports took up station in the city's inner harbour, Brueys for some reason took the naval vessels 24km to the east on 7 July and anchored them in Aboukir Bay. An order from Napoleon stating that they should return to Alexandria apparently did not reach the fleet before Nelson's attack.

Lord St Vincent had no knowledge of the destination of the French fleet from Toulon but there were several possible targets for such a force: Naples, Sicily, Spain, Portugal, even Ireland or Russia. Nelson was ordered to shadow the enemy and destroy them if possible.

After losing touch with the French at Toulon, however, Nelson's task in regaining contact was doubly difficult in that he had no frigates and only one brig which could be used for reconnaissance purposes – he was almost blind operationally. In addition, his flagship *Vanguard* had had her rigging badly damaged in the storm and was still only partially repaired when he resumed station off Toulon on 31 May, only to find that his prey had slipped out in his absence thirteen days before. On 5 June he was joined by Troubridge's reinforcements and at once set off to find and destroy the enemy. By 12 June he passed the southern tip of Corsica and on 17 June he entered Naples where he was told that Brueys had probably gone to Malta.

He learned of the fall of Malta at Messina on 20 June and two days later, at Cape Passaro, he heard that the French fleet had left the island, sailing with a north-west wind. From this Nelson deduced that Alexandria was the enemy's target and he pressed on for this point under full sail, arriving there on 28 June but finding no sign of his quarry. Unknown to him, he had overtaken the slower-sailing French fleet on 25 June at a distance of some sixty nautical miles south of the island of Crete – the lack of frigates was

59

to cost him much time and effort. Assuming he had been mistaken in his target choice, Nelson at once left for Asia Minor and then beat his way back to Sicily, arriving there to water and replenish on 19 July without having seen a ship or having learned anything about French intentions. Still convinced that Napoleon was in Egypt, Nelson set course again for Alexandria and his suspicions were confirmed by information he received off the southern tip of Greece. On 1 August the British arrived off Alexandria to find only the French transports in the harbour but no battle fleet. Shortly after this, however, a British ship of the line sighted Brueys' 17 ships at anchor in Aboukir Bay and reported this long-awaited news to Nelson at once.

Although Brueys knew that the Royal Navy was liable to be hunting for him, he had taken little or no precautions in his deployment in Aboukir Bay either to guard against being surprised or to ensure that he was prepared to fight at short notice. Indeed, when Nelson's ships actually fell on his fleet, over 3,000 of the crews were on land collecting fresh water or engaged on other duties.

## The Battle of the Nile (Aboukir Bay), 1 August 1798

The French fleet of 17 ships of the line was anchored about 3km offshore, in line headed into the NNW wind. To their north-west the shoals extending well past Aboukir Island protected them from a direct approach on that flank. On the island was a battery of French guns. Bruey's flagship *l'Orient* (120) was in the centre of the line; 4 frigates lay between the shore and the line ships. The ships were anchored about 150 metres apart (the whole line thus 2.7km long) and the north-westernmost ship was 1km from the shallows around Aboukir Island. Although Napoleon had given Brueys troops and field artillery to help protect his ships, these were scarcely employed and the ships were anchored so far from the shore as to be out of effective range of the field guns and so far apart as to give each other no mutual support. The guns on board ship were not at action stations and the gun crews were at very reduced strengths due to the absence of most of them ashore.

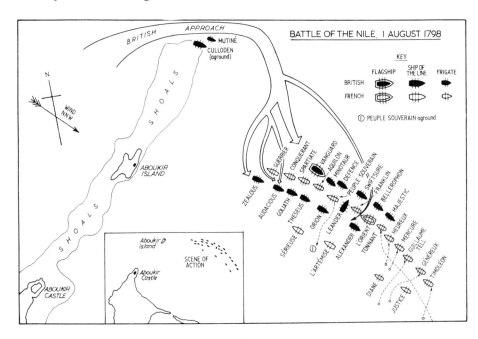

With the appearance of the British fleet at about 4pm, Brueys transferred some of the frigate crews to the line ships and ordered his brigs to try to lure the enemy onto the shoals but this ruse failed; he also ordered his ships to prepare to weigh anchor but as he expected no attack until the next morning he did not actually give the order to weigh.

Nelson's battle plan was to concentrate all his ships against the enemy van and main body, and overwhelm them. The British sounded their way around the shallows (only *Culloden* went aground at about 6.30pm but was later refloated) and moved into their chosen positions. The 2 leading French ships and the battery on Aboukir Island opened fire at about 6.15pm and at 6.30 the leading British ship, *Goliath*, passed the northernmost Frenchman *Guerrier*, saw that the water was over five fathoms deep and decided to break through the French line and to fight them from the shoreward side. She anchored opposite the second French ship *Conquérant* and opened fire; 4 other British ships followed his example and Nelson in *Vanguard* was the first British ship to stay to seaward of the enemy. The British now dropped their stern anchors and the battle proceeded. *Bellerophon* anchored opposite *l'Orient* but within the hour was so badly shot that she had to withdraw; a similar fate was suffered by *Majestic*, when anchored opposite *Tonnant*, and she had to cut her cable and then drifted into *Heureux* before clearing the line.

Sunset was at 6.44pm by which time there was so much gunsmoke about that it was almost impossible to tell how the battle was going. The British ships set night signals as pre-arranged and the firing continued. By now the frigate *Sérieuse* was near to sinking and the 5 ships of the French van were being overpowered by 8 British vessels, but the French centre was holding its own and their rearguard (under Villeneuve) was intact although not contributing to the battle at all. By midnight the *Swiftsure*, *Alexander* and *Culloden*, from Alexandria and the shallows respectively, joined their comrades and worsened the predicament of the immobile Frenchmen.

At 9pm the *Peuple Souverain* cut her cables and drifted south out of the line and *Leander* moved into her place and anchored so as to rake both *Franklin* and *l'Orient* with her fire. By this time the French van had struck their colours and at 10.30pm *l'Orient*, which had been on fire since 8 o'clock, blew up; only about 100 men managed to escape, Brueys having been killed prior to this event. At 11.15pm *Tonnant* and *Franklin* struck their colours, by which time most of the French rearguard had cut their cables and drifted south away from the battle. Those British ships opposite the defeated French van now also let themselves drift south to engage new targets. From about 3am to 5am on 2 August there was a tacit ceasefire and then fighting was renewed. At 9am the frigate *Artémise* blew up and at midday Villeneuve finally set sail with *Guillaume Tell*, *Généreux* and *Timoléon*, although this latter ship then ran aground and was burned by her crew. The other 2 ships and a frigate also escaped – for the moment.

French losses in the battle were 11 ships of the line, 2 frigates and many other vessels; they also had 1,700 dead, 1,500 wounded (of which 1,000 were captured) as well as 2,000 taken prisoner. Nelson had all the prisoners put ashore.

British losses were 218 dead and 678 wounded and most casualties occurred on those ships which fought the French from the deep water side where most of the French guns were ready for action.

The British casualties at the Battle of the Nile were: *Goliath* (74) Capt T. Foley – 27 killed, 41 wounded; *Zealous* (74) Capt S. Hood – 1 and 7; *Orion*

1 August 1798: The Battle of the Nile (*National Maritime Museum*)

1 August 1798: The Battle of the Nile at sunset with HMS *Vanguard* at the rear of the British line (*National Maritime Museum*)

(74) Capt Sir James Saumarez – 13 and 29; *Audacious* (74) Capt D. Gould – 1 and 35; *Theseus* (74) Capt R. W. Miller – 5 and 30; *Vanguard* (74) Rear-Admiral Sir Horatio Nelson KB (wounded), Capt E. Berry – 30 and 76; *Minotaur* (74) Capt T. Louis – 23 and 64; *Defence* (74) Capt J. Peyton – 4 and 11; *Bellerophon* (74) – Capt J. Hopkins (mortally wounded) – 49 and 148; *Majestic* (74) Capt G. B. Westcott (killed) – 50 and 143; *Culloden* (74) Capt T. Troubridge – nil; *Alexander* (74) Capt A. J. Ball – 14 and 58; *Swiftsure* (74) Capt B. Hallowell – 7 and 22; *Leander* (50) Capt T. B. Thompson – 14 wounded.

Unfortunately, Nelson had been wounded during the battle and was not in command on 2 August, otherwise no French ship would have escaped. As it was, the consequences of the battle were impressive enough; in the short term the French Mediterranean fleet was destroyed and their army in Egypt cut off; 6 of the captured vessels were taken back as prizes, 3 others were burned. Strategically the threat to India had been removed, British control of the Mediterranean decisively re-established and the Ottoman Mamelukes became bolder in their resistance to Napoleon. Turkey declared war on France in September 1798 and Britain was able to reform the coalition against the French with Austria, Russia, Naples, Portugal and Turkey, although this did not occur until two months later when news of the victory eventually reached England.

Nelson was made Baron of the Nile and received a Parliamentary address of thanks; his subordinates were also honoured and received prize money.

The 2 French ships of the line which escaped from Aboukir Bay did not survive for long. In early 1800 Rear-Admiral Perrée left Toulon with a small fleet to aid the French garrison on Malta but was intercepted by Nelson and 1 of the Aboukir ships was taken; the other was captured when leaving Malta.

## Further Operations in the Mediterranean 1798–9

Nelson sent Captain Sir James Saumarez with the 6 fit prizes back to Gibraltar with 7 of his own ships as escort while Captain Hood blockaded the French transports in Alexandria with 3 ships of the line. He then left for Naples on 19 August acting on secret instructions and arrived there on 22 September.

A Portuguese squadron had joined the British at Alexandria from where it was sent to Malta (still under French occupation) and where it supported a popular uprising against the garrison. Saumarez delivered muskets and ammunition to the Maltese insurgents at the end of September, then sailed on to Alexandria and at the end of October 1798 Nelson arrived off Malta from Naples.

The French in Valletta were not so easily frightened however and had to be blockaded for two years before surrendering in September 1800. Lord St Vincent had now set up his headquarters in Gibraltar with Nelson in command in the Mediterranean and with Admiral Lord Keith off Cadiz with 15 ships of the line.

In October 1798 a Russo-Turkish fleet under Vice-Admiral Uschakov entered the eastern Mediterranean, occupied the Ionian Islands and besieged Corfu. Nelson attempted to get them to sail to Egypt but to no avail. In mid-November Lord St Vincent sent an expedition to Minorca where Port Mahon was soon reoccupied.

Napoleon, meanwhile, was in Egypt without news from France from July 1798 to February 1799; despite his dangerous position he devised a plan to march through Syria and Mesopotamia to India with his 30,000 men and early in 1799 he advanced through the northern Negev and captured Jaffa and Haifa (nowadays Israeli ports) and then came up to Acre. Here Captain Sir Sidney Smith with a Royal Naval squadron landed in the city and had the defences rapidly organised to oppose this threat. In occupying Acre Smith effectively blocked Napoleon's further advance as his movement was restricted to the narrow coastal strip at this point. Despite the British naval presence and his own lack of warships, Napoleon managed to organise logistic resupply with flotillas of small ships from Alexandria and even brought up siege artillery by sea to help him in his assault on Acre. The siege began in mid-March 1799 and by mid-May a breach had been made and a storm attempt was imminent. These efforts were thwarted by Sir Sidney Smith who bombarded the besiegers and sent reinforcements to hold the breach. The frustrated Napolean had to lift the siege and fall back to Alexandria, holding only the isthmus of Suez. During the siege Napoleon had defeated a Turkish force at Mount Thabor on 16 April 1799.

In June Sir Sidney Smith with his own 2 ships of the line, *Theseus* and *Tiger*, plus 13 Turkish and 100 other vessels landed 20,000 Turkish troops at Aboukir. This venture was short-lived, however, as Napoleon scattered and destroyed this force within a few days on 25 July.

From Sir Sidney Smith, Napoleon received newspapers dated June 1799 in which he read of France's defeats in Germany and northern Italy; this prompted him to abandon his army in Egypt and to return to France with all speed to grasp power for himself.

Smith had to leave Alexandria to go for water in Cyprus on 9 August and Napoleon slipped out with 2 frigates and landed in France two months later Following the overthrow of the Directory he was First Consul and sole head of France by the end of 1799.

# Russian Naval Operations 1798–1801

In 1798 Admiral M. K. Makarov sailed from the Baltic to the North Sea to operate with the Royal Navy blockading the Batavian coast. His fleet consisted of 14 ships of the line, including *Mstislav* and *Alexander Nevski* (74s), *Retvisan*, *Europa*, *Mikhail*, *Joanna*, *Januarius* (66s), *Oemheiten* (62) and 4 frigates. On 11 August 1799, while attacking the Batavian fleet at Nieuwe Diep, Texel, together with Vice-Admiral Andrew Mitchell's ships, the Russian Captain A. V. von Muller II captured the frigate *Washington* (30). The *Washington's* flag is now in the Hermitage Museum, Leningrad.

### Russo-Turkish Operations in the Adriatic 1798

Although normally bitter enemies, Russia and Turkey formed a brief alliance in 1798 to operate against the French presence in the Adriatic.

In September 1798 the Russian Black Sea Fleet under Vice-Admiral F. F. Uschakov sailed through the Dardanelles and joined forces with a Turkish squadron of 4 ships of the line, 6 frigates, 4 corvettes and 14 gunboats. The Russian ships of the line were *Saint Paul*, Vice-Admiral Uschakov, *Saint Peter* (74) First-Captain Seniavin, *Zacharia* and *Elisabeth, Thanks to Supreme God, Holy Trinity* and *Mary Magdalene*. The frigates were *Great Grigori of Armenia, Saint Michael, Saint Nicholas, Holy Spirit, The Holy Virgin of Kazan, Happy, Navarchia, Saint Irene, Red Village* and *Panagia Apotoumengara*.

The allied fleet entered the Ionian Sea and on 12 October Second-Captain Chostak captured the island of Cerigo from its French garrison with his 300

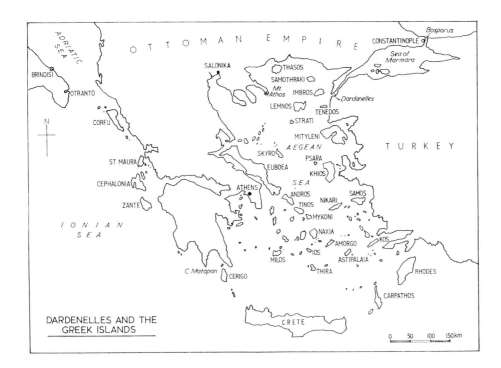

DARDENELLES AND THE
GREEK ISLANDS

marines; 31 guns were also taken. On 24 October they took the island of Zante and another 62 guns. The Russian fleet was then divided into four divisions:

1st under First-Captain Selivacher was sent to blockade Corfu.

2nd under First-Captain Seniavin went to the island of St Maure and thence to the Dalmatian coast.

3rd under Second-Captain Poskotchin attacked the islands of Cephalonia and Ithaca.

4th under Vice-Admiral Uschakov was the main body and proceeded against Corfu.

Next to Malta, Corfu was the strongest natural fortress in the Mediterranean at this time; it had a large French garrison (sent there following the allocation of the Ionian Islands to France at the Peace of Campo Formio in 1797) in 5 forts and a fleet of 9 French sail, all commanded by General de Brigade Chabot and it presented the allies with a major problem.

Two more Russian ships of the line joined the besiegers from the Black Sea in January 1799 and the allies now had 12 ships of the line and 11 frigates concentrated around the island. In March a successful assault was mounted and on 2 May Chabot capitulated and the island surrendered; 2,931 Frenchmen (including four generals), 636 guns, the frigate *Brune* (28), the ex-British frigate *Leander* (50) and 16 smaller vessels fell into allied hands. The *Leander* was returned to the Royal Navy.

All the former Venetian territory along the Dalmatian and Greek coast was now gathered into the Russian-sponsored 'Republic of the Seven Islands'.

In October 1798 Tsar Paul I had become Grand Master of the Order of St John, and Malta, seat of the Order, thus passed into Russian sovereignty, even though still occupied by the French.

Following their capture of Corfu, the Russo–Turkish fleet moved up the

65

2 November 1799: Austro–Russian–Turkish ships attacking French-held Ancona fortress (*National Maritime Museum*)

Adriatic to blockade Ancona on the east Italian coast, assisted by a small flotilla of Austrian ships under a Major Potts. Ancona fell and passed into Austrian hands in November 1799.

The Russians landed 500 marines at Foggia and, together with Italian partisans and British marines, helped to capture Naples. They were also active at Brindisi and Bari, but by the end of 1799 Tsar Paul's relationship with his Austrian allies was increasingly bitter and he left the Second Coalition and ordered Uschakov to withdraw his fleet to the Baltic.

Following the end of the War of the Second Coalition by the Peace of Amiens (25 March 1802) Malta, now occupied by the British, was supposed to return to Russian control but the British never in fact evacuated the island before Tsar Alexander I (Paul's successor) renounced his claim to be Grand Master of the Order of St John and thus Malta remained in British hands.

The Ionian Republic was nominally independent but in fact under Russian control, and Russian naval units cruised in the Mediterranean, keeping contact with the Black Sea Fleet through the Dardanelles, now still open to Russian shipping.

## The Attempted Invasion of Ireland 1798

On 6 September 1798 a French squadron consisting of the *Hoche* (74) (Commodore Bompart) and 8 frigates: *Immortalité, Loire, Romaine* (40s); *Bellone, Coquille, Embuscade, Résolue* and *Semillante* (36s), left Brest with 3,000 troops and a train of artillery to invade Ireland.

On 12 October, off Tory Island they were intercepted by a British squadron under Captain Sir J. B. Warren with *Foudroyant* (80), *Canada, Robust* (74s); *Anson, Magnanime* (44s); *Amelia, Ethalion* (38s), *Melampus* (36).

At 7am the fight began, the *Hoche* struck her colours after a gallant defence at 10.50am having lost 270 killed and wounded from a crew of 1,237. *Bellone* struck next (20 killed, 45 wounded from a crew of 519), then *Embuscade* (15 killed, 26 wounded from a crew of 486), then *Coquille* (18 killed and 31 wounded from a 507 crew). The other 5 frigates stood away westwards.

British losses this day were: *Foudroyant* Capt Sir J. T. Bayard – 9 wounded; *Canada* Capt Sir J. B. Warren – 1 wounded; *Robust* Capt E. Thornborough – 10 killed and 40 wounded; *Anson* Capt P. C. Durham – 2 and 13; *Magnanime* Capt the Hon M. de Courcy – 7 wounded; *Amelia* Capt the Hon C. Herbert – nil; *Ethalion* Capt G. Countess – 1 and 4; *Melampus* Capt G. Moore – 1 wounded; totalling 13 killed and 75 wounded compared with French losses of 425 killed and wounded and 1,870 captured.

The *Résolue* (on her way back to France) was taken by *Melampus* at 1am on 14 October with only token resistance; the *Loire* fought her way out of the clutches of the 32-gun frigate *Mermaid* (Capt James N. Newman) and the 18-gun brig *Kangaroo* (Capt E. Brace). *Mermaid* lost 3 killed and 13 wounded. Next day *Loire*, now without main and fore topmasts, was found by *Anson* (44) who had lost her mizzenmast, main yard and main crosstrees in the action on 12 October. Action began at 10.30am; at 11.45am *Kangaroo* joined in with a broadside and *Loire's* mainmast came down. She struck with a loss of 46 killed and 77 wounded out of a 624 crew. *Anson* lost 2 killed.

*Immortalité* was engaged on 28 October off Brest by the 38-gun frigate *Fisgard* at 11.30am; after a hard fight *Immortalité* struck at 3pm having lost 54 killed and 61 wounded out of 580. *Fisgard* lost 10 killed out of 281. The two remaining frigates, *Semillante* and *Romaine* reached Lorient and Brest respectively in safety.

The expedition had been pitifully weak and had met the disaster it invited.

## Nelson in Naples 1799

Sicily was now put into a state of defence to guard against enemy attacks from the French-controlled mainland. On 13 June 1799 Lord Nelson with 16 ships of the line off Palermo, detached a frigate, a bomb and two brigs to blockade Naples. On land the Austro–Russian forces under the Russian General Suwarow entered northern Italy in mid-April and thrust southwards, overrunning their French enemies and their republican adherents. Cardinal Ruffo defeated the French near Naples on 5 June and by 15 June several small fortified islands in the bay had capitulated to the captain of the British frigate *Sea Horse* (38), Captain James Foote. On 20 June Cardinal Ruffo sent Foote a capitulation for signature; it related to the French and republican-held forts of Castel Nuovo and Castel del Uovo and had already been signed by the cardinal and the local Russian and Turkish commanders. Foote also signed it and the forts were handed over on 22 June. Under the agreed terms, the garrisons of the forts were to be transported on British ships to Toulon but while the ships were being collected for this task, Lord Nelson arrived in Naples with 16 ships of the line and, on the insistence of Lady Hamilton who was aboard the *Foudroyant*, annulled the capitulation on the grounds that no agreement should have been made with Neapolitan rebels without the previous assent of Ferdinand IV, King of the Two Sicilies.

The surrendered rebels were held on board 14 transports in the bay of Naples for over a month on a meagre diet of bread and foul water in direct contravention of a properly concluded capitulation.

The French still held the fortress of St Elmo outside Naples with 800 men and it was decided to attack it with a force of 800 British and 400 Portuguese marines together with 500 Swiss, 450 Russians and 70 Greeks. Siege works began on 3 July and were pushed ahead until 11 July when the garrison capitulated and were returned to Toulon. Losses to the besiegers totalled 37 killed and 84 wounded.

The town of Capua, 24km from Naples, was next attacked on 22 July by a land force of British seamen and marines and Portuguese troops. On 29 June the 2,800 strong French garrison capitulated. Gaeta, a fortress nearby and still in French hands, surrendered on 31 July with 1,498 men, the French being returned to Toulon, the Neapolitan republicans being handed over to their countrymen and most of them executed.

The northern advance up the west coast of Italy continued and on 29 and 30 September 1799 a force of 200 British seamen and marines, together with Neapolitan troops, captured Civita-Vecchia, Corneto and Talfa.

Leghorn had been evacuated by the French on 17 July and the Royal Navy had played no small part in clearing the enemy from Naples, Rome and Tuscany and in restoring the ejected heads of state to their thrones.

## French Atlantic Fleet Operations 1799

On 25 April 1799, Admiral Comte de Bruix slipped out of Brest with 25 ships of the line and 10 other vessels and made for Cadiz. The British blockade squadron off Brest, commanded by Lord Bridport, consisted of 15 ships of the line but had been driven off station by strong north-easterly winds. A British frigate had observed the French, however, and news was soon passed to England where great concern for a renewed invasion attempt was felt. Bridport also sent word to Lord Keith, blockading Cadiz with his 15 ships of the line, who received the news on 3 May.

On 4 May de Bruix arrived with 24 ships of the line, hoping to join up with the score of Spanish ships of the line inside Cadiz harbour. Keith however stood his ground and de Bruix – doubtless aware of the much lower standard of seamanship of his crews – avoided a battle and sailed on into the Mediterranean, passing Gibraltar on 5 May. Lord St Vincent observed this enemy fleet and was at once concerned for the Royal Navy vessels in the ocean which were at this time dispersed as follows: Minorca – 4 ships of the line, Malta – 3, the Levant – 2 and Palermo (Nelson) – 1. Despite the heavy weather, St Vincent sent orders (overland) for Keith to leave Cadiz and join him at Gibraltar. This was done and on 12 May St Vincent left Gibraltar with 16 ships of the line to reinforce his Mediterranean detachments.

Meanwhile, Lord Bridport (off Ushant) had been sent 41 of the 51 Channel Fleet ships and of these he was instructed to send 16 on to the Mediterranean which he did on 1 June.

St Vincent arrived off Minorca and now had 20 line ships under his hand on 19 May and here he heard that de Bruix had been seen on a course for Toulon eight days before; he thus moved to Cape San Sebastian on the Spanish coast.

As soon as Keith left Cadiz, the Spanish fleet slipped out and went to Cartagena; of their 17 ships of the line however, 11 had lost nearly all their masts in the storms en route.

On 30 May, St Vincent heard that the French had left Toulon again; he maintained his position in order to prevent a junction between the two enemy fleets. He was reinforced by 5 line ships from England and so sent 5 others off to join Nelson at Palermo who then had 16 ships of the line in all. On 2 June Lord St Vincent was taken ill and handed over command to

Keith. Admiral de Bruix sailed to Vado to deliver supplies to the Army of Italy but on 6 June he sailed west along the coast to Cartagena where, on 22 June, he successfully joined up with the Spanish fleet.

Keith meanwhile had in fact sailed to Monaco but had then returned to protect his base at Port Mahon on Minorca. On 8 June St Vincent (now recovered) ordered him to go to the Bay of Rosa to frustrate any Franco–Spanish attempt to unify their fleets but this order was now too late. Keith cruised fruitlessly and returned to Port Mahon on 7 July where he found 12 more ships of the line sent from Lord Bridport. He at once set out in pursuit of the allied fleets which had left Cartagena at the end of June with 40 ships of the line, stayed at Cadiz for ten days and then made for Brest which they reached safely on 13 August. Keith arrived off Brest one day later.

Despite the numerical and qualitative superiority of the Royal Navy, the French had succeeded in a long-awaited operation of uniting the Spanish fleet with their own in a French harbour where the Spanish ships now lay as quasi-hostages against political changes. It is not clear, however, whether that was the true or the only aim of this breakout or whether another invasion of Ireland was also to be attempted.

Keith's concern for his vulnerable base at Port Mahon caused him to abandon his station between the French and Spanish fleets; had he remained where originally instructed, it is most likely that he would have intercepted and destroyed the French component at least – a strong object lesson that naval bases should ideally be capable of withstanding maximum expected enemy attack for a considerable period independent of their own fleet.

## Developments in Egypt 1799

Since the Battle of the Nile (1 August 1798) Napoleon and his army had been marooned in Egypt where he was unmolested by the Turks who had no answer to the aggressive tactics of destruction so well executed by the French Ever ambitious, Napoleon now planned to march on to India but first he had to clear his path through the inert Turkish army in the Ottoman province of Syria. The Turkish ruler there, Achmet Djezzat, had given refuge to Ibrahim Bey (ex-ruler of Egypt) in Acre and Napoleon seized this excuse to attack that city. In January 1799 he left Cairo with 13,000 men, 37 cannon and 11 howitzers and with generals Kléber, Bon, Lannes and Murat. The other 17,000 men of his army were spread in various garrisons in Lower Egypt.

On 18 February the French arrived at the defended castle of El Arish. The Royal Navy had effected their reappearance off Alexandria in November 1798 and Commodore Sir Sidney Smith (minister plenipotentiary to the Sublime Porte) then went to Constantinople to co-ordinate Anglo–Russian–Turkish action against the French.

Sir Sidney arrived off Alexandria in *Tigre* (74) on 3 March 1799 and joined *Theseus* (74) and the *en flute* frigate *Alliance*. In the evening he received news of Napoleon's invasion of Syria (he took Jaffa by storm that day) and sent *Theseus* to Acre to assist in the defence of the city. He joined that ship with *Tigre* in Acre on 16 March and began to organise the repair of the dilapidated fortifications. The Turkish garrison was small and was commanded by Djezzat Pasha.

To reach Acre the French had to use the coast road from the south so on 18 March Sir Sidney Smith placed *Tigre* in the bay of Acre, to enfilade this route. They engaged the French advanced guard that day near Mount Carmel and drove them back in confusion. Trying to find an alternative route inland, the French were harassed by Samaritan arabs. The French thrust was thus channelled to strike at Acre's defences on the north east – the strongest side – instead of being able to attack the weaker southern flank.

On 18 March *Tigre* intercepted and captured a French flotilla of 7 gunboats mounting in all 34 guns and loaded with Napoleon's complete siege train brought up from Damietta – indeed Napoleon paid dearly for being so rash as to trust his vital assault weapon to the sea! The siege guns were incorporated into Acre's defence and the gunboats used to enfilade the flanks of the French siege operations.

French logistic supplies continued to be sent from Alexandria to the port of Caïffa (Jaffa).

The French tried to storm a breach in Acre on 1 April but were repelled by the garrison of Turks and British seamen and marines. A storm drove *Tigre* and *Theseus* out to sea that day and when they returned on 6 April it was found that the French had pushed their trenches to the counterscarp and were mining the main tower at the north-east corner of the town. At dawn on 7 April a party of Royal Marines made a sortie into the mine to destroy it while the Turks carried out false attacks to left and right of this real thrust. As proof of their prowess in battle, the Turks brought back 60 French heads from these raids!

Meanwhile, a French squadron of 3 frigates and 2 corvettes under Admiral Perrée reached Jaffa from Alexandria with more siege guns for Napoleon and he also had 4 18pdrs taken from the *Junon* to increase his artillery. These cannon reached Acre overland from Jaffa on 27 April and on 1 May another French attempt was made to storm the north-eastern breach but it was again repulsed, the defenders being aided by the flanking fire of *Theseus*, *Tigre* and the captured gunboats.

On 7 May over 20 transports and some Turkish corvettes appeared off Acre carrying long-awaited reinforcements for the hard-pressed garrison. The French launched a last desperate attempt to carry the city before the men could disembark and by dawn on 8 May the French flag flew over the ruins of the north-east tower. The Turkish reinforcements under Hassan Bey were now half way to the shore from the transports – the race was on and Sir Sidney Smith led a party of seamen to bolster up the Turks around the tower until their countrymen could arrive. He succeeded and held the place until 1,000 men of the Chifflic Regiment (armed and trained like European troops) disembarked and rushed up to stabilise the situation. Another French assault that night was also repulsed. *Theseus* and *Tigre* were now north of Acre, the Turkish vessels to the south. General Kléber's division now arrived from the Jordan river and was preparing to make yet another assault but was caught off balance by the Chifflic Regiment commanded by Lieutenant-Colonel Suliman Aga on the night of 19 May and suffered heavy losses.

Napoleon finally saw that Acre was not to be taken and the siege was lifted on 20 May; a retreat was made next day in such haste that 23 cannon were left behind. He fell back to Cantoura on 21 May; Jaffa on 24 May, rested there for three days and reached Gaza on 30 May. On 2 June Napoleon was at El Arish where he left a garrison, and arrived in Cairo on 14 June. Berthier (famous as Napoleon's chief of staff in later campaigns) gave French losses from March–June 1799 as 500 killed, 1,800 wounded and 700 died from disease but the true figures were probably much greater.

Due to British command of the eastern Mediterranean, the weak Turkish garrison of a dilapidated and neglected fortress were able to hold out against the greatest military genius of the age and thus to stop his planned advance on India through Syria.

# Egypt 1800–01

On 24 January 1800 a convention was signed in El Arish between representatives of the Grand Vizier and General Kléber, who was then the French commander in Egypt since Napoleon had abandoned his men to pursue his own political ambitions in France. This treaty stipulated that the French should evacuate Egypt, embarking at Alexandria, Rosetta and Aboukir but on 20 February Kléber was informed by Sir Sidney Smith that the British government would not permit ships carrying the French army to return to France unmolested and that they could only capitulate as prisoners of war.

Sir Sidney had not been signatory to the Treaty of El Arish but he had signed, together with the French General Desaix and M. Poussielgue, a preliminary document containing the basis of the treaty. This unusual diplomatic reversal came it appears not from the British government as such but from Lord Keith and was contrary to the aims of the British cabinet.

This apparent treachery caused Kléber to decide to attack the Grand Vizier who was entirely innocent of any intrigue. On 20 March 1800 Kléber with 10,000 men attacked the Grand Vizier Jussuf with 60,000 men at the village of Matarich, on the site of the ancient Heliopolis, and after five days' fighting the Turks were decisively beaten, losing over 50,000 men, while French losses were slight.

Kléber re-established himself in Egypt and rejected a renewed British attempt to negotiate a peace treaty during June. Unfortunately for the French, Kléber was assassinated on 14 June in Cairo and his place was taken by General Abdullah Jacques Menou. The situation stabilised until 1801 when the British sent an expedition to Egypt to terminate the existence of this French army.

On 2 February 1801 a squadron of about 60 vessels, including *Foudroyant* (80), *Kent*, *Ajax*, *Minotaur*, *Northumberland*, *Tigre* and *Swiftsure* and carrying an army of 16,000 men under General Sir Ralph Abercromby anchored in Aboukir Bay, east of Alexandria. Due to bad weather, the troops could not disembark until 2am on 8 February. The French army in Egypt now totalled 21,000 fit for service and 900 sick (an incredibly low proportion of sickness in a European army in the Mediterranean even in the Second World War and most unlikely!). There were also 1,000 sailors left in Egypt since their ships were destroyed at the Battle of the Nile and 500 Greek auxiliaries.

The British advanced party of 700 men landed and a detachment of seamen accompanied them for service ashore and were commanded by the ubiquitous Sir Sidney Smith. The French garrison of Alexandria took up position on a ridge blocking the British advance to that city. They numbered 1,500 infantry and 180 cavalry and were joined by other detachments from Rosetta, making the total up to at least 2,500 men under General Friant.

The British regiments involved included the Guards, the Royals, the 54th Foot (Dorsets), 40th (South Lancashires), 23rd (Royal Welsh Fusiliers), 28th (Gloucesters), 42nd (Black Watch), 58th (Northamptons), and the Royal Corsican Rangers.

They landed in a hail of French fire and rushed the hills, driving off the French and taking 4 cannon. British losses were 22 sailors killed and 70 wounded while the army lost 102 killed and 515 wounded, making a total of 124 killed, 585 wounded with 38 missing.

In twenty minutes the bridgehead had been formed and the French

8 February 1801: British troops landing in Egypt – note Turkish mameluke charge in centre of picture (*National Maritime Museum*)

withdrew to Alexandria. By 9 February the whole British force was on shore. On 12 March Abercromby advanced down the narrow isthmus (less than a mile wide in places) towards the city and was blocked by 6,000 French at Mandora; a brief charge and the French fell back again. By now the brigade of seamen with the army was about 1,000 strong. Just before dawn on 21 March the French attacked the British in their desert camp on the isthmus which had the sea to the northern side but a partially dry lake Mareotis to the south over which French cavalry made a flank attack. The French had 9,730 men including 1,380 cavalry with 46 guns. The initial fury of this attack enveloped both British flanks but the remarkably cool behaviour of the redcoats held fast and the French were repelled decisively. British strength was 10,000 men including 300 cavalry with 46 guns. The French recorded their losses as 800 killed, 200 wounded and 400 captured but British accounts put the total loss at 3–4,000 men. The British army lost 243 killed, 1,193 wounded and 34 missing. The naval brigade was split at this battle, the marines occupying Aboukir castle (which had surrendered on 18 March), the sailors being in the battle. They lost 4 killed and 50 wounded including Sir Sidney Smith. General Abercromby was mortally wounded in the thigh, dying aboard the *Foudroyant* on 28 March.

On 26 March a second Turkish squadron arrived in Aboukir Bay carrying 5,000 Turkish and Albanian troops. The Turkish navy now had 6 ships of the line and 8 frigates and corvettes there. Their troops disembarked on 3 April and together with 800 British soldiers under Colonel Spencer captured Rosetta castle, thus opening up access to the Nile delta and its inhabitants who supplied the British with provisions. On 19 April the castle of Jullien, on the banks of the Nile, fell to this Anglo–Turkish force, supported by gunboats of both nations after a three-day siege.

72

Lake Mareotis, south of Alexandria was mainly dry but on 15 April the British cut the Alexandria canal and flooded the lake, thus isolating 6,000 French troops under General Menou in that city. Major-General Hutchinson had taken over from General Abercromby and on 5 May he left a holding force at Alexandria and took an Anglo–Turkish force of 8,000 men from Rosetta to deal with 4,000 French under General Lagrange at El-Aft. Allied gunboats moved up the Nile with him. The French abandoned El-Aft on 7 May and fell back south. Rahmineh was taken by the allies on 9 May but they did not proceed to Giza until 20 June. General Belliard capitulated in Cairo two days later; the treaty was signed on 27 June and the French garrison surrendered and were conveyed to France as agreed. They totalled 8,000 fit men and 1,500 sick and wounded. By 10 August 13,500 French prisoners had been embarked at Aboukir Bay and sent off to France; only Alexandria still held out. The island of Marabou, west of Alexandria, was attacked on 17 August and surrendered on 21 August after having burnt a flotilla of 18 of their own gunboats. The French moved their two 64-gun ships of the line and several corvettes closer up to Alexandria and sank several merchant vessels across the old harbour to prevent British ships getting in.

The allies attacked the city on 26 August and General Menou requested a three-day armistice next day in order to prepare a capitulation. This was agreed to and the city surrendered on 2 September 1801. The garrison of 8,000 soldiers and 1,300 sailors was carried back to France at British expense.

British naval losses at Marabou were 2 killed and 2 wounded; total British losses at Alexandria were 13 killed and 113 wounded.

The following French ships were captured in Alexandria and were given to the Turks: *Causse* (64), *Justice* (40) and an unknown 32-gun Venetian frigate. The *Egyptienne* (44), *Régénérée* (36) and another unnamed 32-gun Venetian frigate were retained by the British.

Thus ended Napoleon's oriental adventure – rendered a total failure by British naval power.

## Malta 1799–1800

Since landing there late in 1798, the French garrison of 3,000 sailors in Malta had been shut up in Valletta fortress; blockaded by a squadron of British, Portuguese and Neapolitan ships and closed in from the land side by Maltese, Neapolitan and British troops. A frigate from Toulon had slipped in with supplies in spring 1799 but by the autumn things were so bad that 36,000 of the 45,000 inhabitants of the city were expelled in order to make available supplies go further. On 1 November 1799 Lord Nelson sent a demand from his flagship *Vanguard* (80) that the garrison under General Vauban should surrender; this was rejected. An aviso ran the blockade in early 1800 and brought the garrison news of Napoleon's appointment as chief consul which did much to raise their morale.

On 15 February 1800, Lord Keith, off Malta with *Queen Charlotte* (100), *Foudroyant* (80); *Audacious, Northumberland, Alexander* (74s) and *Lion* (64) heard that a French squadron, consisting of *Généreux* (74), a frigate, 2 corvettes and several transports carrying 3,000 troops, all commanded by Admiral Perrée, had left Toulon on 7 February with the aim of putting supplies into Valletta. At dawn on 8 February *Alexander* and *Success* (a 32-gun frigate), to the south east of Malta, met and chased this squadron and captured a storeship. At 4.30pm Nelson with *Foudroyant* and *Northumberland* came up and *Généreux* struck her colours; Admiral Perrée was killed.

On 30 March 1800 the *Guillaume Tell* (80) slipped out of Valletta harbour in a southerly gale with Rear-Admiral Denis Decrès aboard and ran for Toulon. She was caught by *Penelope, Lion* (64s) and *Foudroyant* and, after a long struggle, surrendered having lost 200 killed and wounded. *Foudroyant* lost 8 killed and 64 wounded, *Lion* 8 and 38 and *Penelope* 1 and 3.

By August 1800 the French in Valletta were so short of firewood that they broke up their frigate *Boudeuse* to be burned. In a desperate attempt to save the 2 finest ships left (40-gun frigates *Diane and Justice*), they were sent to sea to try and reach Toulon in the evening of 24 August 1800. The *Success* found and chased them and after a short fight forced *Diane* (with only 114 men on board) to surrender. *Justice* got through safely to Toulon.

Valletta capitulated on 5 September; there were 3 warships in the harbour, only one of which, the Maltese *Athénien* (64), was worth taking. Another Maltese 64, the *Dégo* and the French frigate *Cartagénoise* (36) were unfit for service

## Anglo–Russian Cooperation
Since the outbreak of war, a Russian squadron had been in the Channel operating with the Royal Navy. The ships included the *Vsevolod, Admiral Tait-isidore, Asia, Civilot, Cedar, Svernoi Orel* (74s); *Aries, Probedt* (66s); *Pobeda, Elizabeth* (64s); *Narva, Shaftway, Pospheinay* (44s); *Probesna* (40) and *Ratvisian* (?).

## The Expedition to the Helder (Batavian Republic), August 1799
Admiral Lord Duncan, with 10 ships of the line and other vessels, escorted 250 transports carrying 29,000 British troops which were landed at the Helder late in August. The Russians sent 2 ships of the line with transports carrying 1,700 Russian soldiers.

After a brief clash with the Franco–Batavian defenders, Nieuwediep was captured together with 8 small ships of the line on 28 August. The ships, with the guns actually carried at the time, were: *Verwachting* (64); *Broederschap* (56); *Antoinette, Constitutie, Het Duifje, Expeditie, Hector, Unie* (44s); 5 frigates were also taken: *Heldin, Minerva* (28s); *Alarm, Polux* and *Venus* (24s).

Two days later the main Dutch (Batavian) fleet, under Vice-Admiral Storij, anchored in the Vlieter River, capitulated to Vice-Admiral Mitchell: *Washington* (70); *Leiden, Cerberus, Utrecht, Ruyter, Gelderland* (64s); *Beschermer, Batavier* (56s); *Amphitrite, Mars* (44s); *Embuscade* (34) and *Galathe* (16).

On 6 October 1799, however, the Franco–Batavians defeated the Anglo–Russian forces at Castricum and these forces were evacuated. The invaders had lost about 5,000 casualties.

### The British Blockade
Having now no active allies, Britain reverted to the effective and well-tried tactics of keeping all enemy naval ships firmly blockaded in their harbours. This was an exhausting task but the Royal Navy reaped the benefits that ensued from constantly exercising and improving its seamanship, whereas the enemy navies were decaying in enforced idleness with their men, equipment and supplies dwindling. World trade was also subject to rigorous control and search by Royal Naval ships, and neutrality was no safeguard against high-handed and ruthless British action.

Napoleon of course urged his naval commanders to break the blockades if

74

THE NETHERLANDS   1789 – 1806

NORTH
SEA

R Texel
HELDER
CAMPERDOWN
✗ 1797
Zuider
Zee
AMSTERDAM

BATAVIAN
REPUBLIC

The Maas        ○ THE HAGUE
Haringvliet

East Scheldt
Walcheren Island
FLUSHING
West Scheldt

GERMANY

○ ANTWERP

○ BRUSSELS
AUSTRIAN
NETHERLANDS
○ LIÉGE

Absorbed into France
in 1789

LUXEMBOURG

possible as he planned to relieve his abandoned forces in Egypt. It was not until the end of January 1801 that Admiral Ganteaume succeeded in slipping out of Brest during a heavy storm and passed the Straits of Gibraltar two weeks later. By this time Ganteaume had heard that a British expedition was already en route for Egypt and he went to Toulon to pick up the French troops earmarked for his venture and to sail on for Egypt as quickly as possible.

Admiral Warren (blockading Cadiz) at once left his station in pursuit of the French fleet and together with Admiral Keith he frustrated both of Ganteaume's attempted landings. Other French attempts to leave harbours

75

30 August 1799: the surrender to the British of the Batavian fleet in the Vlieter; the *Washington* can be seen at the rear of the line (*National Maritime Museum*)

and to support the Egyptian venture were still-born in face of the rigid British blockades.

In April 1800 Lord St Vincent (now recovered in health) assumed command of the Channel Fleet and with his energy and strict discipline the blockades of the enemy ports were made considerably more effective. Instead of the blockading ships returning to British ports to replenish supplies, auxiliary vessels took victuals, ammunition and reinforcements out to the ships on station.

## Genoa and Cooperation with the Austrians 1800

In March 1800 Lord Keith was off Genoa with *Queen Charlotte* (100), *Audacious, Minotaur* (74s) several frigates, sloops and gunboats cooperating with the Austrians under General von Ott who were besieging that city. On 16 March *Queen Charlotte* caught fire accidentally and burnt out with a loss of 666 out of 820 men.

On 20 May the French made a naval sortie with a 52-oared galley, *Prima* (mounting two very long 32pdrs and several smaller pieces), an armed cutter, three armed 'settees' and several gunboats. After a minor exchange of shots on 20 and 21 May the French returned to harbour. The British attacked these vessels as they lay alongside the mole in Genoa harbour. After dark on 21 May a British raiding party of 100 seamen and marines in 10 boats went into the harbour and captured the galley which had a crew of 257 combatants and over 300 galley slaves chained to the oars. The British lost 5 wounded; the French lost 1 killed and 15 wounded as well as many drowned when they jumped off the galley to escape; 70 were captured.

On 4 June 1800 General Massena consented to evacuate Genoa and retire to Nice but the next day Napoleon, having crossed the Alps with a strong army, entered Milan and reproclaimed the Cisalpine Republic. On 14 June he defeated the Austrians at Marengo under General Melas. General von Ott, having been in possession of Genoa for only three days, had to evacuate hurriedly. Massena reoccupied the city on 24 June, so rapidly that the *Minotaur* only just managed to get out of the harbour in time to avoid capture

Again, the inter-action of warfare on land and at sea is illustrated; here the naval forces were by far the weaker and played a very secondary role, the decisions being achieved far inland.

## The West Indies

From 1799–1802 Britain captured the following West Indian colonies of her enemies: Surinam (1799), Curaçao (1800), The Virgin Islands (1801), St Bartholemew, St Martin and St Eustace (all 1801). At the Peace of Amiens in 1802 all were returned to their previous owners except Trinidad.

## The Clash at Algeciras, 6 July 1801

On 13 June 1801 Rear-Admiral Linois with *Formidable* and *Indomptable* (80s), *Desaix* (74) and the frigate *Muiron* left Toulon for Cadiz but put into Algeciras at 5pm on 4 July on hearing that Cadiz was heavily blockaded.

Rear-Admiral Sir James Saumarez, commanding the British force off Cadiz, learned of the French force and set off in pursuit, finding them close in under the shore batteries at Algeciras on 6 July. Sir James had *Caesar* (80); *Pompée, Spencer, Venerable, Superb, Hannibal* and *Audacious* (74s). There was practically no wind and it was a long business getting the ships into the desired battle positions; the British ships anchored against the French and the action was fought 'on the spot', starting at 8.30am. *Pompée* received broadsides from all French ships whilst creeping into position and by 10am was in a bad state. *Hannibal* was ordered to rake *Formidable* to take the pressure off her sister ship, but went aground while trying to get into position. Soon after this a light north-easterly breeze sprang up and Linois gave the signal for his ships to cut their cables and beach themselves. Before this could be effected, however, the breeze dropped again. By noon *Pompée* had been towed clear and all other ships wallowed ineffectively in the windless sea. Fire from the shore batteries was heavy and well supplemented that of the French ships. *Hannibal* was now dismasted, aground and had to be abandoned. The action ended for the day.

British losses were 130 killed and 240 wounded: *Caesar* Rear-Admiral Sir James Saumarez, Capt J. Brenton – 18 killed, 25 wounded; *Pompée* Capt C. Stirling – 15 and 69; *Spencer* Capt H. d'Esterre Darby – 6 and 27; *Venerable* Capt S. Hood – 8 and 25; *Superb* Capt R. G. Keats – nil; *Hannibal* Capt S. Ferris – 75 and 62; *Audacious* Capt S. Peard – 8 and 32.

The British withdrew to Gibraltar to repair their ships and renew the contest. Linois refloated his ships and sent an aviso to Cadiz asking for urgent assistance.

On 8 July the Spanish Vice-Admiral Moreno with 5 ships of the line and 3 frigates moved out of Cadiz, putting to sea next day. They were shadowed by Capt R. G. Keats with *Superb*, the frigate *Thames* and the brig *Pasley*. *Pasley* went ahead and on the afternoon of 9 July alerted Gibraltar to the enemy approach. The Spanish squadron then anchored in Algeciras and were joined next day by *St Antoine* (74) from Cadiz. The crews of the battered British ships in Gibraltar were working on repairs day and night and by

Sunday 12 July they were finished and none too soon, for at the same time the Franco–Spanish squadron made ready for sea. The wind was from the east and fresh; at 1pm the British left Gibraltar with *Caesar*, *Venerable*, *Superb*, *Spencer*, *Audacious*, *Thames*, a polacre (Mediterranean barque) *Calpé* (14) and the Portuguese frigate *Princesa Carlota* (48). The time was 7.45pm.

The allies had then just cleared Cabrita Point, the *Hannibal* in tow behind a frigate; seeing the British, the frigate with *Hannibal* returned to Algeciras.

The allied ships were: Spanish – *Real Carlos*, *San Hermenegildo* (112s); *San Fernando* (96); *Argonauta* (80); *San Augustin* (74) and the frigate *Sabina* carrying Vice-Admiral Moreno and Rear-Admiral Linois. French – *Formidable*, *Indomptable* (80s); *St Antoine*, *Desaix* (74s) and the frigates *Libre* and *Muiron*.

There followed a night chase and at 11.30pm *Superb* engaged *Real Carlos* who caught fire and fell astern. At midnight *Superb* engaged *St Antoine* who surrendered after 30 minutes; the *Real Carlos* blew up at about 1am after having been engaged by mistake by her sister ship *San Hermenegildo* who was also caught up in the explosion and blew up as well. Of the 2,000 crew, only 300 were saved.

The French ships had not been as well repaired as the British and were limited in their sailing ability. On 13 July the *Formidable* was caught by *Venerable* and *Thames* just south of Cadiz. *Venerable* was partially dismasted in the fight and ran aground on the shoals of San Pedro, 12 miles south of Cadiz, but was later towed free. The rest of the Spanish squadron got safely back into Cadiz.

In these later actions *Superb* lost 14 wounded and *Venerable* lost 18 killed (including her master) and 86 wounded.

## Napoleon's Renewed Invasion Plans 1801–2

Following the Peace of Luneville Napoleon once more concentrated all his energies on preparing an invasion of England – his last enemy.

From mid-July 1801 9 divisions of gunboats and troop transports, together with the necessary land forces, began to gather at Boulogne under command of Rear-Admiral La Bouche-Tréville.

By 1 October 1801, 150 ships and 55,000 men were on the channel coast. One of the inventions proposed for use in this invasion, but not adopted, was a submarine built by an American named Fulton who planned to block the Thames with mines. In 1803 he built a steamtug but his demonstration to the French in Paris in 1803 was not successful and this too was abandoned. He then went to Britain but the Admiralty showed little interest in his devices.

These French invasion preparations were disrupted repeatedly by the Royal Navy under Nelson as Commander, Coastal Defences, after his return from the Battle of Copenhagen.

Simultaneously, Napoleon had been negotiating to end hostilities with England and on 27 March 1802 the Peace of Amiens was signed.

From her recent colonial conquests Britain retained only Trinidad and Ceylon; among those given up were Elba, Minorca, Guyana, St Lucia and Cape Colony. In return France withdrew her troops from Naples, Rome, Portugal and Egypt and recognised the Republic of the Seven Ionian Islands.

This peace, with its exchange of bargaining counters, was unpopular in England where Britain's undoubted and increasing naval supremacy seemed to make such dealings superfluous; the Royal Navy had increased its ships of the line and frigates from 135 each to 202 and 275 respectively, and these

21 July 1801: the British cutting out the French *Chevrette* from the Bay of Camaset
(*National Maritime Museum*)

were in a high state of readiness and training while France's initial 80 and 66 had dropped to 39 and 35 and were in a parlous state of shortages and unpreparedness.

During the brief peace which followed, Bonaparte sent 20 ships of the line and 6 frigates with 20,000 men to Haiti in order to improve seamanship and to re-establish French presence there. Unfortunately these aims were frustrated by native uprisings and raging fever epidemics which destroyed most of the men sent.

England meanwhile re-inforced her West Indian fleet and maintained forces in Malta and Egypt, contrary to the terms of the Peace of Amiens. Within a year the two nations were at war again.

From 1793 to 1801 the maritime trade of France, Holland and Spain had been ruined, whereas that of Britain had boomed and increased by 100% over the peacetime level. The United States of America, and other neutrals, had also enjoyed a trade boom and smuggling had become a business in itself due to Britain's rigorous search for contraband. Hamburg and Bremen became the main entry ports into northern Europe for British goods and Gibraltar and Malta were their counterparts in the south.

## Britain and the Armed Neutrality 1801

Britain's highhanded conduct against the ships of all other nations since 1793 had finally caused Denmark, Norway and Sweden to form the armed neutrality in March 1794.

Continued friction between Denmark and England led in August 1798 to a force of 9 ships of the line 'visiting' Copenhagen to escort a special government emissary; a convention was agreed, to be followed by negotiations

79

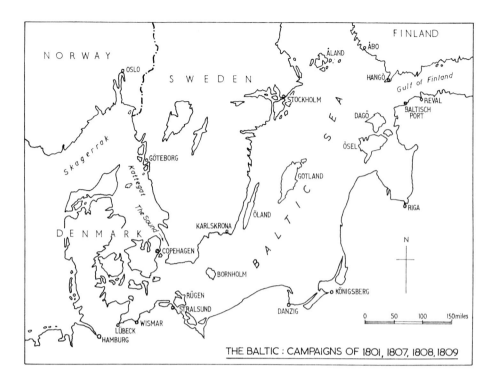

THE BALTIC : CAMPAIGNS OF 1801, 1807, 1808, 1809

in London. This aggressive British act led Tsar Paul I of Russia to sequester all British goods and ships in Russian harbours. Paul was Grand Master of the Order of St John and thus *de jure* ruler of Malta which Napoleon had agreed should be a Russian possession. The British had now occupied the island and this caused Paul to renew the sequestration order and in December 1800 he signed a neutrality pact with Sweden to which Prussia and Denmark also put their signatures. Napoleon supported this second Armed Neutrality as it promised to damage Britain's Baltic trade. The signatories maintained naval contingents and declared the Baltic a *mare clausum*; the British practice of stopping, searching and taking neutral shipping was to be energetically contested.

It was usual for the Russian Baltic fleet to be icebound each winter, thus complete co-operation between these neutral fleets was limited to spring, summer and autumn. This factor caused Britain to push ahead with plans to break the Armed Neutrality before it became too strong and to catch the Danes and Swedes without their Russian allies.

In mid-January 1801 William Pitt declared an embargo over 150 Danish, Swedish and Russian vessels but left those of Prussia alone as he was aware of the vulnerability of the Electorate of Hanover to a Prussian invasion in reprisal. Next, Danish colonies in the West and East Indies were occupied and then the British moved to destroy the Armed Neutrality before it could become a serious menace to her. Logically Denmark was the first to be subdued and this process would also place the Baltic entrance in British hands for the duration of further operations. Following this, Sweden and Russia were to be tackled separately so that their combined fleets were never to be allowed to operate together.

The Danish defences of Copenhagen (see map) included the entire channel 'The Sound' between Zealand and the Swedish mainland. For years the Danes

80

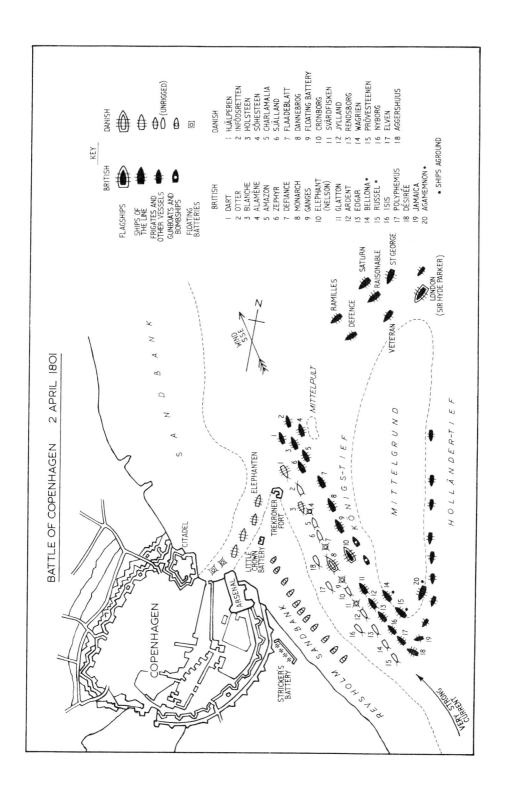

BATTLE OF COPENHAGEN    2 APRIL 1801

KEY

BRITISH

FLAGSHIPS

SHIPS OF THE LINE

FRIGATES AND OTHER VESSELS

GUNBOATS AND BOMBSHIPS

FLOATING BATTERIES

BRITISH

1  DART
2  OTTER
3  BLANCHE
4  ALAMÈNE
5  AMAZON
6  ZEPHYR
7  DEFIANCE
8  MONARCH
9  GANGES
10  ELEPHANT (NELSON)
11  GLATTON
12  ARDENT
13  EDGAR
14  BELLONA ●
15  RUSSEL ●
16  ISIS
17  POLYPHEMUS
18  DÉSIRÉE ●
19  JAMAICA
20  AGAMEMNON ●

● SHIPS AGROUND

DANISH

(UNRIGGED)

DANISH

1  HJÄLPEREN
2  INFÖDSRETTEN
3  HOLSTEEN
4  SÖHESTEEN
5  CHARLAMALIA
6  SJÄLLAND
7  FLAADEBLATT
8  DANNEBROG
9  FLOATING BATTERY
10  CRONBORG
11  SVÄRDFISKEN
12  JYLLAND
13  RENDSBORG
14  WAGRIEN
15  PRÖVESTEENEN
16  NYBORG
17  ELVEN
18  AGGERSHUUS

had kept foreign vessels out of the Great Belt and kept its soundings secret so that the Sound was the only practicable passage. At the north of the Sound was the fortress Kronborg and about thirty kilometres south of this began the shallows (Mittelgrund) which bisected the navigable channel, creating two narrow defiles each about three kilometres long, opposite Copenhagen and between the islands of Amagar and Saltholm. The western channel was called the Königs-Tief, the eastern the Holländer-Tief. East of Saltholm was a third channel, the Flintrinne, and all channels were about six metres deep. On the northern tip of the Revsholm shallows the Danes had built the fort Trekroner; as the channel was 185 metres wide, Trekroner had to be passed at a maximum range of 1,400 metres, minimum 350 metres. Ships of the line could not get closer to the city defences in the east than 1,800 metres.

The Danes had built batteries on Amagar and had anchored hulks and floating batteries in a line along the east side of Amagar. Trekroner had a garrison of 930 men with 66 24pdr ship's guns; the battery Sixtus had 25 18pdrs and 2 mortars; Quintus had 26 cannon and 9 mortars and howitzers; the battery Stricker had 8 36pdrs and 2 mortars. The anchored 'blockships' (dismasted hulks) were reinforced by ships of the line and backed by gunboats in the shallows to their west.

The Danes received news of British naval preparations in Yarmouth on 6 March 1801 and at once began preparing their defences and calling up reserves; 10 ships of the line were equipped to stiffen the static defences. Command of the defence line was conferred on Olfert Fischer and by 1 April the ships were in position although several were in a somewhat dilapidated condition. They consisted of 2 ships of the line, 1 frigate, 7 blockships, 6 gunboats, 1 floating battery (made of masts) and 1 'defence frigate'. They were manned by 5,230 men including 1,350 inexperienced volunteers or pressed men. Olfert Fischer's flagship, the *Dannebrog* (60) lay in the centre of the line which had in all 630 guns. The reserve consisted of 11 gunboats each with 4 guns and propelled by oars, and 2 blockships, 2 ships of the line, 1 frigate and 2 brigs in the inner harbour west of Trekroner. This reserve was commanded by Captain-Commander Steen Andersen Bille and had 268 guns and 2,400 men. 10 ships of the line were on the stocks in varying stages of completion. In laying out the line of blockships the Danes had not brought it close enough to Trekroner for effective mutual support and its southern flank was completely open. It was also possible for enemy line ships to pass between the blockships and Copenhagen itself as they had been anchored too far out in deep water. A further fault was that the reserve was a little too strong and valuable forces were wasted in the inner harbour instead of being used to extend and strengthen the battle line.

The divided command system (Fischer and Bille) and the difficult communications system during the forthcoming battle also detracted from the effectiveness of the defence; Copenhagen city and its citadel each had their own independent commanders as well. Crown Prince Friedrich's spasmodic meddlings in the preparations did not improve matters.

## The British Attack on Copenhagen, 2 April 1801

On 16 March 1801, a special British envoy arrived in Copenhagen and presented the demand that Denmark should at once withdraw from the armed neutrality. The Danes refused to negotiate as long as their vessels were subject to British embargo and after four days the envoy withdrew to join the approaching British squadron. All British ships in Danish ports were

30 March 1801: British fleet passing Copenhagen Sound; note spars for studding sails on outer yardarms (*National Maritime Museum*)

confiscated on 29 March and Danish pilots were forbidden, on pain of death, to aid any British vessel.

Due to the unusually mild winter, the Baltic ports were becoming free of ice earlier than usual; the British plan now was to crush Denmark as swiftly as possible, move on to defeat the Russians at Reval before they were reinforced by their detachments in Kronstadt and then turn on Sweden.

Commander of the expedition was Sir Hyde Parker, a man lacking Nelson's ambition and lust for destruction of the enemy. Nelson had returned from the Mediterranean on 6 November 1800 and had been given command of a division of the Channel Fleet under Lord St Vincent. On 16 January 1801, Nelson was appointed second-in-command to Sir Hyde Parker's Baltic expedition. The British estimated the strength of the Russian Baltic fleet in 1801 at 20 seaworthy ships of the line, the Danish at 10 and the Swedish at 11. They calculated that a force of 20 Royal Navy ships of the line would be sufficient to deal with these threats and during March these and 33 other vessels (frigates, auxiliaries and troop transports) gathered in Great Yarmouth. Sir Hyde Parker's flagship was the *London* (98); Nelson was in the *St George* (98). The expedition left Yarmouth on 12 March and arrived off the Sound on 21 March, having been delayed by heavy blizzards. The fleet had almost 2,000 guns and carried 15,000 men including an army detachment.

It was not until they were off Kronborg that Hyde Parker and Nelson met for a council of war and the commander declared his intention of avoiding the heavily guarded Sound and of passing through the Great Belt to attack Copenhagen from the south. Course was set for this objective but soon abandoned on the strong urgings of the captain of the flagship who was aware of the hazards of passing through the uncharted and complex channels.

Parker then spent 28 March in diplomatic intercourse with the commandant of Kronborg – vital time wasted with no appreciable result. Finally

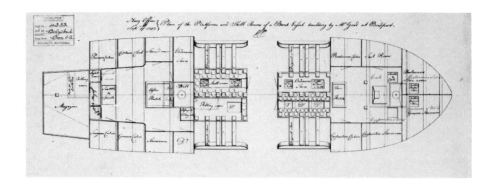

'Plan of the platforms and shell-rooms of a bomb vessel building by Mr Good at Bridport'. This specialist vessel *Belzebub* was equipped as a mobile platform for heavy mortars and contained, in addition to the usual ship's appointments, a magazine of gunpowder, shells and fuses. This, the most dangerous place in the ship, was situated at the stern and well away from the storerooms for filled shells which lie, well protected by timber walls, deep in the midships section (*National Maritime Museum*)

at 5.30am on 30 March, the wind changed to a north westerly and the British weighed anchor and moved south into the Sound; luckily there were no batteries set up on the Swedish shore opposite Kronborg and it was possible for them to pass largely out of range of the Danish fort's guns. Nelson had found his original flagship too awkward in manoeuvring and had transferred to the two-decker *Elephant* and led the van; at midday Parker anchored the fleet off Taarbaek – yet another delay which caused Nelson much annoyance and concern as he had written exhaustively to Parker immediately after their council of war urging maximum speed in the undertaking and stressing the likely penalties for Britain if the raid failed to prevent unification of the three neutral fleets.

Having anchored, Parker and Nelson undertook a reconnaissance of the Copenhagen defences and this was followed by another council of war on the evening of 30 March on board *London*. The original proposal was to have been an attack from the north but Nelson argued strongly for a southerly assault for two main reasons: the current in the Sound ran from south to north thus any damaged ships could drift clear of the fighting and reach safe waters without encumbering their comrades and by placing British ships south of Copenhagen they frustrated any junction with Russian or Swedish reinforcements. Parker accepted this plan and gave Nelson 2 ships of the line to add to his van so that Nelson's assault force consisted of 12 ships of the line, 5 frigates, 12 smaller ships and 7 bombards each with 2 mortars; a total of 36 ships, 1,280 guns (excluding carronades) and 9,400 men. Parker retained 8 line ships (including both three-deckers) and 9 other vessels with 700 guns and 5,500 men.

That night Nelson personally sounded the Holländer-Tief and had the east side of the Mittelgrund sandbank marked. This work continued through the next day and night and at 3.30pm on 1 April Nelson set sail with his force down the Holländer-Tief. At 8pm he anchored in the Svälget, south of the great sandbank, his ships being engaged by Stricker's battery from Amagar but with little effect. Shortly afterwards the Danish bombardment ceased and they omitted to use their gunboats that night which allowed the British to sound the Königs-Tief and to mark some of the west side of the Mittelgrund.

2 April 1801: The Battle of Copenhagen – a Danish view. Note semi-completed ships on slipways, bows first, in the harbour; large wooden ramps have been constructed up their sides to aid supply of materials (*National Maritime Museum*)

Nelson's orders for the attack next morning gave the order of march for his leading ships as *Edgar*, *Ardent*, *Glatton*, *Isis* and *Agamemnon*. The British gunboats were to deploy so as to enfilade the southern flank of the Danish line, shoot the end ship into silence and then to progress northwards up the enemy line in similar fashion.

In contrast to his orders for Aboukir Bay, there was a distinct lack of the concentration of forces in Nelson's plan for his attack at Copenhagen. He also failed to attack the south of the line of blockships from both sides.

The British assault force weighed anchor at 9.30am on 2 April and the first shots of the battle were fired from the blockship *Prövesteenen* at *Edgar* seventy-five minutes later. The 3 ships following *Edgar* had difficulty getting into position and the next in line *Agamemnon* went aground on Mittelgrund trying to overtake her comrades; she took no further part in the battle. *Isis*, *Bellona* and *Russel* were next to come into action and all vessels anchored (with their stern anchors) opposite their designated targets to continue the fire fight. Unfortunately, they anchored at a distance of almost 550 metres from the blockships instead of the desired 300 and their fire was thus less effective than it might have been. *Agamemnon*'s place in the firing line was taken by *Polyphemus* but *Bellona* and *Russel* were so far to the east of the Königs-Tief that they both went aground on Mittelgrund.

Nelson in *Elephant* anchored opposite *Dannebrog*; *Defiance* went aground opposite *Provesteenen* but managed to get off and to reach her appointed position opposite *Själland* and moved later up to fire at *Holsteen*. Five of the British gun brigs were unable to reach their positions at all due to the very strong current.

The British were able to bring 600 guns, 60 carronades and 9,000 men into the combat against 370 guns and 6,000 men in the line of the Danish blockships, and also 66 guns and 1,500 men in batteries on Amagar.

The first Danish ship to fall out of the fight was the *Rendsborg* which went aground but continued firing until 2.30pm. The Commander of the British

85

gunboats, Captain Rose, exploited this gap in the line to enfilade *Wagrien* and *Nyborg* and the latter had to cut her cables at 1.30pm and drifted into Trekroner and sank. At about this time other Danish ships in the south of the line were forced to strike their colours including *Wagrien* and *Jylland* – both very badly damaged. *Prövesteenen* had started the battle with 100 guns, the last 2 serviceable pieces were spiked before the survivors of the 530-man garrison abandoned her and fled to shore. By 3pm the battle in the south had been won but at heavy cost to the British in damaged ships and with 530 dead and wounded.

A fire had broken out on Fischer's flag ship *Dannebrog* at 11.30am and Fischer (with a head wound) transferred his flag to *Holsteen*. *Dannebrog* fought on until 1pm and was abandoned by her crew; the British boarded her but could not control the fire and left her to drift north and burn out. The two adjacent blockships also cut their cables a little later and one subsequently sank; the little *Elven* was fought to a standstill by *Glatton* at 3pm and her commander, Leutnant Möller, was personally praised in his report by Nelson.

Raft battery No 1 had caused *Elephant* considerable damage by closing to within musket range during the battle, but by 2am it too had to cut its cables and leave the line. She drifted into *Sälland* which was also forced to cut her cables, but anchored later behind Trekroner and was the last ship to strike her colours.

Meanwhile on the British side *Monarch*, *Ganges* and *Defiance* were so badly damaged that they drifted out of the line and went aground full in Trekroner's field of fire.

Prior to this, *Charlamalia*, *Söhesteen* and *Holsteen* had struck their colours, the latter at 2.30pm (Fischer had previously transferred his flag to Trekroner). *Infödsretten* struck her colours at 3pm but *Hjälperen* managed to withdraw into the inner harbour.

From *London* Sir Hyde Parker had observed the battle and was very concerned at the heavy damage being suffered, particularly by the 3 ships aground off Trekroner – and he had yet to find and defeat the Russians and Swedes. At 1pm he ordered the signal to break off the action to be hoisted so that Nelson's force should disengage and rejoin him. Nelson replied by hoisting an acknowledgement but, as he could see that he was winning the fire fight, he did not disengage but pressed on. Only *Russel*, with the light division, withdrew from the battle. By this time *Désirée* and *Elephant* had also gone aground and could have fallen easy prey to the still intact Danish gunboat flotilla as could the other 3 stranded ships at Trekroner – Nelson's position was indeed precarious. Nelson now employed his political skill to aid his ships; he sent a conciliatory note to the Danish Crown Prince (now on *Elephant*) offering a mutual cease fire to prevent further loss of life; if this offer were rejected however, he might be forced to set fire to all the blockships that he had taken without being able to evacuate the survivors of their gallant crews. Crown Prince Friedrich sent Kapitän Lindholm back to Nelson to investigate the situation (from his own position he could see little through the thick clouds of gunsmoke). He also sent orders to Fischer to cease firing and Fischer received this order at 4pm. At Lindholm's approach (shortly before 4pm) Nelson hoisted a flag of parley and this too caused a reduction in the Danish fire although it is generally accepted that Nelson had no right to do this. Nelson wrote a second letter to the Crown Prince stating that his motives were humanitarian and he would forego a victory if instead he could achieve an alliance between Denmark and Britain.

During these diplomatic machinations the captains of those British ships which had run aground worked avidly to free their vessels; *Elephant* was floated off at 8pm, *Defiance* at 10pm, *Monarch* next morning but *Désirée* remained stuck fast. Had Trekroner sustained her fire, it is likely that all these ships would have been forced to strike their colours. Indeed, 3 other British ships went aground off Trekroner during the afternoon and evening emphasising the hazardous predicament of the Royal Navy in the Sound.

Nelson now returned to *London* to confer with Sir Hyde Parker and they were later joined here by Lindholm, Crown Prince Friedrich's representative, in order to negotiate an armistice. Parker demanded that Denmark leave the armed neutrality and enter into an alliance with Britain; Lindholm withdrew to receive new instructions, having agreed to a 24-hour truce with immediate effect.

Both sides refurbished their forces for a renewed struggle but the Danes were better able to use the delay as the British fleet was using up its supplies at a fast rate; each ship had about 100 prisoners on board. On the Danish side Fischer was replaced by Steen Bille.

On 8 April Parker reopened negotiations with the Crown Prince, keen to reach an early solution. Luckily for him his opponent was also in a conciliatory mood as he had received news of the assassination of Tsar Paul I on 24 March and knew that his successor, Alexander I, would not be prepared to support him in hostilities with Britain. The British had not yet received this news.

Agreement was reached on 9 April and the main points were that Parker's fleet was to pass through the Sound out of cannon shot of Danish territory; that Denmark was not to be attacked by any other British fleet, that the fleet could renew its provisions in Danish territory, that Denmark's membership of the armed neutrality was temporarily withdrawn and that Parker's fleet was not to interfere with Danish trade. The agreement was to last for 14 weeks and was subject to 14 days' notice.

The British aims had thus been achieved and the fleet, reprovisioned, left the Sound on 12 April to sail into the Baltic. Danish losses in the battle were 480 dead, 570 wounded and 2,000 captured and missing (the prisoners were all returned by 12 April). British losses were 256 killed and 688 wounded.

Of the British ships engaged, many were very badly damaged, and their casualties were: *Elephant* (74) Vice-Admiral Lord Nelson, Capt T. Foley – 10 killed and 13 wounded; *Defiance* (74) Rear-Admiral T. Graves, Capt E. Retalick – 24 and 51; *Edgar* (74) Capt G. Murray – 31 and 111; *Monarch* (74) Capt J. R. Mosse (killed) – 56 and 164; *Bellona* (74) Capt Sir T. B. Thompson (wounded) – 11 and 72; *Ganges* (74) Capt T. F. Freemantle – 7 and 1; *Russel* (74) Capt W. Cummings – 6 wounded; *Agamemnon* (64) Capt R. D. Fancourt – nil; *Ardent* (64) Capt T. Bertie – 30 and 64; *Polyphemus* (64) Capt J. Lawford – 6 and 25; *Glatton* (50) Capt W. Bligh – 18 and 37; *Isis* (50) Capt J. Walker – 33 and 88; *Amazon* (38) Capt H. Rion (killed) – 14 and 23; *Désirée* (36) Capt H. Inman – 4 wounded; *Blanche* (36) Capt G. E. Hammond – 7 and 9; *Alemène* (32) Capt S. Sutton – 5 and 19; *Jamaica* (24) Capt J. Rose – nil; *Arrow* (28) Capt W. Bolton – nil; *Dart* (28) Capt J. F. Devonshire – 3 and 1.

The brigs *Cruiser* and *Harpy* were also present with Nelson's squadron as were the bomb-vessels *Discovery, Explosion, Hecla, Sulphur, Terror, Volcano* and *Zebra*, the fireships *Otter* and *Zephyr* and some gun brigs. The captured prizes were stripped and burned all except *Holsteen* which was taken off and re-christened *Nassau*.

Like Waterloo, the battle of Copenhagen had been a 'damned close-run thing' and was by no means as significant as Aboukir Bay or Trafalgar.

After considerable delay, Sir Hyde Parker took his fleet to Karlskrona where on 22 April he reached an agreement with the Swedes along similar lines to that concluded with the Danes. Nelson was not in agreement with the slow pace of the operation and wanted to tackle the Russians in Reval first; his theory being that by neutralising the major member of the armed neutrality, the minor members would automatically follow suit. This was unnecessary however as Russia's policy towards Britain became much more co-operative with the accession of the new Tsar. Sir Hyde Parker's indecisive conduct had been noticed in London however, and on 21 April he was superseded by Nelson (the order reached the fleet on 5 May). Nelson set sail on 7 May for Reval to confirm the change of heart of the Russian government, if possible before their detachments at Kronstadt and Reval united. He reached the latter port on 12 May to find that the Russians had left three days before. Nelson was now quite seriously ill with influenza and had to leave the Baltic fleet on 19 June to return to Britain to convalesce.

On 2 June Britain had raised her embargo on the ships of the armed neutrality and on 16 June concluded an agreement with Russia that a neutral flag should not protect enemy merchandise and that warring powers had the right to inspect convoys. Peace treaties were signed with Denmark on 23 October 1801 and with Sweden on 30 March 1802. Britain returned captured colonies to Denmark and her fleet left the Baltic in August 1801.

Britain had thus achieved her goals and Nelson's popularity had yet again increased, thanks in part to Tsar Paul I's convenient demise. The Baltic was open to British ships, Denmark evacuated the Hanseatic cities of Hamburg and Lübeck, and Prussia withdrew from Bremen and Oldenburg much to Napoleon's chagrin.

# The Napoleonic Wars 1803-15

The peace signed at Amiens in 1802 was in effect merely an armistice; on 16 May 1803 Britain again declared war on France and 3 days later Admiral Cornwallis was blockading Brest with 10 ships of the line. This time Britain was relatively well prepared for the hostilities. On 18 May Nelson boarded the *Victory* in Portsmouth and sailed for the Mediterranean to assume command of the naval forces there. The British aim was to re-establish undisputed mastery of the seas as quickly as possible, thus frustrating invasion threats, starving her enemies and destroying their trade, while providing excellent opportunities for her own merchant fleet to blossom. Lord St Vincent's well tried blockade policy was once more vigorously applied.

Napoleon's fleet was not prepared for action and really needed a prolonged period of peace in which to rebuild, retrain and replenish. He had sold Louisiana to the United States of America for 80 million francs as he knew he would not be able to defend it against British invasion and now could concentrate what naval forces he had directly against his hated enemy.

A new invasion fleet was soon gathering on France's coast and French troops were marching towards the Channel. Napoleon's plan to improve the state of training of his navy with the Haiti expedition had gone severely wrong, for several thousand trained sailors died of fever and other diseases in the West Indies. Of the 60 available ships of the line, only half were really seaworthy and what men and materials had been available in the dockyards were diverted to support the invasion fleet on the Channel coast.

In Britain an intense programme to build 40 ships of the line, two-deckers with 74 guns each, was set in motion and logistic resupply was simplified by giving each ship guns of only one calibre. The bows of these ships were round instead of slightly pointed and diagonal planking was introduced to give greater rigidity. Later the sterns of ships were rounded instead of being square. Living conditions, discipline, rations and the state of health of ships' crews were however unchanged – as depressing, draconian, insanitary, mono-tonous and brutalising as before. Britain could deploy about 111 ships of the line at the outbreak of war.

As before, the French ships of the line were larger, faster and more heavily armed than the British and were painted all black or had a single red or yellow lateral line. The Spanish four-decker *Santissima-Trinidad* had at Trafalgar four red stripes each with a thinner central stripe.

Napoleon's reply on land to Britain's rapid moves at sea was equally swift and decisive; he occupied Hanover and over-ran southern Italy in order to threaten the Ionian Islands, the Levant and Egypt. Meanwhile, on the Channel coast a fleet of over 2,300 flat-bottomed gunboats each carrying 1–4 guns and 60–100 men was built up and 130,000 troops concentrated in the hinterland around Calais, Boulogne, Dunkirk and Ostend. The Royal Navy repeatedly disrupted these operations with harassing attacks, employing, among other things, towed mines and a type of torpedo device built on a catamaran hull.

In the summer of 1803 the French ships of the line were deployed as follows: Brest – 20, Toulon – 10, Rochefort – 5, Ferrol – 5, Cadiz – 1. In Helder there was a small Batavian squadron, but these forces were insufficient – even if successfully concentrated, fully crewed and well equipped – to wrest control of the Channel from the Royal Navy and to guard the passage of the invasion fleet.

31 January 1804: French gunboats captured by the British off Boulogne; note the way that the victor's flags fly over those of the vanquished (*National Maritime Museum*)

Napoleon's attempts in 1803 to concentrate his navy in Brest were all frustrated by various factors – shortages of supplies and crews, deaths of commanders, bad weather and, of course, the British blockade.

On 18 May 1803, Napoleon was proclaimed emperor and continued to force ahead the planned invasion of Britain with all speed. For 1804 he changed his aim and sought again to invade Ireland but, after an elaborate series of naval moves to elude the British blockade and unite his scattered forces, these ambitions came to nothing.

The British ships of the line on blockading duty were distributed as follows: Brest – 12 (under Cornwallis), Rochefort – 6 (Collingwood), Ferrol – 6 (Pellew then Cochrane), Toulon – 11 (Nelson), Texel – 5. A reserve of 6 ships (Lord Keith) lay in the Downs and 5 more were at Spithead ready to sail at a moment's notice; over 150 frigates, avisos and other vessels were continually passing between these forces carrying orders, supplies, intelligence and personnel.

The blockades were maintained despite all winter storms and the Brest force was continuously on patrol for over two and a half years.

When the problems of controlling the operations of a fleet scattered all over the globe, with a communications system so slow, cumbersome and fragile as was the case in 1803 are considered, the achievements of the Admiralty in London during the Napoleonic wars cannot but be admired.

## The Alliances

Spain had been 'neutral', but in reality under French influence since 1803; when she began to refurbish the French ships in Ferrol, Britain made ready to operate against her and took silver ships off Cadiz. In December 1804 Spain declared war on Britain and on 4 January 1805 she concluded a new treaty with France which placed her firmly in Napoleon's grip.

90

5 October 1804: 4 British frigates, *Indefatigable* (40), *Medusa* (38), *Lively* (38) and *Amphion* (32) in action with 4 Spanish frigates in the Atlantic; 3 of the Spanish ships, *Medea* (40), *Fama* (34) and *Clara* (34), were taken and the fourth *Mercedes* (34) exploded (*National Maritime Museum*)

Britain for her part created the Third Coalition with Sweden, Russia and Austria which was to be ruined on the battlefield of Austerlitz on 2 December 1805 following the capitulation of Mack's Austrian army at Ulm on 15 October.

## The Mediterranean 1803–4

In order to reach Toulon as quickly as possible, Nelson left *Victory* off Brest and sailed in a frigate to reach his goal on 8 July 1803 to take over 8 ships of the line. These vessels were by now beginning to be the worse for wear with continuous operations and were badly in need of a refit. Only the high standard of seamanship of the crews allowed the rigorous blockade to be maintained without a break for over a year during which several minor actions were fought with the French.

## The West Indies 1803–4

In June 1803 the British captured St Lucia and Tobago from the French and in September the Batavian colonies Demerara and Barbice were also taken. The French colony of San Domingo became the negro republic of Haiti. In May 1804 Surinam was captured by the British but their attempted seizure of the capital of Curaçao was beaten off.

## The East Indies 1803–10

French reinforcements under Rear-Admiral Linois had reached Rear-Admiral Rainier in India in July 1803 but no actions of any significance occurred during the ensuing war.

91

15 February 1804: the fleet of the East India Company, homeward bound from China, beating off a French squadron near the Straits of Malacca (*National Maritime Museum*)

## The Trafalgar Campaign 1805

This campaign has been so well covered in countless other books that it will be handled only briefly here.

Spain had declared war on Britain in December 1804 and placed her fleet of about 29 vessels at Napoleon's disposal a few weeks later. In March 1805 Napoleon adopted a plan to unite the Brest and Toulon fleets with the Spanish in the West Indies and to then invade Britain.

Opposing naval dispositions in late March 1805 were as follows:

| Location | Allied ships | British blockaders |
|---|---|---|
| Texel | 9 | 11 (Keith) |
| Brest | 21 | (Cornwallis) |
| | | } 17 |
| Rochefort-Lorient | 3 | } (Gardner) |
| Ferrol | 12 | 8 (Calder) |
| Cadiz | 7 | 6 (Orde) |
| Cartagena | 6 | } |
| | | } 11 (Nelson) |
| Toulon | 11 | } |
| West Indies | 5 | 10 |

Villeneuve slipped out of Toulon while Nelson's ships were off station on 29 March and made for Cartagena intending to join up with the Spanish vessels but as they were not ready for sea he sailed on, passing Gibraltar on 8 April. Nelson had feared another French Egyptian adventure and had sought his prey around Sicily before realising his mistake. On 7 May he passed Gibraltar intending to make for the Channel as Orde had already done from Cadiz. (Orde had been surprised there by Villeneuve on 8 April

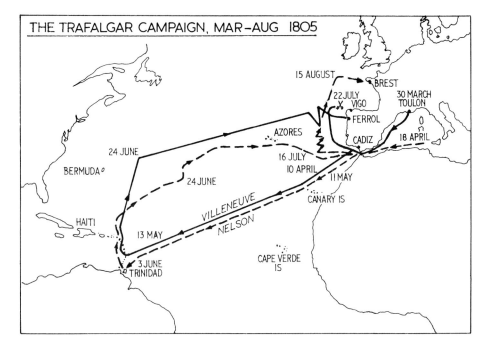

and had moved north to be ready to counter the expected French invasion attempt.)

Villeneuve left Cadiz after staying only 4 hours and took with him 6 Spanish ships of the line, 7 frigates and 4 auxiliaries under Admiral Gravina and went to Martinique which he reached on 14 May. Nelson resolved to follow him which he did on 11 May after having replenished his supplies from Orde's auxiliaries at Lagos.

Villeneuve meanwhile, in response to new orders from Napoleon, had left Martinique on 4 June, picked up Magon and 2 more ships of the line at Guadaloupe and sailed north to return to Europe. On the way he captured a British convoy of 14 ships off Antigua and was at Ferrol on 22 July. Nelson was now only 3 days behind him and headed for Cadiz via the Azores only to learn that he had missed his quarry again. He thus decided to go to Brest where on 15 August he met Cornwallis off Ushant and then proceeded to Portsmouth (18 August) for a well-earned rest.

The admiralty meanwhile sent Admiral Calder with 15 ships of the line and 2 frigates to bring Villeneuve (20 ships of the line and 7 frigates) to battle. At noon on 22 July off Cape Finisterre Calder sighted the enemy and despite poor visibility at once gave chase and attacked, hoping to cut off and overwhelm the allied rear. In this he was only partially successful. By 8.30pm visibility was so bad that Calder hoisted light signals to break off the action, by which time 2 Spanish ships had struck their colours, *San Rafael* (80) and *Firme* (74). Next day the two fleets lay about 16 miles apart and Calder decided to sail for home with his prizes. Villeneuve tried to give chase but lack of wind prevented it. Casualties in the battle were 200 British against 500 allies.

British public opinion was scathing in condemnation of what they saw as Calder's faint-heartedness and a court martial, convened at his request, found that he had not done his utmost to ensure the expected crushing victory.

Shortly after the battle Calder's squadron took up station off Ferrol again but on 1 August a storm blew him away and next day he had to detach 4 ships to Rochefort. When he again came to Ferrol a week later he found Villeneuve with 29 ships of the line in Ferrol and Corunna, ready to put to sea. He at once withdrew on the Channel Fleet at Ushant, arriving there a day before Nelson. Cornwallis however, sent Calder back to Ferrol with 18 ships – a dangerous splitting of his strength in the face of a considerable enemy threat as he kept only 17 himself to blockade Ganteaume who had 21. The British calculated their strength in terms of superior quality as well as actual numbers when allocating naval forces to oppose the French and Spanish.

Villeneuve attempted to join up with Allemand from Rochefort to attack the Channel Fleet but the British captured the frigate carrying exact details of the rendezvous and Allemand missed Villeneuve and sailed on into Vigo. On 20 August Villeneuve put into Cadiz where 10 days later Collingwood and Calder, with 26 ships of the line, blockaded him. Napoleon's invasion plans for 1805 were now completely frustrated and he soon disbanded his great camp at Boulogne to turn his dynamic fury to the task of destroying the incompetent Austrian General Mack at Ulm and later the Austro–Russian army at Austerlitz.

## The Battle of Trafalgar 21 October 1805

As soon as Nelson (at home on leave) heard that Villeneuve was bottled up in Cadiz with the main body of the allied fleet he returned to duty, hoisting his flag on *Victory* on 15 September 1805. On 28 September he assumed command of the fleet off Cadiz. In order to lure the enemy out for a final battle, Nelson took his main body off 50 miles westward leaving only 5 ships of the line and some frigates near to the harbour. He had 27 ships of the line and 2 frigates to oppose the 33 line ships, 4 frigates and 2 brigs of the allies and had always to keep watch on the other enemy ships in Cartagena, Rochefort and Brest.

In order to be ready for instant action, Nelson ordered his ships to sail always in his chosen battle formation – two parallel equal lines each of 16 ships with one vanguard division of the 8 fastest two-deckers ahead. In this way he sought to evade the time-consuming business of changing sailing formation into battle formation – a precaution which was to bring rich rewards.

Inside Cadiz the condition of the allied fleets, and the degree of their cooperation and unity was not improving with the continuing blockade; many of the ships had under-strength crews, and supplies and tackle were in short supply.

On 17 September Napoleon ordered Villeneuve to move the fleet into the Mediterranean, land troops in Naples, raid Malta's supply convoys and then make for Toulon. He also sent Vice-Admiral Rosily to take over from Villeneuve in whom he no longer had confidence. Villeneuve heard of this unofficially and decided to dare all on one desperate throw – to put to sea and do battle with the British. At a council of war on 5 October all his subordinates declared vehemently against such a plan but, when told that the emperor was insistent, they submitted.

On 19 and 20 October, the allied fleet left Cadiz, sailed west-north-west for 20 miles, turned south at 5pm but reverted to their previous course 3 hours later when the British fleet was reported to their south.

Nelson orders his famous signal to be hoisted in the Battle of Trafalgar, 21 October 1805 (*National Maritime Museum*)

At 6am on 21 October Nelson, who had been south to ensure that the allies were not running through the Straits of Gibraltar, sighted the enemy about 25 nautical miles from Cadiz. The wind was light but a storm was in the offing. Nelson's battle plan called for his twin columns to pierce the enemy line at the point of the flagship and to fall on the rear. As it had been well explained to his captains, the very minimum of signals were now needed to bring it to fruition.

By midday Collingwood's *Royal Sovereign* was the first ship to pierce the enemy line, from windward, and she was closely followed by the other ships of her column while *Victory* made for *Bucentaure*, 3 ships ahead of her. Battle was joined and at 1.30pm a marksman in the rigging of *Redoutable* hit and mortally wounded Nelson – shortly afterwards he was carried below. *Téméraire* also laid alongside *Redoutable* and the French ship was soon shot to a wreck and struck her colours. *Téméraire* then moved on to capture *Fougueux*. Ships of the northern column also overwhelmed and took *Bucentaure* (the French flagship) and *Santissima-Trinidad*, strongest ship of the fleet and the only four-decker there. Collingwood meanwhile was severely mauling the allied rear, exactly according to plan. By 4pm 15 ships of the line were out of action and Nelson heard news of his victory just before his death at 4.30pm. Ships of the allied van now entered the battle but the British, although battered, fought back and took *Neptuno* and *San Augustino*, causing the commander of the allied van, Dumanoir, to break off the fight. Gravina, commanding the allied rear, was mortally wounded and also gave orders to his stricken ships to break off the action and withdraw to Cadiz. At 5.30pm the French *Achille*, which had been burning for some time, exploded and the main part of the battle was now over.

The British had taken 18 prizes, one of which *Achille*, had blown up;

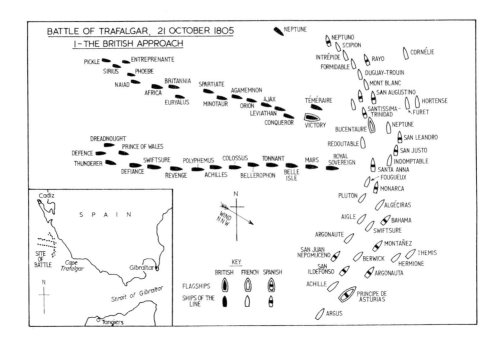

BATTLE OF TRAFALGAR, 21 OCTOBER 1805
1 – THE BRITISH APPROACH

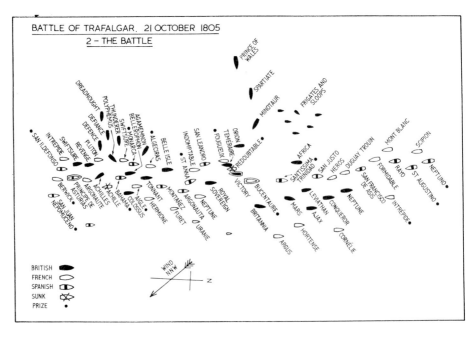

BATTLE OF TRAFALGAR, 21 OCTOBER 1805
2 – THE BATTLE

Death of Nelson in the cockpit of HMS *Victory* in the Battle of Trafalgar, 21 October 1805 (*National Maritime Museum*)

## THE FLEETS AFTER THE BATTLE

*The British Fleet*

| Ship | Guns | Commander | State of Ship | Killed | Wounded |
|------|------|-----------|---------------|--------|---------|
| (L = Lightly damaged, B = Badly damaged, S = Sunk, P = Prize) | | | | | |
| *Van or weather column — Vice-Admiral Nelson* | | | | | |
| *Victory* | 100 | Captain Thomas Masterman Hardy | B | 57 | 75 |
| *Britannia* | 100 | Rear-Admiral the Earl of Northesk | | | |
| | | Captain Charles Bullen | L | 10 | 40 |
| *Téméraire* | 98 | Captain Eliab Harvey | B | 47 | 76 |
| *Neptune* | 98 | Captain Thomas F. Freemantle | L | 10 | 34 |
| *Conqueror* | 74 | Captain Israel Pellew | L | 3 | 9 |
| *Leviathan* | 74 | Captain Henry W. Bayntun | L | 4 | 22 |
| *Ajax* | 74 | Lieutenant John Pilford | L | 2 | 2 |
| *Orion* | 74 | Captain Edward Codrington | L | 1 | 21 |
| *Minotaur* | 74 | Captain Charles J.M. Mansfield | L | 3 | 20 |
| *Spartiate* | 74 | Captain Sir Francis Laforey | L | 3 | 17 |
| *Agamemnon* | 64 | Captain Sir Edward Berry | L | 2 | 7 |
| *Africa* | 64 | Captain Henry Digby | B | 18 | 37 |
| *Rear or lee column — Vice-Admiral Collingwood* | | | | | |
| *Royal Sovereign* | 100 | Captain Edward Rotheram | B | 47 | 97 |
| *Prince of Wales* | 98 | Captain Richard Grindall | L | - | - |
| *Dreadnought* | 98 | Captain John Conn | L | 7 | 26 |
| *Tonnant* | 80 | Captain Charles Tyler | B | 26 | 50 |
| *Mars* | 74 | Captain George Duff | B | 29 | 69 |
| *Belle Isle* | 74 | Captain William Hargood | B | 33 | 93 |
| *Bellerophon* | 74 | Captain John Cooke | B | 27 | 123 |

| | | | | | |
|---|---|---|---|---|---|
| *Colossus* | 74 | Captain James N. Morris | B | 43 | 110 |
| *Achilles* | 74 | Captain Richard King | L | 13 | 59 |
| *Revenge* | 74 | Captain Robert Moorsom | L | 28 | 51 |
| *Swiftsure* | 74 | Captain William G. Rutherford | L | 9 | 8 |
| *Defence* | 74 | Captain George Hope | L | 7 | 29 |
| *Thunderer* | 74 | Lieutenant John Stockham | L | 4 | 12 |
| *Defiance* | 74 | Captain Philip C. Durham | L | 17 | 53 |
| *Polyphemus* | 64 | Captain Richard Redmill | L | 2 | 4 |

Also present were 4 frigates: *Euryalus* — Captain the Hon Henry Blackwood, *Naiad* — Captain Thomas Dundas, *Phoebe* — Captain the Hon Thomas Bladen Capel, *Sirius* — Captain William Prowse (36s); 1 schooner, *Pickle* (10) — Lieutenant John R. Lapenotiere; and 1 cutter, *Entreprenante* (10) — Lieutenant R.B. Young.

Total British casualties were 1,596 men.

---

## The French Fleet — Vice-Admiral P. Ch. J.B.S. Villeneuve

| | | | | | |
|---|---|---|---|---|---|
| *Bucentaure* | 80 | Captain Jean Jacques Magendie | B,P | 197 | 85 |
| *Formidable* | 80 | Rear-Admiral P.R.M.E. Dumanoir le Pelley | | | |
| | | Captain Jean Marie Letellier | L | 22 | 45 |
| *Neptune* | 80 | Commodore Esprit Tranquille Maistral | L | 15 | 39 |
| *Indomptable* | 80 | Commodore Jean Joseph Hubert | L (wrecked later) — all hands drowned | | |
| *Algéciras* | 74 | Rear-Admiral Charles Magon | | | |
| | | Captain Gabriel Auguste Brouard | B,P | 77 | 143 |
| *Pluton* | 74 | Commodore Julien M. Cosmao | L | 60 | 132 |
| *Mont Blanc* | 74 | Commodore G.J. Noel la Villegris | L | 20 | 24 |
| *Intrépide* | 74 | Commodore Louis Antoine Cyprian Infernet | B,P half the crew lost | | |
| *Swiftsure* | 74 | Captain C.E. L'Hospitalier Villemadrin | B,P | 68 | 123 |
| *Aigle* | 74 | Captain Pierre Paul Gourrège | B,P | two-thirds of crew lost | |
| *Scipion* | 74 | Captain Charles Berenger | L | 17 | 22 |
| *Duguay-Trouin* | 74 | Captain Claude Touffet | L | 12 | 24 |
| *Berwick* | 74 | Captain Jean Gilles Filhol Camas | P,S | all lost | |
| *Argonaute* | 74 | Captain Jacques Epron | B | 55 | 137 |
| *Achille* | 74 | Captain Gabriel de Nieport | P,S | 480 casualties | |
| *Redoubtable* | 74 | Captain Jean Jacques Etienne Lucas | P,S | 490 | 81 |
| *Fougueux* | 74 | Captain Louis Baudoin | B,P | 546 casualties | |
| *Héros* | 74 | Captain Jean B.J. Remi Poulon | L | 12 | 26 |

Also present were 5 frigates: *Cornélie, Hermione, Hortense, Rhin, Themis;* and 2 brigs, *Argus, Furet.*

---

## The Spanish Fleet — Admiral don Federico Gravina

| | | | | | |
|---|---|---|---|---|---|
| *Santissima-Trinidad* | 130 | Rear-Admiral don B. Hidalgo Césneros | | | |
| | | Commodore don Fransisco de Uriarte | B,P | 216 | 116 |
| *Principe de Asturias* | 112 | Admiral Gravina | | | |
| | | Rear-Admiral don Antonio Escano | B | 54 | 109 |
| *Santa Anna* | 112 | Vice-Admiral don Ign. Maria D'Alava | | | |
| | | Captain don Josef Guardoqui | B,P | 104 | 137 |
| *Rayo* | 100 | Commodore don Enrique Macdonell | L | 4 | 14 |
| *Neptuno* | 80 | Commodore don Cayetano Valdes | L,P | 38 | 35 |

98

| | | | | | |
|---|---|---|---|---|---|
| *Argonauta* | 80 | Commodore don Antonio Pareja | B,P | 103 | 202 |
| *Bahama* | 74 | Captain don Dioniscio Galiano | L,P | 75 | 66 |
| *Montañez* | 74 | Captain don Josef Salcedo | L | 20 | 29 |
| *San Augustino* | 74 | Captain don Felipe Xado Cagigal | B,P | 184 | 201 |
| *San Ildefonso* | 74 | Captain don Josef Bargas | B,P | 36 | 124 |
| *San Juan de Nepomuceno* | 74 | Captain don Cosme Churruca | B,P | 103 | 131 |
| *Monarca* | 74 | Captain don Teodoro Argumosa | B,P | 101 | 154 |
| *San Fransisco de Asis* | 74 | Captain don Luis de Flores | L | 5 | 12 |
| *San Justo* | 74 | Captain don Miguel Gaston | L | - | 7 |
| *San Leandro* | 64 | Captain don Josef Quevedo | L | 8 | 22 |

Total allied losses 2,600 dead and wounded, 4,400 prisoners.

---

5 French and 6 Spanish ships escaped in the growing storm to Cadiz under Admiral Gravina's command and 4 French ships under Rear-Admiral Dumanoir fled south. Gravina soon died of his wounds and Magon had been killed during the battle.

Collingwood took over the British fleet and sailed westwards to ride out the storm away from the dangerous Spanish coast, all except 4 ships which had already anchored off Cape Trafalgar.

On 23 October, the French Commodore Cosmao put to sea with 5 ships of the line and 5 frigates to try to recapture some of the prizes from the victors, who were so battered and scattered as to be vulnerable. *Redoutable* had sunk on 22 October, *San Augustino* and *Intrépide* had burnt out, *Santissima-Trinidad* and *Argonauta* were scuttled by the British, *Monarca*, *Fougueux*, *Aigle* and *Berwick* were wrecked.

Cosmao had *Pluton*, *Indomptable*, *Neptuno*, *Rayo* and *San Fransisco de Asis*, some of which were damaged but all seaworthy; all the frigates were intact. He retook *Santa Anna* from *Thunderer* (who had time to withdraw her prize crew) but *Neptuno*, although taken in French tow, was wrecked off Rota, as was *Indomptable*, and *San Fransisco de Asis* went aground near Cadiz while *Rayo* was taken by the British *Donegal* after losing her masts and was subsequently wrecked. *Bucentaure* was retaken by Cosmao but wrecked although he did manage to recover *Algéciras*.

On 24 October Collingwood gave the order to withdraw prize crews as the weather was still very rough. Only *Swiftsure*, *Bahama*, *San Ildefonso* and *San Juan de Nepomuceno* were saved.

Dumanoir with his 4 surviving ships now sought to sail back to Rochefort, but on 2 November he was sighted by the British frigate *Phoenix* off Cape Finisterre. He sent *Duguay-Trouin* to destroy the *Phoenix* before it could alert the inevitable British cruisers, but the frigate could not be caught and reached a force of 4 ships of the line commanded by Sir Richard Strachan. A sharp chase across the Bay of Biscay followed with the British gradually overhauling the damaged and leaking French ships which were forced to jettison some of their guns in an effort to increase speed.

On the morning of 4 November, Dumanoir stood at bay after *Scipion* had been overhauled and given broadsides by the frigates *Santa Margarita* and *Phoenix*. Strachan brought up his 74s *Caesar*, *Hero*, *Courageux* and *Namur* and by 4pm had fought the enemy into submission. The *Formidable*, *Duguay-Trouin*, *Mont Blanc* and *Scipion* were all taken and added to the Royal Navy. The *Duguay-Trouin* was renamed *Implacable* and survived until after the Second World War when she was scuttled.

The few surviving French ships in Cadiz were handed over to the British

21 October 1805: HMS *Victory* after the Battle of Trafalgar (*National Maritime Museum*)

The evening after the Battle of Trafalgar, 21 October 1805; the damaged ships wallow in the rising storm (*National Maritime Museum*)

when Spain rose against France in 1808 – *Neptune*, *Algéciras*, *Pluton*, *Héros*, *Argonaute* and *Cornélie*. Only Allemand remained at large with 3 ships and he ran safely into Rochefort on 24 December 1805 having been around Tenerife, raiding commerce.

So ended the Trafalgar campaign; if the battle itself had not been as crushing a British victory as those of the Glorious First of June or of The Nile, it was due to the battered state of the fleet after the fight and the weather, which made survival the only thing which mattered. The subsequent actions, however, gathered in most of the fruits of victory and crippled the French and Spanish fleets so that they were no longer any serious threat to British naval supremacy.

A more vital result of this victory was that Britain, now free to dispose of her naval forces more offensively, was able to take the opportunity of landing an army in Portugal in 1808. This event put the boot well and truly on the other foot as far as Napoleon was concerned and began British involvement in the Peninsular War which lasted until 1813; it cost the French horrific casualties and tied down large armies for five years.

## The Russian Navy in the Mediterranean 1805

In late 1804 anti-Russian movements became noticeable in the Ionian Republic and the Tsar at once sent his plenipotentiary, the Greek Count de Mocenigo, with a division of troops from Sevastopol, 5 ships of the line and 3 frigates under Commodore Alexei Grieg, to stabilise the situation. Grieg's flagship was the *Retvizan* (66) and when he arrived in Corfu in January 1805 he was much dismayed at the neglected state of the ships which had arrived from the Black Sea. Minor difficulties with the ever-present British navy in the area melted away when Russia joined the Third Coalition with England, Austria and Sweden against Napoleon.

While Nelson was chasing the French and Spanish fleets in the Atlantic and destroying them at the Battle of Trafalgar, reinforcements for the Russian Mediterranean fleet were moving from Cronstadt, which they left in September, via England to the Ionian Islands.

The squadron consisted of 5 ships of the line and a frigate under Vice-Admiral Dmitri Nicolaievitch Seniavin who was to become Russian commander in chief in the Mediterranean. They put in at Portsmouth for repairs and stores, left again in November, evaded a French naval squadron attempting to delay them and, on the way to Gibraltar, met the British fleet returning from the Battle of Trafalgar bearing Nelson's body aboard his shattered ship. Seniavin had served 6 years in the British navy and respectfully saluted Admiral Lord Nelson's remains before sailing on.

Anglo-Russian activity in the Mediterranean had meanwhile been high if not completely successful. On 19 November 1805 a joint force of 12,000 Russians under General Lassy and 10,000 British soldiers under Sir John Stuart had landed near Naples to disrupt the French hegemony in the Italian peninsula. Napoleon, hearing of the landing, deposed the King of the Two Sicilies (Ferdinand), replaced him with his brother Joseph and began to assemble forces to expel the intruders. Before his plans against them were complete, however, news reached the allies of the Austro–Russian defeat at Austerlitz in December 1805 and they withdrew from the mainland. The British maintained forces on Capri and Sicily for the next two years, however, much to the annoyance of Joachim Murat who replaced Joseph as King of Naples in 1806 when Joseph left to take over the throne of Spain, from which Napoleon had deposed yet another Bourbon.

101

# Russian Naval Operations in the Adriatic 1806–7

The Russians withdrew from Naples to Corfu where Seniavin joined them in January 1806. His naval force now totalled 45 ships, 8,000 men and 1,154 guns. Ships of the line – *Uriel* (84), *Yaroslav, St Peter, Moscow, Selaphael* – Seniavin's flagship, *St Helena, Krascovia, Asia, St Michael* (74s), *Retvisan* (66) – Rear-Admiral Alexei Grieg; frigates – *Krepkoi* (54), *Venus* (44), *St Nicholas, Avtroil, Derskoi, Great Grigori of Armenia, Kilduin* (26); corvettes – *Diomedes, Kherson, Versons, Alcynae, Dniepr*; brigs – *Argus, Feniks* (18), *Orel, Alexander, Bonasorte, Letun* (12), *Bogoslavni, Jason*. There was also the schooner *Expedition*, the transports *Grigori* and *Paul* and 12 gunboats.

At the same time Commodore Ignatiev was in the Aegean with *Archangel Raphael* (80), *Silnyi, Tverdoi* (74s), *Mostchnoi, Skoroi* (66s); the frigates *Legkoi* (38) and *Vilgelmina* (30); the corvette *Flora* and the brigs *Spitzbergen* and *Strela* (20).

Subsequent to their Austerlitz defeat the Austrians had concluded the Peace of Pressburg with Napoleon in December 1805 and among the territories which they lost were Dalmatia and the Adriatic islands. The French army was now pouring down this coast and seizing the islands to seal Austria off from British naval support and to extend Napoleon's Continental System. Seniavin resolved to dispute this French advance and sent General Baillie with a small division to Cattaro, following on with his main force as soon as he had reorganised things in Corfu.

The Russians were well received by the Montenegrins and thousands flocked to join them in their fight against the French. Encouraged by this, Seniavin requested the Tsar's permission to liberate all of Dalmatia and sent the energetic Baillie north to blockade and harry the French which he did with great effect. Within a short time Baillie had sent some three million francs in prizes back to Cattaro but meanwhile Seniavin had lost the Black Sea squadron and the bulk of General Lassy's troops who had been ordered back to Sevastopol and, by the time Alexander's approval of the Dalmatian invasion plan reached Seniavin, he had insufficient forces to carry it out.

France and Russia signed a peace treaty in July 1806 and the French commander in Dalmatia, General Marmont, sought to gain by diplomatic pressure that which he had lost to the impudent Russians by force of arms. Seniavin, however, refused to recognise the treaty or to give up his position at Cattaro until expressly ordered to do so by the Tsar. Luck was on the side of his obstinancy because in September 1806 he was ordered to continue with his Dalmatian conquest.

Marmont advanced to confront the Russo–Montenegrin force in October, was soundly defeated and pushed back into Ragusa (Dubrovnik). In December 1806 Baillie stormed and captured the fortified island of Curzola while Seniavin and the main body of the fleet sailed boldly into Trieste and rescued 20 Russian merchantmen who had been interned there by the Austrians. Baillie moved on, storming island after island (Castelnovo, Brazo) and chasing Marmont's troops along the coast.

# The Russians in the Aegean 1807

Napoleon's diplomacy came to Marmont's rescue when he succeeded in bringing Turkey into the struggle against Russia; Seniavin left Baillie with 2 ships of the line and the frigates and moved south-east towards the Dardanelles to check the Turkish fleet.

The Russians had precipitated this crisis by their continued interference in the Greek islands – traditionally a Turkish sphere of influence – and by their invasion of Moldavia (a Turkish province) in December 1806.

When Seniavin reached Corfu he was joined by another division of Russian vessels (5 ships of the line and 1 frigate) from the Baltic and now commanded 10 ships of which however two were badly in need of a refit. While in Corfu, Seniavin received orders to cooperate with the British fleet under Vice-Admiral Sir John Duckworth and to secure the Turkish archipelago. He left Corfu with 8 ships to help Duckworth force the Dardanelles. Sir John, however, had been too impatient to await the arrival of his Russian allies and had rashly sailed into the fortified narrows with his 8 ships on 19 February 1807.

## The Forcing of the Dardanelles

In December 1806 Britain's ally Russia had invaded the Turkish province of Moldavia and the British government expected that Turkey would declare war on Russia. Adopting the same doctrine as was to be used so well at Copenhagen later that year, the Admiralty directed Lord Collingwood to send a force to the Dardanelles and to sieze the Turkish fleet, then numbering 12 ships of the line and 9 frigates.

Vice-Admiral Sir John Duckworth was chosen to command this force and was told to force the narrows and to bombard Constantinople if the Turks refused to accede to his demands. He was not however to open the bombardment without prior approval of the British ambassador who sailed with him. Sir John arrived at Malta on 30 January from the Atlantic, left again on 4 February and anchored off Tenedos Island on 10 February with *Royal George* (100), *Windsor Castle* (98), *Canopus* (80), *Repulse, Pompée, Thunderer, Ajax* (74s), *Standard* (64), *Endymion* (40), *Active* (38) and the bombs *Lucifer* and *Meteor*. There he learned that the defences of the Dardanelles were weak and dilapidated and that the Turkish fleet was not seaworthy. He decided to act at once but adverse winds delayed his entry into the narrows until the 19 February.

Whilst waiting, *Ajax* caught fire on 14 February, drifted onto Tenedos and blew up at 5am the next morning with a loss of 250 men.

At 8am on 19 February, *Canopus* led the way past the two castles at the end of the Dardanelles and was fired on; the squadron followed and damage was very slight, casualties being 6 killed and 51 wounded. A little above Abydos castle, on the eastern shore was anchored a Turkish squadron of a 64-gun line ship, a 40-gun frigate, 2 36-gun frigates, 1 32-gun frigate, 4 corvettes with 10–20 guns each, 2 brigs and 2 gunboats. Nearby was a Turkish redoubt with 31 guns.

The British closed up to musket range and engaged the Turks; after a 30-minute battle the Turks cut their cables and ran aground. A corvette and a gunboat were captured, and the other Turkish ships were boarded and burnt by the British who also captured the redoubt, spiked the guns and set the gabions on fire before retiring. British losses in this action were 4 killed and 26 wounded.

At 5pm the British sailed on towards Constantinople and anchored off Prince's Island on 20 February. The British ambassador, Mr Arbuthnot, attempted to land under flag of truce to negotiate the surrender of the Turkish fleet but was refused any chance to talk.

The British dithered and on 27 February there was a skirmish between janissaries and marines in which the British lost 7 killed and 19 wounded. By 1 March the Turks, still silent, had equipped 5 ships of the line and 4 frigates and Sir John Duckworth decided to withdraw rather than to continue the unprofitable operation. On 3 March the squadron sailed down the Dardanelles again; as they came up to the forts at the entrance, the *Royal George* fired a 13-gun salute which prompted a fierce bombardment from both banks in reply. Some of the Turkish stone shot later recovered from the British ships weighed up to 800lb. Losses in this second passage were 29 killed and 138 wounded making a total for the whole expedition of 46 killed and 235 wounded.

Sir John Duckworth had become the naval equivalent of the Grand Old Duke of York – marching his men up and down the hill and achieving nothing by it.

Seniavin came up with Duckworth's damaged squadron off Tenedos but the latter refused to try a joint venture to force the Dardanelles again and sailed off to join Collingwood. Being too weak to undertake the attack alone, Seniavin decided to capture Tenedos and use it as a base from which to blockade the Turks in their own narrows. The island fell easily enough and Seniavin cruised up and down off the Dardanelles for a month but the Turkish fleet remained quietly within its safe anchorage. Leaving a Major Gidionov in charge of an adequate garrison in the fortress of Tenedos, Seniavin tried an old trick to lure the Turks out and sailed off westwards to Imbros. The trick succeeded and on 7 May 1807 8 Turkish ships of the line and 6 frigates left the Dardanelles, descended on Tenedos and landed troops there. Unfortunately for Seniavin, his return to the island was delayed by adverse winds and the Turks reembarked their troops and fled back to the safety of the Dardanelles. On 10 May the Russians caught up with this Turkish squadron under Said Ali Pasha and the Turkish coastal artillery opened up in support of their ships. By nightfall Seniavin managed to destroy 3 Turkish ships which had gone aground on Cape Janissary before the strong currents pushed him out of the Dardanelles. The Turks remained anchored under the castles.

Leaving a detachment under Grieg to maintain the blockade, Seniavin returned to Tenedos while in the Black Sea Rear-Admiral Poustochkine with 6 ships of the line and 3 frigates sealed off the Bosphorus. As the Russians now had complete control of the Black Sea, had blocked the Dardanelles and bottled up the main Turkish fleet, Turkey was now almost helpless and starvation began to be felt in the capital. It was a result of this emergency that the janissaries in Constantinople mutinied, causing the overthrow of the Turkish ruler Sultan Selim III.

Seniavin had been joined by the 2 ships which had completed their refit at Corfu and his force now mustered 10 ships. On 5 June he sent Grieg with 5 ships to Lemnos with the aim of enticing the cautious Turkish fleet to attack the apparently inferior force left under his command. The Turks obliged and left the Dardanelles. Seniavin at once sent a frigate to recall Grieg who rejoined successfully but the Turkish squadron slipped away and lay under their protective coastal batteries. After five days of fruitless waiting Seniavin decided to try the same ploy again, sailed west and then changed course to gain the north-west of Imbros, ready to fall on the emergent Turkish fleet. The enemy swallowed the bait and come out with 10 ships of the line, 6 frigates and 70 galleys to invade and recapture Tenedos. Being confronted by Seniavin, they beat to the shelter of Imbros, formed line of battle and anchored; they ranged 1,196 guns against Seniavin's 768. For four days the Russians were unable to close with the enemy due to adverse weather conditions and on the evening of 14 June the Russians left to sail

around Imbros to catch the Turks from the rear. As soon as they had gone
the Turks, with a following wind, fell on Gidionov on Tenedos, landed 1,000
janissaries on 16 June and demanded that the Russians surrender. Gidionov
refused and 3,500 more janissaries were landed to begin a formal siege. At
this point Seniavin, with 1 80-gun ship, 6 74s, 2 66s, a 60 and 2 26-gun
frigates rounded Imbros and saw that the enemy had left their anchorage
to attack the bait – his plan had succeeded beautifully but adverse winds
then held him back and he did not sight Tenedos until 17 June. As soon
as the Turkish commander saw Seniavin's royals on the horizon to the north,
he realised that he was cut off from the safety of the Dardanelles and,
abandoning the janissaries on Tenedos, he slipped off westwards towards
Lemnos, pursued by the Russian squadron.

## The Battle of Lemnos, 19 June 1807

At dawn on 19 June 1807 Seniavin attacked the Turks off Lemnos. The
Turks formed line of battle with 3 ships in the van, the 3 strongest in the
centre about their admiral and 4 ships in the rear; 5 frigates supported the
main line. Seniavin delegated the assault of the enemy van to Grieg and fell
upon the Turkish centre himself, concentrating 10 ships upon 6 and emulating
Nelson at Trafalgar on a smaller scale.

The Russian ships attacked in pairs and the *Raphael* (80) (the leading
Russian ship) was soon dismasted and drifted into the Turkish line. Seniavin,
in the *Tverdy* (74) came up in support but was soon also unmanageable. The
superior Russian gunnery gradually won the day, however, and the Turks
fell off towards Mount Athos losing their flagship, *Sedd-ul-Bakir* (84) to
Seniavin. Grieg meanwhile had attacked the Turkish van which evaded him,
and had rejoined Seniavin.

The engagement had now lasted some four hours when a calm set in; the
opposing fleets drifted apart, the Turks did not use their galleys and the
artillery duel died away. Throughout the night the Russians strove to close
up to the enemy but next morning the Turks fell away on Thasos. Grieg
managed to overtake and destroy a ship and 2· frigates and the Turks
abandoned and burned another ship and a frigate.

The Turkish fleet at the battle was: ships of the line – *Mesudiye* (120)
Capitan Pasha Seïd-Ali; *Sedd-ul-Bakir* (84) Capitan-Bey Bekir Bey, *Ankay i
Bakir* (84) Real-Bey Cheremet-Bey, *Tavusu-Bakir* (84) Patrum-Bey Houssaïn-
Bey; *Tenfik-Numa, Besaret, Kilit-Bakir* (84s); *Sayadi-Bakir, Heybetendaz*
(74s), *Malbaik-Nesuret* (66); frigates – *Meskeni-Ghazi, Bedrisaffet, Nesim,
Fukizefir* (50s); *Iskenderiye* (44); schooners – *Metelin* (39), *Denuvet* (32),
*Rehberi-Âlem* (28); brigs – *Alemit-Posaret, Melenkay* (18s).

The *Sedd-ul-Bakir* was captured; 2 other ships of the line and 3 frigates
were destroyed; Seïd-Ali lost an arm and his ship suffered 500 killed and
wounded out of a complement of 774.

Seïd-Ali called Capitan-Bey Bekir Bey and two captains of other vessels
on board *Mesudiye* and had them strangled for their poor performance in
the battle! Russian losses were 135 killed and 409 wounded.

Lemnos was the major Russian naval engagement and victory of the
Napoleonic era and was the culmination of a series of bold tactics and
sound seamanship. Seniavin was now master of the archipelago and had thus
achieved the objective of his plans. He returned to Tenedos, concluded a
capitulation with the 4,600 janissaries, and shipped them back to Anatolia
on 28 June.

## Subsequent Political Developments 1807

Seniavin now returned to Cattaro to deliver the *coup de grâce* to the bumbling Marmont in Dalmatia but the Russian–Prussian defeats in early 1807 and the subsequent Treaty of Tilsit between France and Russia of 21 July 1807 obliged Alexander to leave the Third Coalition, accept Napoleon's terms and withdraw from the Adriatic.

Marmont was thus pleasantly surprised to be able to negotiate not just his own survival but even the peaceful occupation of Cattaro as the Russians pulled out.

Seniavin returned to Tenedos to pick up Gidionov and his garrison, slighted the fort, burned the town and laid the island waste. While there, Collingwood arrived with instructions from the Admiralty to assist in bringing the Russians and Turks together (these orders had been overtaken by the conclusion of the Treaty of Tilsit). For two weeks Collingwood negotiated with the Turks to secure the safe return of Seniavin's fleet through the Dardanelles to Russia via the Black Sea but without success and on 30 August Seniavin left to return via the Baltic.

Collingwood, now receiving news of Tilsit by which he understood that the Russian fleet was to be given to Napoleon, began to watch his ex-allies and to keep his powder ready should the need arise to destroy the Russians rather than let them slip into the enemy camp – a typically British act of naval policy employed with great success for hundreds of years including the destruction of French naval units at Oran in World War II.

Of Seniavin's squadron, 3 ships of the line, a frigate, 3 sloops and the prize *Sedd-ul-Bakir* were unseaworthy and he left them with Grieg to look after Russian interests in the Adriatic. Grieg later took the ships to Trieste where they lay inactive for some years.

## Russian Withdrawal from the Mediterranean

Seniavin, with 9 ships, left Corfu in December 1807, carefully shadowed by Collingwood who eventually let them go out into the Atlantic past Gibraltar with expressions of friendship and good luck. Battered by a storm for three weeks, the Russians were obliged to put in at Lisbon where they were at once blockaded by the vigilant British into the summer of 1808, by which time Russian and British ships were fighting each other in the Baltic.

Disgusted by the French conduct in Lisbon, Seniavin opened negotiations with Sir Charles Cotton and on 3 September 1808 concluded a convention whereby the British took his 9 ships into protective custody on condition that the entire complement would be taken to Russia at British expense and that the ships would be returned to Russia six months after cessation of hostilities between the states. Two ships, the *Raphael* (80) and the *Yaroslav* (74), were unfit for sea and were to be repaired in the Tagus while the other 7 ships took on their crews and were taken to England by Rear-Admiral Charles Tyler, arriving at Spithead on 6 October 1808. After a leisurely stay in the country renewing old friendships, Seniavin left England in August 1809 and returned to Russia. Most of his ships, old and in bad repair, were sold, Russia being reimbursed for their original value. Only 2 finally returned to Russia in 1813, *Silnyi* (74) and *Moshtchnoi* (66). The Russian ships in Trieste were 'liberated' from the Austrians by Napoleon in May 1809; 2, *Moskow* (74) and *St Peter* (74), were taken to Toulon where eventually they were reduced to hulks to hold slaves; the *Venus* (44) was given to the Neapolitan navy; the *Spitzbergen* left the Mediterranean but ran into the British blockade off Lisbon and surrendered herself to Spanish hospitality in

Vigo, the *Spyesknyi* (44) and the *Vilgelmina* (30) were detained at Portsmouth while trying to rejoin their Baltic fleet and the *Legkoi* (38), *Strela* (20), *Feniks* (18) and *Letun* (12) remained in French hands.

Major Russian naval activity in the Mediterranean thus ceased for the remainder of the Napoleonic era.

## British Joint Operations in Calabria 1806

In June 1806 King Ferdinand of the Two Sicilies and Rear-Admiral Sir Sidney Smith persuaded General Sir John Stuart to invade Calabria with the aim aim of disrupting French plans for the capture of Sicily.

On 1 July General Stuart landed unopposed in the Gulf of St Eufemia, in the toe of Italy, with 4,800 British infantry; 2 days later he learned that the French General Reynier with 4,000 infantry and 300 cavalry was camped on a wooded hill below the village of Maida about 10 miles away and that he was expected to be reinforced by 3,000 more men at any time. Stuart resolved to attack at once and reached the spot on the morning of 4 July only to find that his enemy had already been reinforced. In order to be able to use his cavalry, Reynier left the woods and moved down into the plain, his infantry in the much-vaunted column formation. The British, in line, were unimpressed with this tactically illogical battle drill and proceeded to destroy the columns with well-aimed volleys of musketry.

British losses were 44 killed and 280 wounded while the French lost over 3,000 men. 'Column' had been decisively beaten, for the first time, by 'line'.

In consequence of this victory the British captured all the coastal forts and all depots of arms and ammunition which had been prepared for the invasion of Sicily. Soon after this the French evacuated Calabria.

## The War Against Commerce 1805–10

Following the Peace of Pressburg on 26 December 1805 Napoleon could, briefly, concentrate his main energies against Britain again although the loss of his navy at Trafalgar effectively crippled any large-scale maritime action on his part for the remainder of the Napoleonic wars. He sought to combat Britain's undisputed command of the world's seas by shutting her trade off from the only viable market – Europe (including Russia) – by a system of customs controls. This cessation of trade of course damaged all commercial undertakings in Europe and was much resented even by France's own business community. It is no wonder that the smuggling of British goods into Europe achieved immense proportions in the following years, either via Heligoland and Hamburg–Bremen, the Baltic or through Portugal, Spain and Italy.

Infuriated at the failure of his 'allies' to enforce his rigid embargoes, Napoleon was driven gradually to absorb them into Metropolitan France (eg the Kingdom of Holland, parts of the Kingdom of Westfalia, Oldenburg, Hamburg, Bremen and Lübeck in 1810) or to make war on them. The most fateful step along this dangerous path was of course his invasion of Russia in 1812. His very ambition secured his downfall as surely as the efforts of his most active enemies.

The tools of Napoleon's policy were his coastguards and the remnants of his fleet; the milestones of his disastrous policy were the Berlin Decrees dictated from Berlin on 21 November 1806 following his crushing defeat of the Prusso–Saxon armies at the twin battles of Jena and Auerstädt on 14 October that year and the Milan Decrees of November and December 1807.

In December 1805 Vice-Admiral Leisségues and Rear-Admiral Willaumez

6 February 1806: Admiral Sir J. T. Duckworth's victory over the French fleet in the bay of San Domingo; 3 French ships were taken by the British, 2 more driven ashore (*National Maritime Museum*)

slipped out of Brest past the blockading British with 11 ships of the line and Leisségues took 5 ships with 1,000 troops to Haiti where he set up base in San Domingo and proceeded to attack British commerce in the West Indies. Vice-Admiral Sir John Duckworth and Rear-Admiral Cochrane with 7 ships of the line surprised Leisségues, who had with him 5 vessels, in San Domingo harbour on 6 February 1806 and after a sharp battle took 3 ships, the other 2 being beached.

Rear-Admiral Willaumez with the 6 other ships from Brest sailed south and raided British shipping in the area of St Helena until May when he moved up to Martinique. One of the French ship commanders in this raiding force was Napoleon's younger brother, Jerome (later King of Westfalia), who successfully evaded British ships and brought his craft home after destroying 6 enemy merchantmen. For this he was promoted to admiral. He had, however, abandoned Willaumez without notifying him of his intentions and Willaumez wasted considerable time waiting for him before returning to Brest via Havana at the end of February 1807, by which time he had only his flagship with him; the other 4 had been badly damaged in a storm off Chesapeake Bay and were still being repaired. The decision to disperse the Brest fleet instead of using it as a concentrated whole had been strategically disastrous.

Another French naval commerce raiding force under Admiral Allemand returned safely home to Rochefort at the end of 1805 having captured 4 British men of war and 42 merchantmen together with 1,200 crewmen.

On the British side meanwhile Commodore Sir Home Popham with 4 ships of the line, 4 transports and 4,000 troops landed in Table Bay in January 1806 and soon captured Cape Town together with large stocks of supplies. In March 1806 he had his squadron and the fortress hoist the Dutch flag to lure in and capture a French frigate.

News reached Popham in April 1806 that the Spanish colonies in Buenos Aires and Montevideo were prepared to defect from the mother country and on his own initiative he took part of his force to Buenos Aires which capitulated on 9 July 1806; a British garrison was left there but it later had

23 August 1806: the British raid Havana (*National Maritime Museum*)

to surrender to native forces who remained loyal to Spain. Popham moved to Montevideo where he was joined by Rear-Admiral Stirling early in 1807, but despite these reinforcements he was forced to abandon the adventure in the autumn and one of his vessels, the schooner *Belem* (12), was actually captured by a local Argentinian hussar regiment ('Húsares de Pueyrredon') on 1 August 1806.

In the West Indies Captain Brisbane with 4 frigates forced the 100-metre wide entrance to the harbour of the capital of Curaçao on the morning of 1 January 1807 despite the fact that this was defended by forts and by 4 ships anchored broadside on in the harbour. He landed troops which stormed four of the defence works while his frigates fought the fifth work into silence. Within four hours the defences were all in British hands for the loss of only 17 men.

The usual British 'harvest of enemy colonies' proceded apace; Madeira, St Thomas, St Croix, Procida, etc were all taken and Rear-Admiral Pellew was also successful in Java. In all quarters of the globe Britain reaped the logical benefits of her mastery of the seas while Napoleon could only thrash about in Europe over-extending the French hegemony of the continent, such as in Italy where he set up the puppet kingdoms of Italy and Naples and, in 1808, in Spain and Portugal – another rash adventure which was to cost him dear in the next five years.

After crushing Prussia and Russia in 1806 and 1807 he persuaded King Friedrich Wilhelm III and Tsar Alexander I to join his continental blockade of British trade; this diplomatic coup was doubtless influenced by the British destruction of the Danish fleet in Copenhagen in September 1807.

Junot's invasion of Portugal in autumn 1807 to enforce the French blockade against British goods was decidedly counter-productive. It led at once to the evacuation on 29 November of the Portuguese court to Brazil on board their fleet of 8 ships of the line, 3 frigates, 3 brigs and 2 schooners, escorted by the British Tajo blockade squadron of 9 ships of the line.

109

8 January 1806: the British, under Sir Home Popham and Sir David Baird, capture the Cape of Good Hope from the Batavians (*National Maritime Museum*)

1 January 1807: a British force of 4 frigates under Captain Brisbane captures Curaçao (*National Maritime Museum*)

Portugal thus moved decisively into the British camp and gave Britain her long-awaited opportunity to land an army unopposed on the European mainland at a spot where it could subsist and nourish local guerrilla forces against the French.

In 1809 France crushed Austria and she too was forced into Napoleon's Continental System. By this time Britain's only active ally was Sweden; even Turkey was at war with her.

Luckily, Napoleon's blockade – which would have been terribly effective had it been fully applied – failed because from the start it did not have the consent even of the French commercial community let alone of any of her vassals and 'allies'.

## The Destruction of the Danish Navy 1807

In secret articles of the Treaty of Tilsit (France, Russia and Prussia 1807) it had been agreed that other nations were to be persuaded to close their ports to British goods and one of these, although she did not know it, was Denmark. Britain came to learn of this plan and resolved to neutralise the Danish fleet before it fell – inevitably as it seemed – into France's power.

In early July 9,000 British troops were landed on Rügen to cause a diversion on the French left flank in Prussia; the French victory at Friedland however caused this operation to be abandoned and the men were re-embarked and used against Copenhagen instead.

Commander of the expedition was Admiral Gambier; Lieutenant-General Lord Cathcart commanded the army contingent and one of his ten major-generals was Arthur Wellesley.

Great secrecy covered the British preparations for the preventive raid on the Danish fleet and on 26 July the main body of the fleet left Yarmouth; on 1 August they were off Vinga, by Gothenburg, and a squadron of 4 ships of the line, 3 frigates and 10 brigs under Commodore Keats was detached into the Great Belt with the task of ensuring that no reinforcements reached Copenhagen from the mainland, the Danish army was in Holstein.

The main body, 25 ships of the line, 40 frigates and other vessels, anchored off Helsingør on 3 August where they were joined by over 380 transports carrying the 29,000 landing troops.

The Danish fleet consisted, in 1807, of 20 ships of the line, 17 frigates and 60 other vessels including 12 brigs and 24 sloops; 3 more ships of the line were almost complete and ready to be launched.

Remarkably, the Danish fleet had no ships ready for immediate use at sea and the British operational security had been so good that the true aim of the expedition surprised all foreign governments and most of Britain as well.

The British next occupied the optical telegraph system between Copenhagen and Kiel and a replacement ambassador, Sir Brooke Taylor, presented himself at the Danish court much to the surprise of everyone there.

Crown Prince Friedrich was still ruling for his sick father but he was in Holstein with the army and now out of contact with the capital.

General-Major von Peymann was commander of the Copenhagen garrison and at the appearance of the British fleet he at once reinforced Trekroner and Kronborg fortresses and sent couriers off to the crown prince.

On 9 August the crown prince sent orders through to the capital to concentrate all land forces and to man the coastal batteries. No sooner had this order been sent than a British proposal that Denmark should join her in an alliance was presented to the crown prince; a condition of the alliance was that the Danish fleet should be delivered into British custody and that

Zealand should be occupied by British troops.

Friedrich referred the offer to the king in Copenhagen and set off at once for his capital, reaching it on 11 August. He at once issued decrees calling up all available reserves and sailed, with his father, to Kolding.

The news of this last move had a very negative effect on the Danish populace and on those left in positions of command. These were Peymann, 72 years old, as overall commander and Commodore Steen Bille as naval commander. Copenhagen was to be defended to the last but the Danes were ordered not to fire the first shot. The fleet was to be destroyed rather than to fall into British hands and all ships were bored through below the water-line and the holes plugged to await the scuttling order.

Within 4 days about 14,000 Danes rallied to the colours; there were 5,000 troops of the line, 2,500 Landwehr men, 1,200 student volunteers, 1,000 manning the coastal defences and 4,000 armed citizens with 284 cannon and 75 mortars. The coastal batteries Sixtus and Quintus, south of Copenhagen, were armed and manned as in 1801, on the site of the old Prövesteenen battery of 1713 3 old line ships had been sunk to form a fort of 90 guns with a garrison of 900 men; its flanks were covered by the famous Raft Battery No 1 and by a gun pram. Two blockships and 3 gun prams were towed across the entrance to the inner roads. By 17 August the floating defences were ready and in the inner roads were 26 vessels – 15 gunsloops, 11 gunboats and 4 mortar barques. The whole sea defences totalled 420 guns with 5,400 men; in addition Sixtus Battery had 46 guns and 600 men. After brief and fruitless negotiations in Copenhagen between Crown Prince Friedrich and three British envoys the decision was made on 14 August to invade Denmark at once but unfavourable winds delayed the landing for 2 days.

### The Bombardment of Copenhagen and the Seizure of the Danish Fleet

The transports with the landing forces were organised into 'brigades', each escorted by a ship of the line; 108 boats were divided into 3 divisions each of 6 detachments, each of 6 boats.

On 15 August the fleet anchored in the evening off Skovshoved, four miles north of Copenhagen; next day the troops were landed here and at Vedbaek, five miles further north, unopposed. By the evening of 17 August Copenhagen had been shut in from the land side by 20,000 men. The fleet meanwhile had been split into two halves, one anchored north of Trekroner, the other sailed south through the Holländer-Tief and anchored off Prövesteenen fort and completed Copenhagen's isolation from the sea. On 21 August the 9,000 British troops from Rügen landed in Kjöge Bay.

During the afternoon of 17 August the fighting began between the Danish gunboats and the British ships which supported their land troops who were now busy building siege batteries. Sorties by Copenhagen garrison were weak and easily repulsed by the British; on 25 August the British occupied the outer works of the city which were under renovation.

During an armistice which lasted from 28–30 August, Sir Arthur Wellesley with 6,000 men defeated a Danish Landwehr force of 10,000 men under Generalleutnant von Castenskjold at Kjöge. The fleet ensured that French forces in Stralsund did not cross to Rügen and threaten the beseiging troops.

Peymann was wounded in a sortie on 31 August but retained command even though bed-ridden.

On 1 September the ultimatum to surrender the fleet was repeated and again rejected by Peymann. At 7.30am on 2 September the British began a 24-hour bombardment of Copenhagen which was renewed at 6pm on 3

5 September 1807: the British army destroys Danish ships under construction in Copenhagen following the bombardment and capitulation of that city (*National Maritime Museum*)

September and maintained during the next day. The new 'Congreve' rockets were fired in salvoes from special ships in this action and proved most effective against an area target like the city in which they started many fires, several of which raged out of control. Civilian casualties mounted, some supplies in the city began to run short and on 5 September Peymann asked for a 24-hour truce in order to arrange a capitulation. Lord Cathcart agreed but now stated that the Danish fleet was to be handed over unconditionally. Peymann called a council of war of civil and military leaders (he was still unable to communicate with the crown prince) and all was agreed on 6 September at 9am. A further British demand, also accepted, was that all cannon in the arsenal were to be handed over as well. The treaty was signed and ratified on the spot and the British troops occupied the citadel and the wharf area for six weeks while evacuating their booty and destroying what they did not take.

The 3 ships of the line and 4 other vessels on the stocks were overturned and destroyed as was a fourth ship of the line in a dock; 3 blockships in the inner roads were burnt and 3 gun prams sunk.

The British did not station a permanent garrison on Zealand and on 21 October they sailed off with their spoils: 16 ships of the line, 10 frigates, 5 corvettes, 8 brigs and about 30 various vessels. Due to heavy storms on the return trip to England, however, 25 vessels were lost at sea. Only 4 of the ex-Danish line ships were eventually taken into British service. The material booty from Copenhagen filled 100 of the transports and was worth three million thalers.

Apart from their fleet and arsenal, the Danes had the following casualties: army – 135 dead and 300 wounded; navy – 53 dead and 50 wounded; civilians in Copenhagen – 1,600 dead and over 1,000 wounded. Some 1,200 servicemen had deserted during the action. Total material loss was calculated at sixteen million thalers.

113

Following their experiences at the hands of the Danish defence in 1801, no ships of the line were used in the bombardment of Copenhagen in 1807. The British plan was well thought out and executed with a ruthlessness which surprised many – the sealing off of Zealand from external aid was particularly effective.

The British had been aided in their work by Peymann's inactivity – although he knew of the time and location of their landings in advance he did nothing to oppose them and he neglected to clear fields of fire on the city glacis and to put the unfinished outworks into a state of defence.

The Copenhagen raid is singular in that a navy used land forces to bring about the neutralisation of a potentially hostile fleet.

## The Gunboat War 1807–14

Crown Prince Friedrich refused to ratify the treaty signed by Peymann with the British and Denmark remained at war with Britain, a fact underlined by a British declaration of war on 4 November 1807.

The Danes now concentrated all surviving naval vessels in Copenhagen and by the end of 1807 they had 2 ships of the line and 29 other vessels, some refloated after having been abandoned by the British after going aground in the Sound. As money and time were both in short supply, short term solutions were found to fill the naval vacuum and small, oar-propelled gunboats were rapidly built in many yards. In 6 years the Danes built 1 ship of the line, 4 frigates, 8 brigs and 317 other vessels, 43 of which were donated by private citizens. The mainstays of the new navy were 160 gun-sloops and 70 gunyawls; the sloops carried 2 24-pdr and 6 4-pdr howitzers, had 30 oars and a sail. Their task was to cause maximum damage to British merchantmen and naval vessels entering and leaving the Baltic and they were supported by artillery batteries set up at strategic points on the coast.

During 1808 French troops under Bernadotte in Fünen were aiming to cross to Zealand and then to invade Sweden, but the presence of a British frigate in their path stopped them. The Danish ship *Prinds Christian Frederick* (64) was sent from Norway to destroy the frigate but she was soon opposed by 2 British ships of the line, a frigate and 2 corvettes off Seirö. After a hard, long fight in which the Danish Kapitän Jessen lost half his crew, the Danish ship was beached at Själlands Odde and surrendered, only to be burnt.

The bickering between British and Danes in the entrance to the Baltic continued; on 6 May 1812 the British ship of the line *Dictator* (68) under Captain Stewart and accompanied by some brigs, spotted the Danish frigate *Najaden* with 3 18-gun brigs anchored in a concealed bay near Lyngoer, near Arendal. Stewart sailed boldly into the narrow harbour mouth, through the many shoals – on which 2 of his accompanying brigs went aground – and beached his vessel alongside *Najaden* so that his broadside was bearing on her. In the short battle which followed *Najaden* lost 68 per cent of her crew, 127 of them killed, and sank. The Danish brigs were towed off to safety by oared gunboats. This minor scale war dragged on until January 1814.

### The Trade War 1807–1814

Britain had evolved a licensing system whereby foreign merchantmen (even those of enemy nations!) could buy immunity from Royal Naval interference and be allowed to join protected British convoys by payment of a certain sum of money. This system enabled barter and exchange of goods to occur despite Napoleon's Continental System.

Apart from this, Danish pirates were active and effective against British merchantmen and took 335 prizes; the British were also busy and took almost 400 in reprisal.

Peace was finally signed between Britain and Denmark on 14 January 1814 in Kiel and The Gunboat War came to an end; Denmark finally lost Heligoland, which the British had occupied in 1807 and since used as a smuggling base to break the Continental System, and ceded Norway to Sweden. In compensation she received Lauenburg. The Danish–Norwegian fleet was divided between Denmark and Sweden; Denmark kept the 2 ships of the line, 2 frigates and 186 other vessels; Sweden received 122 smaller vessels.

Norway refused to be bartered and declared herself independent but on 14 August she was forced to recognise a personal union with Sweden.

### Other Baltic Events
In 1807 Danzig was garrisoned by 12,000 Prussians and Russians in the rear of Napoleon's lines of communication and was laid under siege. The Royal Navy was active in supplying the garrison by sea but 1 British corvette sailed boldly into the estuary of the Vistula, ran aground and had to surrender to the French troops.

Pillau and Kolberg were two other Prussian fortresses which held out successfully against the French in 1807, largely due to their resupply by sea by the Royal Navy.

In 1810 Napoleon added Holland, Oldenburg, part of Westfalia, Hamburg and Lübeck to Metropolitan France and Denmark became his ally. In 1812 Sweden joined Russia against France, and Swedish troops invaded Holstein while Danish and Swedish oared flotillas clashed frequently in the Sound.

The Continental System was most damaging to Prussian trade – in one year the ships using Königsberg's roads dropped from 1,000 to 50; but Baltic trade in ships' supplies to Britain boomed during these war years and in 1809 was at double the volume it had been in 1805.

## The Russo–Swedish War 1808–9
Russia had agreed to act against British interests in the Treaty of Tilsit in 1807 and began to pressurise Sweden also to join Napoleon's camp.

Gustav IV of Sweden refused to renew his membership of the armed neutrality even though he knew that Russian forces were gathering on the Finnish border – then a Swedish province. Sweden had an army of 40,000 men ready at home but due to indecision and lack of preparation Finland was practically undefended and the Russians took possession of it with little difficulty.

The Finnish coastal fortresses of Swartholm and Sveaborg were in good condition and well garrisoned, and the Finnish militia of 23,000 men was well trained.

In 1808 the Swedish Orlogsflotte consisted of 12 ships of the line and 8 frigates (as it had in 1790); the 'Schärenflotte' or shallows-fleet had 190 vessels distributed between Sveaborg, Stockholm, Abo, Gothenburg, Malmö, Uleåborg, Landskrona and the Saimen lake near Wiborg.

In 1795 the Swedes had published a handbook *Sea Tactics for the Army Fleet* which divided the vessels into squadrons, divisions and battalions. A battalion of gunsloops had 24 vessels: 1 hemmema (frigate), 12 gunsloops, 2 mortar barques (each with 1 80pdr mortar), 3 aviso reconnaissance vessels and a 'train' of 3 kitchen and ration vessels, 1 water vessel, 1 ammunition transporter and 1 ambulance vessel.

A galley battalion had 6 galleys in 3 divisions, 6 'espingars' (large boats), 1 reconnaissance sloop and a water vessel. The hemmema served as a protective bastion for the train and specialist vessels.

Many Swedish ships were in poor condition.

## The Russian Fleet

In 1800 Russia was numerically the second largest naval power in the world; in 1808 a third of her vessels were in the Mediterranean and a third were not fit for service. Her Baltic fleet consisted of 9 ships of the line, 7 frigates and a dozen other vessels; by the end of 1808 the total of serviceable vessels had risen to 20 ships of the line and frigates. The shallows fleet (galleons and gunboats) was in a poor state; in Petersburg in 1808 there were 11 floating batteries and 60 gunsloops and yawls. In Svensksund were 10 yawls and a further 34 sloops were on the lakes.

## The Outbreak of War

At the end of February 1808, Russia invaded Finland and found it undefended. The Swedish commander in Finland was Field Marshal Graf Klingspor. On 1 April the Russians formally annexed Finland; later that month they occupied the Aalands Islands and shortly before this the Swedes had evacuated Abo after burning 50 shallows vessels there.

On 21 April the Russian Admiral Bodisco occupied Gothland with 1,700 men and 6 guns; the Swedes at once sent Rear-Admiral Cederström with 6 ships of the line, 2 frigates, some other vessels, 1,900 men and 6 guns to recapture this island and Wisby. Cederström landed at Sandviken on the east of the island on 14 May and in two days forced the Russians to capitulate. After the ice melted he also captured 500 Russians in the Aalands Islands.

The Swedish garrisons in Swartholm and Sveaborg surrendered to the Russians with embarrassing speed even though Admiral Kronstedt (who commanded Sveaborg) outnumbered his beseiegers with his 7,000 garrison and 2,000 guns. He also omitted to burn the warships lying in the harbour.

On the high seas Rear-Admiral Cederström with 11 ships of the line, 2 frigates and 8 smaller vessels left Karlskrona on 17 June 1808 and moved to Abo to counter any further advance by the Russian shallows fleet. The Russian high seas fleet under Admiral Chanichof, left Cronstadt at the end of July 1808 and took up station off Hangö with 9 ships of the line, 6 frigates and 13 other vessels to observe their Swedish counterparts.

Cederström had been replaced by Rear-Admiral Nauckhoff from 1 July 1808 and the Swedish fleet had been reinforced by 2 British ships of the line under Rear-Admiral Hood. The Russians withdrew to Baltischport and were blockaded there.

In August 1808 the Russian Admiral Chanichof tiptoed out with his squadron to reconnoitre the British in Oro Roads. Sir Samuel Hood with the Swedish fleet and 2 British ships at once leapt at him. In the following chase he managed to catch the lagging *Vsevolod* (74). The *Implacable* (74) under Captain Thomos Byam Martin outshot and disabled the Russian but Chanichof returned to save his unfortunate comrade and Martin had to retire. Taking *Vsevolod* in tow with a frigate, the Russians made for nearby Ragerswik where they anchored in safety under the guns of Fort Baltic. The *Vsevolod* ran aground but was then refloated when Sir Samuel Hood with the *Centaur* (74) ran alongside her in only six fathoms and there developed a fierce, hand-to-hand combat which ended without result. The *Centaur* was now joined by the *Implacable* and Captain Rudno on *Vsevolod* struck his colours having lost 303 dead and wounded out of 700 men. The British lost 62 men.

The *Vsevolod* – now a battered, dismasted hulk – was burned. On 30 August Saumarez arrived at Ragerswik with the balance of the allied fleet but Chanichof remained in his lair with his ships anchored across the channel behind moored booms and supported by shore batteries and 6,000 troops. An eight-day gale further disrupted the allied offensive plans but when the wind moderated Saumarez sent in fireships (which failed) and 2 bomb brigs which attacked Fort Baltic. Nothing was achieved however and after a month's blockade Saumarez sailed away. Chanichof then went back to Cronstadt. He was later demoted to a common sailor for this action by the Tsar.

This was the only engagement between major ships in this war.

At the end of August 1808 Nauckhoff was reinforced by Vice-Admiral Sir James Saumarez with 4 ships of the line and a frigate; strong southerly winds defeated the latter's plan to attack the Russian fleet and there was no action. In the autumn the British blockade of Cronstadt was lifted and the Russian fleet re-entered the city early in October.

Between Hangö, Abo and the Aalands Islands lies the 'Schärenhof' – an area of shallows, reefs and tiny islands which formed a serious navigation hazard even in peacetime and were not to be negotiated without constant sounding. The presence of an enemy force in the area rendered the Schärenhof doubly difficult and a considerable obstacle.

The Russian shallows fleet was reinforced by the Swedish vessels taken at the fall of Sveaborg (2 hemmemas, 20 gunsloops and 49 yawls) and in June they advanced to Abo where the Swedish shallows fleet had just arrived with 22 gunsloops and 3,000 soldiers (half of them militia) on transports under General-major Freiherr von Vegesack and had landed on Abo. At the Russian arrival, however, the Swedes withdrew to the Aalands Islands with the gunsloops remaining at Korpo.

King Gustav IV of Sweden was a military dilettante and the Russian successes in this war were as much due to his blunders as to their skill.

## The Clash at Sandöström, 2 August 1808

The Swedish Rear-Admiral Hjelmstjerna (commanding the Army Fleet) with 22 sloops was charged with defence of the Sandöström east of Kimito and with preventing the union of the Russian main body of 90 vessels with a secondary force of 70 vessels coming from Hangö.

At the narrowest point of the Sound the Channel was bisected by an island and it was here that Hjelmstjerna drew up his forces.

General Graf Buxhöwden commanded the Russian forces and he at once set his land forces to work building batteries and trenches on both banks of the Sound. The Swedes landed 1,000 Landwehr soldiers on the south-west side of Kimito to attack these Russian positions in rear and the landing went undetected.

At 3am on 2 August the Russians opened fire but made little headway initially. After five hours, however, they succeeded in breaking the southern end of the Swedish line of sloops and the Swedes fell back. Hjelmstjerna took up the withdrawing ships with his reserve of 6 galleys and 9 gunboats (despite an adverse wind) at 9am. The Swedish Landwehr troops advanced to within 500m of the Russian headquarters but were eventually pushed back by their more experienced regular foes and the action ended with the Russians in possession of the vital waterway.

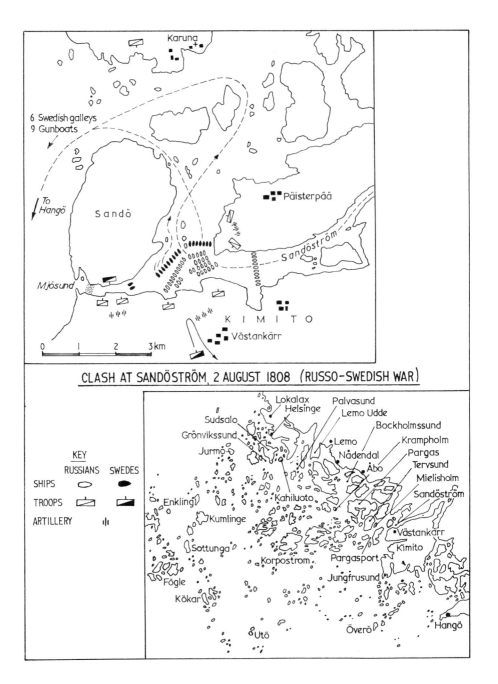

CLASH AT SANDÖSTRÖM, 2 AUGUST 1808 (RUSSO-SWEDISH WAR)

Swedish losses were 173 men and 2 vessels in the fleet and 220 men and 6 guns on land; the Russians lost 350 men and 20 ships. Had the Swedes concentrated their naval forces they would easily have held the Sandöström channel and thus considerably have influenced the course of the war. As it was the Swedes were forced to fall back westwards.

In mid-August the Russians attacked the Swedish Orlogsflotte with 26 vessels and cleared them from the coastal waters so that all Russian shallows fleet vessels could be unified.

In August 1808 the Swedish shallows fleet lay, inactive, at Hangö Udd and the officers of the staff of the 2,000 troops with the fleet evolved a plan to raid the Russian shallows fleet (captured from the Swedes at the fall of Sveaborg) which lay nearby and to remove or destroy it. The main body of the raiding party, commanded by Oberst-Lieutenant Krusenstjerna, was made up of the Swedish Leibregiment and the raid took place on the night of 17–18 August. Aided by a moonless night the Swedes reached their target undetected and captured the hemmema *Styrbjörn* after a brief struggle; the hemmema *Hjalmar* was boarded but could not be held. The Russians now trained all their ships' guns on the *Styrbjörn* which the Swedes had to abandon, making off with only a number of smaller vessels.

By September sickness had reduced Cederström's fleet so badly that the troops were disembarked on the Aalands Islands and the ships sailed back to base.

On 30 August, Hjelmstjerna, who had learned of the detachment of a Russian flotilla to the north, attacked the residual Russian forces in Grönvikssund. The Russians had 20 sloops and 4 yawls anchored by an island and the Swedish Lieutenant-Colonel Brandt with 19 sloops attacked frontally (an operation made difficult by a headwind) and detached 10 sloops to take the Russians in rear. The battle lasted for 6 hours until 7pm and ended with a Russian withdrawal; they were pursued to the Palva Sound. Losses were 242 men and 2 vessels for the Swedes, many more men and 9 sloops for the Russians.

## The Battle at Palva Sound, 18 September 1808

King Gustav sought now to exploit this victory by landing troops in south-west Finland and to cover these landings he ordered Admiral Rajalin to drive the Russian fleet out of the Palva Sound. The Swedes were deployed across the sound with 24 sloops in a broken line to the west, and north-east of this 10 more sloops; the total length of the Swedish line was about 2,300m.

The Russian commander, Rear-Admiral Mäsojedoff, reconnoitred the Swedish position on 17 September; he had 7 large vessels 28 gunsloops and 52 yawls, and with his superior strength he decided on a frontal holding attack coupled with outflanking moves to north and south of the Swedish line.

The Russian advance began at 3am on 18 September – a difficult operation in the narrow waters and made more hazardous by fog. At 5am the battle opened and by 6am the Russian left wing had been driven back. After 3 hours of combat the Swedish left wing was itself in difficulties; 1 sloop blew up and 2 others were badly damaged. The Russians pressed their advantage and the Swedes fell back in good order on Grönvikssund; there was no pursuit.

Russian losses were 200 men and 3 sloops; the Swedes lost 150 men (of these 50 wounded) and 1 sloop.

Undeterred by this failure, Gustav planned more landings and to cover them sent 2 detachments, each of 10 sloops, to the east while Rajalin with 33 sloops covered the landing force in the Grönvikssund. Kapitän von Brunck with 10 sloops guarded the shallow channel by Kahiluoto, a position so strong that all Russian efforts to force it had failed. At night the Swedish vessels closed up to the narrowest point of the defile; by day they took up a more extended position. For 7 days, until 2 October, the Russians tried to force this passage but not only were they successfully resisted but on the last day the Swedes drove them off with double shotted fire from 2 cleverly-placed sloops lying off Kahiluoto island. During this affair the Russians attempted

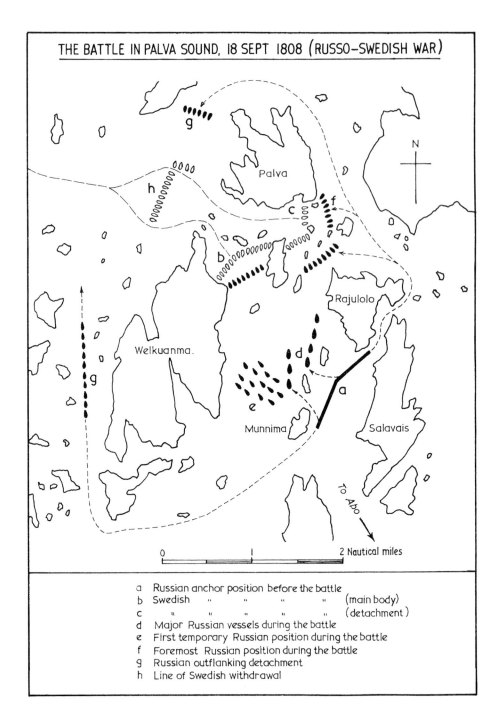

### THE BATTLE IN PALVA SOUND, 18 SEPT 1808 (RUSSO—SWEDISH WAR)

g

h

Palva

f

c

b

Rajulolo

g

Welkuanma.

d

a

e

Munnima

Salavais

To Abo

0                 1                 2 Nautical miles

a   Russian anchor position before the battle
b   Swedish    „        „        „        „    (main body)
c      „        „        „        „        „    (detachment)
d   Major Russian vessels during the battle
e   First temporary Russian position during the battle
f   Foremost Russian position during the battle
g   Russian outflanking detachment
h   Line of Swedish withdrawal

no outflanking moves. The weather had been extremely rough with frequent snowstorms throughout and winter brought naval activity in the Baltic to a halt; sickness had caused many casualties among the fleets.

Finland remained in Russian hands and Buxhöwden had pushed the Swedes well back in the north.

120

**Swedish Material Losses 1808**

When the Russians overran Finland, they found that they had captured the following vessels in the fortresses surrendered by the Swedes.

|  | Sveåborg | Abo | Uleåborg | Total |
|---|---|---|---|---|
| Frigates (hemmema) | 2 | - | - | 2 |
| Floating batteries | 6 | 2 | - | 8 |
| Yachts | 8 | 4 | 2 | 14 |
| Sloops or gunboats | 83 | 43 | 25 | 151 |
| Yawls | 36 | 45 | - | 81 |
| Supply ships | 4 | - | 1 | 5 |
| Ration ships | 1 | 2 | - | 3 |
| Water ships | 1 | 2 | - | 3 |
| Landing craft | 4 | - | - | 4 |
| Hospital ships | 1 | - | - | 1 |
| Scouts | 4 | 4 | - | 8 |
| Totals | 150 | 102 | 28 | 280 |

**The 1809 Campaign**

Despite his reverses in 1808, King Gustav of Sweden determined to push on with the recapture of his Finnish province and had new vessels built for the shallows fleet including 10 new gun schooners and larger gun sloops with covered decks as well as many other vessels of traditional design.

All these military preparations were to be brought to nothing, however, by the divided political state in which Sweden found herself where party intrigue and palace conspiracy sapped the competence of the country's leadership.

On the Russian side Buxhöwden was replaced by General Bogdan Knorring who was ordered by the Tsar to invade the Swedish mainland in winter over the ice of the frozen Baltic. Three separate forces were used, the southernmost crossing via the Aalands Islands towards Stockholm, the central one moving via Quarken and the northernmost one landing at Torneaa. Due to delayed preparations the advances did not start until 10 March, by which time concern was felt for the state of the ice.

In Sweden King Gustav had been forced to abdicate following a coup and in the confusion which followed the Swedish garrison on the Aalands had been withdrawn, thus the Russian advance was unopposed and their advance guard actually landed in Sweden and began to conduct peace negotiations when a southerly wind sprang up which threatened to break up the ice and they withdrew hastily. An armistice was signed however on 21 March and in Sweden Grand-Admiral Herzog Karl von Södermannland was elected King Karl XIII.

The second Russian army crossed the ice to Umeå from 17–21 March and quickly forced the 1,100-man garrison under General Kronstedt to capitulate, but not before they had burnt the 12 sloops which lay in the harbour there.

The third army crossed the border on 18 March and their Swedish foes capitulated on 25 March. The Tsar refused to ratify the armistice however and hostilities were resumed in May by which time the Anglo–Swedish high seas fleet could operate in the ice-free waters and caused the Russian forces to advance with great caution to Umeå.

The Swedish shallows fleet at Stockholm now numbered 10 covered and

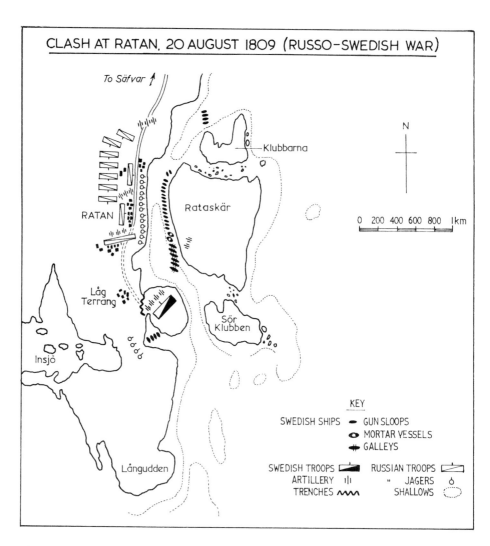

### CLASH AT RATAN, 20 AUGUST 1809 (RUSSO-SWEDISH WAR)

To Säfvar

Klubbarna

Rataskär

RATAN

Låg Terräng

Sör Klubben

Insjö

Långudden

N

0  200  400  600  800  1km

KEY

SWEDISH SHIPS — GUN SLOOPS
MORTAR VESSELS
GALLEYS

SWEDISH TROOPS          RUSSIAN TROOPS
ARTILLERY               " JAGERS
TRENCHES                SHALLOWS

50 open sloops, 40 galleys, 4 frigates and 3 other vessels; around the Aalands the Russians had 17 large vessels, 50 sloops and 64 yawls with 5,000 troops.

The Swedes decided to attack the Russians frontally at Umeå and to take them in rear with seaborne troops; Ober-Admiral Freiherr von Puke was given overall command of the expedition and he arrived on 13 August in Hernösand with 3 ships of the line and 5 frigates to join up with 6 covered and 36 open sloops, 6 galleys, 4 mortar boats and 40 transports with over 11,000 troops under General Graf Wachtmeister. On 15 August the fleet put to sea, each line ship towing a battalion of sloops, the frigates towing the other vessels. In thick fog he reached Ratan next day having covered 120 nautical miles in 36 hours. There he was joined by 2 galleys, 18 sloops and 3 other vessels. The troops disembarked next day and advanced slowly south-west. On 17 August they were confronted by the Russians with 9,000 men under General Kamensky (which Kamensky is not clear – there were several) at Säfvar and beaten after a 10-hour battle in which they lost 1,000 men and were pushed back to Ratan. Wachtmeister's incompetence was the cause of this surprising defeat

23 August 1809: pictorial plan of the British expedition into the West Scheldt and Walcheren (*National Maritime Museum*)

At Ratan on 20 August Puke drew up the gunsloops, galleys and mortar vessels in the Ratan Sound (180–250m wide) so that their heavy bow guns could be brought to play on the advancing Russians. He had prepared entrenchments across the narrow neck of the small peninsula east of the village of Låg Terräng as a last-ditch defensive position and Wachtmeister hurried to take refuge within this protection despite Puke's orders not to do so. The weaker Russians (2,000 fewer than the Swedes) pursued him vigorously but their assaults on the peninsula were all thrown back by the enfilading fire brought to bear by 4 gunsloops anchored in the inlet south of the peninsula.

The incompetent Wachtmeister was saved but he had failed utterly to overpower a numerically inferior enemy and the Swedish troops re-embarked.

Kamensky in his turn was forced to evacuate Umeå as the main Swedish army approached; Puke's seaborne raid to destroy the Elf bridge and so cut the Russians' retreat failed to achieve its aim. By mid-September the Swedish offensive died of mismanagement and on 17 September 1809 Sweden signed the humiliating Treaty of Fredrikshamn by which she lost Finland and part of Norbotten down to the Torneaa-Elf river and the Aalands Islands after having ruled them for 700 years.

## British Operations in the Baltic 1809

At the beginning of June Admiral Saumarez arrived at Karlskrona with 10 ships of the line and 17 other vessels; he carried out landings in the bay of Finland and blockaded Riga, Reval and Kronstadt. He also set up a battery of guns at Porkala and captured 7 Russian shallows vessels; Russian coastal traffic was constantly harried by the British and came to a virtual standstill. All this British action failed to help Sweden in her struggle with Russia, however; she had already declined from the first rate power she once was and the campaigns of 1808 and 1809 almost completed her reduction, the final blow coming in 1814 when she ceded her Pomeranian province to Prussia. Scandinavian domination of the Baltic was thus brought to an end.

## Further Operations in the Mediterranean 1808–10

### The Capture of Capri October 1808

The island was occupied by a British force 2,000 strong under General Hudson Lowe and was known as the 'Little Gibraltar' due to its craggy nature and defensive works. Joachim Murat, king of Naples, who could see the British flag on the island from the windows of his palace in Naples, determined to take the place.

On the night of 3–4 October 1808, 1,500 men embarked from Naples and 500 from Salerno in a total of 60 transports escorted by a frigate, a corvette and 36 gunboats. Commander of the expedition was General Lamarque, Murat's chief of staff.

The breeze died during the night and it was not until 3pm next day that the force landed on Capri at Marina Grande and at Tragar Point. The assailants proceeded to scale the steep cliffs of Anacapri which Hudson Lowe had deemed inaccessible. The British garrison was a battalion each of the Corsican Rangers and the Maltese Rifles.

By the afternoon of 5 October the eastern part of Capri was in French hands and they had taken 780 prisoners. The British garrison was confined to the citadel. Next day, the French disembarked their artillery at Tibère. On 7 October a British squadron of 2 frigates, 4 corvettes and 16 sloops penetrated the Capri channel and bombarded the French positions without great effect. By 15 October a breach had been made in the citadel wall and next day Hudson Lowe capitulated to General Lamarque. The island was given over to the French in return for which the British garrison was allowed to leave the island unmolested.

Murat was furious with Lamarque for concluding this capitulation, but reported his conquest in glowing terms to his brother-in-law, who coolly

124

replied: Capri ayant été prise par mes troupes, je dois apprendre cet événement par mon ministre de la guerre, á qui vous devez en rendre compte.' (Napoleon to Murat, 4 November 1808, Correspondence No 14,436). The king was insulted at having been treated as a simple French marshal.

### Moves Against Naples 1809

In its ceaseless efforts to bring discomfort to Napoleon and his allies, the British government sent more troops, under General Stuart, to join Sicilian and Neapolitan renegades in an attack on Murat's kingdom. The force totalled 14,000 men and embarked on 23 May 1809.

On 11 June (after many delays) the force sailed from the ports of Messina and Milazzo in 200 transports with a 50-vessel naval squadron as escort. They disembarked 400 irregulars and 3,000 soldiers at Reggio and Palmi to lay siege to Scylla and as a diversion the Royal Navy harassed the Adriatic coast.

As soon as the telegraph announced the enemy's presence to Naples, great concern raged. Having only 11,000 Neapolitan troops at his disposal, Murat appealed to the French General Partouneaux, commander of the imperial troops in Calabria, for assistance.

At this time Napoleon had just incorporated the Holy See into France as one of his departments (for which he was excommunicated by Pope Pius VII) and unrest was likely in that area, thus causing a potential threat to Murat's rear.

The emperor ordered Murat to send General Salicetti to reinforce General Miolli's troops who had occupied Rome.

Stuart did not press his invasion too hard; on 26 June he captured the weakly defended islands of Ischia but did not achieve much more.

At sea, the Neapolitan frigate *Cérès*, a corvette and some gunboats from Gaëte, all commanded by Commandant Bausan, were attacked by a superior British force including the frigate *Cyane*; 8 Neapolitan gunboats were captured, 5 others sunk and Bausan took refuge in the port of Baïae. Shore batteries prevented a British naval *coup de grâce* and the remains of the battered Neapolitan navy withdrew into Darsena.

General Stuart dithered timorously in his position, his indecision compounded by arrival of the news of the Austrian defeat at Raab on 14 June 1809. This and the news of the Austrian defeat at Wagram and the subsequent signing of the treaty at Znaim on 12 July 1809 ended his dilemma and he re-embarked his force and evacuated the isles of Ischia on 26 July.

On 23 December 1809 Salicetti died suddenly after having dined with Maghella, his prefect of police. The minister had been cordially hated by the populace and, although poisoning was suspected, the autopsy confirmed death from natural causes.

### The Attack on Sicily 1810

On 30 November 1809 Murat arrived in Paris at the invitation of the emperor (his brother-in-law) and was joined there shortly afterwards by his wife. He returned to Naples on 15 February 1810 and began preparing an assault on British-held Sicily. Napoleon, sceptical about the quality of the Neapolitan armed forces, instructed his minister of war, Clarke, to write to Murat urging great care in the planning of his operation.

Due to the low strength of the Neapolitan navy, 1 frigate and 1 corvette, construction of gunsloops was begun.

Murat assembled his troops in the area of Otranto. The army consisted of about 35,000 men (18,000 of them French troops) organised into two divisions commanded by Generals Partouneaux and Lamarque. The Neapolitans were commanded by General Cavaignac and formed one division which included the guard.

In the various Calabrian ports, 300 transports and 60 gunboats assembled but no men-of-war were available for escort duties.

The commander of all French troops involved was General Grenier and in this capacity he received orders directly from Paris; with his other duties as Murat's chief of staff, friction must often have been caused by this dual-rôle.

The British commander in Sicily was General Stuart who had 14,000 British troops, many of them from the King's German Legion. He also had about 7,000 Sicilians of doubtful combat value. Admiral Martin defended the Straits of Messina with 3 ships of the line, 8 frigates and 100 gunboats. Stuart asked for reinforcements but this request was refused.

Murat published a proclamation and had it distributed to the Sicilians urging them to rise and throw their English oppressors into the sea. He also promised his soldiers five days' pillage in the captured towns. His opponents, the deposed Ferdinand de Bourbon (ex-king of The Two Sicilies) and Stuart set up their base across the 3km-wide Straits of Messina and watched the invasion preparations carefully.

Imperial faith in the proposed adventure was waning however; Napoleon instructed Clarke to send an officer of his staff to the King of Naples telling him that the expedition would fail due to lack of transport capacity and naval power (Napoleon to Clarke, 23 May 1810, Correspondence No 16,499). Indecision reigned in Murat's camp; Grenier was against the venture and many other generals just dithered. On 30 June a rehearsal of the embarkation was carried out and on 15 August a parade of the whole army was held in honour of Napoleon's birthday. A sharp bombardment of this opportune target by the Royal Navy, who had complete control of the sea in the area, caused proceedings to be abruptly terminated.

In spite of this crippling drawback, Murat ordered his army to embark the assembled transports on 5 September. A heavy bombardment from the waiting British men-of-war forced the abandonment of this operation but on 17 September, in the temporary absence of the enemy ships, Murat re-embarked his army although Grenier refused to permit the divisions of Lamarque and Partouneaux to go aboard ship. Part of Cavaignac's Neapolitan division (3,000 men) thus crossed to Sicily alone and landed at Scaletta on 18 September. Surprise was complete and the landing was achieved without loss. The alarm was given by the natives however, and the Sicilians all took to the hills with their weapons in a guerrilla style operation previously planned by General Campbell. Allied reinforcements rushed to the town and soon the invaders were hard pressed. A withdrawal was the only course possible and Cavaignac had to sacrifice Murat's favourite regiment, the 'Royal Corse' to cover the re-embarkation of the rest of his division. Luckily for the Neapolitans, the Royal Navy was becalmed and could not interfere with their flight. Cavaignac lost 5 transport barges and left 41 officers and 900 men of the 'Royal Corse' as prisoners on Sicily.

Murat was furious and laid the blame for the failure on Grenier's refusal to embark his troops. On 27 September the camp was evacuated and the army returned to its previous garrisons. Murat published an order of the day stating that his raid on Sicily had been in accordance with imperial wishes but this move only brought down more misery on him when the emperor

126

instructed Clarke to convey his displeasure to the king on 13 October (Correspondence No 17,042).

## The Attack on Basque Roads (Isle d'Aix), 11/12 April 1809
On 2 February 1809 the French Rear-Admiral Williamez took advantage of

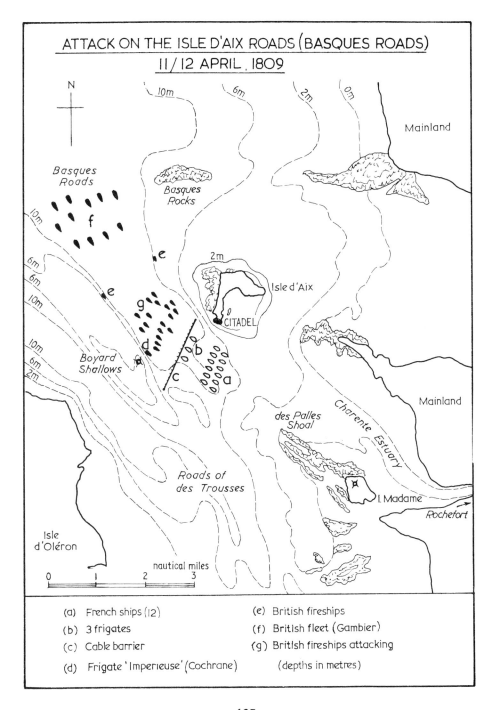

**ATTACK ON THE ISLE D'AIX ROADS (BASQUES ROADS)**
**11/12 APRIL, 1809**

(a) French ships (12)
(b) 3 frigates
(c) Cable barrier
(d) Frigate 'Imperieuse' (Cochrane)
(e) British fireships
(f) British fleet (Gambier)
(g) British fireships attacking

(depths in metres)

11 April 1809: a British fireship in action against French ships lying blockaded behind the cable barrier in Basque Roads which the fireship has just cut through (*National Maritime Museum*)

the temporary absence of Admiral Gambier's blockading squadron to slip out of Brest harbour with 8 ships of the line and 4 other vessels. His aim was to join up with the divisions from Lorient and Rochefort and sail to the West Indies. Off Lorient he was supposed to be joined by 3 ships of the line and 3 frigates but the British drove off the 3 ships of the line and captured the frigates. After 3 days' manoeuvring, Williamez managed to bring his division into the safety of Basque Roads on 26 February where he was joined by 3 ships of the line from Rochefort. The British at once blockaded him and were joined in mid-March by Gambier who then had 11 ships of the line, 8 frigates and 18 other vessels. He at once sent word to the Admiralty in London suggesting that he should attack the French with fireships. This was approved and Captain the Lord Cochrane – a particularly bold and successful officer – was sent out in a frigate to join Gambier and to organise and control the attack. Cochrane joined Gambier on 26 March with his frigate and 12 fireships. With him was William Congreve with supplies of his new rockets (which were used to such good effect in the bombardment of Copenhagen in 1807). Gambier gave Cochrane 6 frigates, 11 brigs, 8 fireships and 3 'bombships' (small vessels each loaded with about 1,500 barrels of gunpowder) for the planned attack. Due to the narrow waters with their many shoals and strong currents, Gambier was unwilling to risk his line ships too close inshore to support the assault.

Williamez had now been replaced by Allemand and the French division of 11 ships of the line and 4 frigates lay in the Charente estuary behind an 80cm thick cable boom (supported by many large buoys) laid across the narrow channel between the islands of Aix and Oleron. On Aix was an extensive citadel containing 30 heavy guns and 2,000 men charged with giving flanking fire in support of the boom; on Oleron were similar batteries. 300m behind the boom were 3 frigates anchored in line abreast, bows towards the British, and 70 ships' boats patrolled the boom itself. Allemand felt quite safe in his lair and his opinion was shared by Napoleon who considered it impregnable; the British had other ideas.

In the afternoon of 11 April Cochrane anchored his frigate *Impérieuse* just north of the Boyard shallows with 3 other frigates to the north east, all ready to take off the crews of the fireships. Two brigs were anchored at the sides of the channel (e–e) to indicate by means of fire signals the clear channel for the fireships in the planned night attack. At 7.30pm on 11 April, 2 hours after ebb tide and in a stormy north-west wind, the 2 bombships bore down on the boom followed by 20 fireships. Due to the prevailing wind, the French patrol boats had fallen back from the boom – it was unguarded. The 2 bomb-ships were caught up in the cable and cut it with their explosions; at about 8.30pm several of the fireships drifted through the resulting hole onto the French line. The 3 French frigates cut their cables and sailed south east towards their own line ships who in turn cut their cables and drifted, in the dark and in great confusion, onto the shallows of Palles.

On the morning of 12 April only 2 French line ships and 1 frigate were still capable of manoeuvre, the rest were stuck fast in the shallows. Cochrane attacked at once with his frigates but Gambier was initially loth to risk his line ships; eventually he sent support and after a short bombardment 2 French line ships struck their colours, while 2 others and a frigate were set on fire and abandoned by their crews. The other ships were refloated at high water and drifted up the Charente. Gambier stayed in position until 29 April but nothing more of consequence was achieved.

The results of the raid were that one of the French commanders was tried by court martial and shot, another cashiered and 3 were given varying periods of arrest. The French navy suffered considerable loss of material and morale.

Cochrane was elevated to Knight Commander of the Order of the Bath, and the Royal Navy's superiority at sea was heavily emphasised. Gambier was subject to criticism for his cautious conduct.

## The East Indies 1810

In 1810 the British sent a squadron under Vice-Admiral Bertie to attack the French-held island of Mauritius; the raid was successful and the island, a valuable base, passed into British control. The French ships captured by the squadron on 6 December 1810 were: *Astree*, *Bellone*, *Minerve* and *Manche* (40s); *Iphigenie* and *Nereide* (ex-British 36s); the prison ships *Ceylon*, *Charlton* and *United Kingdom* (30s), *Victor* and *Entreprenente* (14s), 1 brig and 5 gunboats.

## The Peninsular War 1808–13

Although not involving any large naval actions, it was Britain's supremacy at sea after Trafalgar which permitted the landing of British armies in Portugal in August 1808 at Porto Novo on the Maceira River. On 21 August Wellington beat the French at Vimiera, a village only 3km inland, and secured his bridgehead. His superior, Sir Hugh Dalrymple, concluded the infamous Convention of Cintra with the French commander, Junot, whereby 24,000 beaten French were repatriated to France on British ships complete with all their booty! Wellington and Dalrymple were called back to Britain for a court of inquiry and Sir John Moore was left in charge of the army. He made a thrust into Spain with 35,000 men to help the Spanish, who were now Britain's allies, having risen in revolt against Napoleon's brother Joseph who had been placed on the Spanish throne by the emperor. Napoleon

31 July 1810: Royal Navy attacking Dutch lateen-rigged gunboats in Java (*National Maritime Museum*)

turned on Moore with superior forces but the British army was able to scuttle north-west to Corunna and Vigo where they were evacuated by the fleet on 17 January 1809. Without command of the sea, this British army would have been lost.

In April 1809 Wellington, cleared of all blame by the court of inquiry, landed in Lisbon with another British army to liberate Portugal and to co-operate with the Spanish in their struggle against the French. For the next four years not only was this army to be kept well supplied with ammunition, equipment, food, remounts and reinforcements, but massive logistic support was also to be sent to the reforming Portuguese and Spanish armies and guerrillas. The Iberian peninsula was an ideal theatre for naval support and combined operations and the Royal Navy was able to keep the fires of the Spanish revolt burning well all around the coastal areas. In the winter of 1810–11 the navy was to guard the flanks of the Lines of Torres Vedras, across the Lisbon peninsula, with Wellington's Anglo–Portuguese army safe within the fortifications and the French besiegers, under Marshal Masséna, starving slowly outside them. Finally the French had to withdraw in March 1811 and the British began an advance that was to continue up through Spain into France in 1814. From 4 May to 30 June 1811 the French besieged Tarragona in north-eastern Spain but the continued resupply of the city from the sea and the presence of a squadron of 8 British ships under Commodore Codrington strengthened the defence and permitted them to resist the siege successfully.

On 2 June 1813, Wellington's Anglo–Portuguese–Spanish army beat the French decisively at Vittoria in northern Spain and he ordered his logistic resupply from Britain to be transferred from Lisbon to Santander and, from the time of its capture in September 1813, to San Sebastian on the Spanish Biscay coast, so that time and effort could be saved on land resupply routes.

June 1809: Wellington lands at Lisbon with army reinforcements (*National Maritime Museum*)

20 September 1811: a defeat for the French navy under Napoleon's eyes, off Boulogne. HMS *Naiad* (Captain P. Casteret) and the brigs *Castilian, Renaldo* and *Redpole* defeated a French squadron of 7 prams (flat-bottomed boats) each carrying 12 24pdr guns, and 15 brigs; one of the largest prams, *Ville de Lyons,* was captured (*National Maritime Museum*)

May 1811: the USS *Constitution* (44) battering HMS *Little Belt* (22) during one of the many individual ship-versus-ship actions which were characteristic of the Anglo–American war. Remarkably, the *Little Belt* seems to have survived to fight another day (*National Maritime Museum*)

Had Britain not had control of the seas, it is likely that the Spanish uprisings would have been suppressed or that the war would have dragged on for much longer.

# The Anglo–American War 1812–15

### The High Seas

The cause of this conflict was Britain's continuous high-handed action against neutral shipping in the Napoleonic wars. At the outbreak of hostilities the American navy consisted of only 3 very large frigates each mounting 66 guns, including 30 24pdrs below decks and 20 carronades on deck; they weighed 1,600 tons, carried 460 crewmen and were built in 1799. There were also 4 normal frigates of 48 guns and 1,300 tons displacement, 9 corvettes and brigs each with from 12 to 28 guns and some smaller vessels including about 100 gunboats. These large frigates were strongly built, fast ships, heavier and more strongly armed than their British equivalents.

Naval personnel numbered 5,750; three-quarters were American citizens, 8 per cent were British and the rest were Scandinavians, Germans, French and other European nationalities. The American navy had been founded in 1798 and had enjoyed excellent training in the wars against the Barbary pirates. Their gunnery in particular was good, better than that of the British.

At the outbreak of war the Royal Navy had 1 ship of the line and 6 frigates scattered along the American eastern seaboard. One of the first

29 December 1812: USS *Constitution* (44) making off out of gun range after having raked HMS *Java* (44) several times. The weight of broadsides were 1490lbs for the *Constitution* and 1034lbs for *Java;* the crews were 485 and 377 respectively. The engagement ended with *Java*'s capture after a gallant defence (*National Maritime Museum*)

clashes took place on 23 June 1812 off Chesapeake Bay when the lone British frigate *Belvidera* (36) ran into an American squadron of 2 frigates and 2 other vessels. Action was joined and things looked serious for the *Belvidera* when a gun barrel burst on one of the American vessels; *Belvidera*'s shots increased the chaos and, by jettisoning her anchors, boats and water ballast, she managed to escape.

The British *Alert* (16) was taken by the USS *Essex* (32) on 13 August and on 19 August the large American frigate *Constitution* (44) clashed with the British frigate *Guerrière* (38) and captured her in a fierce two-hour battle in which the Americans lost 7 dead and 7 wounded and the British had over 80 casualties. Two such further victories followed; on 18 October *Frolic* (18) was taken by USS *Wasp* (18) and on 25 October the *Macedonian* (38) was taken by USS *United States* (44); the Royal Navy, and the world, realised that they had met their match at last. Orders were given that no single Royal Navy frigate was to engage an American foe! From now on they hunted in packs and more ships were detached from blockade duty in Europe to bolster up the shaky situation in the new world. The *Constitution* took the *Java* (38) on 29 December to end the year on a high note for the Americans.

On 1 June 1813 British morale received a boost however when the British frigate *Shannon* (52), Captain Broke, met the *Chesapeake* (36), Captain Lawrence, off Chesapeake Bay. Broke enfiladed his enemy and raked her from astern; in ten minutes of furious artillery fire Lawrence was killed, Broke personally led the boarding party and in five minutes he had taken the

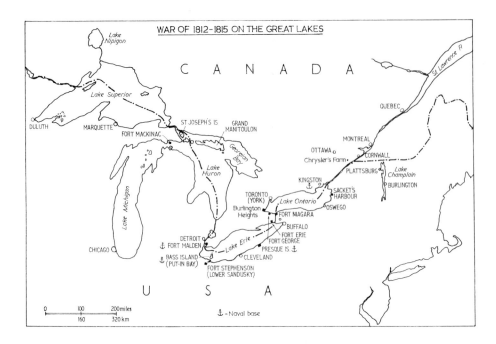

WAR OF 1812-1815 ON THE GREAT LAKES

ship. Casualties were 148 American dead and wounded to 83 British. The *Chesapeake* had been hit by 362 shots in the brief battle, the *Shannon* by only 158. The British ship had been on active service for seven years at the time of the battle whereas the American vessel and crew were only recently commissioned; the higher state of training of the British secured the victory. The USS *Hornet* (18) captured the *Peacock* (18) on 25 January and the latter subsequently sank.

By now the British began a serious blockade of American ports so that the American naval vessels found themselves increasingly subject to the same sapping, enforced idleness that the French, Dutch and Spanish navies had long since become used to.

British troops were landed at several points and in August 1814 even Washington was taken by the redcoats. American corvettes slipped out past the blockading ships however and raided British commerce right up to the mouth of the Channel.

On 14 February 1814 the *Constitution* took the 16-gun British *Picton* and on 29 April the *Epervier* (18) was taken by USS *Peacock* as was the *Ballahou* (4) by the American privateer *Perry*. The USS *Wasp* ranged into the Channel and on 28 June took the *Reindeer* (18).

In February 1815 the *Constitution* captured 2 small British frigates off Madeira, *Levant* (22) and *Cyane* (20), but both were subsequently retaken. By now the American navy was expanding at a great rate; 3 ships of the line had now been built and naval strength stood at 225 officers, 500 cadets, 15,000 sailors and 3,000 marines. There was also a steam-powered, paddle-driven frigate, the *Fulton*, with the single paddle-wheel built into the centre of the vessel to give protection.

Hostilities were ended by the Peace of Ghent in February 1815.

### The Battles on Lake Erie and Lake Champlain 1813 and 1814

The struggle between Canada and the United States of America in this war

134

developed largely into a small-scale naval war along the huge inland lakes which formed so much of the populated borders between the states at this time.

However, like the much dramatised operations of the legendary Lawrence of Arabia in World War I, these actions were very much 'a side show of a side show' in military terms and on the British–Canadian side only about 6,500 men were involved (8th, 41st, 49th and 100th Foot plus artillery and engineers numbering 4,450 men, plus about 2,000 Canadian militia), while the Americans deployed about 8,000 regulars and militia; varying numbers of Indians fought for both sides during the conflict.

The theatre of war stretched from Quebec to Lake Superior along the waterways and it was inevitable that aquatic mobility would become vital when the rough, undeveloped nature of the terrain is considered.

The Americans intended to make the first major moves in the campaign, aimed at Detroit and Niagara in order to pre-empt any Indian offensives on their vulnerable western areas, but the British commander of Upper Canada, Major-General Isaac Brock, learned of these plans and frustrated them when on 26 July 1812 he ordered Captain Charles Roberts, commanding the British garrison on St Joseph's Island, to capture the American post at the north-west extremity of Lake Huron.

This was quickly done and all the Indian tribes of the north-west threw in their lot with the British.

On the American side, Brigadier William Hull was in charge of the force on the Maumee River and sent a schooner to Detroit which was captured by the British, revealing all the American war plans.

Hull now crossed the Detroit River to advance on Fort Malden only to have his land communications cut by Brock. On 6 August the Indians under Tecumseh ambushed 200 Americans and Hull fell back to Fort Detroit where he was besieged by a British force under Colonel Proctor from Fort Malden to whom Hull surrendered on 16 August after a one-day siege. Brock now threw his main weight eastwards towards Fort George to confront the other American force under General Henry Dearborn.

At this time the British had naval superiority on Lakes Erie and Ontario and could thus move, communicate and manoeuvre with ease. Now the Americans sent Captain Isaac Chauncey and Lieutenant Jesse D. Elliot from New York to take command of their naval affairs on the Great Lakes and a new vigour flooded into the American offensive. On 8 October Elliot raided Fort Erie and captured 2 British brigs *Detroit* and *Caledonia* and thus tipped the scales of naval supremacy on Lake Erie in America's favour.

A further, and more serious, blow to British fortunes occurred on 13 October when General Brock was killed in a minor skirmish at Queenstown Heights near Niagara. His clear strategic view was not shared by his successor, General Sheaffe.

The winter enforced a pause in the war but in April 1813 the British opened the season with some partially successful operations at the south-west end of Lake Erie which eventually led to no permanent gains.

Meanwhile, in the east, Dearborn concentrated 4,000 men from Lake Champlain on Sacket's Harbour and 3,000 on Buffalo; he embarked the former and captured York, capital of Upper Canada, on 27 April. The Americans then joined their two forces near Niagara and attacked Fort George which the British evacuated, falling back to Burlington Heights. The Americans followed up, were ambushed and fell back again ten miles to Forty Mile Creek.

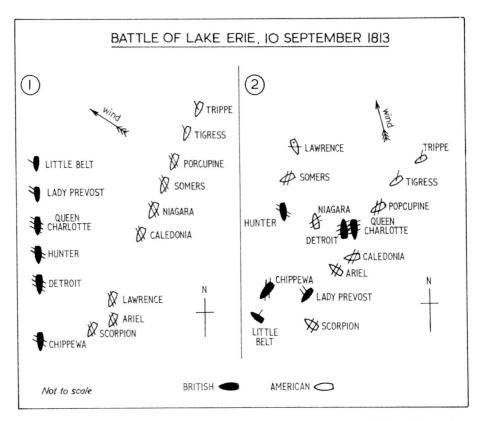

BATTLE OF LAKE ERIE, 10 SEPTEMBER 1813

In an effort to restore the situation 600 Americans under Colonel Boerstler advanced on 50 men of the 49th Foot and some Indians at de Cou's House, near Fort George, but again fell into an ambush and were forced to surrender.

By now Captain Sir James Yeo had been sent out by the admiralty to take over British naval operations on the Great Lakes and he took over the small fleet at Kingston. After one or two minor skirmishes the main naval phase of the war opened on Lake Erie when in June Captain R. H. Barclay, RN, based at Fort Malden, blockaded the American naval station at Presque Island until 2 August when unaccountably he sailed away, allowing the Americans under Captain Perry to move out of the harbour within two days – quite an effort because each ship had to be unloaded and lifted over the bar at the harbour mouth. Barclay sailed to Fort Malden and took over his new vessel, the *Detroit*. Meanwhile, Perry had set up his new operations base at Put-in Bay on Bass Island where he blocked the British supply lines to Fort Malden, where food shortages were already apparent. Barclay decided to fight rather than give in but as his crews were mainly 'Canadian peasants and soldiers' he was not confident of success; the main disadvantage on the British side, however was that they were outnumbered by their foes and outgunned in terms of weight of broadsides as can be seen opposite.

On 9 September 1813 Barclay set out to find the enemy and seek a decision; next day he found them at anchor and at 11.45am the *Detroit* opened fire on *Lawrence* to good effect and within two hours every gun on *Lawrence* was out of action and the greater part of her crew dead or wounded.

| Vessel | Tonnage | Crew | Guns |
|---|---|---|---|
| Detroit (flagship) | 490 | 150 | 3 x 24pdrs |
| | | | 2 x 18pdrs |
| | | | 6 x 12pdrs |
| | | | 8 x 9pdrs |
| Queen Charlotte | 400 | 126 | 14 x 24pdrs |
| | | | 3 x 12pdrs |
| Lady Prevost | 230 | 86 | 10 x 12pdrs |
| | | | 3 x 9pdrs |
| Hunter | 80 | 45 | 2 x 12pdrs |
| | | | 2 x 6pdrs |
| | | | 4 x 4pdrs |
| | | | 2 x 2pdrs |
| Little Belt | 90 | 18 | 1 x 9pdr |
| | | | 2 x 6pdrs |
| Chippewa | 70 | 15 | 1 x 9pdr |
| Totals | 1,360 | 440 | 63 |

PERRY'S AMERICAN SQUADRON

| Vessel | Tonnage | Crew | Guns | |
|---|---|---|---|---|
| Lawrence (flagship) | 480 | 136 | 2 x 12pdrs | 18 x 32pdrs |
| Niagara | 480 | 155 | 2 x 12pdrs | 18 x 32pdrs |
| Caledonia | 180 | 53 | 2 x 24pdrs | 1 x 32pdr |
| Ariel | 118 | 36 | 4 x 12pdrs | 2 x 32pdrs |
| Somers | 94 | 30 | 1 x 24pdr | |
| | | | 1 x 24pdr | |
| Scorpion | 86 | 35 | 1 x 24pdr | |
| Porcupine | 83 | 25 | 1 x 32pdr | |
| Tigress | 96 | 27 | 1 x 32pdr | |
| Trippe | 60 | 35 | 1 x 24pdr | |
| Totals | 1,677 | 532 | 55 | |

On the British side, Captain Finnis of *Queen Charlotte* had been killed and there was no suitable officer to take his place although Lieutenant Irvine tried gallantly to fill the vacuum. By 2.30pm both *Lawrence* and *Detroit* were shot to hulks and the action slackened. The battle could now be won by anyone who could bring an undamaged ship into action and it was the Americans who had the vital ingredient for success in the shape of the *Niagara* which had until now been in rear. She came up, Perry transferred to her and *Lawrence* struck her colours. *Niagara* now positioned herself between *Chippewa* and *Lady Prevost* on the one side and *Detroit, Queen Charlotte* and *Hunter* on the other and poured broadside after broadside into her already badly battered foes. *Detroit* lay bows-on to *Niagara* and, being completely helpless could not move and thus was raked repeatedly. *Queen Charlotte* struck, *Detroit* was now being raked from astern as well and she too struck, as did *Little Belt* and *Chippewa* a little later. The battle was over and control of Lake Erie had passed decisely into American hands.

Casualties were: British 41 killed and 94 wounded; American 27 killed and 96 wounded.

The effects of this victory were to sound the death knell of the British possessions at Detroit and Fort Malden and of Proctor's operations on the Sandusky river. It also severely shook Indian allegiance to the British and it opened the way for a renewed American invasion of Canada.

Proctor fell back destroying forts Detroit and Malden but was caught by superior American forces under General Harrison at Moravian Town on 5 October and beaten. In this battle Chief Tecumseh was killed.

In the east meanwhile the Americans had moved against Montreal in two forces, one under General James Wilkinson, replacing General Dearborn, sailing down the St Lawrence supported by a squadron of warships; the other, under General Hampton, coming overland from Lake Champlain. Hampton was ambushed by a small force near Chateaugay, severely trounced and fell back to Plattsburg. Wilkinson set out down the St Lawrence on 1 November, landed 2,000 men near Cornwall on 10 November and 1,800 further downstream next day. This latter force attacked the British Colonel Morrison with 900 men of the 49th and 89th Foot at Chrysler's Farm but was repulsed, counter-attacked and again repulsed. The eastern thrust at Canada then fizzled out and the Americans subsequently evacuated Fort George which was immediately repossessed by the British who proceeded to surprise and capture Fort Niagara on 19 December 1813. Prior to abandoning Fort George the American militia commander, McClure, had burnt the nearby Canadian settlement of Newark, driving 400 women and children

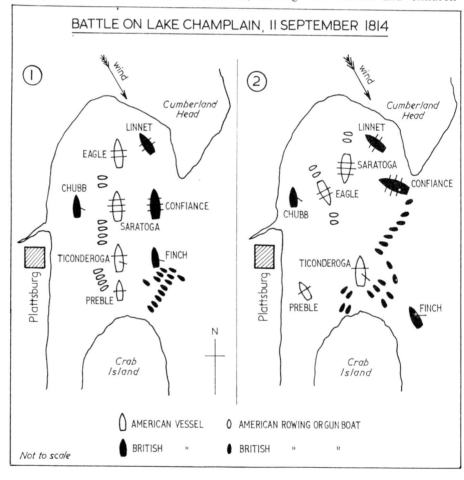

BATTLE ON LAKE CHAMPLAIN, 11 SEPTEMBER 1814

'from their houses into the snows of a Canadian winter'. In their new advance the British occupied Fort Lewiston (south of Fort Niagara), Black Rock and Buffalo, drove out the inhabitants and destroyed every settlement on the Buffalo River. 'The whole of the frontier, in fact, was laid in ashes as reprisal for the burning of Newark'.

The fiasco of their eastern operations largely negated all the hard-won advantages which the Americans had gained by their victory on Lake Erie. In March 1814 a renewed attempt to force the door was made by the American General Brown against Kingston but he misread his orders and bungled the whole affair.

On 25 July the 'best' battle of the whole war was fought at Lundy's Lane, one mile north-west of Niagara Falls; about 2,800 men were engaged on each side and the British won the day. Losses were 878 British killed and wounded; 860 Americans killed and wounded, 117 captured. The Americans fell back to Fort Erie which the British besieged from 3 August to 27 September, whereupon the Americans blew up the fort and withdrew altogether from British territory.

In 1814, with the war in Europe won, the British began to reinforce their army and navy forces in Canada and the centre of activity moved eastwards to Lake Champlain. Here at Plattsburg the Americans had built a fortified position which the British, under General Prevost, attacked without success on 7 August with land forces while their naval squadron under Captain George Downie advanced to Isle la Motte. The American squadron on Lake Champlain was at Plattsburg under Captain Thomas Macdonough.

Prevost decided on a joint assault on Plattsburg. The vital feature of this campaign was that Lake Champlain was the main logistic artery of both armies, thus whoever gained naval supremacy would win. The day was to be decided by the opposing fleets no matter how small they were in comparison to their land forces.

The balance of these naval forces was as follows:

### BRITISH (DOWNIE)

| Vessel | Tonnage | Crew | Guns |
|---|---|---|---|
| Confiance* (flagship) | 1,200 | 325 | 6 x 32pdrs<br>31 x 24pdrs |
| Linnet | 350 | 125 | 16 x 12pdrs |
| Chubb | 112 | 50 | 10 x 18pdrs<br>1 x 6pdr |
| Finch | 110 | 50 | 8 x 32pdrs<br>3 x 24pdrs<br>7 x 18pdrs<br>4 x 6pdrs |
| 12 gunboats | 630 | 387 | 2 x 18pdrs each |
| Totals | 2,402 | 937 | 110 |

*Confiance (also shown as Confidence) was brand new and, in fact, still being fitted out on the morning of the decisive battle.

Apart from heavier broadsides, the main American advantage was in their commander, an experienced naval officer, well acquainted with the winds, currents and soundings of Lake Champlain where he had been in command since 1813.

| Vessel | Tonnage | Crew | Guns |
|---|---|---|---|
| *Saratoga* (flagship) | 734 | 240 | 12 x 32pdrs |
| | | | 6 x 24pdrs (long) |
| | | | 8 x 24pdrs (short) |
| *Eagle* | 500 | 150 | 12 x 32pdrs |
| | | | 8 x 18pdrs |
| *Ticonderoga* | 350 | 112 | 5 x 32pdrs |
| | | | 4 x 18pdrs |
| | | | 8 x 12pdrs |
| *Preble* | 80 | 30 | 7 x  9pdrs |
| 10 gunboats | 580 | 350 | 6 x 24pdrs |
| | | | 6 x 18pdrs |
| | | | 4 x 12pdrs |
| Totals | 2,244 | 882 | 86 |

Macdonough anchored his squadron one mile from the Plattsburg shore, thus out of effective range of land artillery pieces should the British succeed in taking the place. He anchored his vessels so that they could be 'sprung', ie swung around so as to bring fire to bear where desired.

Before dawn on 11 September 1814 the British squadron weighed anchor and stood out for Plattsburg Bay; at 7.30am they reached the place and Downie reconnoitred the American position in a small boat prior to attacking. *Confiance*'s first salvo raked *Saratoga* with terrible effect but then the north-easterly wind failed and Downie was killed by being struck by one of his ship's guns dismounted by *Saratoga*'s reply. The *Chubb* drifted through the American line and struck her colours and *Finch* failed to reach her predetermined position. She was then crippled by a broadside from *Ticonderoga* and went ashore off Crab Island.

Four British gunboats closed with *Ticonderoga* and tried to board her but were repulsed at only boatshook range and very badly mauled in the process. Some of the other British gunboats, manned by militia, took flight soon after the start of the action or the battle may well have had a different outcome.

By 10.30am *Confiance*, having become unmanageable and been raked by broadsides from *Saratoga* and *Ticonderoga* for some time, struck her colours, followed shortly by *Linnet* who was by then little more than a wreck herself. The American victory was complete and decisive. Losses were 54 killed and 115 wounded for the British, 52 killed and 58 wounded for the Americans.

The land attack, which was to have coincided with Downie's assault, was misdirected by a guide, did not find the ford on the Saranac River, and was called off.

Control of Lake Champlain was now firmly in American hands and while they were too weak to invade the reinforced Canada, they were completely safe from any British invasion threat from their northern flank. The situation remained static for the rest of the year.

# Part Three
# The National Navies

# Austria

For hundreds of years the Venetians controlled the Adriatic but in 1382 Austria–Hungary gained a foothold when Trieste joined her empire. The leading naval powers in the Mediterranean then were Venice, Genoa, Turkey and the Order of St John (on Malta). Throughout the sixteenth, seventeenth and eighteenth centuries there were repeated attempts by Austria to found a viable navy but success always slipped from her grasp, mainly due to lack of funds – the empire was constantly engaged in a vital struggle against Turkey – and lack of sufficient experienced officers.

Emperor Karl VI was, however, able to make a decisive advance into the naval sphere when in 1733 he engaged the Italian Conte Luca Pallavicini to form and command a naval flotilla in Trieste. Pallavicini collected some Neapolitan galleys and 'tartanen', (lateen-rigged coastal craft) and sailed them to Trieste which he put into a state of defence. Austria had her first naval base. In 1738 however, the ships were sold off and their men and equipment used to form the Danube flotilla.

The next naval advance occurred in 1764 when Algiers declared war on Austria and the latter was forced hurriedly to have 2 30-gun frigates built in Porto Rè, but they were poorly manned and equipped and achieved nothing in their short life. In 1772 the Empress Maria Theresa abandoned the idea of maintaining a navy and the ships were sold off, the men discharged.

Having always been a land power, Austria was finding the transition to a martime power extremely difficult and unrewarding.

In 1776 the Hungarian Littoral (Dalmatia) achieved independence in naval matters from their Austrian colleagues in Trieste. Whereas the Austrians were always timid in face of Venetian supremacy at sea, the Hungarians had no such inhibitions and their shipbuilding at once began to gather momentum in Zadar, Split and Ragusa (Dubrovnik). On the mercantile side, however, even the Austrians began to be more adventurous when they founded the 'Trieste–East India Trading Company' and opened factories in East Africa, India and the Nicobar Islands from 1777 to 1786. In the latter year the company was allowed to collapse however and the potential colonies fell into other hands.

There were in this later period Neapolitan and Dutch vessels which flew the imperial Austrian flag and were often referred to as 'the Austrian fleet' but they were, in fact, basically national warships operating under nominal imperial control.

In 1798, when Austria annexed Venice, those few Austrian ships in Trieste and Dalmatia were combined with the Venetian fleet to form the first official 'Austrian–Venetian Navy'.

In 1806 Venice fell to Italy and the remaining Austrian naval forces were termed 'The Trieste Navy'. From 1809 to 1814 Austria lost all her Adriatic provinces and thus had no naval forces.

## The First Trieste Navy 1786–97

The first warships of this force were 2 20-gun cutters, *Le Ferme* and *Le Juste*, bought in Ostend in 1784 and sailed into Trieste on 4 October 1786. The commander of the *Le Juste* was a certain Captain Botts, an Englishman who, in spite of only being able to speak his mother tongue, was appointed commander of the infant navy. The passage crews were paid off and new

143

crews recruited from the 'sea companies' and the gunners of the Liccaner and Ottochaner Border Infantry Regiments.

The men on the cutters fell into two categories – the 'ship's equipage' which consisted of 1 captain, 2 lieutenants, 1 boatswain, 2 gun masters, 2 carpenters, 1 sailmaker, 2 mates, 2 quartermasters, 1 boat commander, 1 sea cadet, 1 surgeon, 1 corporal, 1 gunner, 1 ration master, 33 sailors, 4 ship's youths, and 3 ship's boys; and the 'Crew' which comprised 1 lieutenant, 1 corporal, 1 gunner, 1 drummer, 1 cadet and 17 soldiers (marines). The uniform of the Border Infantry was a bicorn for officers and cadets (round, black sailors hat for on-board wear), tobacco-brown coat with sky-blue Swedish cuffs and collar, sky-blue waistcoat and breeches. Leatherwork was black. The new naval flag was the red-white-red horizontal stripes with an open heraldic royal crown.

From 1788 to 1789 Austria was again at war with Turkey and in order to increase her power at sea several gunboats were built and various merchant-men were armed. The model for the gunboats was the design which had proved itself during the siege of Gibraltar and was put forward to the Emperor Joseph by the Neapolitan Naval Minister, Acton. Each had a 24pdr bow gun and later 2 sideguns were added; the crew was a commander, 30 sailors and 2 gunners. Due to limited seagoing properties, they were scarcely ever used.

Captain Botts was still naval commander and the cutters, each accompanied by an armed merchantman, patrolled the Istrian coast and went down the Adriatic to Ragusa and the Gulf of Cattaro. Periodically naval equipment and manpower were transferred to the Danube Flotilla.

Although there were no notable naval actions in 1788–9, the cutters and the armed merchantmen, S. Giovanni and Citta di Vienna, gave valuable help to the successful withdrawal of an Austrian force under Major Vukassovich out of Montenegro.

When Emperor Leopold II took the Austrian throne in 1790, he immediately reduced even this tiny naval force, largely due to pressure from the government of Trieste who grudged the annual outlay of 60,000 gulden for its upkeep.

In 1791 the Le Juste was sold for 9,900 gulden and in 1792 the Le Ferme and two feluccas were also disposed of for 1,320 gulden. The 'fleet' now consisted of 3 gunboats used for the protection of Trieste harbour. The commander was Major George Simpson who had 66 men to crew and administer his craft.

The impending outbreak of the Revolutionary wars with France, however, caused the Austrians to reconsider their naval policy and the Le Ferme (now converted to a brigantine) and 3 feluccas were brought back into service. One felucca and all its crew was lost at sea in a storm off the Neapolitan coast in November 1792.

In 1793 Emperor Franz II (1792–1806) ordered an increase in naval strength to 1 brigantine, 2 schebecks (two or three-masted vessels with lateen sails found in the Mediterranean), 2 feluccas and 7 gunboats and by 1796 there were an additional 9 gunboats. The appearance in the Adriatic of 6 British frigates during the year caused the governor of Trieste once more to call for reductions in his own country's naval budget. The naval commander, Major Simpson, submitted a report to the Emperor on the quality of the existing ships in which he complained that, as they could only venture out of harbour in fair weather and in absolutely calm conditions, they were prac-tically useless for naval defence purposes.

Despite this, however, they did enter combat on 26 March 1797 in the

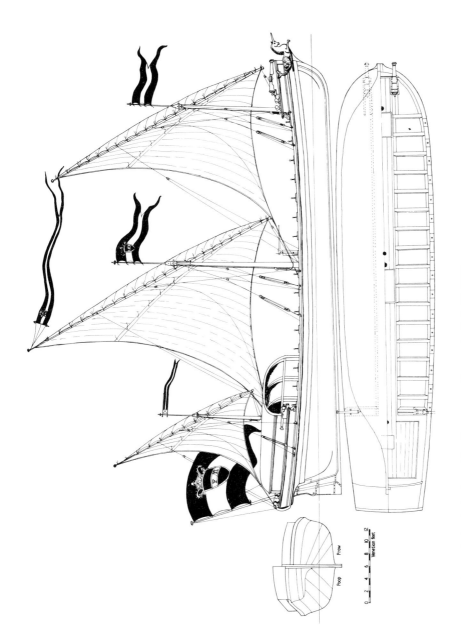

Poop    Prow

0  2  4  6  8  10  12
Venetian feet

Austrian schebeck designed by Francesco Vincenzio Rubelli 1798

neutral Venetian harbour of Quieto when attacked by a superior French squadron in violation of the laws of the sea. Simpson had 2 schebecks and 12 gunboats and was supported by the Venetian ship of the line *L'Eolo*. After a short cannonade the French withdrew.

In 1798 naval affairs were taken from the unwilling hands of the Trieste government and given to the imperial foreign office but in 1801, when their incompetence had also been established, the department was handed over to the central military planning staff.

## The First Austrian–Venetian Navy 1797–1806

Following the Peace of Leoben between France and Austria on 28 April 1797 Venice, from the Oglio to the Po and all her Istrian and Dalmatian provinces, fell to Austria. Napoleon is said to have remarked 'Austria will never be a naval power!' and he was to be ably, but unwittingly, supported in the fulfilment of this prophecy by the ineptness of the Austrian government.

Prior to evacuating Venice, Napoleon sent all the serviceable ships of that fleet to join the French Adriatic fleet and had all others sabotaged and rendered unusable. Austria assumed control of Venice on 18 January 1798 and that same day a flotilla of Austrian ships under command of the Englishman, Naval Lieutenant-Colonel James Ernest von Williams (ennobled with the 'von' in recognition of his services in command of the Danube Flotilla against the Turks 1788–9 and of the Rhein Flotilla against the French in the war of the First Coalition) entered the harbour. They were the corvette *Austria* (18), the schebeck *Henrici* (14), the gunboats *Centauro*, *India*, *Dragone*, *Ceffea*, *Corvo* and *Colombo*, and the feluccas *Lepre* and *Fenice*.

The ships left by the French had either been scuttled or overturned on the stocks. Of the sunken vessels the following were salvaged: the floating battery *Idra*, the frigate *Bellona*, the brigs *Oveste* and *Pilade*, 11 gunboats and all the various minor craft. The bombarde *Distruzione* was later converted to the brig *Orione* and the historic ship of the Doges of Venice *Bucintaro*, which had been stripped of all decoration by the French, was converted to a floating battery.

Of those ships overturned on their stocks the following were salvaged: 4 frigates, 1 schebeck, 9 galliots, 1 galley, 1 dredger, 8 gunboats and 6 feluccas; 10 ships of the line and 1 frigate were damaged beyond repair. All galleys were withdrawn from service in 1802.

Austria was thus now in possession of a fair-sized naval force and generous naval base facilities. Proven, capable naval commanders were available in the shape of Williams and Major Chevalier Joseph de L'Espine, a French emigré naval officer, but for some reason the Austrian governor of Venice, Feldzeugmeister Graf Wallis, passed them over and recommended that command go to the former Proveditore Generale of Dalmatia, Andrea Querini. This man was duly installed as President of the Venetian Arsenal and it is largely due to his lack of understanding of naval affairs that the potential of the Austrian fleet in this period was never realised. The 'Venetian Navy' was now placed under command of the Imperial Austrian foreign office, while the 'Trieste Navy' was allotted to the command of the Army of Italy and Querini who, although ordered to assume command of both 'fleets', strenuously refused on the grounds that he did not wish to accept the increased responsibility.

In 1800 Emperor Franz II sent officers to England, Denmark and Sweden in order to gather ideas as to how to improve the efficiency of his navy, but not much was achieved before Venice was once again taken from him.

The Venetian–Dalmatian infantry (Schiavoni) were organised into a regiment of marines in 1799, but disbanded in 1800 after a mutiny. The officers of this formation who had no participation in the mutiny were taken into the Marine Infantry Battalion (six companies) which was raised in 1802 Also in this year the Marine Artillery Battalion of six companies was raised from the Venetian Artillery regiment for manning the guns on board ship.

During the War of the Second Coalition an Imperial Austrian flotilla under Major Potts cooperated with a Russian–Turkish squadron in the Adriatic along the Italian coast and performed valuable service.

In Autumn 1799 Ancona fell into Austrian hands and in the harbour were 3 ex-Venetian ships of the line, *Beyrand*, *Laharpe* and *Stengel*, and 5 smaller craft all now flying the French flag; they were added to the Austrian navy. Although General Klenau, Austrian commander on the Genoese Riviera, frequently requested naval assistance in his campaign, his pleas went unheard and many excellent opportunities for combined operations were lost, although a small naval force did take part in the blockade of Genoa in 1800.

After the Peace of Luneville, Erzherzog Karl was appointed to reorganize military and naval affairs and he in turn gave the detailed naval problems to Oberst Graf Ludwig Folliot de Crenneville, an ex-officer of the French navy. In January 1802, Querini was removed from office and a naval cadet training school was reopened in Venice (from 1774–97 it had been the Scuola di Marina) as was a naval architectural school (founded 1777 as Scuola di Architettura Navale). New naval regulations were issued.

Ships' boys (10–15 years of age) were also officers' batmen and were responsible for cleaning the ship or, in action, replenishing ammunition supplies for the guns. Sailors were required to keep themselves 'clean, to comb their hair daily and to shave once a week'.

Rations consisted of wine, biscuit, salt meat, oil, vegetables, flour and dried fish. Those men sick also received sauerkraut, sauerampfer, plums, rice, eggs, chicken and mutton.

In February 1804, the following ships were in service with the Austrian navy: brigs *Oreste* and *Pilade*; schebeck *Tritone*; martegana *Nereide*; and a gunboat. The impending war of 1805 caused the commissioning of the corvette *Aquila*, the brigs *Eolo* and *Oriane* and the schooner *Indagatore* but all too little and too late. After the defeats of 1805 Austria had to give up Venice and Friule, Istria, Dalmatia and Albania. She was left only with the cities of Trieste and Rijeka.

## Uniforms
Information is scarce and incomplete.

### Naval Officers
Bicorn with black cockade, gold loop and button and black within gold rosettes in the corners; dark-blue, single-breasted coat with light-blue cuffs, light-blue breeches, knee boots. Gilt-hilted sabre in steel sheath with black and gold fist-strap and tassels.

### Sailors
No set uniform.

### Marines
Officers as for naval officers except tobacco-brown coats with brass buttons

and light-blue collars and pointed cuffs. Soldiers wore the shako with brass anchor badge under a black within yellow pompom, tobacco-brown coats with light-blue facings and brass buttons. Belts were black.

**Naval Artillery**
Bicorns with black within yellow corner tassels, pike-grey coats, red facings, yellow buttons, white belts and breeches, black gaiters.

## The Second Trieste Navy 1806–9
The serviceable vessels remaining in Austrian possession in Trieste in 1806 were 23 gunboats, 4 schebecks, some brigs, a galliot and 3 smaller vessels; 7 gunboats on Lake Garda fell into French hands. The brigs were *Pilade*, *Eolo*, *Delphino*, *Oreste*, *Oriane* and *La Speranza*; the galliots *Cibele* and *Diana;* the martegana *Nereide;* the felucca *Lepra*; the schebecks *Lampo* and *Re Pirro* and 10–12 gunboats.

From 1808–9 Feldmarschall-lieutenant Zach was commissioned to review the organisation and uniform of the navy but little was achieved due to lack of funds.

Austria had joined Napoleon's Continental System and a hostile British squadron stood at Lissa and thus paralysed any large-scale naval activity.

In the war of 1809 the brig *Delphino* captured a French gunboat and a battery at Rovigno and, together with other Austrian and British ships, skirmished successfully against the French.

When the French entered Trieste on 16 May 1809 the Austrian vessels sailed for Lussinpiccolo with most of the vital naval stores loaded in merchantmen. Due to the French victory at Wagram, however, Austria was forced to give up all her Adriatic coastal possessions to France at the Peace of Schönbrünn and the Austrian navy ceased to exist. The majority of the naval officers and men were transferred to the new Italian navy.

The British fleet, however, controlled the Adriatic, especially after their victory in the Battle of Lissa in 1811 and frequently supported Austrian land operations near these coasts.

## The Second Austrian–Venetian Navy
In April 1814, Austria re-occupied her Adriatic provinces and Venice and the considerable fleet at the latter city was handed over to her. Feldmarschall-Lieutenant de l'Espine was placed in charge of naval affairs and the existing Venetian naval personnel were taken into Austrian service.

The following ships were taken over: 4 ships of the line in service and 6 under construction; 2 frigates in service and 5 under construction, and 2 corvettes in service. Austria seems, once again, to have mishandled her chances to become a naval power as those ships of the line on the stocks were dismantled and 2 of those in service, *Castiglione* and *Monte San Bernadino* were destroyed by fire; the other 2 were converted to frigates. Only the frigates *Piave* (later *Austria*) and *Principessa di Bologna* (later *Lipsia*), 1 brig and 1 schebeck were retained in service condition, the others being stripped and laid up.

There were no further naval actions during 1814–15.

# Denmark

Denmark-Norway occupied a position in the Baltic in 1792 as significant as that of Turkey on the Black Sea – she could completely control access to the inland sea and in both cases it was the Russian fleet which could be bottled up if desired.

In 1790 the Danish navy consisted of 38 ships of the line with from 90–50 guns each – smaller vessels than those of Britain, France and Spain – 20 frigates each with 42–40 guns, 60 schebecks and some minor vessels. There were 12,000 seamen. The ships were in good repair and well designed, the crews well trained and in excellent spirits. After the events of 1801, and the harshly enforced British policy of taking the ships of all neutral and enemy powers, the Danish fleet by 1807 had shrunk to 20 ships of the line and 17 frigates with a large number of smaller vessels.

From 1805 onwards the newly-constructed Danish gunsloops were almost exact replicas of the successful Swedish vessels with the difference that, whereas the Swedes used lateen sails, the Danes had 2 lug sails with a foresail and small jigger. The same rig was applied to the Danish gunyawls which were otherwise copies of the equivalent Swedish vessels. It is likely that the English naval architect Chapman had a hand in their design.

After 1807, the ships of the line and frigates almost disappeared but the Danes were still lively and active in their strategically important waters by use of a large fleet of gunyawls and other light vessels which they used to excellent effect even against ships of the line.

In 1798 the 'Marine Corps' of 6 companies was raised for military duties on board ship and in the naval strongpoints; in 1803 this was increased to a 'Marine Regementet' of 4 battalions but by 1810 it was reduced to 1 battalion which became the 1st Battalion of the 3-battalion strong 'Köbenhavns Infanteri Regementet'. It had 5 companies each of 166 men.

Coastal defence was also aided by the formation in 1801 of a 'Kystmilits' (Coastal Militia) organised on local bases as a home guard. It was disbanded after the end of the 1801 war with Britain.

## Uniforms

### Flag Officers
*Full Dress*: Bicorn with gold edging, tassels, loop and button, black cockade; dark-blue, double-breasted frockcoat with red collar and cuffs, two gold lace embroidered loops to collar sides, three to each cuff, fringed gold epaulettes on the right shoulder only, gold buttons. White waistcoat and breeches, hussar boots with gold trim and tassel. Gold-hilted sword in black sheath. *Undress*: For everyday wear dark-blue breeches were worn. The sword belt was black with gold embroidery, the sword knot gold and crimson. In 1802 gold Hungarian thigh knots were added to the dark-blue breeches.

In 1801 silver discs were added to the fields of the epaulettes to indicate rank but the exact system is not known. The ranks of the Danish naval officers in descending order of seniority were—flag: admiral, vice-admiral, contre-admiral; senior: commandör, commandör-captajn, captajn; junior: captajn-lojtnant, premier-lojtnant, seconde-lojtnant.

In 1793 the adjutants of the admirals received the following uniform: plain bicorn with black cockade, gold loop and button, gold tassels; dark-blue

Danish Naval Officer: dark-blue coat, red facings, gold buttons and epaulettes – note single star on epaulette strap. A naive contemporary watercolour by G. Pragen from the Heimat Museum Altona, Hamburg. Altona was Danish during the Napoleonic Wars and this plate was painted in Glückstadt in 1809 (*Author's collection*)

double-breasted coat with dark-blue collar, red cuffs and lapels all piped white. The collar bore two gold lace loops of particular design, the cuffs three such loops and the lapels seven. The golden, fringed epaulettes were apparently abandoned by these officers in 1793. White waistcoat and breeches, straight-topped boots, sword and belt as before.

## Junior Officers

As for flag officers but without the gold embroidery to collar and cuffs and with a narrower gold hat edging. In 1801 the waistcoat and breeches became white; small, fringed golden epaulettes were worn on both shoulders (instead of only on the right) with silver discs on them to denote rank. By 1802 the breeches were dark-blue again with gold Hungarian thigh knots. In 1812 officers below flag rank lost their epaulettes and gold hat edging. Rank was now shown by a series of bars and rosettes in gold above the cuff (exact details not known). The gold thigh knots were also discontinued.

## Naval Cadets

Bicorn as for officers, dark-blue, double-breasted frockcoat with dark-blue lapels, collar, cuffs and turnbacks all edged white and with gold buttons and rectangular gold buttonholes to collar (2), cuffs (3) and lapels (7); white waistcoat, plain dark-blue breeches, plain hussar boots; no epaulettes.

## Sailors

The non-commissioned ranks (in descending order) were: höjbadsmand, skebmand and matroser while the artillery ranks were konstabler, kanoner and underkanoner. Uniform consisted of a black leather 'kasket' with high, round-topped front flap and no peak. The flap bore a crowned, brass oval plate bearing an anchor for sailors, a flaming grenade for gunners. A hip length, dark-blue, double-breasted jacket with red collar, lapels and round red cuffs, brass buttons, dark-blue trousers and black shoes completed the outfit.

## Marines

Officers wore plain bicorns with black cockade, gold loop, button and tassels, white plume; red, double-breasted frockcoat with dark-blue collar, lapels and cuffs; red, rectangular cuff flaps, white turnbacks, gold buttons, no epaulettes. White waistcoat and breeches, plain-topped hussar boots, black sword belt with rectangular gold plate, gilt hilted sword with gold and crimson fist strap, gold and crimson sash tied on the left; Malacca cane with gold tip and knob.

## Other ranks

Lacquered leather 'top hats' (very similar to those adopted in 1802 by the Royal Marines of the British fleet) with white headband, black cockade at top left side of the crown, white plume, white loop and brass button. Short-skirted, double-breasted red tunic with dark-blue collar, lapels and cuffs; only the front corners of the skirts were turned back to show the white lining. White belts and white gaiter-breeches for parades, grey gaiter-breeches for everyday wear.

# France

French men-of-war were generally larger than their British counterparts, faster and more heavily armed. In 1783 the French had introduced the carronade (a British invention) into their naval armoury but other British artillery innovations (such as the use of a flintlock to fire the guns instead of the dangerous old slow match) were only adopted in 1802. The French navy had 80 ships of the line and 70 frigates in 1790 but by no means all were ready for service at sea. French naval officers were generally better in theoretical knowledge than their British counterparts but far behind them in practical seamanship.

In mid-1789 the French Revolution had broken out, Louis XVI was deposed in September 1792, condemned to death on 19 January 1793 and guillotined just two days later. France became a republic and was torn apart with internal struggles as the old establishment was destroyed and a new elite was created to take its place

It was the rabid, contagious nature of the new, bloodthirsty state which caused its monarchial neighbours to declare war on it in the hope of crushing the revolution before its dangerous philosophies were exported to disturb the status quo in other lands.

The new revolutionary authorities felt honour-bound to purge every organ of the old order and the upper echelons of the armed forces were subject to particularly thorough scrutiny in the hunt for 'Aristos' who had to be rooted out and destroyed for politically expedient reasons regardless of their contribution to the national defensive effort in the perilous state of war in which France now found herself. Many of the old aristocracy left their homeland of their own accord, of course, sickened by the bloody excesses of their new rulers. These 'emigrés' took service with Britain, Austria, Russia and other states and fought against their own motherland. Their going, either voluntarily or otherwise, left great gaps in the command structures of the French army and navy and those that remained (only 25 per cent of the 1790 strength by June 1791) were harassed by political commissars, 'Representatives of the People', who overturned their military decisions for often whimsical reasons and conducted witch hunts to find scapegoats for the ensuing military disasters.

Even prior to the Revolution the officers of the French navy came from two very different sources – from the aristocracy and from officers of the merchant navy – known as 'blue officers' by their aristocratic comrades. This marriage of officers from vastly different social and educational backgrounds led to almost intolerable situations on board ship, with 'blue officers' practically refusing to take orders from their aristocratic superiors. The sharp class differences led to indiscipline, insubordination and disobedience which badly affected the operations of the ships.

The next casualty in the 'civil war' which raged in France at this time was the Marine Artillery Corps (5,400 highly trained experts) which was disbanded as being too elitist and the servicing of the guns was entrusted to politically reliable men who lacked even the most basic necessary training. The entire French nation was in turmoil and it is no wonder that the administration and logistics of the armed services suffered as well. The army was saved by the emergence of Lazare Nicolas Marguerite Carnot who conjured an army and its logistic support system out of nothing; but the navy – always of minor

concern to that continental power – found no such saviour and its performance throughout the period 1792–1815 reflected its neglected state and the
lack of interest and understanding of the new rulers.

## The French Navy January 1793 (After James)

As the French often changed the names of ships to suit revolutionary
fervour, the ships are shown with their original names first with any
subsequent names in brackets. New ships are marked with an asterisk.

### In Brest

Ready for sea: *Royal Louis (Républicain)* (110); *Languedoc (Anti-fédéraliste,
Victoire)* (80); *Entreprenant, Eole, Jupiter (Batave, Jupiter), Leopard, Patriote,
Phocion (Ferme), Themistocle, Tourville, Trajan (Gaulois) Vengeur* (74s).
Fitting for sea: *Etats-de-Bourgogne (Cote-d'Or, Montagne, Peuple, Océan)*
(120); *Majestueux* (110); *Indomptable\*, Juste, Résolution* (80s); *Borée
(Agricole), Duguay-Trouin* (74s).
In good condition: *Sans-Pareil* (80); *Achille, America\*, Audacieux\*, Brave,
Jean-Bart\*, Fougueux\*, Suffren\* (Redoubtable), Superbe, Téméraire, Tigre\*,
Zélé* (74s).
In want of repair: *Bretagne (Revolutionnaire), Invincible, Terrible* (110s);
*Auguste (Jacobin, Neuf-Thermidor), St Esprit (Scipion)* (80s); *Argonaute,
Diadême (Brutus), Hercule, Illustre, Magnanime, Neptune, Northumberland,
Pluton, Sceptre (Convention), Victoire* (74s).
Unserviceable: *Citoyen* (74).

### At Rochefort

Ready for sea: *Généreux, Apollon (Gasparin), Orion (Trente-un-Mai)* (74s).
Fitting for sea: *Séduisant* (74).
In good condition: *Aquilon\*, Jemmappes, Impetueux\*, Lion (Formidable?),
Mont Blanc\*, Révolution\** (74s), *Sphynx* (?).
Unservicable: *Marseillois* (74).

### At Toulon

Ready for sea: *Dauphin-Royal (Sans-Culottes, Orient)* (120); *Tonnant* (80);
*Censeur, Commerce de Bordeaux (Timoléon), Lys (Tricolour), Scipion* (74s).
Fitting for sea: *Triomphant* (80); *Destin, Dictateur (Liberté), Duquesne,
Héros, Heureux, Pompée* (74s).
In good condition: *Commerce de Marseille* (120); *Couronne (Ça-Ira)* (80).
In want of repair: *Censeure, Mercure, Alcide, Conquérant, Guerrier, Puissant,
Souverain (Souverain Peuple), Suffisant* (74s).

There were also the following frigates but their location and condition is
not known: *Pomone\** (44); *Aréthuse, Carmagnole\*, Concorde\*, Cybèle,
Driade, Junon, Méduse, Melpomène, Nymphe, Perle, Prosperine, Sibylle,
Thétis* (40s); *Aigle, Alceste, Althée, Andromaque, Aurore, Bellone, Boudeuse,
Calypso, Capricieuse, Cléopâtre, Confiante, Courageuse, Danaë, Embuscade,
Engageante, Fée, Félicite, Fidelle, Fine, Fortunée, Friponne, Galathée\*,
Gloire, Gracieuse, Hélène, Hermione, Inconstante, Insurgente, Iphigénie,
Lutine, Médée, Modeste, Précieuse, Preneuse, Prudente, Railleuse, Résolue,
Réunion, Sémillante\*, Sensible, Sérieuse, Sultane, Surveillante, Topaze,
Tribune, Unité, Vestale, Victorieuse* (38s); *Iris, Montreal, Richmond* (32s);
*Badine, Baïonnaise, Belette, Bienvenue, Blonde, Brune, Calliope, Fauvette,
Mignonne, Républicaine, Tourterelle* (28s).

ARMAMENT OF FRENCH SHIPS

| Type and crew | Guns (1st or main deck) | | Guns (2nd deck) | | Guns (3rd deck) | | Guns (quarterdeck) | | Guns (forecastle) | | Guns (poop) | | Total |
|---|---|---|---|---|---|---|---|---|---|---|---|---|---|
| | No | Calibre (lb) | No | Calibre (lb) | No | Calibre (lb) | No | Calibre (lb) | No | Calibre (lb) | No | Calibre (lb) | |
| 120-gunner (1098 crew) | 32 | 36 | 34 | 24 | 34 | 12 | 14 | 8 | 6 | 8 | 4* | 36* | 124 |
| 110-gunner (1037 crew) | 30 | 36 | 32 | 24 | 32 | 12 | 12 | 8 | 4 | 8 | 4* | 36* | 114 |
| 80-gunner (840 crew) | 30 | 36 | 32 | 24 | - | - | 12 | 12 | 6 | 12 | 6* | 36* | 86 |
| 74-gunner (690 crew) | 28 | 36 | 30 | 24 | - | - | 12 | 8 | 4 | 8 | 4* | 36* | 78 |
| 40-gun frigate (330 crew) | 28 | 18 | - | - | - | - | 10 / 2* | 8 / 36* | 2 / 2* | 8 / 36* | - | - | 44 |
| 38-gun frigate (320 crew) | 26 | 18 | - | - | - | - | 10 / 2* | 8 / 36* | 2 / 2* | 8 / 36* | - | - | 42 |
| 36-gun frigate (300 crew) | 26 | 12 | - | - | - | - | 8 / 2* | 6 / 36* | 2 / 2 | 6 / 36* | - | - | 40 |
| 32-gun frigate (275 crew) | 26 | 12 | - | - | - | - | 4 / 2* | 6 / 36* | 2 / 2 | 6 / 36* | - | - | 36 |
| 28-gun frigate (200 crew) | 24 | 8 | - | - | - | - | 6* | 36* | 2 | 6 | - | - | 32 |

*carronade

An indecisive encounter during 1793 between HMS *Scourge* (16) and *Sans Culottes* – a French vessel of 22 guns

# Uniforms

### Flag Officers
*Full Dress*: Bicorn with gold lace edging 8cm wide, gold loop, button and hat tassels, blue-within-white-within-red cockade, tricolour plumes (red, white and blue); dark-blue, single-breasted frockcoat with knee-length skirts with red collar and cuffs. The collar, cuffs and coat front were covered in gold embroidery and edged in gold lace. The gold buttons bore a trophy of arms under a helmet and crossed by an anchor. The gold embroidery was an elaborate oak-leaf pattern. White, single-breasted waistcoat, dark-blue breeches with elaborate gold embroidery to the thigh fronts, gold trimmed hussar boots. Gold and white sash tied on the left and ending in gold tassels; gold, fringed epaulettes. The gold hilted sabre was carried on a gold and black leather belt. In about 1800 a system of rank badges worn on the epaulette fields was introduced; this consisted of silver, five-pointed stars, four (in diamond formation) for an admiral, three (in triangular formation) for vice-admirals (who wore red and gold waist sashes), two for rear-admirals (who wore sky-blue and gold waist sashes).

The tricolour plumes on the bicorns were later replaced by white feathers. *Undress*: Hat as above but without plumes, dark-blue, single-breasted coat with dark-blue collar, cuffs and lining, gold buttons and embroidery 4cm wide; white waistcoat, plain dark-blue breeches. Epaulettes as before. It was also permitted to wear a totally plain dark-blue coat with gold embroidery only to collar and cuffs and with epaulettes. The sash was also worn in undress.

### Junior Officers
*Full Dress*: Bicorn with gold edging 18mm wide, gold loop, button and

155

tassels, tricolour cockade. Dark-blue, single-breasted coat, red collar and dark-blue cuffs; gold buttons bearing an anchor, white waistcoat and dark-blue breeches; black sword belt with gold buckle bearing an anchor; boots. Gold epaulettes according to rank.

By 1805 the full dress of junior officers had altered in the style of the coat as follows: red collar with two elaborately embroidered gold anchors on each side; ten-button front with the top two, bottom two and centre three buttonholes extended to either side with the same elaborate gold anchors and two such vertical anchors on each red cuff. White waistcoat, breeches and stockings.

*Undress*: Some illustrations c1793 show plain bicorn with tricolour cockade, gold loop and button, gold tassels; dark-blue, single-breasted coat closed with four buttons, red collar, waistcoat and breeches, epaulettes according to rank, dark-blue cuffs with three buttons and one gold lace ring (for lieutenants); black baldric with gold anchor badge, boots and sword with gold fist strap.

*Epaulette ranks*: Captain – two fringed epaulettes with an anchor embroidered on the field; frigate captain (lieutenant) – a fringed epaulette on the left, contre epaulette on the right; other lieutenants wore these epaulettes in the reverse order.

By 1802 captains in undress wore double-breasted dark-blue coats with red collars, and three-button cuff flaps, dark-blue cuffs, gold buttons and epaulettes as before. The collar and cuffs were edged in wide gold lace, the red cuff flaps in narrow gold lace. With this they wore white waistcoat and breeches and gold-trimmed hussar boots. The gold-hilted sabre was carried on a black and gold embroidered belt.

**Medical Officers**

Bicorn with 18mm wide gold lace edging, cockade loop and button as for officers; bright-blue, single-breasted frockcoat closed with nine gold buttons; collar and cuffs were black velvet for doctors, red for surgeons and dark green for apothecaries. The buttons bore an anchor around which a serpent twined, surrounded by branches of oak and laurel. Waistcoats and breeches were bright-blue for doctors, red for surgeons, dark-green for apothecaries. The coat buttonholes were embroidered according to the profession of the wearer and the gold sword knot strap had black stripes for doctors, red for surgeons and dark-green for apothecaries.

**Sailors**

Uniforms were introduced in 1804 as follows. Black, glazed leather hat with tricolour cockade, yellow loop and button at the top lefthand side of the crown. This hat was very similar to that worn by the Royal Marines of the British Navy from 1802. On the front was painted a yellow anchor. The dark-blue, double-breasted jacket was hip length with brass buttons, dark-blue collar and cuffs; red, single-breasted waistcoat, dark-blue, wide-legged trousers, black shoes with brass buckles.

Boatswains wore plain cocked hats with tricolour cockade, yellow loop and button and a dark-blue tailcoat with brass buttons and collars in the colour of their branch of service: 'crewing' the ship – navy-blue; gunners – red; pilots – gold; carpenters – crimson; sailmakers – white; armourers and black-smiths – black; pursers – light-blue.

Badges of rank for the crew were as in the army – diagonal bars worn on the lower sleeves: corporal – two red bars, helmsman (sergeant) – one gold bar, quartermasters – two gold bars on a backing of cloth in their branch colour.

## Other Branches of the Navy

An order of 27 April 1800 reorganised the naval departments and the French coast was divided into 6 Prefectures. On 26 September 1800 4 instructional companies for apprentice gunners were set up, 2 at Brest, 1 each at Rochefort and Toulon. By July 1802 the marine corps included 7 half brigades (later called regiments) of artillery and 3 of artificers. 20 companies of conscript marine artificers were raised by a decree of 14 March 1803 and on 5 June 1805 the 20 battalions forming the 7 regiments of marine artillery were reduced to 12 which on 9 December 1805 were retitled 'Imperial Corps of Marine Artillery'. 100 companies of coastal artillery were raised by order of 28 May 1803 and soon increased to 145 companies each of 122 men. On 15 January 1808 the conscript artificers were reduced to 18 companies, a pointer to the waning role of the French navy and this trend was sharply increased by an imperial decree of 19 February 1812 whereby 40,000 naval personnel were to be used on Napoleon's disastrous Russian campaign. The uniforms of other branches of the navy were as follows.

**Marines of the Imperial Guard** (one battalion, raised in 1804)
*Officers*: Bicorn with tricolour, loop, button and tassels as before, red plume for parades. Dark-blue, single-breasted coat (surtout), dark-blue collar, cuffs and turnbacks. The collar was edged all around with gold lace, the pointed cuffs had gold lace only on the top. The coat closed with seven gold buttons. There were gold anchors in the turnbacks and gold epaulettes were worn according to rank with a gold aiguilette on the right shoulder. The waistcoat was white, the breeches dark-blue with gold thigh decoration and gold-trimmed hussar boots. The sword was carried on a white waistbelt under the coat. The button bore the crowned eagle of the Imperial Guard.
*Other Ranks – Full Dress*: Shako with orange top and bottom bands and removable black peak; in 1804 the cockade was worn at the lower left side with orange loop and brass button extending to the top band and orange cords and red plume added for parades. By 1806 the cockade, loop and button had moved to the top front centre of the shako and by 1812 the shako front was decorated by a brass, crowned imperial eagle superimposed on a vertical anchor. For full dress a dark-blue dolman (hussar's waist-length jacket) with dark-blue collars edged all around with orange braid, red pointed cuffs edged in orange braid, five rows each of about twenty brass ball buttons, linked with about twenty rows of orange lace; the whole garment was edged in orange braid and the rear seams were also decorated and piped orange. On the shoulders were brass scales. Legwear was either close fitting dark-blue breeches with orange thigh knots and side-stripes or wide-legged dark-blue trousers with similar decoration. Hussar boots with orange trim were worn with the breeches, black shoes and gaiters with the trousers. Leatherwork was black and the square buckleplate and the pouch lid bore initially an anchor, later the eagle and anchor as on the shako. The side-arms were bayonet and sabre with brass hilt in black, brass filled scabbard; on the hilt was an orange fist strap.
*Other Ranks – Service Dress*: Shako as above; waist-length, double-breasted dark-blue jacket with dark-blue collar and cuffs, both edged orange; brass buttons and shoulder scales; plain blue trousers, shoes and black gaiters.
    The rank badges were not bars but chevrons, point up, above each cuff.

Marines of the French Imperial Guard in Hamburg. This contemporary plate by
C. Suhr shows an officer (left) and trumpeter (centre) in light-blue costume
with crimson and white trumpet cords, and a marine. Note the detail of the sabre
handles – like an anchor's fluke and quite distinctive (*Staatsarchiv, Hamburg;
Author's collection*)

### Drummers
As for the men except: red and gold shako cords, sky-blue dolman and
breeches with red and gold lace, gold trefoils instead of shoulder scales.

### Marines
*Other Ranks*: Shako with red top trim, cords and plume, tricolour cockade,
yellow loop and button over brass eagle and anchor plate; short, dark-blue,
double-breasted jacket with yellow buttons and red patches to the front of

French sailors on the bank of the Alster in Hamburg. A contemporary plate by
C. Suhr showing details of the costume actually worn, not necessarily in accordance
with regulations. Note that the drummer has his drum bandolier under his pouch
bandolier –this is most unusual (*Staatsarchiv, Hamburg; Author's collection*)

the dark-blue collar, red woollen epaulettes, wide, dark-blue trousers, black
shoes, gaiters and belts, brass picker equipment on the bandolier.
*Officers*: As for those of the Marines of the Imperial Guard but with red
collar, round cuffs and turnbacks; two gold laces to collar, gold anchors on
turnbacks, gold lace to chest buttons. Dark-blue breeches, black boots.

## Musicians
Bicorn with tricolour cockade, gold loop and button, white plume; sky-blue
tunic and collar, red, pointed cuffs, red lapels and turnbacks all edged gold.
Seven gold laces to buttonholes on lapels, gold anchors in the turnbacks,
vertical pocket flaps edged gold, gold trefoils on the shoulders. Light-blue
breeches, gold-trimmed hussar boots.

**Bataillone de Flotilla** (rank badges as for other naval branches)
Shako with tricolour cockade, yellow loop and button under red pompon and above brass eagle and anchor plate, yellow cords; single-breasted, hip-length dark-blue tunic, dark-blue collar and cuffs (the latter edged yellow) with rectangular, dark-blue cuff flaps having three brass buttons, dark-blue shoulder straps edged yellow, horizontal pocket flaps edged yellow; front and bottom of jacket edged yellow, dark-blue trousers with yellow side-stripe, black gaiters, belts and shoes.

**Bataillone de Haut Bord** (rank badges as for the other naval branches)
Shako with red pompon over tricolour cockade with yellow loop and button over brass lozenge plate bearing the eagle, red cords; dark-blue frockcoat with dark-blue collar and lapels, red, pointed cuffs and long red turnbacks bearing dark-blue anchors in the corners, brass buttons. Red edging to vertical pocket flaps, dark-green epaulettes with red half moons; red waistcoat, dark-blue breeches, black gaiters with red top edging; black belts.

## Naval Artificers
Shako as above with red pompon and brass lozenge plate; dark-blue, hip-length, double-breasted tunic with short red turnbacks containing dark-blue anchors. Black collar, lapels and cuffs with rectangular cuff flaps all edged red. Red fringed epaulettes, red piping to vertical pocket flaps.

## Coastal Artillery
Shako with cockade, loop and button, brass eagle plate, red pompon with red tuft above it; dark-blue frockcoat with green collar and lapels, dark-blue cuffs and white, rectangular cuff flaps, white turnbacks with dark-blue grenades; white, fringed epaulettes, brass buttons, green edging to vertical pocket flaps, white belts, green waistcoat and breeches, black gaiters.

In 1813 the 2ᵉ Régiment of Marines fought at the Battle of Möckern (Leipzig) on 17 October with six battalions and lost an eagle to the Mecklenburg Hussars.

# Great Britain

According to *Steel's Original and Correct List of the Royal Navy*, in April 1794 the Royal Navy consisted of the following vessels:

|  | Line | Fifties | Frigates | Sloops, etc | Total |
|---|---|---|---|---|---|
| In port and fitting | 41 | - | 36 | 32 | 109 |
| Guard, hospital and prison ships at the several ports | 5 | 3 | 2 | - | 10 |
| English and Irish channels | 15 | 1 | 22 | 25 | 63 |
| Downs and North Sea | - | - | 2 | 1 | 3 |
| West Indies | 9 | 1 | 18 | 11 | 39 |
| Jamaica | 1 | 1 | 3 | 4 | 9 |
| America and Newfoundland | - | - | 4 | 6 | 10 |
| East Indies | 2 | 1 | 7 | 1 | 11 |

| | | | | | |
|---|---|---|---|---|---|
| Africa | 1 | - | - | 2 | 3 |
| Gibraltar and Mediterranean | 17 | 2 | 22 | 5 | 46 |
| Total in commission | 91 | 9 | 116 | 87 | 303 |
| Receiving ships | 8 | 1 | 1 | 2 | 12 |
| Serviceable and repairing | 22 | 2 | 7 | 4 | 35 |
| In ordinary (mothballed) | 22 | 7 | 16 | 25 | 70 |
| Building | 10 | 3 | 6 | 2 | 21 |
| Grand total | 153 | 22 | 146 | 120 | 441 |

## SHIPS AND THEIR CREWS

| | |
|---|---|
| 1st Rate (100 guns or more) | — 875-850 men |
| 2nd Rate (98-90) | — 750-700 men |
| 3rd Rate (80-64) | — 650-500 men |
| 4th Rate (60-50) | — 420-380 men |
| 5th Rate (44-32) | — 300-220 men |
| 6th Rate (30-20) | — 200-160 men |

When an admiral's flag was hoisted on a 1st Rate, her complement of men was increased to 875, when a vice-admiral's to 870 and when a rear-admiral's to 865.

Sloops, bombs, fireships, armed ships and storeships were commanded by masters and commanders; cutters, schooners, brigs, armed vessels, armed transports, armed storeships and surveying sloops were commanded by lieutenants; yachts were commanded by post-captains.

# Royal Navy 1794

In the following alphabetical list of ships of the Royal Navy in April 1794, each ship's name is preceded by a character and certain other symbols also appear in explanation of the role or build of the ship.

ASSp – armed storeship
AT – armed transport
B – building
Bb – bomb
Bg – brig
C – in commission
Corv – corvette
Cut – cutter
FS – fireship
GS – guardship
Gy   galley
HS – hospital ship

Lug – lugger
O – in ordinary (not in commission)
PS – prison ship
Sch – schooner
Sp – sloop
SS – storeship
Sur Sp – surveying ship
Ten – tender
Yt – yacht
+ – hired
† – rigged as brig
‡ – rigged as cutter

Ships captured from enemy nations are marked *; their names are followed by a code letter indicating previous ownership and followed by their previous names (if any); A = American; Bat = Batavian; E = Spain; F = France; the date is the date of capture.

Ships for receiving stores on board were stationed at Portsmouth, Plymouth, Chatham and Sheerness and were termed 'Receiving Ships' (R).

Ships 'in ordinary' in each port were divided into 6 or 8 divisions and a master appointed to each division. Each ship had a boatswain, a gunner, a carpenter, a purser and a cook with their servants and the following number of seamen who had been rated able for 6 calendar months:

| | |
|---|---|
| 100 and more guns – 36 men | 50 – 14 |
| 98 or 90 – 32 | 44 – 12 |
| 80 – 30 | 38 or 28 – 10 |
| 74 or 70 – 26 | 24 or 20 – 8 |
| 64 – 20 | sloops – 6 |
| 54 – 16 | cutters, brigs, etc – 4 |

Locations of ships are shown by abbreviations as follows:

| | |
|---|---|
| Ch = Chatham | N = Nore |
| Cnl = Channel | Po = Portsmouth |
| Cv = on convoy to | Py = Plymouth |
| Df = Deptford | Sh = Sheerness |
| EI = East Indies | Spit = Spithead |
| G = Gibraltar | WI = West Indies |
| J = Jamaica | Wo = Woolwich |
| M = Mediterranean | |

| | Ship | Guns | Station | Year built |
|---|---|---|---|---|
| O | Atlas | 98 | Py repairing | 1782 |
| C | Albion | 74 | Ch | 1763 |
| C | Alcide | 74 | M | 1779 |
| C | Alexander | 74 | Cnl | 1773 |
| C | Alfred | 74 | With Admiral Bowyer | 1778 |
| C | Arrogant | 74 | N | 1761 |
| C | Audacious | 74 | Spit | 1785 |
| C | Africa | 64 | Spit | 1781 |
| C | Agememnon | 64 | M | 1781 |
| C | America | 64 | Spit | 1777 |
| O | Anson | 64 | Ch serviceable | 1743 |
| C | Ardent | 64 | M | 1783 |
| C | Argonaut *F | 64 | Py refitting | 1782 |
| C | Asia | 64 | Cv to WI | 1764 |
| C | Adamant | 50 | Cv to WI | 1779 |
| B | Antelope | 50 | Sh | - |
| C | Assistance | 50 | Cv to M | 1781 |
| O | Acteon | 44 | Po | 1779 |
| C | Adventure | 44 | Spit | 1784 |
| C | Argo | 44 | Cv to St Helena | 1781 |
| C | Assurance | 44 | M | 1780 |
| O | Apollo | 38 | Df fitting | 1794 |
| C | Arethusa | 38 | With Admiral Macbride | 1781 |
| C | Artois | 38 | Df fitting | 1794 |
| C | L'Aigle *F | 36 | M | 1782 |
| C | Active | 32 | Ireland | 1780 |
| O | Aeolus | 32 | Ch repairing | 1758 |
| C | L'Aimable *F | 32 | M | 1782 |
| C | Alarm | 32 | WI | 1758 |
| O | Amazon | 32 | Py repairing | 1773 |
| C | Amphion | 32 | Spit | 1780 |
| C | Andromache | 32 | Ireland | 1781 |
| O | Andromeda | 32 | Py fitting | 1784 |
| C | Aquilon | 32 | G | 1786 |
| C | Astrea | 32 | Cv to M | 1781 |
| C | Alligator | 28 | WI | 1786 |
| C | Aurora | 28 | Bristol Channel | 1777 |
| C | Ariadne | 20 | M | 1776 |

| C | Albicore, Sp | 16 | N | 1793 |
|---|---|---|---|---|
| C | Alert, Sp | 16 | Cnl | 1793 |
| O | Ariel, Sp | 16 | Po | 1779 |
| O | Atlanta, Sp | 14 | Po | 1776 |
| O | Alecto, FS | 12 | Po | 1779 |
| O | Ætna, Bb | 8 | Wo repairing | 1781 |
| C | Assistant, Ten | 8 | Df | 1791 |
| | | | | |
| C | Britannia | 100 | M | 1762 |
| C | Barfleur | 98 | Cnl | 1768 |
| C | Boyne | 98 | WI | 1790 |
| O | Blenheim | 90 | Py | 1761 |
| C | Bedford | 74 | M | 1775 |
| C | Bellerophon | 74 | Spit | 1786 |
| C | Bellona | 74 | Spit | 1760 |
| C | Berwick | 74 | M | 1779 |
| O | Bombay Castle | 74 | Py repairing | 1782 |
| C | Brunswick | 74 | With Admiral Bowyer | 1790 |
| C | Belliqueux | 64 | Cv to WI | 1780 |
| O | Bienfaisant | 64 | Py repairing | 1759 |
| O | Bristol | 50 | Ch Church ship | 1775 |
| C | Beaulieu | 40 | WI | 1791 |
| O | Belle Poule *F | 36 | Ch repairing | 1779 |
| C | Blanche | 32 | WI | 1786 |
| C | Blonde | 32 | WI | 1787 |
| C | Boston | 32 | Cv to Newfoundland | 1762 |
| O | Boreas, SS | 28 | Sh | 1774 |
| C | Brilliant | 28 | Cnl | 1779 |
| C | Bien Aimé, ASSp | 20 | EI | 1793 |
| C | Bonetta, Sp | 16 | Po | 1779 |
| O | Brisk, Sp | 16 | Po | 1784 |
| C | Bulldog, Sp | 14 | Africa | 1782 |
| O | Brazen, Cut | 14 | Py | 1781 |
| C | Birbice, Sch | ? | WI | ? |
| C | Black Joke, Lug | 10 | Spit | 1793 |
| | | | | |
| C | Cambridge, GS | 80 | Py | 1750 |
| C | Caesar | 80 | Cnl | 1793 |
| C | Canada | 74 | Po | 1766 |
| C | Captain | 74 | M | 1787 |
| O | Carnatic | 74 | Py repairing | 1783 |
| B | Centaur | 74 | Wo | ? |
| C | Colossus | 74 | Po | 1787 |
| O | Conqueror | 74 | Ch repairing | 1775 |
| C | Courageux | 74 | M | 1761 |
| C | Culloden | 74 | Py | 1783 |
| O | Cumberland | 74 | Ch | 1774 |
| O | Chichester, R | 74 | Py | 1753 |
| C | Le Caton, HS, *F | 64 | Py | 1782 |
| O | Crown | 64 | Po | 1782 |
| C | Centurion | 50 | EI | 1774 |
| C | Chatham | 50 | Py Convalescent ship | 1758 |
| C | Charon | 44 | Spit | 1783 |
| C | Chichester, SS | 44 | Po fitting | 1785 |
| C | Concorde, *F | 36 | Po | 1783 |
| C | Crescent | 36 | With Admiral Macbride | 1784 |
| C | Castor | 32 | Ostend | 1785 |
| C | Ceres | 32 | WI | 1781 |
| C | Cleopatra | 32 | Po | 1780 |
| C | Carysfort | 28 | St George's Channel | 1767 |
| C | Circe | 28 | Cnl | 1785 |
| C | Cyclops | 28 | M | 1779 |
| O | Champion | 24 | Wo serviceable | 1779 |
| O | Camel, ASSp | 24 | Wo | 1782 |

| | | | | |
|---|---|---|---|---|
| C | *Camilla* | 20 | Py fitting | 1776 |
| B | *Cerberus* | ? | Southampton | ? |
| O | *Cygnet*, Sp | 18 | Po | 1776 |
| O | *Calypso*, Sp | 16 | Po | 1783 |
| C | *Cormorant*, Sp | 16 | Cnl | 1794 |
| C † | *Childers*, Sp | 14 | Df | 1778 |
| C | *Comet*, FS | 14 | Spit | 1783 |
| C | *Conflagration*, FS | 14 | M | 1783 |
| O | *Cockatrice*, Cut | 14 | Po | 1782 |
| C | *Catherine*, Yt | 8 | Df | 1720 |
| O | *Chatham*, Yt | 8 | Ch | 1741 |
| C | *Chatham*, Ten | ? | EI | 1790 |
| | | | | |
| B | *Dreadnought* | 98 | Po | - |
| O | *Duke* | 98 | Py repairing | 1777 |
| C | *Defence* | 74 | With Admiral Macbride | 1763 |
| O | *Defiance* | 74 | Ch refitting | 1783 |
| C | *Diadem* | 64 | M | 1782 |
| C | *Dictator* | 64 | to Africa | 1783 |
| O | *Director* | 64 | Ch | 1784 |
| C | *Diomede* | 44 | EI | 1781 |
| C | *Dolphin*, HS | 44 | M | 1781 |
| O | *Dover* | 44 | Po | 1784 |
| O | *Diamond* | 38 | Df fitting | 1791 |
| O | *Diana* | 38 | Df fitting | 1794 |
| C | *Daedalas* | 32 | Virginia | 1780 |
| C | *Druid* | 32 | Cruising | 1783 |
| C | *Dido* | 28 | M | 1784 |
| C | *Daphne* | 20 | Cv to Downs from Py | 1776 |
| C | *Dorset*, Yt | 10 | Dublin | 1753 |
| C | *Dromedary*, SS | 24 | WI | 1779 |
| C † | *Drake*, Sp | 14 | Sh | 1779 |
| C | *Discovery*, Sp | 10 | Nootka Sound | 1790 |
| C+ | *Daedalus*, SS | ? | Botany Bay | - |
| C | *Deptford*, Ten | 8 | On impress service | 1788 |
| | | | | |
| O | *Edgar* | 74 | Ch | 1773 |
| C | *Egmont* | 74 | M | 1766 |
| O | *Elephant* | 74 | Po | 1789 |
| O | *Elizabeth* | 74 | Po | 1768 |
| C | *Excellent* | 74 | Po | 1786 |
| O | *Eagle* | 64 | Ch repairing | 1777 |
| O | *Essex*, R | 64 | Po | 1763 |
| O | *Europe* | 64 | Py repairing | 1769 |
| C | *Europa* | 50 | J | 1782 |
| C | *Expedition* | 44 | On ordnance service | 1781 |
| C | *Experiment* | 44 | WI | 1780 |
| C | *Enterprise* | 28 | Tower to receive men | 1774 |
| C | *Eurydice* | 24 | Spit | 1784 |
| C | *La Eclair* *F | 20 | M | 1793 |
| C | *Echo*, Sp | 16 | Coasting convoy | 1784 |
| C | *L'Espion*, Sp *F | 16 | Py | 1793 |
| C | *Expedition*, Cut | 10 | Cnl | 1775 |
| C | *Experiment*, Lug | 10 | Cruising | - |
| | | | | |
| O | *Formidable* | 98 | Py repairing | 1777 |
| B | *Foudroyant* | 80 | Py | - |
| O | *Fame* | 74 | Py | 1759 |
| C | *Fortitude* | 74 | M | 1780 |
| O | *Fortunée*, PS *F | 40 | Langstone | 1779 |
| C | *Flora* | 36 | With Admiral Macbride | 1780 |
| C | *Fox* | 32 | G | 1780 |
| C | *Fairy*, Sp | 16 | Africa | 1778 |
| C | *Favourite*, Sp | 16 | Df fitting | 1794 |

| | | | | |
|---|---|---|---|---|
| C | *Fly*, Sp | 16 | Cruising | 1776 |
| C † | *Fortune*, Sp | 16 | Cruising | 1778 |
| C | *Fury*, Sp | 16 | Cruising | 1790 |
| C † | *Falcon*, Sp | 14 | Cnl | 1782 |
| C | *Ferret*, Sp | 14 | Cnl | 1784 |
| O | *Flirt*, Sp | 14 | Df | - |
| C | *Flying Fifth*, Sch | ? | J | - |
| | | | | |
| C | *Glory* | 98 | With Admiral Bowyer | 1788 |
| C | *Gibraltar* *E | 80 | Spit | 1780 |
| C | *Ganges* | 74 | Py refitting | 1782 |
| O | *Goliath* | 74 | Po repairing | 1781 |
| O | *Grafton* | 74 | Po serviceable | 1771 |
| O | *Grampus* | 50 | Df repairing | 1782 |
| C | *Gladiator*, HS | 44 | Po | 1783 |
| C | *Gorgon* | 44 | M | 1784 |
| O | *Greyhound* | 32 | Limehouse repairing | 1783 |
| C | *Grana*, HS *E | 28 | Ch | 1781 |
| C | *Le Goelan*, *F | 14 | J | 1793 |
| | | | | |
| B | *Hibernia* | 110 | Py | - |
| C | *Hannibal* | 74 | Py refitting | 1786 |
| C | *Hector* | 74 | With Admiral Macbride | 1779 |
| C | *Hero*, PS | 74 | R. Medway | 1753 |
| C | *Hebe*, *F | 38 | Cnl | 1782 |
| C | *Hermione* | 32 | J | 1782 |
| C | *Heroine* | 32 | EI | 1783 |
| C | *Hind* | 28 | G | 1785 |
| C | *Hussar* | 28 | Halifax | 1784 |
| C | *Hawke*, Sp | 16 | Cnl | 1793 |
| O | *Hazard*, Sp | 16 | Ch | 1794 |
| C | *Hornet*, Sp | 16 | Df fitting | 1794 |
| C | *Hound*, Sp | 16 | J | 1790 |
| C † | *Helena*, Sp | 14 | Spit | 1778 |
| | | | | |
| C | *Impregnable* | 90 | Spit | 1786 |
| C | *Illustrious* | 74 | M | 1789 |
| C | *Invincible* | 74 | Cruising | 1765 |
| C | *Irresistable* | 74 | WI | 1782 |
| O | *Indefatigable* | 64 | Po serviceable | 1784 |
| C | *Inflexible*, SS | 64 | Spit | 1780 |
| C | *Intrepid* | 64 | Py for J | 1770 |
| O | *Isis* | 50 | Sh | 1774 |
| C | *L'Impereuse* *F | 40 | G | 1793 |
| C | *Inconstant* | 36 | M | 1783 |
| C | *Iphigenia* | 32 | J | 1780 |
| C | *Iris* | 32 | N | 1783 |
| C | *Inspector*, Sp | 16 | WI | 1782 |
| C | *Incendiary*, FS | 14 | Py refitting | 1782 |
| | | | | |
| O | *Jupiter* | 50 | Sh repairing | 1778 |
| B | *Jason* | 38 | Df | - |
| C | *Juno* | 32 | M | 1780 |
| | | | | |
| C | *King's Fisher*, Sp | 18 | Cruising | 1782 |
| O | *Kite*, Cut | 14 | Po | 1778 |
| | | | | |
| O | *London* | 98 | Po | 1766 |
| C | *Leviathan* | 74 | Spit | 1790 |
| C | *Lion* | 64 | To China Sept 1792 | 1777 |
| O | *Leander* | 50 | Po | 1780 |
| C | *Leopard*, GS | 50 | Downs | 1790 |
| C | *Latona* | 38 | Cnl | 1781 |

165

| | | | | |
|---|---|---|---|---|
| C | *Leda* | 36 | M | 1783 |
| C | *Lowestoffe* | 32 | M | 1762 |
| B | *Lively* | 32 | Northam | - |
| C | *Lapwing* | 28 | Wo fitting | 1785 |
| C | *Lizard* | 28 | Lisbon | 1757 |
| C | *Lark*, Sp | 16 | Wo fitting | 1794 |
| O | *Lynx*, Sp | 16 | Wo serviceable | 1794 |
| C | *Liberty*, Cut | 16 | Cruising | 1779 |
| C | *Lutin* *F | 16 | Newfoundland | 1793 |
| C | *Lutine*, Bb | ? | M | - |
| | | | | |
| O | *Magnificent* | 74 | Po serviceable | 1766 |
| C | *Majestic* | 74 | With Admiral Rowley | 1785 |
| C | *Marlborough* | 74 | Spit | 1767 |
| B | *Mars* | 74 | Df | - |
| C | *Minotaur* | 74 | Cnl | 1793 |
| C | *Monarch* | 74 | Cnl | 1765 |
| C | *Montague* | 74 | With Admiral Bowyer | 1779 |
| C | *Magnanime* | 64 | Py repairing | 1780 |
| O | *Modeste*, R *F | 64 | Po | 1759 |
| O | *Monmouth* | 64 | Po repairing | 1773 |
| O | *Medway*, R | 60 | Py | 1755 |
| C | *Medusa*, GS | 50 | Cork | 1785 |
| C | *La Modeste* *F | 40 | M | 1793 |
| C | *Minerva* | 38 | EI | 1780 |
| C | *Melampus* | 36 | With Admiral Macbride | 1785 |
| C | *Magiciene* *F | 32 | WI | 1781 |
| C | *Meleager* | 32 | M | 1785 |
| C | *Mermaid* | 32 | Sh | 1785 |
| O | *Maidstone* | 28 | Sh repairing | 1758 |
| O | *Medea* | 28 | Po repairing | 1778 |
| O | *Mercury* | 28 | Po | 1780 |
| C | *Myrmidon*, Slopship | 20 | Py | 1780 |
| O | *Merlin*, Sp | 20 | Sh repairing | 1777 |
| C | *Martin*, Sp | 14 | Cruising | 1789 |
| C | *Megaera*, FS | 14 | Spit | 1782 |
| C | *Mutine*, Cut *F | 14 | Cnl | 1778 |
| C | *Mary*, Yt | 10 | Df repairing | 1723 |
| C | *Medina*, Yt | 10 | Isle of Wight | 1771 |
| C | *Marie Antoinette*, Sch *F | 10 | J | 1793 |
| | | | | |
| B | *Neptune* | 98 | Df | - |
| O | *Namur* | 90 | Py | 1756 |
| O | *Nassau* | 64 | Py repairing | 1785 |
| C | *Nonsuch* | 64 | Ch | 1774 |
| C | *La Nymphe* *F | 36 | With Admiral Macbride | 1780 |
| C | *Niger* | 32 | Spit | 1759 |
| C | *Nemesis* | 28 | M | 1780 |
| C | *Narcisus* | 20 | Df fitting | 1781 |
| C | *Nautilus*, Sp | 16 | WI | 1784 |
| C | *Nimble*, Cut | 14 | North Sea | 1781 |
| | | | | |
| B | *Ocean* | 98 | Wo | - |
| C | *Orion* | 74 | Cnl | 1787 |
| C | *L'Orseau* *F | 36 | Spit | 1793 |
| C | *Orpheus* | 32 | EI | 1780 |
| C † | *Orestes*, Sp *Bat | 18 | Spit | 1781 |
| C † | *Otter*, Sp | 14 | Sh | 1782 |
| | | | | |
| O | *Prince George* | 98 | Ch serviceable | 1772 |
| C | *Princess Royal* | 98 | M | 1773 |
| B | *Prince of Wales* | 98 | Po | - |
| O | *Prince* | 98 | Po | 1788 |
| C | *Le Pegase*, HS *F | 74 | Po | 1782 |

| | | | | |
|---|---|---|---|---|
| C | Powerful | 74 | J | 1783 |
| O | Polyphemus | 64 | Ch serviceable | 1782 |
| O | Prothee *F | 64 | Po repairing | 1780 |
| O | Prudent | 64 | Py repairing | 1768 |
| O | Prince Edward, R *Bat | 60 | Ch | 1781 |
| O | Portland | 50 | Po repairing | 1770 |
| O | Princess Caroline, R *Bat | 50 | Sh | 1781 |
| C | Phaëton | 38 | Cnl | 1782 |
| O | La Prudente *F | 38 | Po serviceable | 1779 |
| O | Perserverence | 36 | Po | 1781 |
| O | Phoenix | 36 | Wo | 1783 |
| C | Pallas | 32 | Cnl | 1794 |
| C | Pearl | 32 | Milford | 1762 |
| C | Penelope | 32 | J | 1783 |
| C | Pegasus | 28 | Spit | 1779 |
| C | Pomona | 28 | Spit | 1778 |
| C | La Prompte *F | 28 | Po | 1793 |
| C | Proserpine | 28 | Spit | 1777 |
| C | Porcupine | 24 | Py | 1779 |
| O | Prosperity, ASSp, R | 22 | Sh | 1782 |
| C | Perseus | 20 | Py refitting | 1776 |
| O | Peterell, Sp | 16 | Ch fitting | 1794 |
| C | Providence, Sp | 16 | Wo | 1791 |
| B | Pylades, Sp | 16 | Rotherhithe | - |
| C | Pluto | 14 | Newfoundland | 1782 |
| C | Pilote, Cut *F | 14 | Cruising | 1778 |
| O | Portsmouth, Yt | 8 | Po serviceable | 1755 |
| O | Princess Augusta, Yt | 8 | Df | 1710 |
| C | Placentia, Sp | ? | Newfoundland | 1790 |
| | | | | |
| C | Queen Charlotte | 100 | Spit | 1790 |
| C | Queen | 98 | Spit | 1769 |
| C | Quebec | 32 | Madeira | 1781 |
| | | | | |
| C | Royal George | 100 | Cnl | 1788 |
| C | Royal Sovereign | 100 | Spit | 1786 |
| C | Royal William | 84 | Spit | 1719 |
| C | Ramillies | 74 | With Admiral Bowyer | 1785 |
| C | Resolution | 74 | With Admiral Macbride | 1770 |
| C | Robust | 74 | Po refitting | 1764 |
| O | Royal Oak | 74 | Po repairing | 1769 |
| C | Russel | 74 | Cnl | 1764 |
| C | Raisonable | 64 | Po | 1768 |
| O | Repulse | 64 | Po serviceable | 1780 |
| C | Ruby | 64 | Spit | 1775 |
| O | Rippon, R | 60 | Py | 1758 |
| O | Renown | 50 | Ch repairing | 1774 |
| C | Romney | 50 | M | 1762 |
| O | Rainbow, R | 44 | Wo | 1761 |
| C | Regulus | 44 | Spit | 1785 |
| C | Resistance | 44 | EI | 1782 |
| C | Roebuck | 44 | WI | 1774 |
| O | La Reunion *F | 38 | Po | 1793 |
| C | Romulus | 36 | G | 1785 |
| C | Resource | 28 | WI | 1778 |
| C | Rose | 28 | WI | 1783 |
| C | Redoubt, Floating battery | 20 | Ostend | 1793 |
| O | Le Robert *F | 20 | Py refitting | 1794 |
| O | Racehorse, Sp | 16 | Sh | 1783 |
| O | Ranger, Sp | 16 | Df | 1794 |
| B | Rattler, Sp | 16 | Northam | - |
| C | Rattlesnake, Sp | 16 | WI | 1791 |
| C | Ranger, Cut | 14 | Cnl | 1787 |
| C | Rattler, Cut | 14 | Py | - |

167

| | | | | |
|---|---|---|---|---|
| C | *Resolution,* Cut | 14 | Cnl | 1779 |
| O | *Royal Charlotte,* Yt | 10 | Df | 1749 |
| | | | | |
| C | *St George* | 98 | M | 1785 |
| C | *Sandwich,* GS | 98 | N | 1759 |
| C | *Saturn* | 74 | Po refitting | 1786 |
| C | *Suffolk* | 74 | Spit | 1765 |
| O | *Sultan* | 74 | Po repairinng | 1775 |
| C | *Swiftsure,* GS | 74 | Cork | 1787 |
| C | *St Albans* | 64 | Cv to WI | 1764 |
| C | *Sampson* | 64 | Cv to St Helena | 1781 |
| C | *Sceptre* | 64 | WI | 1781 |
| O | *Scipio* | 64 | Ch fitting for a HS | 1782 |
| O | *Standard* | 64 | Py repairing | 1782 |
| C | *Stately* | 64 | Po refitting | 1784 |
| O | *Salisbury* | 50 | Po | 1769 |
| O | *Serapis* | 44 | Ch serviceable | 1781 |
| C | *Severn* | 44 | Py refitting | 1786 |
| C | *Sheerness* | 44 | North Sea | 1787 |
| B | *Sea Horse* | 38 | Rotherhithe | - |
| O | *Santa Leocadia* *E | 36 | Wo repairing | 1781 |
| C | *Santa Margarita* *E | 36 | WI | 1779 |
| C | *Sole Bay* | 32 | WI | 1785 |
| C | *Southampton* | 32 | Cnl | 1757 |
| B | *Stag* | 32 | Ch | - |
| C | *Success* | 32 | WI | 1781 |
| C | *Syren* | 32 | Py refitting | 1782 |
| C | *Sybil* | 28 | Df fitting | 1779 |
| C | *Squirrel* | 24 | St George's Channel | 1785 |
| C | *Sphynx* | 20 | Sh | 1775 |
| C | *Savage,* Sp | 16 | Cruising | 1778 |
| C | *Scorpion,* Sp | 16 | Cv to WI | 1785 |
| C † | *Scourge,* Sp | 16 | N | 1779 |
| C | *Serpent,* Sp | 16 | Cnl | 1789 |
| C | *Shark,* Sp | 16 | Po | 1780 |
| O † | *Swallow,* Sp | 16 | Po | 1781 |
| C | *Swift,* Sp | 16 | Po for EI | 1793 |
| C | *Sea Flower,* Cut | 16 | WI | 1782 |
| C † | *Scour,* Sp | 14 | G | 1781 |
| C † | *Speedy,* Sp | 14 | G | 1782 |
| C | *Swan,* Sp | 14 | Cv to Wi | 1767 |
| C | *Spitfire,* Sp | 14 | Cruising | 1782 |
| C | *Speedwell,* Cut | 14 | Spit | 1780 |
| C | *Sprightly,* Cut | 14 | Cnl | 1778 |
| O | *Sultana,* Cut | 14 | Py | 1780 |
| C | *Spider,* Cut *F | 12 | Cnl | 1782 |
| C | *Spitfire,* Sch | 8 | J | 1793 |
| | | | | |
| B | *Téméraire* | 98 | Ch | - |
| C | *Terrible* | 74 | M | 1785 |
| C | *Theseus* | 74 | Ch | 1786 |
| C | *Thunderer* | 74 | Ch fitting | 1783 |
| C | *Tremendous* | 74 | With Admiral Bowyer | 1784 |
| O | *Triumph* | 74 | Po repairing | 1764 |
| O | *Trident* | 64 | Po serviceable | 1768 |
| B | *Tiger* | 50 | Po | - |
| C | *Trusty* | 50 | Cork | 1782 |
| C | *Thetis* | 38 | Cnl | 1782 |
| C | *Thalis* | 36 | Po | 1782 |
| C | *Terpsichore* | 32 | WI | 1786 |
| C | *Tartar* | 28 | M | 1756 |
| C | *Thisbe* | 28 | Spit | 1783 |
| C | *Triton* | 28 | Po fitting | 1773 |
| O | *Termagent,* Sp | 18 | Sh | 1781 |

168

| | | | | |
|---|---|---|---|---|
| O | *La Trompeuse* *F | 18 | Py | 1794 |
| C | *Thorn*, Sp | 16 | N | 1779 |
| C | *Trespassy*, SS | ? | Newfoundland | 1790 |
| O | *Trimmer*, Sp *F | 16 | Sh | 1782 |
| C | *Tisiphone*, Sp | 12 | M | 1781 |
| O | *Tyral*, Cut | 12 | Cnl | 1781 |
| C | *Terror*, Bb | 8 | Spit | 1779 |
| | | | | |
| C | *Union*, HS | 90 | Sh | 1756 |
| C | *Ulysses* | 44 | WI | 1779 |
| B | *Unicorn* | 32 | Ch | - |
| | | | | |
| B | *Ville de Paris* | 110 | Ch | - |
| C | *Victory* | 100 | M | 1765 |
| C | *Valiant* | 74 | Cnl | 1759 |
| C | *Vanguard* | 74 | WI | 1787 |
| O | *Venerable* | 74 | Ch serviceable | 1784 |
| C | *Vengeance* | 74 | WI | 1774 |
| C | *Victorious* | 74 | Ch fitting | 1785 |
| C | *Veteran* | 64 | WI | 1787 |
| O | *Vigilant* | 64 | Po serviceable | 1774 |
| C | *Venus* | 32 | With Admiral Rowley | 1758 |
| C | *Vestal* | 28 | North Sea | 1779 |
| O | *Viper* *F | 18 | ? | 1794 |
| C | *Vulture*, Sp (Slopship) | 14 | Po | 1776 |
| C | *Viper*, Cut | 12 | Cnl | 1780 |
| C | *Vesuvius*, Bb | 8 | WI | 1776 |
| | | | | |
| C | *Windsor Castle* | 98 | M | 1790 |
| O | *Warrior* | 74 | Po serviceable | 1781 |
| O | *Warspite*, R | 74 | Po | 1758 |
| O | *Warwick*, R | 50 | Ch | 1767 |
| C | *Woolwich* | 44 | WI | 1785 |
| C | *Winchelsea* | 32 | WI | 1764 |
| O † | *Wasp*, Sp | 16 | Sh | 1782 |
| C † | *Weazle*, Sp | 12 | Cnl | 1783 |
| C | *Woolwich*, Ten | 10 | On impress service | 1788 |
| O | *William & Mary*, Yt | 8 | Df | 1694 |
| | | | | |
| O | *Yarmouth*, R | 64 | Py | 1754 |
| | | | | |
| O | *Zealous* | 74 | Ch serviceable | 1786 |
| C | *Zebra*, Sp | 16 | WI | 1780 |

By 1799 the Royal Navy had been joined by the following ships (ships marked * had been captured and their previous nationality is indicated by the code letters: Bat=Batavian; E=Spanish; F=French; their former names if any are then shown:

C *Ajax* (80); C *Aboukir* *F *Aquilon* (74); C *Achilles* (74); C *Agincourt* (64); C *Ardent* (64); C *Alkmaar* *Bat (56); C *Abergavenny* (54); B *Antelope* (50); C *Amelia* *F *Prosperine* (44); C *Anson* (44); C *Acasia* (40); O *Ambuscade* *F (47); B *Active* (38); B *Amazon* (38); C *Apollo* (38); B *Amethyst* (38); C *Amphion* (32); C *Alemene* (32); C *L'Aurore* *F PS (32); C *Albion* ASSp (22); C *Ann* ASSp (22); O *Arab* *F (22); C *Alliance* *Bat (22); C *Albatross* Bg (18); C *Arrow* Sp (18); C *Atalante* *F Sp (16); O *Avenger* *F (16); C *Amaranthe* *F (14); O *L'Arrogante* *F (14); O *L'Audacieux* *F (14); C *Amboyna* *Bat Bg (10); C *Alert* Cut; C *Alexander* Sch (6); C *Ant* Sch; O *Belleisle* *F *Formidable* (74); C *Brakel* *Bat (54); C *Braave* *Bat (40); C *Boadicea* (38); O *La Bellone* *F (36); C *Borcas* Sp (28); C *Le Babet* *F (20); C *La Bonne Citoyenne* *F (20); C *Beaver* Sp (18); O *Belette* Sp (18); C *Bonette* *F (18); C *Busy*

Bg (18);   C *Bittern* Sp (16);   C *Barbara* Sch;   C *Buffalo* SS (12);   C *Canopus* *F *Franklin* (80);   C *Camperdown* *Bat *Jupiter* PS (74);   C *Centaur* (74); B *Conqueror* (74);   B *Courageux* (74);   C *Le Conquerant* *F (74);   C *Cambrian* (44);   C‡ *Clyde* (38);   C *Calcutta* AT (24);   C *Coromandel* AT (24); C *La Constance* *F (24); C *Cormorant* *F (20); C‡ *Cameleon* Bg (18); C *Cyane* (18); C† *Corso* *E (18);   C *Cynthia* Sp (16);   *Cruizer* Bg (18); C *Cygnet* Cut (14);   O *Le Coureur* *F (14);   C *Campbell* Sch; C *La Certain* *F (–); C *Crache Feu* *F (3);   O *Carouse* Sch (2);   C *Confederacy* Bb Ten; C *Dragon* (74);   C *Dordrecht* *Bat GS (64);   C *Diomede* (50);   O *La Decades* *F (44);   C *Doris* (36);   C *Dryad* (36);   O *Daphne* *Bat *Sirene* (26);   C *Daphne* (20); C *Danaë* *F (20); C *Dart* Sp (18); C *Diligence* Bg (16); C *Dather* (16); C *Driver* (16);   C *Deux Amis* *F (14);   C *Dauphin Royal* Sch;   C *Dispatch* Ten (6); B *Europe* (98);   C *Endymion* (44);   C *Ethalion* (38);   C *Emerald* (36);   C *Eugenie* *F Bg (8);   C *L'Espior* *F Sp (16);   C *Echo* (14);   C *Euphrosyne* Bg (14);   C *L'Espiegle* *F Bg (12);   C *Explosion* Bb (8);   C *Fisgard* *F *La Resistance* (38);   ? *La Fortune* *F (18);   ? *La Fulmiuante* *F Cut;   C *Le Guerrier* *F *Peuple Souverain* (74);   C *Gelykheid* *Bat PS (68);   C *Glatton* (54);   C *Grampus* SS (54);   O *La Gentille* *F (40);   O *La Gloire* *F (40); C‡ *Glenmore* (36);   C *Gaiete* *F Corv (20);   C *General Small* (8);   C *Garland* Ten (6);   C *Goonang Api* FS;   O *L'Hercule* *F (74);   C *Haarlem* *Bat (68);   O *Hercules* *Bat (64);   C *Hindostan* (54);   C *Hydra* (38);   B *Hussar* (38);   C *Hyaena* (24);   C *Hermes* AS (24);   C *Harpy* Bg (18);   C *Havick* *Bat (18);   C *Hobart* (18);   C *Hound* Bg (18);   C *Hope* *Bat *Star* Sp (14);   C *Harlequin* Sch;   C *Hecla* Bb (8);   O *Hannah* Ten;   C *Hebe* (6); O *L'Immortalité* *F (42);   O *Janus* *Bat *Argo* (32);   C *Jamaica* *F *Percante* (26);   C *Jalouje* *F Bg (18);   C *Kent* (74);   C‡ *Kite* Bg (18);   C‡ *Kangaroo* Bg (18);   C *Lancaster* (64);   O *La Loire* *F (46);   B *Lavinia* (44);   O *Leighton* ASSp (22); C *Monmouth* (64); C *Madras* (54); C *La Melpomene* *F (44); C *La Minerve* *F FS (42); C‡ *Maidstone* (32); C *Marsouin* *F (26); C *Musette* *F FS (24);   O *La Marie* *F (14);   C *La Mutine* *F Corv (14); C *Merlin* Sp (16);   O *Miermin* *Bat (16);   C *Montego Bay* Sch (10);   C *Mary* Ten (6);   C *Northumberland* (74);   C *Naiad* (38);   B *La Nereide* *F (36);   O *Narcissus* (32);   C *Overyssel* *Bat GS (64);   C *Osprey* Sp (18); C *Prince Frederick* *Bat *Revolution* (64);   *La Prevoyante* *F (40);   C+ *Prince of Wales* AT (38);   C *Phoebe* (36);   C *Penelope* (36);   C *Proselyte* *Bat *Jason* (32);   C *Princess* *Bat *Williamstadt* GS (26);   C *La Perdrix* *F (24);   C *Plymouth* Yt (8);   C‡ *Pelican* Bg (18);   C *Penguin* *Bat *Comet* (18);   C *Plover* Sp (18);   C *Pheasant* (18);   C *Pyl* *Bat (16);   C *Pedro* Sch; C *Plymouth* (8);   C *Porpoise* ASSp (10);   C *Plymouth* NT (8);   O *Plymouth* Ten;   C *Renown* (74);   B *Revenge* (74);   C *La Renomée* *F (44);   ? *La Revolutionnaire* *FS (44);   ? *La Raison* *FS (24);   C‡ *Racoon* Bg (18); C *Republican* *F Sch (18);   *La Raileur* *F (18);   C *La Renard* *F (18);   C *Rambler* Sp (14);   C *Rosario* *E FS (14);   C *Rattler* Sp (16);   C *Recovery* Sch (10);   C *Requin* *F Bg (12);   C *Revenge* (8);   C *Royalist* Sch;   C *Regard* NT (6);   O *San Josef* *E (112);   C *Salvador del Mundo* *E (112);   C *San Nicolas* *E (80);   C *San Domingo* *E PS (74);   C *San Ysidro* *E PS (74); C *Superb* (74);   C *La Spartiate* *F (74);   C *La Seine* *F (42);   C *Santa Dorothea* *E (42);   C *Saldanha* *Bat R (38);   C *Sensible* *F (36);   C *Sirius* (36);   C‡ *Shannon* (32);   C *Surprize* *F *L'Unite* (24);   O *Sardine* *F Sp (22);   C *Scourge* *F *Robuste* Sp (22);   C *Selby* Sp (22);   C *Sphynx* (20);   C‡ *Sea Gull* Bg (18);   C *Spy* *F *L'Espion* (18);   C‡ *Star* Bg (18); C‡ *Swallow* Bg (18);   C *Stork* (18);   C‡ *Sylph* Bg (18);   C *Snake* Sp (18); C *Speedwell* Bg (14);   C *Spencer* Sp (14);   C *Speedy* Sp (14);   C *Strombolo*

Bb (8); C *Sulphur* Bb (8); C *Supply* NT; O *Téméraire* (98); C *La Tigre* *F (80); ? *Le Tonnant* *F (80); C *Tromp* *Bat A en flute (54); C *Tamer* (38); C *Thulen* *Bat *Tholen* A en flute (36); C *Trent* (36); C *Thames* (32); C *Triton* (32); ? *La Tourterelle* *F (30); C *Teranagant* (18); C *Transter* *F (14); C *Tartarus* Bb (8); C *Thude* Bb (8); C *Thomas* Sch; C *Thetis* Sch (8); C *L'Unite* *F (36); C *L'Uranie* *F (8); C *Ville de Paris* (110); O *Vryheid* *Bat PS (74); C *La Virginie* *F (44); O *Vindictive* *Bat *Bellona* (28); C *La Volage* *F (24); C *Victor* (18); O *Le Victoire* Lug (14); C *La Victorieuse* *F (12); C *Volcano* Bb (8); C *Virginia* Sch (4); C *Venus* NT (6); C *Wassenaer* *Bat en flute (64); C *William* ASSp (22); C *Weymouth* AT (26); C *Xenophon* ASSp (22); C *York* (64); C *Zealand* *Bat GS (64); C *Zephyr* Sp (14).

This made a total of ships as shown in the following table:

| | Line | Fifties | Frigates | Sloops, etc | Total |
|---|---|---|---|---|---|
| In port and fitting | 32 | 7 | 69 | 165 | 273 |
| Guard, hospital and prison ships at the several ports | 35 | 4 | 9 | - | 48 |
| English and Irish Channels | 9 | 3 | 23 | 46 | 81 |
| Downs and North Sea | 11 | 1 | 9 | 17 | 38 |
| West Indies | 3 | - | 14 | 29 | 46 |
| Jamaica | 7 | 1 | 16 | 11 | 35 |
| America and Newfoundland | 2 | 1 | 5 | 7 | 15 |
| Cape of Good Hope and East Indies | 9 | 4 | 11 | 15 | 39 |
| Africa | - | - | 2 | - | 2 |
| Portugal, Gibraltar and Mediterranean | 38 | - | 18 | 13 | 69 |
| Total in commission | 146 | 21 | 176 | 303 | 646 |
| Receiving ships | 9 | 1 | 7 | - | 17 |
| Serviceable and repairing | 1 | - | 5 | 1 | 7 |
| In ordinary | 22 | 1 | 28 | 39 | 90 |
| Building | 14 | 2 | 10 | 2 | 28 |
| Grand totals | 192 | 25 | 226 | 345 | 788 |

TOTALS OF VESSELS CAPTURED FROM ENEMY POWERS IN THE WAR UP TO JANUARY 1799

| Guns | 120/110 | 84/80 | 74 | 68/64 | 56/54 | 44/40 | 38/36 | 32 | 28 | 26/24 | 22/20 | 18 | 16/14 | 12/8 | 6 and less | Totals |
|---|---|---|---|---|---|---|---|---|---|---|---|---|---|---|---|---|
| French | 3 | 12 | 35 | - | - | 35 | 23 | 11 | 7 | 16 | 28 | 19 | 34 | 20 | 25 | 268 |
| Spanish | 2 | 2 | 4 | - | - | 2 | 3 | 2 | - | - | 1 | 3 | 3 | - | 3 | 25 |
| Dutch | - | - | 2 | 9 | 4 | 2 | 3 | 3 | 2 | 5 | 1 | 2 | 5 | 7 | 7 | 52 |
| Totals | 5 | 14 | 41 | 9 | 4 | 39 | 29 | 16 | 9 | 21 | 30 | 24 | 42 | 27 | 35 | 345 |

In addition 597 privateers of all nations had been captured, thus giving a grand total of 942 foreign vessels taken.

ORDNANCE CARRIED BY THE VARIOUS SHIPS OF THE BRITISH NAVY

| Rated | Guns | No of guns | | | | | | | No of carronades | | | |
|---|---|---|---|---|---|---|---|---|---|---|---|---|
| | | 42pdr | 32pdr | 24pdr | 18pdr | 12pdr | 9pdr | 6pdr | 32pdr | 24pdr | 18pdr | 12pdr |
| 1st | 100 | 28 | - | 28 | - | 30 | - | 18 | 2 | 6 | - | - |
| 2nd | 98 | - | 28 | - | 30 | 40 | - | - | 2 | - | 6 | - |
| 3rd | 80 | - | 26 | - | 26 | - | 24 | - | 2 | - | 6 | - |
| | 74 | - | 28 | - | 28 | - | 18 | - | 2 | - | 6 | - |
| | 70 | - | 28 | - | 28 | - | 14 | - | 2 | - | 6 | - |
| | 64 | - | - | 26 | 26 | - | 12 | - | - | 2 | 6 | - |
| | 60 | - | - | 24 | - | 26 | - | 10 | - | - | - | - |
| 4th | 50 | - | - | 22 | - | 22 | - | 6 | - | 6 | - | 6 |
| | 44 | - | - | - | 20 | 22 | - | 6 | - | - | 8 | - |
| 5th | 36 | - | - | - | 26 | 2 | 8 | - | 8 | - | - | - |
| | 32 | - | - | - | - | 26 | - | 6 | - | 6 | - | - |
| | 28 | - | - | - | - | - | 24 | 4 | - | 6 | - | - |
| 6th | 24 | - | - | - | - | - | 22 | 3 | - | 2 | 6 | - |
| | 20 | - | - | - | - | - | 20 | - | - | - | - | 8 |
| Sloops | 18 | - | - | - | - | - | - | 18 | - | - | - | 8 |

DIMENSIONS OF BRITISH NAVY SHIPS, CREWS AND DRAUGHTS

| No of guns | Length of gundeck (m) | Beam (m) | Complement | | Draught (m) |
|---|---|---|---|---|---|
| | | | Sailors | Marine officers* | |
| 112 | 57.0 | 15.9 | 875 | | 7.2 |
| 100 | 55.8 | 15.6 | 875 | 1 captain | 7.2 |
| 98 | 54.0 | 15.0 | 750 | 3 subalterns | 6.9 |
| 90 | 53.25 | 14.7 | 750 | | 6.9 |
| 80 | 54.6 | 14.9 | 650 | | 5.4 |
| 74 | 54.6 | 14.6 | 650 | | 5.4 |
| 74 | 50.7 | 14.1 | 650 | | 5.4 |
| 64 | 50.7 | 13.35 | 650 | 1 captain, 2 subalterns | 5.4 |
| 50 | 43.8 | 12.2 | 420 | 2 subalterns | 4.8 |
| 44 | 42.2 | 11.6 | 300 | | 4.8 |
| 38 | 43.2 | 11.7 | 300 | | 4.8 |
| 36 | 42.6 | 11.4 | 300 | | 4.8 |
| 32 | 37.8 | 10.6 | 300 | 1 subaltern | 4.5 |
| 28 | 36.0 | 10.1 | 200 | | 4.5 |
| 24 | 34.4 | 9.7 | 200 | | 4.5 |
| 20 | 32.4 | 9.0 | 200 | | 4.5 |
| 18 | 33.0 | 8.9 | 125 | 1 sergeant | 3.9 |
| 16 | 31.8 | 8.4 | 125 | 1 sergeant | 3.9 |

*Marine soldiers were allocated at the scale of one per gun carried by the ship

A British squadron 'under press of sail, chasing to windward'. This plate shows clearly the action of the running rigging in altering the position of the yards to give the vessel forward motion even though the wind is not from astern (*National Maritime Museum*)

Royal Navy admiral's full dress uniform 1812–25. The colour scheme is dark-blue coat, white facings and gold buttons; the buttons bear a crowned, fouled anchor within a beaded ring, all within laurel leaves (*National Maritime Museum*)

# Uniforms 1792–1815
## (after *Dress Regulations* 1787 and 1805)

**Flag Officers**

*Full Dress*: Bicorn with wide gold edging, gold tassels in the corners, black silk cockade, gold loop and button. Flag officers wore their hats from side to side, other officers wore them fore and aft. Navy-blue frockcoat, white lapels and cuffs (navy-blue from 1795), white lining. The collar was edged all round with gold braid about 2.5cm wide, the same lace edged the lapels and the cuffs and the lower coat-front as well as the pocket-flaps. The nine lapel buttonholes were also edged in gold lace as were the three on each cuff and on each pocket-flap. In addition to the gold cuff edging, rank was shown by gold cuff-rings; an admiral had three, vice-admirals two and rear-admirals one. The gold buttons bore a fouled anchor within a laurel wreath within a beaded ring. Epaulettes were often worn by Royal Navy officers at this time although it was not until 1795 that they were officially introduced. They had a plain, gold strap, gold bullion fringes and eight-pointed silver stars on the straps denoted rank. Admirals wore two epaulettes each with three stars, vice-admirals had two stars and rear-admirals one. Waistcoat, breeches and stockings were white; the black shoes bore brass buckles. Black and gold sword belt, gold sword strap with navy-blue stripes, black and gold scabbard.

*Undress*: Bicorn as above; navy-blue coat of same style as above but the only gold lace was the rings denoting rank on each cuff. All other details as above.

**Captain**

*Full Dress*: Bicorn as above but narrower gold lace edging, navy-blue coat as for flag officers' full dress but with no gold buttonholes and instead of the plain, round cuff there was a trident-edged, navy-blue cuff flap edged in gold lace and bearing three buttons. Captains of under three years post wore only one epaulette without stars (on which shoulder is not known); more senior captains wore two. The cuff and cuff flap bore one gold band inside the outer gold edging. All other details as above. The gold buttons bore a fouled anchor within an oval rope design all within a roped edge.

*Undress*: As for captain's full dress except that the coat bore no gold lace and the cuffs were plain round with three buttons. Hessian boots were often worn in this form of dress. In 1812 a crown was added over the fouled anchor on the buttons.

**Lieutenant**

*Full Dress*: Plain bicorn with black cockade, gold loop, button and hat tassels, navy-blue coat with gold loop and button to each side of the navy-blue collar, white lapels, plain round cuffs (with three buttons) and lining; white waistcoat, breeches and stockings, black shoes with brass buckles. The button design was as for captains. Swords were carried either on a black and gold waistbelt or on a black baldric over the right shoulder and had an oval gilt plate bearing a fouled anchor. No epaulettes.

*Undress*: Hat as before, navy-blue coat with white piping to top of collar (some sources show a button and buttonhole to each side), blue lapels piped white, round cuffs piped white; white waistcoat and breeches, black Hessian boots.

British Marines 1802, 1807 and 1810. On the left are a private and an officer in the old uniform (red with white facings); the officer has a gold gorget and crimson silk waist-sash. In 1802 the men abandoned the bicorn for the top hat and the facings changed to royal blue; the plumes were white over red. They used the well known Brown Bess musket (*National Maritime Museum*)

### Midshipmen

Plain bicorn with black cockade and loop, gold button, single-breasted navy-blue coat with similar collar and round cuffs having three buttons. The coat closed with nine brass buttons bearing the fouled anchor but without the roped border. To each side of the collar was a rectangular white patch with in the rear corner a button and a false white buttonhole running towards the front. White lining, waistcoat and breeches; boots. The dirk was carried on a black leather baldric.

### Warrant Officers

Plain bicorn with black cockade, loop and tassels, brass button; navy-blue, double-breasted coat with eight brass buttons on each lapel, three on each round cuff, three under each pocket-flap and two at the rear waist. The buttons bore a fouled anchor. The coat was lined white and the waistcoat, breeches and stockings were also white. Black shoes with brass buckles.

### Sailors

There were no uniforms for British sailors in the period under review although within each ship most men dressed alike and an unofficial uniform could

175

British troops landing from Arab dhows at Ras el Khyma in the Persian Gulf on 13 November 1809 during a drive to crush the pirates then rampant along that coast (*National Maritime Museum*)

often be seen consisting of a black lacquered straw hat with the name of the ship painted on the front in white letters, short, navy-blue double-breasted jacket with two rows of brass buttons, dark-blue (or white in summer) trousers with wide legs, chequered shirt and a neckerchief.

In 1805 new uniforms were introduced for two more officials of the navy's ships, the physician and the surgeon, who till then had worn warrant officers' uniforms.

### Physician
*Full Dress*: Plain cocked hats with black cockade, loop and tassels, gold button. Navy-blue coat with similar collar edged all round with two gold laces each 1.25cm wide; round dark-blue cuffs also with two such lace rings and three buttons (between the rings). The brass buttons bore an anchor without the fouling cable. Navy-blue lapels; white waistcoat, breeches and stockings. No epaulettes.
*Undress*: As above except navy-blue breeches.

### Surgeons
As for physicians except that the navy-blue collar bore a gold button and twisted loop if the man served aboard ship, two such loops if he served ashore; the cuffs bore only three buttons. The gold buttons bore a plain anchor within an oval if serving afloat, an anchor with an entwined serpent if ashore (also with the letters 'HS').

### Royal Marines
*Officers*: Bicorns with black cockade, gold loop, button and tassels; long-tailed, double-breasted red coat with royal-blue collar, cuffs and lapels, gold lace and buttons, white breeches and stockings or boots. They carried their swords on white baldrics with gold buckleplate.

176

*NCOs*: Badges of rank were as in the army; white chevrons, point down, on the upper right arm as follows: lance-corporal – 1, corporal – 2, sergeant – 3, colour-sergeant – 3 under a union jack and crossed sabres, sergeant-major – 4. Sergeant major's and sergeant's chevrons were in gold lace; sergeant-majors had double-breasted, officer-style coats with long skirts and instead of white lace edging and tufts to their shoulder straps these were in gold. They had no white edging to collar and no white cuff lace but to each side of the collar was a button and buttonhole.

*Drummers*: Dark-blue swallow's nests edged white and had several white lace chevrons, point up, on each sleeve.

*Other Ranks*: In 1802 the marines were made a royal corps and the facings of their red coats changed from white to royal-blue. They wore army-style coats with brass buttons arranged in pairs on the chest, cuffs and under the pocket-flaps. The ten buttons on the chest were set on square-ended white lace buttonholes, this lace bearing narrow dark-blue stripes. These button-holes appeared also on the dark-blue cuffs. The collar and dark-blue shoulder straps were edged in white lace. At the outer ends of the shoulder straps were white, worsted tufts. Turnbacks were white as were belts and breeches. The square belt-plate on the chest was brass and bore an anchor. White gaiters were worn for full dress, otherwise they were black with black leather buttons. Until 1802 the headgear was a bicorn with black cockade, white loop and brass button but in that year the well known 'top hat' of lacquered black leather with white headband and brim binding was intro-duced. It had a black cockade held by a button at the top lefthand side of the crown and above this was a white over red tuft.

# The Kingdom of Italy

From 1806 Venice passed into the control of the Kingdom of Italy and with her a small rump of a navy – left behind by the French when they evacuated in 1797. In 1808 the navy consisted of 3 frigates but with 6,000 personnel!

## Uniforms 1806

### Officers
Top hat with brass, rhombic front plate, dark-green, single-breasted, long-tailed coat with dark-green facings and silver buttons, silver piping to collar, cuffs and turnbacks, silver epaulettes, dark-green breeches and short boots with silver trim.

### Sailors – ('Battaglione del Flottiglia')
Corsican hats with the lefthand brim upturned and bearing the green-white-red Italian cockade over a white loop and button; dark-green, waist-length jacket with a single row of silver buttons, dark-green trousers and black shoes, white bandoliers.

### Naval Gunners
As for the sailors except: silver hat badge of crossed cannon barrels on an

Review of the Italian Navy in Venice by Napoleon on 29 November 1807. This plate is by Baron Alessandro Zanoli and is at variance with the uniform regulations in some minor details; artistic licence may have caused him to insert in the background more large ships than the infant kingdom actually possessed at that time. All uniforms are dark-green and all buttons white; the figures from left to right are: a Two marines of the Royal Guard; red facings, green plumes. b Soldier of line infantry; buff facings, red over white over green plume. c Naval gunner; black facings. d Officer, Marines of the Royal Guard (with drawn sabre); silver epaulettes and gorget with gold crest, red facings. e Naval officer (rear view); green facings, silver epaulettes. f The Emperor and officers of the Collegio di Marina. g Sailors (in column); green facings. h Soldier, Venice City Guard; shako with brass rhombic shako plate, red over white over green plume, light-blue coat, red facings, red-white-red cockade. j Gunners of the Coastal Artillery (in line); brass cap plate of crossed cannon barrels on an anchor, black fur crest, red plume, green facings, waistcoat and trousers, white belts, black gaiters. k Naval veterans; bicorn, buff facings edged red. l Marine; green facings piped white. m Private, Dalmatian Infantry Regiment; white metal rhombic shako plate, red cords, red over green plume, red facings, white waistcoat, green breeches, black gaiters (*Author's collection*)

anchor, double-breasted coat with white piping to collar and lapels, black collar and cuffs.

**Marines**

*Other Ranks*: Top hat with cockade at the top lefthand side, dark-green, double-breasted tunic with dark-green facings and white buttons, white piping to collar, lapels, cuffs and turnbacks, dark-green trousers, black shoes, white bandoliers.

*Officers*: Similar dress but with long coat-skirts, dark-green breeches in silver-trimmed hussar boots and silver-fringed epaulettes.

**Marines of the Guard**

*Other Ranks*: As for marines except – cockade worn at top front centre of the top hat, over a rhombic brass plate bearing an anchor and under a carrot-shaped, light-green pompon, red collar and cuffs, light-green fringed epaulettes, red waistcoat with two rows of white buttons, dark-green breeches in short, black gaiters with red top trim.

*Officers*: Silver top band to their hats, the rhombic plate was silver and above the cockade was a white-over-red-over-green plume; they wore silver fringed epaulettes, silver gorget with gold crest, long coat-skirts, and silver-trimmed hussar boots.

# Naples 1792-1806

## The Kingdom of the Two Sicilies

This kingdom is colloquially referred to as 'Naples', thus causing confusion with the state formed by Napoleon from 1806–14 and bearing the title 'Kingdom of Naples'.

According to Fulton the Sicilian navy of 1792 consisted of 4 ships of the line, each with 74 guns, *Tancredi, Guiscardo, Samnita* and *Parthenope*; 6 other ships of the line with 50 guns each, 10 frigates and 12 sloops mounting in all 1,000 cannon of various calibre and having 5,000 seamen.

When King Ferdinand was thrown out of the mainland portion of his kingdom in 1799 for a short time, he gave orders for that part of the fleet which was left in Naples to be destroyed; it seems that these orders were only partially carried out. In 1806, when once again he was forced to leave the mainland, most of the navy was taken off to Sicily and only a few sloops and gunboats fell into the hands of King Joseph, first monarch of the Kingdom of Naples.

In the period 1808–14, when mainland Naples was a Napoleonic satellite state, this navy suffered a steady drain of vessels taken or destroyed by the Royal Navy.

According to data kindly provided by the Italian Naval Historical Office, the navy of the Kingdom of the Two Sicilies consisted in 1792 of the following vessels: Ships of the line – *Guiscardo, Parthenope, Samnita, San Gioacchino, Tancredi*; the following were added at the dates shown: *Capri* (1810), *Gioacchino* (1812), although from the names they would appear to have belonged to the mainland Kingdom of Naples; Frigates – *Aretusa, Cerere, Minerva, Pallade, Santa Dorotea, Santa Teresa, Sibilla, Sirena*; later additions were *Venere* (1808); *Cristina* (ex *Letizia*) (1812). Brigs – *Leopoldo, Lipari, Sparviero, Stromboli, Vulcano*; later additions were *Aquila* (?), *Calabrese* (1810), *Indagatore* (1812); Corvettes – *Aurora, Fama, Flora, Fortuna, Cialatea, Stabia*; Galleys – none in 1792 – they appeared later as: *Gioia* (?), *Diana* (1799), *Delfino* (1808), *Lampo* (1810), *Luisa* (1810), *Oceano* (1811); Packets – *Leone, Tartaro*; a later addition was *San Antonio* (1812); Polacca – *Colomba* appeared later (1808).

## Uniforms 1800

Neapolitan naval uniforms were dark-blue with gold buttons and lace and rather French in style.

179

**Marines**
*Full Dress*: single-breasted, long-skirted dark-blue coat, red collar, shoulder straps, cuffs and turnbacks, yellow buttons and cuff lace; white waistcoat, red waist sash, white breeches in short black gaiters.
*Service Dress*: Austrian kasket with brass FR (Ferdinandus Rex); short, dark-blue, double-breasted tunic with red collar, cuffs and shoulder straps and yellow buttons; dark-blue trousers, white belts, brass anchor badge on pouch; sabre and bayonet.

A portrait of Giovanni Acton, Neapolitan War Minister under King Ferdinand, shows a dark-blue frockcoat, red collar and cuffs, liberal gold lace decoration to collar, cuffs, coat-front and pockets; red waistcoat laced gold, red breeches and stockings, black shoes. Another portrait of an officer in the navy (c1800?), Gaetano Filangieri, shows the dark-blue coat but with light-coloured facings (white?) and gold buttons and epaulettes.

# Naples 1806-14

## The Kingdom of Naples

In 1806 the mainland portion of the Kingdom of the Two Sicilies was taken by Napoleon and created a kingdom with his brother, Joseph, as its monarch. When Joseph was promoted to become King of Spain in 1808 his place on the throne was taken by Joachim Murat, one time Duke of Kleve-Berg and French grand-admiral. Although the Neapolitan navy consisted only of a handful of sloops and gunboats – Ferdinand had removed most of it to Sicily and given orders for the rest to be burned at his evacuation of the mainland portion of his kingdom – Murat ensured that the crews were smartly dressed. A battalian of Marines of the Guard was raised.

## Uniforms 1806

**Marines of the Guard**
*Marines*: Black bearskins with red cords and plumes, dark-blue tunics with red collar, lapels, cuffs and turnbacks, dark-blue cuff flaps and yellow buttons. On each side of the collar were two yellow laces and all buttons on lapels, pocket flaps and cuff flaps had yellow lace buttonholes. They wore red epaulettes, white belts and breeches and long black gaiters.
*Officers*: The same uniform but with gold bearskin cords, gold-fringed epaulettes, gold-trimmed hussar boots and carried swords with gold fist straps.

# The Netherlands 1795-1815

When France invaded the Republic of the United Netherlands in 1795 and converted a previously hostile state into an ally named 'The Batavian Republic', it was not so much the acquisition of territory or ground forces which was important but much more the sealing off of another length of European coastline against Great Britain and the transfer to France's credit of a considerable navy. This consisted of 6 ships of the line with 74 guns, 23 with 70–60 guns and 9 with 60–50 guns, 7 frigates with 50–40 guns, 11 with 40–30 guns, 16 corvettes with 30–20 guns, 33 brigs or schooners with 18–5 guns and 72 gunboats with 3–1 guns. These figures exclude ships under construction.

The strength of the navy was from 25–30,000 men including the 2 regiments of marines 'Douglas' and 'Westerloo', which were then transferred to the land army establishment as 1st Battalion, IV Half-Brigade and 2nd Battalion, III Half-Brigade respectively. Their places were taken by the 'Korps Mariniers' raised in 1796 and distributed among the vessels in so-called 'Ship's Detachments'.

In 1806 this Korps was 1,763-men strong and it was augmented on 14 August by an elite formation, the 'Korps Koninklijke Grenadiers van de Marine'. On 6 February 1814, after liberation from French rule, a new 'Korps Mariniers' was set up and this formation is the direct ancestor of the Royal Dutch Marine Corps of today.

In 1806 the Dutch fleet was distributed as follows: In Dutch waters were 1 ship of the line with 90 guns, 3 with 74 guns, and 5 with 70–60 guns; 4 frigates with 11 guns; 2 corvettes with 5 guns; 15 brigs and schooners with 18–5 guns. In Flushing and Boulogne, under French command, were 55 galleys with 20–6 guns; 207 gunboats with 3–1 guns and 94 transports. This

29 March 1793: Batavian gunsloops and other vessels blocking the Dordrecht Channel (*National Maritime Museum*)

181

flotilla was prepared for the projected invasion of England in 1805 which was abandoned prior to Trafalgar.

In the East Indies were 5 ships of the line with 70–60 guns; 5 frigates with 40–30 guns; 3 corvettes with 30–20 guns and 6 brigs or schooners with 18–5 guns.

## Battle History

August 1795 – Clash off the Norwegian coast with the Royal Navy.

1796 – A Batavian squadron surrendered to the British in Soldanha Bay in South Africa.

11 October 1797 – Battle of Camperdown (see page 55).

13 October 1800 – Capture of a British cutter by the Batavian gunboat *De Adder* off Wattum on the River Ems.

15 May 1804 – Batavian squadron of 19 schooners, 47 gunboats and 2 French gun barges, under command of Rear-Admiral Carl Hendrik ver Huell, Count of Sevenaer, runs the British blockade of Flushing and moves to Ostend.

30 March 1807 – Capture of the anchored British brig *The Ferreter* in the eastern estuary of the Ems by the Dutch gunboat *Ambleteuse.*

April 1809 – Recapture of the Dutch gunboat *Blankenburg* off the East Friesian coast.

1810–13 – Continued coastal defence duties.

Apart from these events there were numerous skirmishes in the Atlantic and in Indonesia in which the British usually came off best.

THE BATAVIAN FLEET — APRIL 1795

(A = Amsterdam, M = Maze, Z = Zeeland, F = Friesland, NK = Noorderkwartier)

| Ship | Guns | Year built | Station |
|---|---|---|---|
| Ships of the Line | | | |
| Admiraal Generaal | 74 | 1763 | A |
| Williem de Eerste | 74 | 1782 | M |
| Jupiter | 74 | 1782 | A |
| Vrijheid | 74 | 1782 | A |
| Prins Maurits | 74 | 1783 | A |
| Staten Generaal | 76 | 1786 | M |
| Under construction — no name | 74 | - | A |
| Zuid-Beveland | 60 | 1746 | Z |
| Amsterdam | 68 | 1763 | A |
| Revolutie | 60 | 1777 | M |
| Admiraal de Ruiter | 68 | 1778 | A |
| Wassenaar | 68 | 1781 | M |
| Hercules | 66 | 1781 | M |
| Gelderland | 68 | 1781 | A |
| Utrecht | 68 | 1781 | A |
| Rotterdam | 68 | 1782 | M |
| Dordrecht | 68 | 1782 | M |
| Admiraal Tjerk Hiddes de Vries | 68 | 1782 | F |
| Zeeland | 64 | 1782 | Z |
| Westfriesland | 68 | 1782 | NK |
| Noordholland | 68 | 1783 | NK |
| Hersteller | 68 | 1783 | NK |
| Verwachting | 68 | 1783 | NK |
| Zevenwolder | 68 | 1784 | F |
| Cerberus | 68 | 1784 | A |
| Pluto | 68 | 1785 | NK |
| Haarlem | 68 | 1785 | A |

| | | | |
|---|---|---|---|
| *Leijden* | 68 | 1786 | A |
| *Gelijkheid* | 68 | 1788 | A |
| *Overijssel* | 68 | ? | A |
| Under construction — no name | 68 | 1795 | NK |
| *Broederschap* | 56 | 1769 | A |
| *Admiraal Piet Hein* | 56 | 1774 | A |
| *Admiraal MH Tromp* | 54 | 1777 | M |
| *Batavier* | 56 | 1779 | A |
| *Goes* | 50 | 1781 | Z |
| *Alkmaar* | 56 | 1782 | NK |
| *Delft* | 54 | 1782 | M |
| *Brakel* | 56 | 1782 | M |
| *Beschermer* | 56 | 1784 | NK |

Frigates

| | | | |
|---|---|---|---|
| *Medea* | 40 | 1781 | A |
| *Castor* | 40 | 1781 | M |
| *Pollux* | 40 | 1781 | M |
| *Monnikendam* | 40 | 1782 | NK |
| *Tholen* | 40 | 1782 | Z |
| *Hector* | 46 | 1784 | A |
| *Braave* | 40 | 1789 | M |
| *Ceres* | 36 | 1766 | M |
| *Amazoon* | 36 | 1768 | A |
| *Jason* | 36 | 1770 | M |
| *Eensgezindheid* | 36 | 1779 | F |
| *Medemblik* | 36 | 1779 | NK |
| *Jager* | 36 | 1786 | NK |
| *Alliantie* | 36 | 1787 | A |
| *Wilhelmina* | 36 | 1787 | Z |
| *Zephyr* | 36 | 1788 | A |
| *Argo* | 36 | 1789 | A |
| *Erfprins van Brunswijk* | 36 | 1790 | A |

Corvettes

| | | | |
|---|---|---|---|
| *Walcheren* | 24 | ? | Z |
| *Venus* | 24 | 1768 | A |
| *Valk* | 24 | 1770 | A |
| *Alarm* | 24 | 1773 | A |
| *Enkhuyzen* | 24 | 1779 | NK |
| *Dolphijn* | 24 | 1780 | A |
| *Pallas* | 24 | 1781 | F |
| *Zeepaard* | 24 | 1782 | A |
| *Therijs* | 24 | 1785 | A |
| *Bellona* | 24 | 1786 | M |
| *Waakzaamheid* | 24 | 1786 | NK |
| *Sirena* | 24 | 1786 | F |
| *Minerva* | 24 | 1787 | Z |
| *Scipio* | 24 | 1789 | M |
| *Triton* | 24 | 1789 | A |
| *Nehalennia* | 24 | 1795 | Z |
| Under construction — no name | 24 | 1795 | A |

Brigs and Schooners

| | | | |
|---|---|---|---|
| *Diana* | 8 | ? | Z |
| *Brak* | 14 | 1781 | M |
| *Vlugheid* | 12 | 1781 | F |
| *Kemphaan* | 18 | 1781 | M |
| *Mercuur* | 18 | 1782 | A |
| *Postillon* | 6 | 1783 | M |
| *Havik* | 18 | 1784 | A |
| *Lynx* | 12 | 1784 | A |
| *Meermin* | 16 | 1784 | Z |
| *Panther* | 14 | 1784 | M |

| | | | |
|---|---|---|---|
| *Pijl* | 16 | 1785 | A |
| *Courier* | 6 | 1787 | M |
| *Vlieg* | 6 | 1788 | A |
| *Mug* | 6 | 1788 | A |
| *Snelheid* | 10 | 1789 | NK |
| *Comeet* | 18 | 1789 | A |
| *Echo* | 18 | 1789 | A |
| *Gier* | 12 | 1795 | M |
| *Orangespruit* | 6 | 1688 | NK |
| *Jager* | 10 | 1747 | M |
| *Hyaena* | 20 | 1782 | NK |
| *Maasnymph* | 16 | 1784 | M |
| *Zeehond* | 16 | 1785 | M |
| *Hoop* | 14 | 1785 | M |
| *Voorzorg* | 8 | 1792 | M |
| *Kijk-uit* | 8 | 1792 | M |
| *St Lucie* | 3 | 1793 | M |
| *Levrette* | 6 | ? | A |
| *Mesiante* | 6 | ? | A |
| Name not known | 10 | ? | A |
| Name not known | 8 | ? | ? |
| Name not known | 8 | ? | NK |
| Name not known | 3 | 1793 | ? |

THE BATAVIAN FLEET AT THE BATTLE OF CAMPERDOWN 11 OCTOBER 1797

Commandant: Vice-Admiral de Winter (captured)

| Vessel | Guns | Commander |
|---|---|---|
| *Gelijkheid* | 68 | Kap-Luit Ruijsch |
| *Beschermer* | 56 | Kap Hinxt |
| *Hercules* | 64 | Kap Rijsoort |
| *Tjerk Hiddes de Vries* | 68 | Kap Zegers |
| *Vrijheid* | 74 | Vice-Admiral de Winter |
| *Staten-Generaal* | 74 | Schout bij nacht Story |
| *Wassenaer* | 64 | Kap-Luit Holland |
| *Batavier* | 56 | Kap-Luit Souter |
| *Brutus* | 74 | Schout bij nacht Bloijs van Treslong |
| *Leijden* | 68 | Kap Musquetier |
| *Mars* | 44 | Kap Kolf |
| *Cerberus* | 68 | Kap Jacobson |
| *Jupiter* | 72 | Vice-Admiral Reyntjes |
| *Haarlem* | 68 | Kap Wiggers |
| *Alkmaar* | 56 | Kap-Luit Krafft |
| *Delft* | 54 | Kap Verdooren |
| *Monnikendam* | 44 | Kap-Luit Lancaster |
| *Embuscade* | 36 | Kap Nuijs |
| *Heldin* | 32 | Kap Dremesnil |
| *Waakzaamheid* | 24 | Kap Van Mierop |
| *Minerva* | 24 | Kap Eilbrecht |
| *Daphne* | 18 | Kap Frederiks |
| *Ajax* | 18 | Kap Arkenbout |
| *Galathe* | 18 | Kap Reverij |
| *Atalante* | 18 | Kap Pels |
| *Het Haasje* | 6 | Kap Harteveld |

**Ships taken by the British**

| | |
|---|---|
| *Monnikendam* | *Hercules* |
| *Haarlem* | *Gelijkheid* |
| *Jupiter* | *Tjerk Hiddes de Vries* |

| | |
|---|---|
| *Alkmaar* | *Vrijheid* |
| *Delft* | *Galathe* |
| *Wassenaar* | |

Killed: Kap Van Rossum (*Vrijheid*), Kap Holland.
Wounded: Vice-Admiral Reijntjes (died 9 November in England); Kap Rijsoort (died 24 October in England); Schout bij nacht Storij, Schout bij nacht Bloijs van Treslong, Kap Hinxt (died 20 October).

### SUMMARY OF THE BATAVIAN FLEET IN 1801

| Type of ship | Guns |
|---|---|
| 2 Ships of the line | 76 |
| 8 Ships of the line | 68 |
| 1 Frigate | 44 |
| 2 Frigates | 32 |
| 2 Frigates | 24 |
| 4 Corvettes | 20-18 |
| 53 Brigs, Schooners and Gunboats | |
| 1 Cutter | |
| 4 Galleys | |
| 1 Guardship | 68 |
| 2 Guardships | 20 |
| 2 Coastships | ? |
| 2 Transports | ? |
| *Under Construction* | |
| 1 Ship of the line | 90 |
| 2 Ships of the line | 80 |
| 1 Ship of the line | 68 |
| 4 Frigates | 32 |
| 2 Aviso | 6 |
| 2 Schooners | ? |

96

### DUTCH FLEET IN 1806 AT THE TIME OF THE CREATION OF THE KINGDOM OF HOLLAND

| Type of ship | Guns | Crew |
|---|---|---|
| 1 Ship of the line | 90 | 650 |
| 3 Ships of the line | 76 | 550 |
| 4 Ships of the line | 68 | 480 |
| 6 Frigates | 40 | 450 |
| 6 Frigates | 32 | 230 |
| 3 Corvettes | 20 | 200 |
| 2 Corvettes | 22 | 120 |
| 3 Brigs | 18 | 99 |
| 4 Brigs | 16 | 55 |
| 2 Galleys | 7 | 20 |
| 15 Schooners | 7 | 40 |
| 55 Schooners | 7 | ? |
| 207 Gunboats | 3 | ? |
| 94 Transports | - | ? |

405

*Under Construction*

| | |
|---|---|
| 1 Ship of the line | 90 |
| 3 Ships of the line | 76 |
| 2 Ships of the line | 68 |
| 1 Frigate | 40 |
| 2 Frigates | 32 |
| 2 Corvettes | 22 |
| 2 Schooners | 7 |

not known

418

DUTCH FLEET IN 1810 AT THE TIME OF HOLLAND BEING ABSORBED INTO FRANCE

| Type of ship | Guns | |
|---|---|---|
| 2 Ships of the line | 90 | * |
| 3 Ships of the line | 80 | * |
| 3 Ships of the line | 80 | ** |
| 1 Ship of the line | 76 | * |
| 3 Ships of the line | 68 | * |
| 1 Ship of the line | 68 | ** |
| 3 Frigates | 50 | ** |
| 5 Frigates | 32 | * |
| 1 Frigate | 32 | *** |
| 1 Frigate | 40 | ** |
| 6 Corvettes | 20 | * |
| 3 Brigs | 14 | * |
| 4 Brigs | 12-6 | *** |
| 2 Hulks | 18 | * |
| 27 Schooners | 7 | * |
| 18 Schooners | 7 | *** |
| 2 'Boeyers' | 4 | * |
| 65 Gunboats | 3 | * |
| 95 Gunboats | 3 | *** |
| 3 Coastboats | 3 | * |
| 1 Coastboat | 3 | *** |
| 15 'Hengsten' | 1 | * |
| 28 Landing boats | 1 | * |
| 1 Bombard | 15 | * |
| 1 Galliot | 7 | *** |
| 2 Galleys | 7 | *** |

296

* = in service
** = under construction
*** = under repair

# Uniforms

Data is incomplete on the uniform detail at the beginning of the period.

### Full Dress

On 7 July 1795 new naval uniform regulations were published; they varied only slightly from those previously in force in the Republic of the United Netherlands and the uniforms remained dark-blue with red facings and gold buttons and lace; even the old pattern of gold lace decoration to the coats of admirals was retained.

*Vice-Admiral*: Bicorn with white cut-feather edging, black silk cockade, gold loop, tassels and button with an anchor badge. Dark-blue, single-breasted coat with red standing, turn-over collar, red Swedish cuffs, dark-blue lining, gold buttons and double wavy gold embroidery to collar, cuffs, lateral pocket-flaps and coat-front; no epaulettes. Red waistcoat, dark-blue knee breeches, white stockings; gold sword knot.

*Rear-Admiral* (Schout bij nacht): As above but single wavy gold embroidery instead of double.

### Alterations to Uniform 1798

White feather hat edging replaced by a 3cm wide gold braid and red, white and blue plume was added; collar and cuffs changed to dark-blue, white waistcoat and knee breeches.

Apart from this full dress, an everyday 'service dress' was introduced. It was a dark-blue, double-breasted frockcoat with seven gold buttons on each lapel, dark-blue collar and cuffs (the latter each with two gold buttons) dark-blue lining; gold, fringed epaulettes with two silver stars for vice-admiral, one for rear-admiral; plain bicorn with black cockade, gold loop and button.

### Junior Officers – Full Dress 1795

As for flag officers except – plain bicorn with cockade, loop and button, no gold embroidery to coat, red cuff flaps. The colour of lapels and coat lining varied according to rank.

*Kapitein ter Zee*: Two gold bullion epaulettes, gold embroidery to all button-holes and two gold loops on the collar, double, van-dyked gold braid to collar and cuffs.

*Kapitein-Liutenant ter Zee*: As above except two gold epaulettes with thin fringes, single van-dyked gold braid to collar and cuffs.

*Liutenant ter Zee 1 Klasse*: As above except one gold epaulette with thin fringes worn on the left, no gold edging to collar and cuffs.

*Liutenant ter Zee 2 Klasse*: One gold epaulette worn on the left with thin fringes, no collar and cuff lace, no gold buttonhole embroidery.

The buttons bore crossed anchors and a spear with a Phrygian cap on top. All kadets wore officers' uniform but without epaulettes and gold embroidery and this plain uniform was the everyday service dress of naval officers except that from 1797 they wore epaulettes according to rank. In 1798 new dress regulations and rank designations were issued and the Liutenante ter Zee were renamed Eerste Luitenant and Ordinaris Luitenant.

### Junior Officers – Full Dress 1798

In 1797 gold epaulettes were introduced:

*Kapitein ter Zee*: Red lapels and lining.

*Kapitein-Luitenant ter Zee*: Blue lapels and lining.

Both the above ranks had gold embroidered buttonholes to collar (two), lapels (seven), below the lapels (two) and cuff flaps (three).

*Eerste Luitenant*: Red lapels and lining, gold buttonholes only on the lapels. The buttons bore crossed anchors and a staff with a Phrygian cap.

*Ordinaris Luitenant*: Blue lapels and lining, gold buttonholes to the lapels.

*Luitenant der Marine and Kadet 1 Klasse*: Blue lapels and lining, no gold buttonholes.

*Kadet 2 Klasse*: As before but red collar, cuffs and cuff flaps.

*Kadet 3 Klasse*: As for 2 klasse but blue cuffs and cuff flaps.

**Changes to Uniform**

*Kapitein ter Zee*: Two with bullion fringes.

*Kapitein-Luitenant ter Zee*: As above but with one red stripe along strap and cross band.

*Eerste Luitenant*: As above but two red stripes.

*Ordinaris Luitenant*: Two gold epaulettes with thin fringes.

*Luitenant der Marine*: As above but with one red stripe.

*Kadet 1 Klasse*: As above but with two red stripes.

*Kadets 2 and 3 Klasse*: No epaulettes.

### Flag Officers 1806

In 1806 admirals were retitled 'generaals ter zee' and received gold bullion epaulettes for wear both in full dress and in service dress; their coats became double-breasted with dark-blue lapels. The wavy gold embroidery was ordered to be replaced by simpler gold braid.

The white, cut-feather hat edging was re-introduced for flag officers, waistcoat and knee-breeches remained white. The service dress was a bicorn with black feather edging, dark-blue 'surtout' with gold braid along the coat-edges and to the edges of collar, cuffs and pocket-flaps; the buttonholes were also edged in gold braid but no epaulettes were worn with service dress.

These published regulations are contradicted by several existing portraits of Dutch admirals which show thick, gold, oak-leaf embroidery (as worn by French generals of the period) to collar, cuffs, coat-edging and pocket-flaps. Similar embroidery can be seen to the white waistcoat.

The silver stars on flag officers' epaulettes, forbidden by the 1806 regulations, seem to have been retained in practice. Collars and cuffs remained red.

### Junior Officers – Full Dress 1806

Regulations were again changed in 1806 and altered the pattern of the gold epaulettes worn by officers as follows.

*Kapitein ter Zee*: Two with bullion fringes.

*Kapitein-Luitenant ter Zee*: A bullion-fringed epaulette on the right, on the left a contre epaulette.

*Luitenant ter Zee 1 Klasse*: Two fringed epaulettes.

*Luitenant ter Zee 2 Klasse*: A fringed epaulette on the left, a contre-epaulette on the right.

*Kadet ter Zee 1 Klasse*: A contre epaulette on the right with white silk stripes.

The buttons now bore the Netherlands lion holding nine arrows over a vertical anchor. Kadets 2 and 3 klasse wore no epaulettes.

On 6 June 1808 new naval uniform regulations were issued, the main points of which were to change all red uniform items to dark-blue and to introduce new pattern gold embroidery, half an inch wide and in the form of a cable. This embroidery was henceforth to be restricted to the buttonholes (two on the collar, nine on the lapels and two under them, two on the cuffs, two under the pocket-flaps and two at the small of the back). Skirts were now turned over and embroidered with golden anchors in the outer corners, golden lions in the inner corners. For service dress the knee-breeches were dark blue and worn with short boots having fawn cuffs. On 7 November 1806 it was ordered that all kadets should have light-blue standing collars and that their buttons should bear crowned, crossed anchors with the peripheral inscription KADETTEN-INSTITUUT.

188

Dutch marines in Hamburg 1805. A rare contemporary illustration by C. Suhr of Hamburg. The plumes are black over red; shako top band, badge and buttons yellow; facings, epaulettes, piping and sabre knots red. The left hand figure wears a white waistcoat, that on the right a pink one – probably each battalion had its own colour (*Staatsarchiv, Hamburg; Author's collection*)

### NCOs and Sailors – 1795–1807

Schipper, stuurlieden (mates) and constapels-majoor wore all dark-blue uniforms; 'timmerleiden' (artificers) had the same style but in brown with black waistcoat and breeches.

In March 1807 these modest costumes were enriched for certain ranks (opper-schipper, opper-stuurleiden, opper-timmerleiden and constapel-majoor) by the addition of light-blue standing collars and light-blue cuffs both edged

189

with half-inch wide gold lace. Other NCOs wore sailors' uniform but with diagonal bars of gold or yellow lace over the cuffs to indicate rank: bootsmann (boatswain) and 2 schipper – two gold stripes; kwartiermeesters – one gold stripe; 2 kwarteermeister – two yellow stripes.

The regulations of 27 October 1806 described the sailors' dress uniform as a round hat, all dark-blue jacket with copper, crowned-anchor buttons, red waistcoat and dark-blue or white trousers (for winter or summer wear). This was changed by the regulations of 18 March 1807 when the collar became light-blue edged with yellow, yellow piping to all seams, red waistcoat piped yellow and yellow piping to the dark-blue trousers, light-blue piping to the white trousers.

### Marines
Black shako with yellow top and bottom bands, clear anchor badge in brass on the front, black cockade, yellow loop and button and red plume with black tip on the top left side; dark-blue tunic of French infantry style with dark-blue lapels, red collar, cuffs, piping and epaulettes, yellow buttons. Narrow dark-blue trousers, black boots and bandoliers, brass sabre hilt, red fist strap.

Special regulations were issued on 4 October 1806 for the 'Koninklike Marinegrenadiere' – Corsican hat with the left brim upturned and over this a yellow loop and button, cockade and red, drooping plume, brass grenade badge to the front; red jacket with light-blue collar, cuffs and sash, yellow piping and buttons, red epaulettes, long, light-blue sailors' trousers, short white gaiters, black bandoliers supporting cutlass and ammunition pouch; carbines or (on board ship) a brace of pistols.

### Legal, Medical and Administrative Personnel
In 1795 these officials dressed as for luitenants (1 klasse for provost-general, 2 klasse for chirurgyen-major and 1 schryver) but without epaulettes; in 1797 epaulettes were introduced for the provost-general, whose uniform was as for ordinaris luitenant, and for the chirurgyen-major and 1 schryver who dressed as for the luitenant der marine. Epaulettes were again abandoned in 1798 and in 1805 the chirurgyen and schryvers were given light-blue coats and breeches and white waistcoats, the collars and cuffs being edged in gold and being red for 1st klasse officials, light-blue for those of 2nd and 3rd klasse.

# Portugal

## Vessels in Service 1789–1815

(The Portuguese source consulted lists ships with the armament they carried at the time mentioned; it thus occurs that a ship may appear with, say 22 guns and 24 guns on different occasions.)
Passing through the Straits of Gibraltar on 18 April 1789 were:
Ship of the line – *Conceicao* (90) Capitao-de-mar-e-guerra Joaquim José dos Santos Cassao; frigates – *Minerva* (48) Capitao-de-mar-e-guerra Manuel de Cunha Souto Maior, *Fénix* (54) Capitao-de-mar-e-guerra Paulo José da Silva

Gama; brigs – *Galgo* (20) Capitao-tenente Herculano José de Barros e Vasconcelos, *Lebre* (24) Capitao-tenente Daniel Thompson; cutter – *Coroa* (20) Capitao-tenente Mateus Pereira. On 21 March 1793 the force operating with the Royal Navy in the Channel commanded by Tenente-General José Sanches de Brito consisted of: (1st Division) ships of the line – *Conceicao* (90) Comandante, Chefe de divisao Joao Caetano Viganego, *Maria I* (74) Chefe de Divisao Pedro de Scheverin, *Vasco da Gama* (74) Capitao-de-mar-e-guerra D. Domingos Xavier de Lima; frigate – *Graca* (54) Capitao-de-fregata Alvaro Sanches de Brito; brig – *Serpente do Mar* (24) Capitao-tenente Filipe Alberto Patroni.

(2nd Division) ships of the line – *Rainha de Portugal* (74) Chefe de esquadra António Januáris do Vale, *Santo António e S. José* (74) Capitao-de-mar-e-guerra Fransisco de P. L. de Sousa, *Na Sa do Bom Sucesso* (64) Capitao-de-mar-e-guerra José Caetano de Lima; frigate – *Ulisses* (40) Capitao-de-fregata Joao Gomes da Silva Teles; brigs – *Sem Nome* (?) Tenente do mar Antonio Pusich, *Voador* (?) Capitao-tenente Daniel Thompson.

This force visited Britain, calling at the Isle of Wight, Spithead, where they were reviewed and complimented as being 'solid, elegant and well navigated', and returned to Lisbon on 19 September. While in England there was a severe outbreak of fever in the fleet.

Several Royal Naval officers were recruited for service in the Portuguese navy and they were allocated to the following ships: *Conceicao* – Lieutenant Crawford Duncan; *Vasco da Gama* – Lieutenants Isaac Smith and Donald Campbell; *Maria I* – Lieutenant Thomas Pacy; *Fenix* Captain Samuel Wickham. Other British officers listed on 11 October 1793 as serving with the Portuguese Navy were: Captains John Dilkes, Stuarte Roe and Donald Campbell, First Lieutenants Thomas Stone, Philip Hancorn, Callis Hawford, John Douglas and Sampson Michell (sic) and Lieutenants John Guijon and Matheus Welsh.

On 16 June 1794 a ship of the line, the *Santo Antonio e S. José*, was in Lisbon naval arsenal.

On 23 December 1794 the *Principe Real* was completed and christened.

By 1 April 1795 the Portuguese navy listed the following active ships: ships of the line – *Principe Regente, Maria I, Rainha de Portugal, Vasco da Gama, Conde D. Henrique, Medusa, Princesa da Beira, Infante D. Pedro, S. Sebastiao, Na Sa do Bom Sucesso, Na Sa de Belém*; frigates – *Tritao, Minerva, Na Sa da Graca, Principe do Brasil, Princesa do Brasil, Princesa Carlota, Golfinho, Cisne, Venus, Ulisses*; brigs – *Lebre, Falçao, Voador, Giavota, Sem Nome, Serpente do Mar*; corvettes – *Polifemo, Gloria, Neptuno, Aguia*; 'navios' – *Principe, Princesa*.

On 25 December 1795, the following ships went to Brazil: *Principe Real* (90); *Maria I, Vasco da Gama, Princesa da Beira* (74s); *Tritao* (44); *Ulisses* (40). They reached Baia on 9 February 1796 and were joined by the *Infante D. Pedro* (64); *Minerva* (48); *Venus, Thetis* (36s); *Serpente do Mar, Falçao* (22s). Certain changes in armament in some ships had by then taken place as the *Principe Real* is listed as having 106 guns and the *Princesa da Beira* as having only 64 while the *Ulisses* has only 36.

In India at this time were the ships of the line *Belém, Na Sa da Conceicao, Santo António e Ásia Felis* (30s); the frigates *Princesa do Brasil* and *Torta* (36); and the corvettes, *Santo Antonio, Polifemo*.

On 27 July 1797 a training and instruction squadron was formed on the Tejo under command of the Admiral Marques de Nisa and consisting of the following ships of the line – *Principe Real* (90); *Medusa* (74); *Alfonso de*

*Albuquerque, S. Sebastiao* (64s) with Captain Sampson Michell.

In May 1798 a squadron under Contra-Almirante Marques de Nisa was sent into the Mediterranean to co-operate with the British fleet there. It consisted of ships of the line – *Principe Real* (90), *Rainha de Portugal* (74), *Alfonso de Albuquerque, S. Sebastiao* (64s); a frigate, *Benjamin* (26); and the brig *Falco* (24). They participated in the chase of the French fleet prior to the Battle of the Nile; on 21 September they blockaded Malta and from late November until mid-January 1799 the *S. Sebastiao, Benjamin* and the brig *Falcao* with 4 British ships of the line blockaded Toulon and other ports in the Gulf of Genoa. This Portuguese squadron also helped in the evacuation of Naples and the *Rainha de Portugal* took two daughters of Louis XV, the Princesses Adelaide and Victoria, from Brindisi to Trieste.

### The Flight of the Royal Family

On 14 August 1807 Napoleon presented his ultimatum to Portugal to close her ports to British shipping and to confiscate British goods. Portugal refused and was invaded by a Franco–Spanish force under Junot on 20 November. The Portuguese royal family—Queen Maria I, the Prince Regent Joao (Prince of Brazil), the Prince of Beira and the Infantes Don Miguel and Don Pedro Carlos—left Lisbon on 27 November to take refuge in Brazil. They were carried on the *Principe Real* (90) with a crew of 950, and were escorted by the ships of the line – *Conde D. Henrique* (74) 753 men, *Rainha de Portugal* (74) 669 men, *Medusa* (74) 669 men, *Principe do Brasil* (74) 663 men, *D. Joao de Castro* (64) 663 men, *Alfonso de Albuquerque* (64) 634 men, *Martin de Freitas* (64) 634 men; frigates – *Minerva* (48) 349 men, *Golfinho* (40) 300 men, *Urania* (40) 329 men; brigs – *Voador* (24) 136 men, *Lebre* (24) 133 men, *Vinganca* (18) 97 men; schooners – *Curiosa* (12) 43 men, *Furao* (8) 60 men. Following the main squadron were frigate – *Princesa Carlota* (48); brigs – *S. Bonaventura* (?), *Condessa de Resende* (20) 90 men; the corvettes – *Thetis* (36) 100 men, *Princesa da Beira, S. Joao Magnanimo* (26); schooner *Ninfa* (6).

The following ships were left in Portugal in unserviceable condition: ships of the line – *Maria I* (74), *Vasco da Gama* (74) (her artillery had been transferred to the *Martin de Freitas*), *Princesa da Beira* (74) (converted to a floating battery), *S. Sebastiao* (64); frigates – *Amazona* (50), *Fénix* (46), *Pérola* (44); *Tritao* (44) and *Venus* (36); brig – *Gaivota do Mar* (24); corvette – *Princesa Real* (26).

Junot repaired what ships he could and renamed some (as shown in brackets after the old name). The Franco–Portuguese navy consisted of *Vasco da Gama, Maria I (Cidade de Lisboa), Princesa da Beira (Portuguesa), S. Sebastiao (Brasil), Tritao, Venus, Princesa Carlota, S. Benjamin* and *Giavota do Mar*. The schooner *Curiosa* was captured and taken into the French navy.

When the French evacuated Portugal under the terms of the Convention of Sintra on 30 August 1808, the vessels reverted to national control. The Portuguese navy was apparently involved in no further hostilities before 1815.

# Uniforms

### Naval Officers (1795)

Bicorn with red and blue cockade, gold loop and button (gold edging in full dress according to rank – further details unknown); dark-blue frockcoat with elaborate gold embroidery around the dark-blue collar and cuffs, down the coat-front and around the dark-blue turnbacks. Waistcoat and breeches and stockings were white; black shoes. On each lower sleeve were gold buttons and chevrons – presumably this decoration was limited to admirals. On the right shoulder was a gold cord and button.

A portrait of Almirante Marquês de Nisa, commander of the Portuguese auxiliary squadron serving with the Royal Navy in the Mediterranean in 1798–1800 and presumably showing full dress – gives a gold-edged bicorn, red and blue cockade, gold brooch, powdered and queued hair, red coat with red collar, dark-blue lapels, cuffs and turnbacks with gold braid edging, gold buttonholes to collar (one each side), lapels (seven) and cuffs (three), gold knots above each cuff and to the sides of the waist; crimson waist sash, dark-blue turnbacks, white breeches and stockings, gold-fringed epaulettes. No details of sailors' uniforms are known.

### Marine Officers
High-fronted army shako with brass oval front-plate over a brass front-band, gold cords, black fur crest running over the shako from back to front. Single-breasted, dark-blue tunic with red collar, cuffs and turnbacks, silver buttons and silver epaulettes, white breeches, knee boots. Crimson silk waist sash with silver tassels, white baldric over right shoulder with sword in black sheath on left hip.

### Marines
High-fronted army shako with brass oval front plate over a brass front-band, yellow cords and a black fur crest running over the hat from front to back. The single-breasted, dark-blue tunic had red collar, cuffs, shoulder-straps and turnbacks and white buttons and was worn with dark-blue breeches having a wide red side-stripe and short black gaiters with red top trim. Belts were white.

# Prussia

Despite her pre-eminent status as a European land power in the eighteenth century and a large merchant fleet (the Hanseatic League), Prussia had no navy to speak of.

There was only a para-military force of small craft designed for coastguard duties and enforcement of the Continental System. This naval impotence can be traced to a decision by Frederick the Great not to begin naval development which he feared might detract from the importance of his army.

## Uniforms

### Steuermann
Black round hat, dark-blue, short, single-breasted jacket with red collar and Swedish cuffs, five rows of yellow buttons, gold aiguilette on right shoulder. Dark-blue trousers.

### Kapitän eines Kustenwachschiffs (Captain of a coastguard vessel)
Bicorn with cockade, loop button and silver hat tassels; dark-blue, single-

breasted frockcoat with red collar, turnbacks and Swedish cuffs, gold aiguilette on right shoulder; dark-blue trousers, sabre in black and gold sheath on black waistbelt (under coat) with gold fittings. No sash, portepee or shoulderstraps were worn, thus emphasising the non-military status of the officers of this organisation.

# Russia

The officers' rank structure was: admiral, vice-admiral, rear-admiral, captain commodore, 1st captain, 2nd captain, captain-lieutenant, lieutenant and midshipman (mitschman). NCOs ranks were steuermann (helmsman), boatswain, boatswain's mate, skipper, skipper's mate, sailor. Paymaster, surgeon and other functionaries were classed as senior NCOs. The officer cadets, 'gardemariny' had NCO status.

The topmost naval organ was the Admiralty College in St Petersburg and its chairman equated to minister of naval affairs. The College advised the Tsar on naval matters but all decisions were taken by the monarch alone.

In the period under review the Russian navy was organised into 3 fleets – the Baltic, the Black Sea and the Caspian Sea; the personnel were grouped in so-called 'ship's equipages' which were administrative units for shore-based purposes rather than tactical or functional formations related to service afloat in a particular ship. They were about the same strength as an army regiment (about 1,000 men) and each had its own set of colours (flags).

The Baltic Fleet contained 52 ship's equipages (nos 1–52), the Black Sea Fleet had 31 (nos 53–83) and the Caspian Sea Fleet had 3 (nos 84–86). Apart from the ship's equipages there were 'rowing equipages' for the numerous oared vessels of the fleets.

If sailors were employed on land service (eg 1812, 1813) this occurred on a ship's equipage basis. On 16 February 1810 the Guards (Naval) equipage was raised from the court oarsmen and yachtsmen, rather after the fashion of the marines of the French Imperial Guard. It fought at the Battle of Kulm (Bohemia) on 30 August 1813 and the 75th (Black Sea) Equipage also saw land service in this campaign.

When Tsar Paul I came to the throne in November 1796 he commanded that the Baltic Fleet should consist of 3 divisions each of 3 squadrons; the 1st squadron or Main Body was commanded by an admiral, the 2nd or Van was commanded by a vice-admiral and the 3rd or Rearguard by a rear-admiral. In 1789 the Baltic fleet had 33 ships of the line and 13 frigates at sea, as well as 24 large galleys, 80 gunsloops and 56 other vessels.

## Marines and Artillery
In 1796 there were 2 regiments of marines and 2 battalions of bombardiers with the Baltic Fleet; with the Black Sea Fleet there was a corps of grenadiers and a battalion of bombardiers. During 1796 these were reorganised into the 1st and 2nd Admiralty Battalions and the 1st–8th Fleet Battalions, and in 1797 a 9th Fleet Battalion was raised; 1 battalion was attached to each of the 9 squadrons of the Baltic Fleet. By 1802 there were 12 Fleet Battalions (9 in the Baltic, 3 in the Black Sea) but in 1804 they were reorganised yet

again into 4 regiments of marines each of 1 grenadier and 2 musketier battalions totalling 2,067 men per regiment. In 1805 another regiment was raised in Astrakhan for service with the Caspian Sea Fleet and in 1813 the marine battalions were transferred to the army establishment. On 9 February 1811 the 1st–3rd Marine Regiments were posted to the newly formed 25th Division of the Army of Finland; the 4th Marines went to the 28th Division.

The Baltic Fleet was concentrated mainly on the island of Cronstadt in the Gulf of Finland (one hour's sailing time from St Petersburg) with detachments at Baltischport near Reval and Dunamünde near Riga.

The Black Sea Fleet's main base was Sebastopol; that of the Caspian Sea Fleet was Astrakhan. An independent company of marines was also raised at Okhotsk, on the coast of the Sea of Okhotsk.

THE RUSSIAN BALTIC FLEET 1805

| Ship | Guns | Year built | Station (if known) | Comment |
|---|---|---|---|---|
| Ships of the Line | | | | |
| Januarius | 66 | 1780 | | |
| Bogoslavni Gospodia (Thanks be to God) | 66 | 1783 | | |
| Rostislav (Mighty) | 100 | 1784 | | |
| Izazlev | 66 | 1784 | | Zacharia and Elisabeth? |
| St Helena | 74 | 1785 | Corfu | |
| Mtsislav (Revenge) | 74 | 1785 | | |
| St Peter | 74 | 1786 | | |
| St Nicholas | 100 | 1789 | | |
| Alexiev | 74 | 1790 | | |
| St Michael (possibly the 74 én flute) | 66 | 1791 | | formerly Orlov |
| Prince Carl | 66 | 1791 | | |
| Oemheiten | 66 | 1791 | | ex-Swedish? |
| Retvisan | 66 | 1791 | Corfu | (R/Adm Greig) |
| Europa | 66 | 1793 | | |
| Vsevelod | 74 | 1796 | | |
| Svernoi Orel (Northern Eagle) | 74 | 1797 | | |
| Peter(sberg) | 74 | 1799 | | |
| Moscow | 74 | 1799 | | |
| Yaroslav | 74 | 1799 | | |
| Blagodat (Gratitude) | 130 | 1800 | | |
| St Anne | 74 | 1800 | | |
| Archangel Michael | 66 | 1800 | | |
| Archangel Gabriel | 110 | 1802 | | |
| Archangel Raphael | 80 | 1802 | | |
| Archangel Uriel | 80 | 1802 | | |
| Archangel Selaphael | 74 | 1803 | | |
| Silnoi (Strong) | 66 | 1804 | | |
| Mostchnoi (Powerful) | 66 | 1804 | Archangel | |
| Skoroi (Speedy) | 66 | 1804 | | |
| Chabroi (Courage) | 120 | 1804 | Reval | to Corfu with Seniavin |
| Smeloi (Bold) | 88 | 1804 | | |
| Tverdoi (Resolute) | 74 | 1804 | | |
| Frigates | | | | |
| Archipelago | 44 | 1789 | | |
| Venus | 44 | 1789 | | ex-Swedish |
| Narva | 44 | 1790 | Reval | |

195

| | | | | |
|---|---|---|---|---|
| *Reval* | 36 | 1794 | | |
| *Emmanuel* | 40 | 1797 | | |
| *Legkoi (Light)* | 38 | 1798 | | |
| *Schtschastlivi (Happy)* | 44 | 1798 | | |
| *Tickvinskaya Bogoreditza (Heavenly Clouds)* | 44 | 1799 | | |
| *Tosmanskaya (Theodosia)* | 44 | 1799 | Reval | |
| *Speshnoi (Hurried)* | 50 | 1801 | | |
| | 32 | 1804 | Archangel | a sloop |
| *Malaya Neval (Little Neva)* | 50 | ? | | gun frigate reduced to 22 for the Guard Marines and Naval Cadet Training |

Oared Frigates

| | | | | |
|---|---|---|---|---|
| *Constantine* | 38 | 1796 | Roggersholm | |
| *Nicholas* | 38 | 1796 | | |
| *Bogoslavni (God is Great)* | 38 | 1798 | | |
| *Emmanuel* | 24 | 1800 | | |

Cutters and Sloops

| | | | | |
|---|---|---|---|---|
| *Mercury* | 22 | 1788 | | ex-English |
| *Dispatch* | 20 | 1796 | | |
| *Vestnyi (News)* | 22 | 1800 | Riga | |
| *Gonets* | 22 | 1800 | | |
| *Strela (Arrow)* | 20 | 1800 | | |
| *Astroll* | 24 | 1800 | (refit/?) | ex-Swedish |

Small Vessels

| | | | | |
|---|---|---|---|---|
| *Neptune* | 18 | 1789 | Reval | ex-English |
| *Veliki Knyaz (Great Prince)* | 12 | 1799 | Reval | |
| *Pochodnaya (Cruiser)* | 8 | 1789 | Kronstadt | yacht |
| *Utka (The Duck)* | 8 | 1793 | Roggersholm | |
| *Tchnaika (The Gull)* | 8 | 1793 | Roggersholm | |
| *Gremaschtschaya (Thunder Peal)* | 8 | 1793 | Kronstadt | |
| *Nepobedimaya (Invincible)* | 6 | 1793 | | |
| *Etna* | 6 | 1794 | | |
| *Sopka (Vigilant)* | 6 | 1794 | | |
| *Kotka (Cat Isle)* | 12 | 1794 | | |
| *Kutsam (Whale Isle)* | 12 | 1794 | | |
| *Tschapura* | 8 | 1798 | Roggersholm | |
| *Roggersholm* | 8 | 1801 | Petersburg | |
| *Ceres* | 10 | 1802 | Petersburg | |
| *Luisa Ulrica* | 8 | | Petersburg | |
| *Pallas* | 14 | | Petersburg | |
| *Snapop* | 12 | | | ex-Swedish |
| *Expedition* | 6 | | | |
| *Bjorn Jarn Syda* | 48 | | | schebeck — ex-Swedish, a lateen-rigged galley |

## Russian Shallow-water Vessels in the Baltic

The Russians built galleys for use in the Baltic long after they had ceased to be produced in Sweden (which was 1749), but it was not until the war of 1788 that they began to copy the new, experimental Swedish vessels (hemmema, turuma, udema and pojama). Russian galleys built in 1796 were 38.1m by 6.3m, propelled by 22 oars and armed with 3 heavy guns forward and 1 at the stern. Half galleys, or 'tschaiks' were also built and were 21.3m long with 11 pairs of oars.

Rowing frigates, schebecks, half-schebecks and 'secret vessels' were also built. The rowing frigate was similar in size to the hemmema, 39m by 9.6m with a 3.3m draught and carrying 38 guns. The schebeck or turuma, of which 8 were built, was 36m long, 4 were 9m wide and had a draught of less than 2.55m, the others were 10.2m and drew 3.45m. The larger ships carried 32 guns each, the others 50, but of smaller calibre. Some of these schebecks were turuma-rigged; others had a lateen sail on the foremast and square sails on the main and mizzenmasts. All were propelled with 40 oars.

The half-schebecks were 22.8m by 5.7m and were sometimes referred to as schooners but seem to have had lug sails on both masts or a lateen forward and a gaff sail aft with a square sail above it. They carried 2 18pdrs forward and 2 aft.

The 3 'secret vessels' built seem to have been modelled on the udema and were 36m by 8.4m wide, propelled by 22 pairs of oars and apparently carried 44 guns.

In 1808 the Russians captured 2 Swedish hemmema at the fall of Sveaborg and only two months later launched their own version, very similar to the captured vessels. It was 43.2m by 11m, with 32 guns; the number of oars is not known. One of these ships was launched as late as 1823.

Although following the lead from the Swedes in building large, oared ships, the Russians had been producing gunsloops in quantity since 1764. These were 21.3m long and 4.2m wide with 10 pairs of oars and 8 guns and were made obsolete by the new Swedish gunsloops of 1775. They did however copy the Swedish gunboats of Chapman's design and started building in 1788. The larger class, equating to sloops, were from 18.6m to 20.4m long and 4.2m or 4.5m wide with 1 or 2 heavy guns and 14 or 15 pairs of oars.

In 1809 and 1812 they built larger boats 24.3m by 5.1m with 2 or 3 guns. Oared Russian gunboats were in action against the British off Abo as late as 1854.

The Russian gunyawl equivalent was 13.5m by 4.2m with 9 pairs of oars and 1 gun.

THE RUSSIAN BLACK SEA FLEET 1805

| Ships of the line | Guns | Year built | Station |
|---|---|---|---|
| Jagudial | 110 | 1800 | Sevastopol |
| Ratnyi | 110 | 1802 | Sevastopol |
| Pravyi (Right) | 76 | 1804 | Kherson |
| Isodor | 74 | 1794 | Sevastopol |
| Simon & Anna | 74 | 1799 | Sevastopol |
| Pobeda (Victory) | 74 | 1797 | Sevastopol |
| St Michael | 74 | 1798 | Sevastopol |
| Krascovia | 74 | 1799 | Sevastopol |
| Mary Magdalene | 74 | 1799 | Sevastopol |
| Varachael | 66 | 1800 | Sevastopol |
| Asia (*possibly a 74 en flute) | 66* | 1796 | Sevastopol |
| Krepkoi (Firm) | 54 | 1801 | Corfu |
| Michael | 50 | ? | Kherson |
| Nazareth | 44 | ? | Corfu |
| Pospechnoi (Rash) | 36 | ? | Corfu |
| Voinyi (Warrior) | 32 | ? | Kherson |

There were also 40 gunboats (of unknown armament) mostly in Nikolaiev and a corvette at Kherson.

Vice-admiral Uschakov's fleet in 1805 consisted of the ships of the line *St Paul, Holy Trinity, Zacharia and Elisabeth*; the frigates *Great Grigori of*

*Armenia, St Michael, St Nicholas, The Holy Virgin of Kazan, Navarchia, Krepkoi, Avtroil, Derskoi, Kilduin* and the sloops *Dniepr, Argus, Letune, Grigori* and *Paul.*

RUSSIAN BLACK SEA FLEET 1805 (MISCELLANEOUS)

| Ship | Type | Guns | Year built | Station |
|---|---|---|---|---|
| *Feniks (Phoenix)* | Galley | 4 | 1787 | |
| *Roshestvo* | Bomb ship | 4 | 1787 | Corfu |
| *Foma* | Brig | 6 | 1788 | Kazan |
| *Paul* | Brig | 6 | 1788 | Nikolaiev |
| *Mohilev* | Galley | 4 | 1788 | |
| *Joseph* | Brig | 12 | 1790 | |
| *Mokryi* | Brig | 6 | 1790 | Ochakov |
| *Nikolai* | Sloop | 6 | 1790 | Corfu ex-Turkish |
| *Radion* | Brig | 8 | 1790 | |
| *St Irene* | Sloop | 8 | 1795 | Corfu |
| *Krasny-Selo* | Sloop | 8 | 1795 | Corfu |
| *Panagia Apotoumengara* | Sloop | ? | | |
| *Maria Theresa* | Yacht | 6 | 1797 | Odessa |
| *Galet* | Galley | 8 | 1798 | |
| *Bogoslavni (God is Great)* | Brig | 6 | 1798 | |
| *Tvardya (Resolute)* | Yacht | 8 | 1803 | Nikolaiev |
| *Bonnasorte* | Brig | 12 | ? | Corfu captured from French |
| *Kynaz Constantine (Prince Constantine)* | Galley | 4 | ? | Corfu |
| | Brig | 12 | ? | |
| *Yakov* | Lanzon | 4 | ? | ex-Turkish |
| *Nikon* | Lanzon | 4 | ? | Nikolaiev |
| *Constantine* | Lanzon | 4 | ? | |
| *Platon* | Galley | ? | ? | |
| *Albert* | Galley | ? | ? | Nikolaiev |
| *Helena* | Cruiser | ? | ? | Nikolaiev |

RUSSIAN CASPIAN SEA FLEET 1805

| Ship | Type | Guns | Year built |
|---|---|---|---|
| *Sokoi (The Falcon)* | Brig | 12 | 1794 |
| *Pobeda (Victory)* | Brig | 12 | 1794 |
| *Kazan* | Brig | 10 | 1796 |
| *Maria* | Brig | 6 | 1796 |

Two unnamed frigates each with 18 guns built in 1798
All based at Astrakhan

SEA OF OKHOTSK FLEET 1805

*Cherni-Orel (The Black Eagle)* – a 10-gun brig, plus 2 other brigs and 8 galliots.

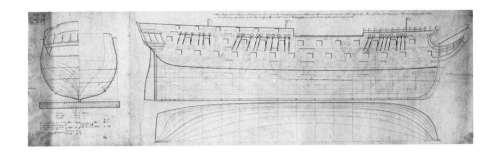

Plan and profile of *Pobedonosetz* (64). Designed in Britain in 1806 for Admiral Macocusca, the keel was laid in Archangel on 20 August 1807 (No 80); she was launched on 29 May 1809 and sent to Cronstadt on 10 August 1812; note the unusual diagonal reinforcing beams (*National Maritime Museum*)
Dimensions (all quoted in 'Russian feet')
Length – 163ft
Beam – 44ft 8in
Depth – 17ft 6in

# Uniforms 1792–6 (Catherine II)

### Ship's Officers
Tricorn with broad gold edging, black, white and orange cockade, gold loop, tassels and buttons; white frockcoat with dark-green collar, cuffs and lapels; gold buttons and lace; dark-green waistcoat and breeches, white stockings. In full dress, admirals had single-breasted coats with no lapels. Rank was shown for admirals by varying widths of gold lace embroidery on the coat and waistcoat edges, and to collars, cuffs and pocket-flaps. Other officers wore this gold lace only on the waistcoat. There were no epaulettes. Officers of naval artillery and logistic services had black facings; otherwise they dressed as above.

### Naval Cadets and Midshipmen
Plain bicorns with cockade, gold loop, button and tassels, dark-green coat and breeches, white collar, cuffs, lapels and waistcoat, gold lace and buttons.

### Senior Ratings – Steuermann (helmsman), bootsmann, (boatswain) and skipper (boatswain's mate):
Plain versions of the officers' uniforms and in reversed colours, ie green coats faced white.

### Sailors
Peculiar black hat with the brim turned up all round and a simple, dark-green, single-breasted tunic and breeches or, for summer, white and light-blue striped linen tunic and trousers with bare feet.

### Marines
Army-style uniforms; for officers this was a bicorn with gold edging, loop, button and tassels, silver, orange and black cockade, dark-green coat with red collar, cuffs and lapels, white turnbacks, gold lace and buttons; red waistcoat, white breeches, boots. They had silver and gold gorgets according to rank; silver waist-sashes and sword-knots with black and orange stripes.

199

## Other Ranks

Peculiar but simple and very functional 'Potemkin Uniform'. It consisted of a low-crowned black helmet with peak and narrow brass front-band, yellow hair crest running from ear to ear and two long red flaps hanging down the back of the neck. The hip-length, double-breasted tunic was dark green with red collar, lapels and cuffs and red edging to the turned-back tips of the front-skirts, red trousers, with yellow side-stripe, white belts, black shoes.

## Uniforms 1796–1815

On the first day of his reign (17 November 1796) Tsar Paul I commanded that the white coats of the naval officers should be replaced by dark-green, single-breasted garments with white collar, dark-green cuffs and cuff-flaps. On the cuff-flaps were two horizontal lace loops which indicated the wearer's division and squadron as follows: *1st Division* – gold lace; *1st Squadron* – hanging tassel at the end; *2nd* – horizontal; *3rd* – no tassel. *2nd Division* – silver lace, the squadrons as above. *3rd Division* – mixed gold and silver lace, the squadrons as above. Officers aboard galleys had no such laces.

The bicorn was edged with white cut feathers for admirals, who also wore a white plume; gold loop, button and tassels, cockade as before. Waistcoat and trousers white, buttons gold. Other officers had plain bicorns.

On 18 May 1801 a new style coat was introduced; it was double-breasted and worn closed over with two rows each of eight gold buttons; the collar was white and white piping was added to the dark-green cuffs and cuff-flaps. The cuff-flaps lace was as before. Admirals now received gold lace embroidery to their collars in addition to their cuff-flap lace; senior officers (1st and 2nd captains and captain-lieutenants) now wore white plumes to their hats.

An order of 2 May 1803 modified this uniform considerably; the collar became dark-green piped white; the turnbacks dark-green and officers now had gold anchor embroidery to collars and cuffs and rank badges, in the form of stiffened golden shoulder-straps, were introduced.

*Admirals*: Collar edged gold, with interlocking gold lines within the edging and a large, fouled anchor on each side; the cuff edged gold and covered in intertwined gold lace; three gold fouled anchors on the flap. Gold shoulder-straps bearing three black, imperial eagles one above the other; vice-admirals had two such eagles, rear-admirals one. The design of the Soviet admirals' gold shoulder-boards in 1979, with their black-rayed stars has a direct link back to this item of dress.

Other officers had the same gold anchors and entwined lines but no gold edging to collar and cuffs; senior officers (1st and 2nd captains) had plain gold shoulder-straps, the captain-lieutenant only one (on the right shoulder). Lieutenants had dark-green shoulder-straps edged gold, mitschman (midshipman) had no shoulder-straps.

In 1807 these shoulder-straps were replaced by golden-fringed epaulettes, distributed according to rank as the shoulder-boards had been. From 1811 they were worn as follows: admirals – heavy bullion fringes with black eagles as before; captain-commodores – plain with heavy bullion fringes; senior officers – two epaulettes with thin gold fringes; junior officers – two with no fringes.

Apart from the embroidered full dress, officers had plain, unembellished service dresscoats or 'vicemundir' apparently even without the white piping to collar and cuffs.

Up to 1811 naval officers carried gold-hilted swords but after this date a lightly curved sabre was introduced; it had a three-bar gold guard and was carried in a black sheath with gold fittings on a black bandolier. On board ship many officers wore a short, straight-bladed dagger instead of the sabre.

*Gardemariny*: It is known that in 1807 they wore plain bicorns with cockade, gold loop button and tassels, plain, dark-green, double-breasted coat with gold buttons and a golden anchor on the dark-green shoulder-straps. The dark-green breeches were worn in gold-trimmed hussar boots.

*Ratings 1802*: Black top hat with (for NCOs) a black and orange loop and gold button on the left-hand side; hip-length, dark-green, double-breasted jacket with white collar and white piping to dark-green cuff. Until 1811 the two rows each of six buttons were covered in dark-green cloth, but after this they were brass.

The shoulder-straps were in the divisional colour: 1st – white; 2nd – blue; 3rd – red. From 1811 onwards they bore the ship's equipage number in yellow. Legwear was long, dark-green bell bottoms.

Badges of rank were golden lace to collar and cuffs for senior NCOs, to cuffs only for junior ratings. The blue and white striped fatigue dress on board remained unchanged.

In 1811 a peakless, flat-topped, dark-green cap replaced the top hat; it had white piping to headband and crown.

From 1811–13, as sailors gradually took over the role previously played by the marines, they were issued with the famous 'kiwer' shako with single-flamed brass grenade badge and brass chinscales, and black bandoliers on which to carry the ammunition pouch.

Drummers and musicians had their jackets decorated with wide yellow lace on collar, cuffs, cuff-flaps, sleeve-seams, jacket-front and bottom and with six yellow chevrons, point up, on each sleeve, eight double lace bars on the chest.

*The Guard Equipage 1810–15 – Officers*: As for other naval officers but with golden edging to collar, cuffs and cuff-flaps. Their vicemundir bore two gold lace loops on each side of the collar, three on each cuff-flap. From 1811 onwards they wore army-pattern shakos bearing a gilt badge of the imperial double eagle upon crossed anchors (as previously worn by the men of the guard equipage on their top hats).

*Ratings*: As for the other ratings but with white piping to collar, cuffs and cuff-flaps. The collar and cuff-flaps bore two and three orange lace bars respectively. Shoulder-straps were red. Until 1811 they wore a top hat with brass double eagle over crossed anchors badge; in this year they received the kiwer shako with the same badge. Brass anchor badge to ammunition pouch and sabre.

Musicians dressed as for those of the rest of the equipages but with orange guards' lace instead of yellow.

*The Artillery Detachment of the Guards Equipage*: As above except – black collar and cuffs, red shako cords.

*Marines 1796*: Grenadier companies wore the brass-fronted mitre-cap with double eagle badge, the backing was in the battalion colour (see below) with white trim and headband and brass grenade badges. Fusilier companies wore a gold-edged bicorn with brass button but no cockade.

The dark-green jacket had red collar, lapels and cuffs, dark-green cuff flaps, white turnbacks. On the cuff-flaps were three laces in the battalion colour. White waistcoat and breeches, black gaiters.

The battalion facings were: 1st Admiralty (St Petersburg) – red; 2nd Admiralty (St Petersburg) – sky blue; The Fleet Battalions, 1st (Cronstadt) – white; 2nd (Cronstadt) – blue; 3rd (Cronstadt) – yellow; 4th (Reval) – violet;

Russian collar and cuff embroidery, Guard Marine Equipage 1810–11 (*Author's collection*)

Artillery Commando of the Russian Lifeguard Marine Equipage; left – gunner, right – bombardier (*Author's collection*)

5th (Reval) – orange; 6th (Reval) – green; 7th (Cronstadt) – black; 8th (Cronstadt) – grey; 9th (Cronstadt) – lilac; the Black Sea battalion facings, 1st – blue; 2nd – buff; 3rd – orange. It is known that due to resupply difficulties, the marines with the fleet in the Mediterranean in 1798–9 wore dark-blue coats with cylindrical headgear, the lower part of which was white, the upper in the battalion colour.

In 1801 the battalion facing colours changed as follows: Baltic battalions: 1st – red; 2nd – white; 3rd – yellow; 4th – raspberry; 5th – turquoise; 6th – pink; 7th – light green; 8th – grey; 9th – lilac. Black Sea battalions: 1st – blue; 2nd – buff; 3rd – orange.

An order of 29 April 1803 made collar, cuffs and turnbacks all dark-green with white piping; the individual regiments were distinguished by the colour of the shoulder-straps, 1st – red; 2nd – white; 3rd – yellow; 4th dark-green piped red. The Caspian Sea Battalion (raised 1805) had pink shoulder-straps.

From 1803 the army shako replaced the grenadier cap and the bicorn; leatherwork was black. Officers wore gorgets and waist-sashes as for infantry officers of the army; from 1807 they adopted the shako in place of the bicorn. From 1811 onwards all marine regiments wore red shoulder-straps with the divisional numbers ('25' or '28') on them in yellow.

*Naval Artillery*: As for the fleet but with black collar and cuffs.

# Spain

An interesting view of this navy can be achieved from the following contemporary accounts. Firstly, in Fulton's *Torpedo Warfare and Submarine Explosions*, published in New York in 1810, the strength of the navy in about 1790 is given as 72 ships of the line with from 112–58 guns, 41 frigates and 109 sloops and other vessels.

Bradford, in his *Sketches of Military Costume in Spain and Portugal* published in London in 1814 gives us this portrait of the service:

> The naval establishment of Spain, a leading feature in a military view of this kingdom, a short sketch is subjoined.
>
> The service of the navy is divided into 3 grand departments, Cadiz, Ferrol and Carthagena.
>
> The highest rank in the Spanish navy is that of captain general, of which in 1808 there were 3; next are the lieutenant generals, about 25 in number; the chiefs of squadrons (Xefe de esquadra) hold the next rank, of these, in 1808, there were only 28; the brigadiers form the last class of superior officers, in number 34, these 4 ranks appear similar to our admirals, vice-admirals, rear-admirals and commodores.
>
> There are 6 classes of subordinate officers, viz. captains of ships, (ships of the line) captains of frigates; lieutenants of ships; lieutenants of frigates; ensigns of ships and ensigns of frigates: there are also three companies of marine cadets, one hundred in each, who become officers by seniority.
>
> Attached to the navy is a corps of engineers and constructors, composed of directors and officers of different degrees, who all hold rank in the navy;

it is commanded by a general officer, and is the only one of the kind in Europe.

The marine artillery consists of 16 brigades, distributed in the 3 departments; each brigade is composed of 2 captains, 1 lieutenant, 1 ensign, 24 serjeants and corporals, 16 bombardiers, 48 cannoniers and 74 assistants, etc.

The marines, who are convertible into an efficient land force, consist of 12 battalions of 6 companies each, also distributed in the 3 departments; each company has 2 captains, a lieutenant, an ensign and 168 men: the officers are taken from the navy.

Each of the 3 departments is divided into provinces, and these again into subdivisions; in these the sailors are registered and classed; the department of Ferrol comprehends 11 provinces; that of Carthagena, 10; and that of Cadiz, 9. In 1792, the first of these departments had on its register 19,685 sailors, the second 26,733, and the third had 17,300 men; there were also 464 pilots.

The naval force of Spain consisted in 1798 of 16,420 marines; 64,363 sailors, and 20,197 artificers; previous to the battle of Trafalgar she had 50 sail of the line, 30 frigates and about 100 other vessels, and must be considered from her peculiar situation and established resources a respectable naval power.

The Spanish colonies are in the best state of defence. According to the latest and most correct accounts, it is found there is in New Spain 9,500 troops of the line, 24,000 militia, without taking notice of the armed inhabitants, who form a numerous and respectable force; in the isle of Cuba 1,560, in Florida 2,000, Porto Rico 4,400, in the province of Venezuela, or the captain generalcy of the Caracas, 9,000, New Grenada 11,000, in the Rio de la Plata 21,000, in Peru 11,200, in Chili 3,350, in the Phillipine Island 12,000; in all, comprehending some lesser stations, the aggregate may be 129,055.

In 1792, the Spanish fleet had 76 ships of the line but only 56 were in serviceable condition and the dockyards were so bad as to be described as derelict by British observers. The ships scarcely ever put to sea, crews were at half strength, money was short, corruption rife and morale very poor. These were the symptoms of the canker in Spain at that time—Godoy, 'Prince of Peace'— who was the king's favourite and who controlled the land and abused his powers.

# Uniforms

### Flag Officers
*Full Dress*: Bicorn with wide gold-braid edging, red cockade, gold loop and button, red plume; navy-blue, double-breasted frockcoat with red collar, red lining and cuffs; gold buttons and embroidery to collar, lapels, cuffs, pocket-flaps and edges of skirts. For admirals this gold embroidery was three rows of braid with diagonal oakleaves crossing them at intervals of about 2cm.

A red silk waist-sash was worn, fastened on the left and ending in two heavy gold tassels (with three rows of embroidery and oak leaves around them) and gold fringes. Red waistcoat, white breeches and stockings; the sword-belt was gold on red Morocco leather.

*Service Dress*: As above except no plume; plain blue collar, narrow gold edging to collar, lapels, cuffs and skirts, gold embroidery as before to cuffs and to the red lining of the lapels; red breeches and white stockings.

## Captains

*Full Dress*: As for flag officers' full dress except gold edging to collar and lapels, pocket-flaps, cuffs and skirts; rings of plain gold lace on the cuff; red breeches.

*Service Dress*: As for flag officers' service dress but without the oak leaf embroidery; white stockings and shoes or boots.

## Midshipmen

Bicorn with thin gold edging, red cockade and plume; dark-blue double-breasted coat with red collar, lapels and cuffs; gold edging to lapels, gold shoulder-cord on the right. Red waistcoat, white breeches for full dress, dark-blue for service dress; black sword-belt, black Hungarian boots.

## Naval Artillery

*Officers*: Bicorn with red cockade and plume, gold edging, loop and button; dark-blue, double-breasted coat with dark-blue lapels piped red; red collar with gold anchor badge, red cuffs and turnbacks, gold epaulettes and buttons; white waistcoat and breeches, knee boots. Gold-hilted sword in black leather sheath on white belt and slings worn under waistcoat. Red silk waist-sash.

*Other ranks*: Bicorn with red cockade and plume, dark-blue double-breasted coat with dark-blue lapels piped red, red collar, shoulder-straps and cuffs, dark-blue cuff-flaps, brass buttons; on the collar a yellow anchor. White waistcoat and breeches in summer (dark-blue breeches in winter), black gaiters, white bandoliers. On the pouch lid a brass anchor.

There were no uniform regulations for sailors until 1840.

## Marines

Marines wore a bicorn with red cockade, yellow loop and button, dark-blue coat with red collar, lapels, cuffs, turnbacks and shoulder-straps, dark-blue, three-button cuff-flaps, brass buttons bearing an anchor. On the collar was a yellow anchor badge and in the turnback corners were small, dark-blue heart-shaped pieces of cloth. The white waistcoat bore two rows of brass buttons; breeches were white, bandoliers were black, the short gaiters were black. The belt-plate was brass and bore an anchor. Marine officers wore gold-edged bicorns with red cockade and plume, gold loop and button; their coats were as above but long-skirted, double-breasted, edged in gold down the front and lined red. The lapels were worn open at the top and the buttonholes were edged gold and the cuffs were edged gold. They wore gold-fringed epaulettes, white breeches and hussar boots with gold trim. Their sword-belts were black and the gold buckle-plate bore an anchor.

# Sweden

Sweden had once included the Baltic provinces around Riga and Reval and in 1792 she still controlled Finland although this too was to be taken from her in the period under review. The nature of the Baltic, much of it shallow and strewn with reefs, rocks, tiny islands and a coastline split by many inlets, gave a theatre of war ideal for amphibious forces, and both Sweden and her massive neighbour and traditional enemy, Russia, had developed special naval forces to operate in this environment.

These special, light, highly manoeuvrable, shallow-draught craft existed alongside the conventional men-of-war of the high seas fleet and required their protection if moving away from the shoreline.

## Naval Recruitment

Recruitment for both sections of the Swedish navy – the High Seas Fleet Örlogsflottan, and Army Fleet 'Armens Flottan' (also termed the Schärenflotte) – came from two sources; firstly recruits enlisted for bounties and secondly from the contingents of men supplied under the 'indelta' or national service system. Apart from the pure sailors there were the marines, recruited to serve the ships' guns and to perform the military duties such as landing parties. Officers for both marine regiments and for many positions in the army fleet were drawn from the army itself.

## High Seas Fleet

The Swedish High Seas Fleet on 23 August 1808 consisted of the following serviceable ships: *Gustav IV Adolf* (78), *Vlädislaff* (76), *Adolf Fredrik*, *Dristigheten*, *Faderneslandet*, *Gustav III* (74s), *Fredrik Adolf*, *Äran*, *Man-ligheten*, *Forsiktigheten*, *Tapperheten* (64s); frigates *Euridice* (46), *Chapman* (44), *Camilla*, *Bellona* (42s), *Janamas* (34) and the cutter *Dolphin*. Others joined the fleet later.

## Army Fleet

Galleys had been built and used by Sweden and Norway since the sixteenth century and were introduced in order to enable naval co-operation with land forces along the Baltic shores. This could not be achieved by using conventional sailing ships due to the shallow, rocky, treacherous nature of much of the coastal waters which presented serious hazards to the relatively unmanoeuvrable sail-driven vessels.

Galleys were of shallower draught and smaller displacement than ships of the line but were fast and manoeuvrable even if there were no wind. In the mid-eighteenth century the Swedes built much larger, hybrid vessels resembling brigs, barques and schooners, all of which were propelled by oars if circumstances dictated. They were named after various parts of the Finnish coast (then under Swedish sovereignty) such as Hemmema, Turuma, Udema and Pojama. They were of a size between a sloop and a frigate and were designed by the Englishman Chapman – the outstanding naval architect of the century. This difference in role from conventional high seas vessels led to the formation of a specific Army Fleet in 1756 designed to operate with the Swedish land forces along the Baltic coast. It was quite separate from the High Seas Fleet and it had three main tasks: first to fight its Russian equivalent force; second to support with men, supplies and artillery fire the Swedish land forces; third to transport that army as needed. Naturally these craft were no match in combat with conventional naval ships on the high seas and had to be protected if moving on open waters.

At outbreak of the war with Russia in 1788 the Army Fleet comprised the Swedish squadron, at Stockholm, with 28 galleys and 28 espingers, 30 gun sloops and 3 yachts, while the Finnish squadron at Helsingfors had 3 hemmema, 8 turuma, 3 udema, 40 gunsloops and many logistic vessels. The Swedish Örlogsflottan had at this time 17 ships of the line, 8 frigates and 8 other vessels. By 1808 the Army Fleet had 150 vessels and the Örlogsflottan had 12 ships of the line and 8 frigates.

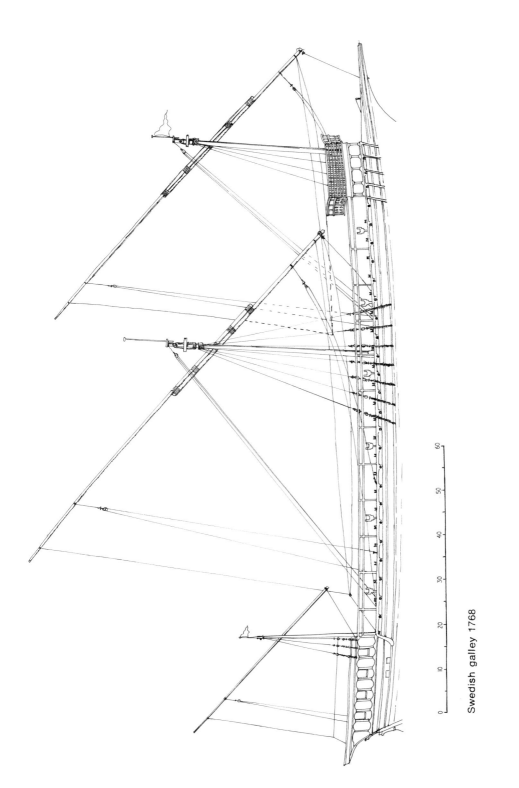

Swedish galley 1768

0    10    20    30    40    50    60

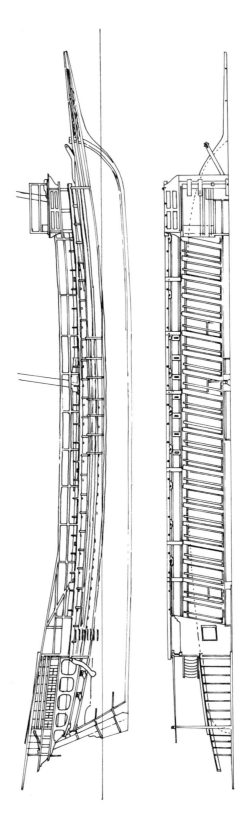

Plan of Swedish galley

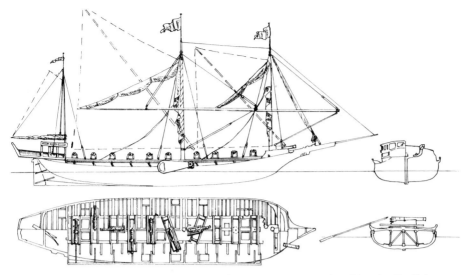

A Swedish udema. The design for this peculiar vessel was completed by the Englishman Chapman on 3 May 1760. The shallow-draught boat was capable of being run aground and was built to be driven by sail or by oars. It was armed with 10 12pdr guns arranged along the keel line and capable of being used to either port or starboard. The greatest disadvantage of this craft was that, if the guns were being used, neither sails nor oars could be employed. For this reason the booms of the lugsails were designed to be carried high above the gundeck when not in use. The dotted lines show the lugsails when set

The original turuma (very similar to a schebeck) built in 1770 was 36.9m long by 9m wide and carried 19 pairs of oars pivoting in crutches on a narrow outrigger above the maindeck ports. It had a cut-down, three-masted square rig without topgallants and carried 18pdr cannon. Originally this vessel had been intended to be lateen-rigged but square-rigging was used on all of these larger oared vessels. The udema was the most revolutionary, and the least successful, design. Her main armament, 9 12pdrs, was carried on a narrow central battery along the keel line with traversing carriages allowing them to be fired to either side; 2 18pdr pieces were mounted on the forecastle and 2 8pdrs on the poop. Her 18 pairs of oars were worked from the same deck that carried the guns and so the ship could not be simultaneously fought and rowed. She was 35.4m long by 8.4m wide, three-masted with a 'polacca barque' rig without topgallants.

Next smaller in size was the pojama, 27m long by 7.8m wide with 16 pairs of oars and a bomb-ketch-type of rig, 2 masts, with square sails only on the fore and with no topgallants. She was armed with 12 3pdr swivel guns amidships and a pair of 24 pdrs at the bow and on the stern which could also be brought to bear broadside.

The largest of these new vessels was the hemmema which first came into service in 1788–90. Her length was 42.6m, width 10.5m and had a draught of 3m: she carried 20 pairs of oars worked through ports, in pairs, between the gunports. She had 24 36 pdrs and 2 12 pdrs on the same deck as the oars. Her riggings was as a frigate without royals.

Two more such vessels were built in 1809 and had the same dimensions but only half the number of oars; they carried 22 36pdrs and 10 24pdrs. It was Chapman again who designed the smaller gunsloops and gunyawls,

209

introduced into service in about 1775. The original gunsloops carried 2 heavy guns, 1 fore and 1 aft, on carriages which could be slid down into the vessel when not firing so that stability could be increased. In 1789 these guns were 24pdrs but the vessels also carried 4 3pdr swivels amidships. Dimensions were 20m by 4.4m and there were 2 masts carrying lateen sails as well as 14 or 15 pairs of oars.

The smaller gunyawl was 12.3m by 3m and had 2 masts with standing lugsails as well as oars. They each had a single heavy gun, usually a 24pdr, mounted in a fixed carriage firing aft. The hull was double-ended and progress under oars was as rapid backwards as forwards. The stern was cut right down near water level to give the gun a clear field of fire and to allow it to be mounted amidships for maximum stability.

It had been hoped that the hemmema, turuma, udema and pojama would replace ships of the line in the Baltic but they proved to be too small for that role and also unwieldy in the shallows and not able to cooperate effectively with the smaller, faster gunsloops and gunboats; construction of them was thus discontinued.


# Uniforms

As with the Swedish army of this period, reliable data on uniforms is scarce and fragmentary.

**Flag and Deck Officers** (both fleets)
From 1779–93 King Gustav III introduced a uniform for High Seas Fleet officers closely modelled on Swedish national costume; a top hat with left brim turned up, held by a gold loop and button under a yellow over light-blue feather plume, gold hat cord. Very short-skirted, close-fitting jacket in dark-blue with similar lapels turned back and each held by seventeen gold buttons, gold-fringed epaulettes, dark-blue breeches with gold thigh-knots and short boots. The waist-sash was light-blue and yellow, striped along its length. The waistcoat was white. A white brassard was worn tied about the upper left arm. Ship's architects had black collar, lapels and cuffs instead of the deck officer's dark-blue. All officers had gold fist-straps to their sabres.

Officers of the Army Fleet were dressed as above except that they had light-blue piping to top edges of collar and Swedish cuffs, and instead of epaulettes they had light-blue 'wings' decorated with gold lace and gold fringes.

From 1793 the national costume gave way to a more casual uniform with gold oak leaves embroidered around the collar and cuffs of admirals. The top hat was replaced in full dress by a plumed bicorn with white cut-feather edging, gold lace, loop and button and yellow over light-blue plume. The long-skirted, single-breasted coat was dark-blue. The golden buttons bore the anchor.

Deck officers wore the top hat as before, dark-blue, double-breasted, long-tailed coats with white piping to collar, cuffs, rectangular cuff-flaps and front edges, gold buttons, white breeches and boots. The sabre was carried on a white leather waist-belt over the coat and it was fastened with a rectangular gold plate bearing the Swedish crest. Gold epaulettes were worn on both shoulders and the white brassard on the upper left arm.

**Admirals 1810–15** (both fleets)
In 1810 a new uniform for admirals was introduced; top hat with wide gold

## SHIPS OF THE LINE OF THE SWEDISH HIGH SEAS FLEET

### IN ACTION AGAINST RUSSIA 1808-9

| Name | Total guns max usual | 36 lb | 24 lb | 18 lb | 12 lb | 8 lb | 6 lb | Crew | Length (m) | Beam (m) | Draught fully armed (astern) (m) | Date launched, captured or bought | Date lost or broken up | Where built | Naval battle year |
|---|---|---|---|---|---|---|---|---|---|---|---|---|---|---|---|
| Fredrik Adolf | 64 62 | - | 24 | 26 | - | - | 12 | 567 | 50.19 | 13.51 | 6.24 | 1774 | 1825 | Karlskrona | 1808 |
| Adolf Fredrik | 74 70 | - | 26 | 28 | - | 16 | - | 610 | 51.7 | 13.9 | 6.3 | 1775 | 1825 | Karlskrona | 1808-9 Flagship in the battle of Ratan 1809 |
| Gustav III | 74 70 | - | 26 | 28 | - | 16 | - | 610 | 51.7 | 13.9 | 6.3 | 1777 | 1825 | Karlskrona | 1808-9 |
| Aran | 64 62 | - | 26 | 28 | - | - | 8 | 567 | 49.6 | 13.59 | 5.79 | 1784 | 1874 | Karlskrona | 1808 |
| Försiktigheten | 64 62 | 26 | 28 | - | - | - | 8 | 567 | 49.6 | 13.59 | 5.79 | 1784 | 1825 | Karlskrona | 1808 and the battle of Ratan 1809 |
| Manligheten | 64 62 | - | 26 | 28 | - | - | 8 | 567 | 49.6 | 13.59 | 5.79 | 1785 | 1864 | Karlskrona | 1808-9 |
| Tapperheten | 64 62 | - | 26 | 28 | - | - | 8 | 567 | 49.6 | 13.59 | 5.79 | 1785 | 1825 | Karlskrona | 1808 |
| Vlädislaff | 76 ? | ? | ? | ? | ? | ? | ? | 660 | 52.8 | 14.1 | 5.95 | 1788 | 1819 | Arkangelsk | Captured from the Russians 1788. 1808 under Swedish flag |
| Gustav IV Adolf | 78 74 | 28 | 30 | - | 16 | - | - | 695 | 55.9 | 14.7 | 6.6 | 1799 | 1876 | Karlskrona | Flagship 1808 |

All ships were built by Chapman, except the *Vlädislaff*

band, gold button, loop and cockade surmounted by a yellow over light-blue plume on the left side; single-breasted, long-skirted dark-blue coat with dark-blue standing collar and Swedish cuffs, white skirt lining and gold oak leaf embroidery to collar, cuffs, lower sleeves, jacket-front and pocket-flaps. No epaulettes were worn. The white brassard fell into apparent disuse in 1810 and the conventional bicorn reappeared to replace the top hat so beloved of the Swedes.

### Sailors 1792–3 (both fleets)
Black tophats, short dark-blue, double-breasted coats. blue knee-breeches and white stockings or grey pantaloons.

### Marines 1792–3
The marines of the High Seas Fleet (Örlogsflottan Volontär Regementet) wore top hats with yellow band, button loop and plume, dark-blue national costume piped yellow along all seams, yellow buttons, white breeches and white leather equipment. The short boots had yellow trim to the top. Their equivalents in the Army Fleet wore the same dress but with white hat band and long white over light-blue plume curving over the hat crown. Their jackets had no yellow piping and over the thighs of their breeches they wore white 'scharawaden' with a blue stripe around the upper edge.

### Marines 1793–1815
Marines of the High Seas Fleet at this time wore the old top hat, short-skirted, double-breasted dark-blue coat with brass buttons, white pantaloons and leather work. Marines of the Army Fleet were differentiated by a brass hat band bearing a crowned 'G' and the date 1790 (Second Battle of Svensksund) and a white hat-loop and plume.

Officers of the High Seas Fleet wore the white waist-belt with gold buckle-plate, officers of the Army Fleet wore light-blue and yellow silk waist-sashes with heavy tassels tied to the left side.

### Sailors 1793–1815
Sailors were dressed as for marines throughout the period 1792–1815 but with yellow collar and cuffs and yellow waistcoats, white or dark-blue pantaloons, black waist belt with brass buckles.

# Turkey

In 1790 the Turkish fleet consisted of 30 ships of the line with from 74–50 guns, 50 frigates with from 50–10 guns and 100 galliots. The total cannon numbered 3,000 and there were 50,000 seamen, mainly Greeks from the Aegean Sea. The French ambassador in Constantinople reported to General Napoleon Bonaparte in 1796 that 'The Ottoman naval force is composed of 27 three-deckers and 20 frigates. This fleet is the most beautiful fleet in Europe'.

Turkish men-of-war had higher intervals between decks than was usual with European ships and it is said that this was to permit the men to be able

First rate Turkish ship of the line, 1790s, which carried over 80 guns; a plate from the Topkapi Museum, Istanbul

to wear their high and elaborate headgear. This sacrifice to military fashion made the vessels very high and thus less stable and unable to carry great quantities of sail without being in danger of capsizing.

Intercourse with British naval officers in the later stages of the Napoleonic wars is said to have led to a significant increase in the efficiency of the Turkish fleet. Although their naval tactics were still far behind those of the British, their courage and tenacity were never questioned and it was said that if they could handle their ships like they handle their scimitars, they would be formidable foes.

Naval uniform as such did not exist, even admirals were distinguished only by certain items of dress such as their headgear and their boots – the most senior grades wearing yellow boots, the next junior group red and the lesser officers black.

The capitan pasha, supreme commander of the Turkish navy, wore a high, domed white hat with a yellow scarf upon it, dark-green robe with long, false sleeves and brown fur trim to shoulders and front and to the ends of the short, genuine sleeves, green under-tunic and yellow boots. The flag of the capitan pasha was crimson and bore a silver sabre with two blades, the names of disciples of the prophet in the four corners and some passages of the Koran around the border, all in silver.

The 31st Ortah of Janissaries, who carried out the duties of marines, were governed by the same lax sartorial rules although each man carried the Ortah badge (an anchor) tattooed on his forearm.

Turkish Admiral Capitan Pasha; white turban with yellow scarf, green robes with brown fur, yellow boots (*Author's collection*)

In 1801 28 Turkish vessels were placed under command of the Russian Vice-Admiral F. F. Uschakov; they included 4 ships of the line, 6 frigates – *Houssain*, *Abbas*, *Zeyner*, *Suleiman*, *Herim* and *Akhmet*; 4 corvettes – *Moustapha*, *Houssain*, *Ali-Bey* and *Mehmet* and 14 gunboats.

The Turkish commander was Abdul Kadyr-Bey. After the capture of Corfu, 2 May 1799, the Turks took the French frigate *Brune* (28) as part of their spoils.

A 64-gun Turkish ship of the line of the period 1789–1807 when Sultan Selim III ruled the Ottoman Empire; a plate from the Topkapi Museum, Istanbul

# The United States of America

Although Congress was full of justified patriotic ardour and indignation at Britain's high-handed actions at sea and declared war on her, the means with which to wage that war had not been at all well prepared. It was to be mainly a naval conflict from 1812–15 but the American navy consisted in 1812 of only 17 ships ready for service with a total tonnage of some 15,300 tons. These ships carried in all 442 guns and 5,025 men were available for service both afloat and in the shore bases. There was no real dockyard as such although one was being established at Norfolk, Virginia. The heaviest available ships were frigates but they had the advantage of being larger and better armed than equivalent British vessels – a factor which, when linked with the skill and daring of their crews, was to make them the most dangerous opponents that the Royal Navy had ever encountered. The vessels were the frigates *Constitution, President, United States* (44s); *Congress, Chesapeake, Constellation* (36s); *Essex* (32); the corvette *Adams* (28); the sloops *Hornet* and *Wasp* (18s); the brigs *Oneida* (26) on Lake Ontario, *Argus* (18) and *Siren* (16); and the schooners *Enterprise, Nautilus, Vixen* (12s), *Viper* (10). Unserviceable were the frigate *New York* (36) and the corvette *Boston* (28).

There were other, minor vessels on the coast and on the great lakes, and by 1815 2 ships of the line were nearing completion, but it was with these tiny forces that the Americans challenged the world's greatest naval power.

215

# Uniforms

**Officers**

Cocked hats with black cockade, dark-blue coat with red lapels collar and cuffs, dark-blue cuff-flaps, yellow buttons and lace, red waistcoat, dark-blue breeches, white stockings.

**Marines**

Cocked officers' hat or shako, dark-green coat with white collar and cuffs, dark-green cuff-flaps, silver buttons and lace, white waistcoat and breeches, black gaiters, white belts.

# Appendix 1:

# Ship Losses of the Major Navies 1793-1802

(Reprinted directly from *History of the Royal Navy* by William, Lord Clowes, London 1899, 6 vols. Note that there is some discrepancy in the spelling of the ships' names.)

ROYAL NAVY

| Year | Date | H.M. Ship | Guns | Fate |
|------|------|-----------|------|------|
| 1793 | May 27 | *Hyaena* ........... | 24 | Taken by *Concorde*, 40, in W. Indies |
| | June 1 | *Advice,* cutter ...... | 4 | Wrecked on Key Bokell, Honduras |
| | Oct. 4 | *Thames* ........... | 32 | Taken by three French frigates, going to Gibraltar. Retaken, June 7, 1796 |
| | Nov. 20 | *Scipion* .......... | 74 | Accidentally burnt off Leghorn |
| | Dec. 16 | *Pigmy,* cutter ...... | 14 | Wrecked on the Motherbank |
| | " 18 | *Vigilante,* cutter .... | 4 | Taken by the French at Toulon |
| | " 18 | *Alerte* ............ | 14 | Taken by the French at Toulon |
| | " 18 | *Conflagration,* f.s. .. | 14 | Burnt on evacuation of Toulon |
| | " 18 | *Vulcan,* f.s. ........ | 14 | Expended at Toulon |
| | " 18 | *Union,* gunboat .... | .. | Blown up at Toulon |
| | | *Vipère,* cutter ...... | 4 | Wrecked in Hyères Bay |
| 1794 | Jan. 7 | *Moselle* .......... | 24 | Taken on entering Toulon by mistake |
| | " 30 | *Amphitrite* ....... | 18 | Wrecked in the Mediterranean |
| | Feb. | *Spitfire,* cutter ..... | 6 | Capsized off San Domingo, with all hands |
| | Mar. 8 | *Convert (ex Inconstant)* ..... | 32 | Wrecked on Grand Cayman |
| | Apr. 11 | *Prosélyte,* floatg. batt | 24 | Sunk by batteries at Bastia |
| | " | *Ardent* ........... | 64 | Accidentally blown up off Corsica, with all hands |
| | May 8 | *Placentia* .......... | .. | Lost at Newfoundland |
| | " 10 | *Castor* ........... | 32 | Taken by Adm. Nielly's squadron off Cape Clear |
| | " | *Alert* ............ | 16 | Taken by *Unite*, 40, off Ireland |
| | June 28 | *Rose* ............. | 28 | Wrecked on Rocky Point, Jamaica |
| | " | *Speedy* ........... | 14 | Taken by French frigates, off Nice |
| | " | *Ranger,* cutter ...... | 14 | Taken by a French squadron, off Brest |
| | July 14 | *Hound* ........... | 16 | Taken by *Seine* and *Galatée*, coming from W. Ind. |
| | Aug. 24 | *Impétueux* ........ | 74 | Accidentally burnt at Portsmouth |
| | " | *Scout* ............ | 16 | Taken by two French frigates, off Cape Bona |
| | Nov. 6 | *Alexander* ........ | 74 | Taken by a French squadron off Sicily |
| | " 26 | *Pylades* .......... | 16 | Wrecked on Isle of Nest, Shetlands |
| | " 26 | *Actif,* brig ........ | 10 | Foundered off Bermuda |
| | | *Espion* ........... | 16 | Taken by three French frigates |
| | Dec. 22 | *Daphne* .......... | 20 | Taken by two French men-of-war. Retaken, Dec. 28, 1797 |
| 1795 | Mar. 7 | *Berwick* .......... | 74 | Taken by the French fleet in the Mediterranean |
| | " 14 | *Illustrious* ........ | 74 | Wrecked near Avenza |
| | May 1 | *Boyne* ........... | 98 | Accidentally burnt at Spithead |
| | | *Mosquito,* floatg. batt. | 5 | Lost on coast of France with all hands |
| | June | *Flying Fish,* schoon. | 6 | Taken in W. Ind. by two French privateers |
| | Aug. 2 | *Diomede* ......... | 44 | Wrecked near Trincomale |
| | Oct. 7 | *Censeur* .......... | 74 | Taken by a French squadron off C. St. Vincent |
| | Nov. 12 | *Flèche* ........... | 14 | Wrecked in San Fiorenzo Bay |

| Year | Date | H.M. Ship | Guns | Fate |
|---|---|---|---|---|
| | Dec. 9 | *Nemesis* .......... | 28 | Taken by two French men-of-war at Smyrna. Retaken, March 9, 1796. |
| | " 11 | *Shark*, Dutch hoy ... | 4 | Carried by her crew into La Hougue |
| | " 29 | *Amethyst* ......... | 38 | Lost at Alderney |
| 1796 | .. | *Scourge* .......... | 16 | Foundered off the Dutch coast |
| 1796 | Feb. 11 | *Lela* ............. | 36 | Capsized in a squall. |
| | " 12 | *St. Pierre* ........ | .. | Wrecked off Pt. Negro |
| | Aprl. 4 | *Spider*, hired lugger | .. | Collided with *Ramillies* |
| | " 11 | *Ça Ira* ........... | 80 | Accidentally burnt in San Fiorenzo Bay |
| | May 13 | *Salisbury* ......... | 50 | Wrecked near San Domingo |
| | June 10 | *Arab* ............ | 16 | Wrecked near Point Penmarck |
| | July 15 | *Trompeuse* ....... | 16 | Wrecked near Kingsale |
| | " | *Active* ........... | 32 | Wrecked in the St. Lawrence |
| | | *Sirène* ........... | 16 | Wrecked in the Bay of Honduras |
| | Aug. 27 | *Undaunted* (ex *Aréthuse)* ..... | 38 | Wrecked on Morant Keys |
| | | *Bermuda* ......... | 14 | Foundered in Gulf of Florida |
| | Sept. 22 | *Amphion* ......... | 32 | Accidentally burnt in Hamoaze |
| | Oct. 2 | *Experiment*, brig ... | 10 | Taken by the Spaniards in the Mediterranean |
| | " 3 | *Narcissus* ......... | 20 | Wrecked off New Providence |
| | " 10 | *Malabar* .......... | 54 | Foundered coming from W. Ind. |
| | " 20 | *Poulette* .......... | 26 | Burnt at Ajaccio, as unserviceable |
| | " 20 | *Bellette* .......... | 24 | Burnt at Ajaccio, as unserviceable |
| | Nov. 3 | *Helena* ........... | 14 | Foundered on Dutch coast, with all hands |
| | " | *Berbice*, brig ....... | 8 | Wrecked at Dominica |
| | " | *Vanneau*, brig ...... | 8 | Wrecked at Porto Ferrajo |
| | Dec. 7 | *Réunion* .......... | 36 | Wrecked in the Swin |
| | " 14 | *Vestale* ........... | 36 | Retaken, after capture, on Dec. 13 |
| | " 19 | *Courageux* ........ | 74 | Wrecked below Ape's Hill |
| | " 21 | *Bombay Castle* ..... | 74 | Wrecked in the Tagus |
| | " 24 | *Cormorant* ........ | 18 | Accidentally blown up at Port au Prince |
| | " 27 | *Hussar* ........... | 28 | Wrecked near Isle Bas |
| | " 31 | *Curlew* ........... | 18 | Foundered in the North Sea |
| 1797 | Jan. 2 | *Vipère* ........... | .. | Foundered off the Shannon |
| | " | *Hermes* ........... | .. | Foundered at sea |
| | " 14 | *Amazon* .......... | 36 | Wrecked near Isle Bas |
| | Feb. 24 | *Bloom*, tender ...... | 14 | Taken by the French, off Holyhead |
| | " 24 | *Brighton*, tender .... | 14 | Taken by the French off Holyhead |
| | Apr. 27 | *Albion*, floatg. batt. | 60 | Wrecked in the Swin |
| | " | *Tartar* ........... | 28 | Wrecked off San Domingo |
| | May 17 | *Providence*, discovery ship ...... | 16 | Wrecked in the Pacific |
| | " | *Lacedomonian* ..... | 12 | Taken by the French in the West Indies |
| | " | *Port Royal*, schoon. | 10 | Taken in the West Indies |
| | June 15 | *Fortune* .......... | 16 | Wrecked near Oporto |
| | July 24 | *Fox*, cutter ........ | .. | Destroyed before Santa Cruz |
| | " 31 | *Artois* ............ | 38 | Wrecked on the French coast |
| | " 31 | *Mignonne* ......... | 32 | Burnt as unserviceable at Porto Ferrajo |
| | Sept. 22 | *Hermione* ........ | 32 | Carried by mutinous crew into La Guaira |
| | Nov. 16 | *Tribune* .......... | 32 | Wrecked off Halifax |
| | " | *Hope*, hired lugger .. | 10 | Run down in the Channel |
| | Dec. 27 | *Hunter* ........... | 18 | Wrecked on Bog Island, Virginia |
| | " | *Growler* .......... | 12 | Taken off Dungeness by two French row-boats |
| | | *Swift* ............. | 18 | Foundered in the China Seas |
| | | *Pandour* ......... | 14 | Foundered in the North Sea |
| | | *Resolution* ........ | 14 | Foundered at sea |
| | | *Marie Antoinette*, schoon. .......... | 10 | Carried by mutinous crew into a French W. I. port |
| 1798 | Jan. 3 | *George* ........... | 6 | Taken by two Spanish privateers |

| --- | --- | --- | --- | --- |
| | Feb. 3 | *Raven* ........... | 18 | Wrecked at the mouth of the Elbe |
| | Apr. 4 | *Pallas* ........... | 32 | Wrecked on Mount Batten Point |
| | " 12 | *Lively* ........... | 32 | Wrecked near Rota Point, Cadiz |
| | May 23 | *De Braak* ......... | 16 | Capsized in the Delaware |
| | June 23 | *Rover* ........... | 16 | Wrecked in the Gulf of St. Lawrence |
| | " 29 | *Pique* ........... | 36 | Wrecked on the French coast |
| | July 18 | *Aigle* ........... | 38 | Wrecked off Cape Farina |
| | " 24 | *Resistance* ........ | 44 | Accidentally blown up in the Strait of Banca |
| | " 26 | *Garland* ......... | 28 | Wrecked off Madagascar |
| | " | *Princess Royal,* cutter | 8 | Taken by a French privateer |
| | Aug.15 | *Etrusco,* armed transport .... | 24 | Foundered coming from the West Indies |
| | " 18 | *Leander* .......... | 50 | Taken by the *Généreux,* 74. Retaken, March 3, 1799 |
| | " 26 | *Crash* ........... | 12 | Taken on the coast of Holland. Retaken, August 11, 1799 |
| | Oct. 13 | *Jason* ........... | 38 | Wrecked near Brest |
| | Nov.12 | *Petrel* ........... | 16 | Taken by three Spanish frigates, Retaken, November 13, 1798 |
| | " 26 | *Medusa,* armed transport .... | 50 | Wrecked on the coast of Portugal |
| | " | *Margaret,* tender ... | .. | Lost off the Irish coast |
| | Dec. 3 | *Kingfisher* ........ | 18 | Wrecked on Lisbon Bar |
| | " 10 | *Colossus* ......... | 74 | Wrecked off Sicily |
| | " 14 | *Ambuscade* ....... | 32 | Taken by *Bayonnaise,* 28 |
| | | *Hamadryad* ....... | 36 | Wrecked off the Portuguese coast |
| | | *Neptune,* lugger .... | 6 | Run down off Beachy Head |
| | | *Caroline,* tender .... | .. | Lost in the East Indies |
| 1799 | Jan. 7 | *Apollo* ........... | 38 | Wrecked on coast of Holland; crew saved |
| | " 12 | *Weazel* ........... | 14 | Wrecked in Barnstaple Bay; nearly all lost |
| | Feb. 1 | *Proserpine* ........ | 28 | Wrecked in the Elbe; nearly all saved |
| | " 2 | *Nautilus* .......... | 16 | Wrecked off Flamborough Head; crew saved |
| | | *Charlotte,* schooner | 8 | Taken by the French off Cape François. Retaken, Nov. 22 |
| | | *Mosquito,* schooner | 6 | Taken by Spanish frigates off Cuba |
| | | *Grampus,* storeship (54) .............. | 26 | Wrecked on Barking Shelf; crew saved |
| | Mar.18 | *Torride* .......... | 2 | Taken by French, Egypt. Retaken same day |
| | Apr.22 | *Brave,* lugger, hired . | 12 | Run down in the Channel; crew saved |
| | May 8 | *Fortune* .......... | 10 | Taken by French frigates; coast of Syria |
| | " 8 | *Dame de Grâce,* gunboat .......... | .. | Taken by French frigates; coast of Syria |
| | " 23 | *Deux Amis* ........ | 14 | Wrecked on the Isle of Wight; crew saved |
| | June 6 | *William Pitt,* lugger . | 14 | Taken by Spanish gunboats; Mediterranean |
| | July 7 | *Penelope,* cutter, hired ............ | 18 | Taken by *N.S. del Carmen;* Mediterranean |
| | Aug.28 | *Contest* .......... | 14 | Wrecked on the coast of Holland; crew saved |
| | Sept.28 | *Blanche,* storeship (32) | 18 | Wrecked in the Texel; crew saved |
| | " 28 | *Fox* .............. | 14 | Wrecked in the Gulf of Mexico; crew saved |
| | Oct. 9 | *Lutine* ........... | 36 | Wrecked off Vlieland; nearly all lost |
| | " 12 | *Trincomale* ....... | 16 | Blown up in action; crew lost |
| | " 14 | *Nassau,* storeship (64) .............. | 36 | Wrecked on coast of Holland; nearly all saved |
| | " 19 | *Impregnable* ....... | 98 | Wrecked near Langstone; crew saved |
| | " 25 | *Amaranthe* ........ | 14 | Wrecked on coast of Florida; 22 lost |
| | Nov. 5 | *Orestes* ........... | 18 | Foundered in the East Indies; crew lost |
| | " 16 | *Espion* (ex *Atalante*), st. sh. (38) ........ | 16 | Wrecked on the Goodwin; crew saved |
| | Dec. 5 | *Sceptre* ........... | 64 | Wrecked in Table Bay; 291 lost |

| Year | Date | H.M. Ship | Guns | Fate |
|---|---|---|---|---|
| | '' 25 | *Ethalion* ......... | 38 | Wrecked off Penmarch; crew saved |
| 1800 | Jan. 5 | *Mastiff* ........... | 12 | Wrecked near Yarmouth; nearly all saved |
| | '' 21 | *Weymouth,* armed transport .......... | 26 | Wrecked on Lisbon Bar; crew saved |
| | '' 26 | *Brazen* ......... | 18 | Wrecked near Brighton; all but one lost |
| | Mar. 10 | *Repulse* .......... | 64 | Wrecked off Ushant; nearly all saved |
| | '' 17 | *Queen Charlotte* .... | 100 | Accidentally burnt off Leghorn; nearly all lost |
| | '' 17 | *Danaë,* (ex *Vaillante*) | 20 | Carried by mutinous crew into Brest |
| | May 17 | *Trompeuse* ........ | 18 | Supposed foundered in Channel; crew lost |
| | '' 17 | *Railleur* .......... | 14 | Supposed foundered in Channel; crew lost |
| | '' 17 | *Lady Jane,* hired cutter ........... | 8 | Supposed foundered in Channel; crew lost |
| | '' 20 | *Cormorant* ........ | 20 | Wrecked on coast of Egypt; crew saved |
| | July 7 | *Comet,* f.s. ........ | .. | Expended in Dunquerque Road |
| | '' 7 | *Falcon,* f.s. ........ | .. | Expended in Dunquerque Road |
| | '' 7 | *Rosario,* f.s. ....... | .. | Expended in Dunquerque Road |
| | '' 7 | *Wasp,* f.s. ......... | .. | Expended in Dunquerque Road |
| | Aug. 10 | *Dromedary,* storeship | 24 | Wrecked near Trinidad; crew saved |
| | Sept. 6 | *Stag* ............. | 32 | Wrecked in Vigo Bay; crew saved |
| | '' 26 | *Hound* ........... | 18 | Wrecked near Shetland; crew lost |
| | '' | *Diligence* ......... | 18 | Wrecked near Havana; crew saved |
| | Oct. 9 | *Chance* (ex *Galgo*) .. | 18 | Foundered in W. Indies; nearly all lost |
| | '' 13 | *Rose,* hired cutter ... | 10 | Taken by the Dutch in the Ems |
| | '' | *Martin* ........... | 16 | Supposed foundered in N. Sea; crew lost |
| | Nov. 4 | *Marlborough* ...... | 74 | Wrecked near Belle Isle; crew saved |
| | '' 9 | *Havik* ............ | 16 | Wrecked off Jersey; crew saved |
| | '' 23 | *Albanaise* ........ | 14 | Carried by mutinous crew into Malaga |
| | '' | *Active,* cutter ...... | 12 | Taken by French and Dutch in the Ems. Retaken, May 16, 1801 |
| | Dec. 2 | *Sir Thomas Pasley,* brig .............. | 16 | Taken by two Spanish gunboats, Mediterranean |
| | | *Urchin,* gun vessel .. | .. | Foundered in Tetuan Bay |
| 1801 | Jan. 1 | *Requin* ........... | 10 | Wrecked near Quiberon; crew saved |
| | '' 9 | *Constitution,* hired cutter ............ | 12 | Taken by two French cutters. Retaken same night |
| | '' 29 | *Incendiary,* f.s. ..... | 14 | Taken by the squadron of M. Gantheaume |
| | Feb. 2 | *Légère* ........... | 18 | Wrecked near Cartagena, S. America; crew saved |
| | '' 10 | *Sprightly,* cutter .... | 12 | Taken by the squadron of M. Gantheaume |
| | '' 13 | *Success* ........... | 32 | Taken by the squadron of M. Gantheaume |
| | '' 14 | *Telegraph,* hired brig | 16 | Supposed foundered off Cape Ortegal |
| | '' 27 | *Bulldog,* bomb ..... | 18 | Taken by the French at Ancona. Retaken, Sept. 16, 1801 |
| | '' | *Charming Molly,* cutter ............ | .. | Foundered coming from St Marcou |
| | '' | *Lurcher,* hired cutter | 12 | Taken by a French privateer |
| | Mar. 16 | *Invincible* ........ | 74 | Wrecked on Hasborough Sand; nearly all lost |
| | '' 23 | *Blazer* ........... | 12 | Taken by the Swedes at Warberg; restored |
| | '' 24 | *Fulminante* ........ | 10 | Wrecked on coast of Egypt |
| | '' 25 | *Scout* ............ | 18 | Lost on the Shingles, Isle of Wight; crew saved |
| | '' | *Nancy,* hired cutter . | 6 | Taken by a French privateer |
| | June 9 | *Meleager* .......... | 32 | Wrecked on the Triangles, Gulf of Mexico; crew saved |
| | '' 24 | *Swiftsure* ......... | 74 | Taken by the squadron of M. Gantheaume |
| | '' | *Forte* ............ | 44 | Wrecked at Jeddah; crew saved |
| | '' | *Speedy* ........... | 14 | Taken by the squadron of M. Linois |
| | July 5 | *Hannibal* .......... | 74 | Taken by the squadron of M. Linois |

| Year | Date | | H.M. Ship | Guns | Fate |
|------|------|----|-----------|------|------|
| | '' | 7 | *Augustus,* gun-vessel | 1 | Wrecked in Plymouth Sound; crew saved |
| | '' | 21 | *Jason* ............. | 36 | Wrecked near St Malo; crew saved |
| | '' | | *Iphigenia* ......... | 32 | Accidentally burnt at Alexandria; crew saved |
| | Aug.11 | | *Lowestoft* ........ | 32 | Wrecked off Inagua, W. Indies; crew saved |
| | Sept. 4 | | *Proselyte* ......... | 32 | Wrecked off St Martin, W. Indies; crew saved |
| | Oct. 25 | | *Bonetta* .......... | 18 | Wrecked on the Janlines, Cuba; crew saved |
| | Nov. | | *Utile* ............. | 16 | Capsized in the Mediterranean; crew lost |
| | '' | | *Cockchafer,* hired lugger ............ | 8 | Foundered of Guernsey; crew saved |
| | '' | | *Friendship,* gun-vessel ............ | 2 | Foundered off Guernsey; crew saved |
| | | | *Babet* ............ | 20 | Supposed foundered in the W. Indies; crew lost |
| 1802 | Mar. 2 | | *Sensible* .......... | .. | Wrecked off Ceylon; crew saved |
| | '' | 29 | *Assistance* ........ | 50 | Wrecked near Dunquerque; crew saved |
| | | | *Scout* ............ | 18 | Foundered off Newfoundland; crew lost |
| | | | *Fly* .............. | 14 | Foundered off Newfoundland; crew lost |

FRENCH NAVY

| Year | Date | French National Ship (*Added to the Royal Navy) | Guns | Fate **M** Medals granted in 1849, in pursuance of *Gazette* notice of June 1st, 1847 **M** Flag-Officers' and Captains' gold medals |
|------|------|-----------------------------------------------|------|-------------|
| 1793 | Feb. 15 | *Léopard* .......... | 74 | Foundered in Cagliari Bay |
| | | *Vengeur* (supposed) . | 74 | Wrecked near Ajaccio |
| | Apr. 16 | *Goéland* .......... | 14 | Taken by *Penelope,* 32, Capt. B. S. Rowley, W. Ind. |
| | May 21 | (Unknown) ........ | 36 | Destroyed by the Spaniards at St Pietro |
| | '' 28 | *Prompte** ......... | 20 | Taken by *Phaeton,* 38, Capt. Sir A. S. Douglas, B. of Biscay |
| | June 3 | *Curieux,* brig ...... | 14 | Taken by *Inconstant,* 36, Capt. Aug. Montgomery, W. Ind. |
| | '' 6 | *Vanneau* .......... | 6 | Taken by *Colossus,* 74, Capt. M. Pole, B. of Biscay |
| | '' 9 | *Eclair** ............ | 22 | Taken by *Leda,* 36, Capt. Geo. Gampbell, Medit. |
| | '' 18 | *Cléopátre* (*as *Oiseau)* ....... | 36 | Taken by *Nymphe,* 36, Capt. E. Pellew, off Start. **M** |
| | July 23 | *Lutine* ........... | 12 | Taken by *Pluto,* 14, Com. J. N. Morris, Newfoundland |
| | Aug.29 | *Commerce de Marseilles** ........ | 120 | Taken at Toulon by Lord Hood |
| | '' '' | *Pompée** .......... | 74 | '' '' '' |
| | '' '' | *Puissant** ......... | 74 | '' '' '' |
| | '' '' | *Scipion** ......... | 74 | '' '' '' |
| | '' '' | *Arethuse* (*as *Undaunted)* .... | 40 | '' '' '' |
| | '' '' | *Topaze** .......... | 36 | '' '' '' |
| | '' '' | *Perle* (*as *Amethyst)* | 40 | '' '' '' |
| | '' '' | *Aurore** .......... | 36 | '' '' '' |
| | '' '' | *Lutine** as 32 ....... | 36 | '' '' '' |
| | '' '' | *Alceste* ........... | 36 | '' '' '' (Given to Sardinians) |
| | '' '' | *Poulette** ......... | 26 | '' '' '' |
| | '' '' | *Belette** ......... | 28 | '' '' '' |
| | '' | *Prosélyte** ........ | 36 | '' '' '' |

| Year | Date | French National Ship (*Added to the Royal Navy) | Guns | Fate — M Medals granted in 1849, in pursuance of Gazette notice of June 1st, 1847. M Flag-Officers' and Captain's gold medals |
|---|---|---|---|---|
| | ,, ,, | *Moselle* .......... | 20 | ,, ,, ,, |
| | ,, ,, | *Embroye* (?) ....... | 20 | ,, ,, ,, (Given to Neapolitans) |
| | ,, ,, | *Mulet* ............ | 18 | ,, ,, ,, |
| | ,, ,, | *Sincère* ........... | 18 | ,, ,, ,, |
| | ,, ,, | *Petite Aurore* ...... | 18 | ,, ,, ,, (Given to Spaniards) |
| | ,, ,, | *Tarleton* .......... | 14 | ,, ,, ,, |
| | Sept | *Convention Nationale* ........ | 10 | Taken by Commod. John Ford, San Domingo |
| | Oct. 11 | *Impérieuse** ....... | 38 | Taken by V.-Ad. John Gell, off Genoa |
| | ,, 17 | *Modeste** .......... | 36 | Taken by *Bedford,* 74, Capt. R. Man (3) etc., off Genoa |
| | ,, 20 | *Réunion** .......... | 36 | Taken by *Crescent,* 36, Capt. J. Saumarez, off Cherbourg, **M** |
| | Nov.25 | *Inconstante* (*as *Convert*) ...... | 36 | Taken by *Penelope,* 32, and *Iphigenia,* 32, off San Domingo |
| | ,, 27 | *Blonde* ............ | 28 | Taken by *Latona,* 38, and *Phaeton,* 38, off Ushant |
| | ,, 30 | *Espiègle** .......... | 16 | Taken by *Nymphe,* 36, and *Circe,* 28, off Ushant |
| | Dec. 18 | *Triomphant* ....... | 80 | Destroyed at the evacuation of Toulon |
| | ,, ,, | *Destin* ............ | 74 | ,, ,, ,, |
| | ,, ,, | *Centaure* .......... | 74 | ,, ,, ,, |
| | ,, ,, | *Duguay Trouin* ..... | 74 | ,, ,, ,, |
| | ,, ,, | *Héros* ............. | 74 | ,, ,, ,, |
| | ,, ,, | *Liberte* (ex *Dictateur*) | 74 | ,, ,, ,, |
| | ,, ,, | *Suffisant* .......... | 74 | ,, ,, ,, |
| | ,, ,, | *Thémistocle* ....... | 74 | ,, ,, ,, |
| | ,, ,, | *Tricolor* (ex *Lys*) .... | 74 | ,, ,, ,, |
| | ,, ,, | *Victorieuse* ........ | 36 | ,, ,, ,, |
| | ,, ,, | *Montréal* .......... | 32 | ,, ,, |
| | ,, ,, | *Iris* .............. | 32 | ,, ,, ,, |
| | ,, ,, | *Auguste* .......... | 24 | ,, ,, ,, |
| | ,, ,, | *Caroline* .......... | 24 | ,, ,, ,, |
| | ,, 30 | *Sans Culotte* ....... | 22 | Taken by *Blanche,* 32. Capt. Christ. Parker (2), W. Ind. |
| | ,, ,, | *Révolutionnaire* .... | 20 | ,, ,, ,, ,, |
| | ,, ,, | *Vengeur* .......... | 12 | ,, ,, ,, |
| 1794 | Jan. 12 | *Trompeuse** ....... | 18 | Taken by *Sphinx,* 20, Capt. Rich. Lucas, off C. Clear |
| | ,, 23 | *Vipère** ........... | 16 | Taken by *Flora,* 36, Capt. Sir J. B. Warren, Channel |
| | Feb. 19 | *Minerve* (*as *San Fiorenzo*) ......... | 38 | Taken at San Fiorenzo |
| | ,, ,, | *Fortunée* .......... | 36 | Destroyed at San Fiorenzo |
| | Mar.16 | *Actif** ............ | 16 | Taken by *Iphigenia,* 32, Capt. Pat. Sinclair, W. Ind. |
| | ,, ,, | *Espiègle** .......... | 12 | ,, ,, ,, ,, |
| | ,, 17 | *Bienvenue* (*as *Undaunted*) ........ | 28 | Taken by V.-Ad. Sir J. Jervis, at Martinique **M** |
| | ,, ,, | *Avenger* . | 16 | ,, ,, ,, ,, |
| | ,, 28 | *Liberté* ............ | 14 | Taken by *Alligator,* 28, Capt. Thos. Surridge, Jamaica |
| | Apr.23 | *Pomone** .......... | 44 | Taken by Commod. Sir J. B. Warren, off Isle Bas |
| | ,, ,, | *Babet** ............ | 20 | ,, ,, ,, ,, |
| | ,, ,, | *Engageante** ....... | 36 | Taken by *Concorde,* 36, Capt. Sir R. J. Strachan, Channel |
| | Apr. 23 | *Guadeloupe* ....... | 16 | Taken by V.-Adm. Sir J. Jervis, Guadeloupe |

| Year | Date | French National Ship (*Added to the Royal Navy) | Guns | Fate — *M* Medals granted in 1849, in pursuance of *Gazette* notice of June 1st, 1847 — **M** Flag-Officers' and Captain's gold medals |
|---|---|---|---|---|
| | May 5 | *Duguay Trouin* ..... | 28 | Taken by *Orpheus,* 32, Capt. Hon. Newcome, E. Ind. |
| | ,, 5 | *Atalante* (*as *Espion*) | 36 | Taken by *Swiftsure,* 74, Capt. Chas. Boyles, near Cork |
| | ,, 5 | *Inconnue* .......... | 16 | Taken and burnt by Lord Howe |
| | ,, 21 | *Flèche** ........... | 14 | Taken at Bastia by Lord Hood |
| | ,, 23 | *Moselle** .......... | 18 | Taken by *Aimable,* 32, Capt. Sir H. Burrard off Hyères. |
| | ,, ,, | *Courier,* cutter ..... | 10 | Taken and scuttled by Lord Howe, Channel |
| | ,, 25 | *Republicain* ........ | 20 | Taken and burnt by Lord Howe, Channel |
| | ,, 29 | *Castor** ........... | 32 | Retaken by *Carysfort,* 28, Capt. Fras. Laforey, off Land's End |
| | June 1 | *Juste** ............ | 80 | Taken by Lord Howe, Ushant 150 leagues E. ½ N. |
| | ,, ,, | *Sans Pareil** ....... | 80 | ,,  ,,  ,,  ,, |
| | ,, ,, | *Amerique* (*as *Impétueux*) ........ | 74 | ,,  ,,  ,,  ,, |
| | ,, ,, | *Achille* ........... | 74 | ,,  ,,  ,,  ,, |
| | ,, ,, | *Northumberland* ... | 74 | ,,  ,,  ,,  ,, |
| | ,, ,, | *Impétueux* ......... | 74 | ,,  ,,  ,,  ,, |
| | ,, ,, | *Vengeur* .......... | 74 | Sunk. Taken by Lord Howe, Ushant 150 leagues E. ½ N. |
| | ,, 17 | *Sibylle** .......... | 40 | Taken by *Romney,* 50, Capt. Hon. W. Paget, at Miconi. *M* |
| | ,, 18 | *Narcisse,* cutter ..... | 14 | Taken by *Aurora,* 28, Capt. W. Essignton, off Shetland |
| | Aug.10 | *Melpomène** ....... | 40 | Taken by Lord Hood, at Calvi |
| | ,, ,, | *Mignonne** ........ | 28 | ,,  ,,  ,, |
| | " " | *Auguste,* brig ...... | 4 | ,,  ,,  ,, |
| | ,, ,, | *Providence,* brig .... | 4 | ,,  ,,  ,, |
| | ,, ,, | *Ça Ira,* g.b. ........ | 3 | ,,  ,,  ,, |
| | ,, 23 | *Volontaire* ......... | 36 | Driven ashore and destroyed, near Penmarck |
| | ,, ,, | *Alerte* ............ | 12 | Driven ashore and destroyed, off P. du Raz |
| | ,, | *Sirène** ........... | 16 | Taken by *Intrepid,* 64, and *Chichester,* 44, San Domingo |
| | ,, | *Reprisal* .......... | 16 | Taken by V.-Ad. Sir John Jervis, W. Ind. |
| | Sept. 7 | *Quartidi* .......... | 14 | Taken by Commod. Sir E. Pellew, off Sicily |
| | Oct. 21 | *Révolutionnaire** ... | 44 | Taken by Commod. Sir. E. Pellew, off Brest |
| | ,, 30 | *Jacobin* (*as *Matilda*) | 24 | Taken by *Ganges,* 74, and *Montagu,* 74, W. Ind. |
| | ,, | *Revenge* (*as *Hobart*) | 18 | Taken by *Resistance,* 44, Capt. Edw. Pakenham, S. Sunda |
| | Nov.30 | *Carmagnole,* schooner .......... | 10 | Taken by *Zebra,* 16, W. Ind. |
| | Dec. 2 | A sloop ........... | .. | Taken by *Beaulieu,* 40, Capt. E. Riou, W. Ind. |
| | ,, 27 | *Républicain* ........ | 110 | Wrecked near Brest |
| | ,, 30 | A schooner ........ | .. | Taken by *Blanche,* 32, Capt. Robt. Faulknor (3), W. Ind. |
| 1795 | Jan. 5 | *Duquesne* ......... | 36 | Taken by *Bellona,* 74, Capt. Geo. Wilson, W. Ind. |
| | ,, 6 | *Pique** ............ | 36 | Taken by *Blanche,* 32, Capt. Robt. Faulknor (3), W. Ind. *M* |
| | ,, 8 | *Espérance* ......... | 22 | Taken by *Argonaut,* 64, Capt. A. J. Ball, America |

*(The June 1 entries from Juste through Impétueux are bracketed together and marked **MM**)*

223

| Year | Date | French National Ship (*Added to the Royal Navy) | Guns | Fate — M Medals granted in 1849, in pursuance of Gazette notice of June 1st, 1847 — **M** Flag-Officers' and Captain's gold medals |
|---|---|---|---|---|
| " | | *Neptune* | 74 | Wrecked in Audierne Bay |
| " | | *Scipion* | 80 | Foundered in a gale |
| " | | *Neuf Thermidor* | 80 | " " " |
| " | | *Superbe* | 74 | " " " |
| " | | *Duras* | 20 | Taken by *Bellona,* 74, and *Alarm,* 32, W. Ind. |
| Feb. | 10 | *Iphigénié* | 36 | Taken by the Spaniards, Medit. |
| " | 20 | *Requin** | 12 | Taken by *Thalia,* 36, Capt. Rich. Grindall, Channel |
| " | 26 | *Curieuse,* schooner | 12 | Taken by *Pomone,* 44, Capt. Sir J. B. Warren, off Groix |
| Mar. | 2 | *Espion* (*as *Spy*) | 18 | Taken by *Lively,* 32, Capt. Geo. Burlton, off Brest |
| " | 13 | *Tourterelle** | 28 | Taken by *Lively,* 32, Capt. Geo. Burlton, off Ushant *M* |
| " | 14 | *Ça Ira** | 80 | Taken by V.-Ad. W. Hotham (1), off Genoa |
| " | " | *Censeur** | 74 | Taken by V.-Ad. W. Hotham (1), off Genoa }*M* |
| | | *Temeraire,* cutter | 20 | Taken by *Dido,* 28, Capt. Geo. Hen. Towry, Medit. |
| " | 27 | *Républicaine* | 22 | Taken by R.-Ad. J. Colpoys, Channel |
| " | " | *Speedy** | 14 | Taken by *Inconstant,* 36, Capt. Thos. Fras. Fremantle, Medit. |
| " | 29 | *Jean Bart* (*as *Arab*) | 18 | Taken by *Cerebus,* 32, and *Sta. Margarita,* 36, Channel |
| Apr. | 10 | *Gloire** | 36 | Taken by *Astraea,* 32, Capt. Lord Hen. Paulet, Channel *M* |
| " | 11 | *Gentille** | 36 | Taken by *Hannibal,* 74, Capt. John Markham, Channel |
| " | 15 | *Jean Bart* (*as *Laurel*) | 26 | Taken by Commod. Sir J. B. Warren, off Rochefort |
| " | 16 | *Expédition* | 16 | Taken by Commod. Sir J. B. Warren, off Belle Isle |
| " | 23 | *Galatée* | 36 | Wrecked near Penmarck |
| May | 9 | *Eclair,* g.v.* | 3 | Taken by Capt. Sir R. J. Strachan, coast of France |
| " | " | *Crache Feu,* g.v.* | 3 | Taken by Capt. Sir R. J. Strachan, coast of France |
| " | 17 | *Prévoyante,* en flûte (40)* | 24 | Taken by *Thetis,* 38, and *Hussar,* 28, Chesapeake |
| " | " | *Raison,* en flûte (24)* | 18 | Taken by *Thetis,* 38, and *Hussar,* 28, Chesapeake }*M* |
| " | 28 | *Courier Nationale* | 18 | Taken by *Thorn,* 16, Com. Robt. W. Otway, W. Ind. |
| " | 28 | *Prompte* | 28 | |
| " | 30 | *Liberté* | 20 | Sunk by *Alarm,* 32, Capt. David Milne, off Puerto Rico |
| June | 23 | *Tigre** | 74 | Taken by Lord Bridport, off Lorient |
| " | " | *Alexandre** | 74 | " " " |
| " | " | *Formidable* (*as *Belleisle*) | 74 | " " " }*M* |
| " | 24 | *Minerve** | 40 | Taken by *Lowestoft,* 32, and *Dido,* 28, Medit. *M* |
| " | | *Perdrix** | 24 | Taken by *Vanguard,* 74, Capt. Simon Miller, off Antigua |
| July | 3 | *Vesuve,* g.v.* | 4 | Taken by *Melampus,* 36, and *Hebe,* 38, off St. Malo |

| Year | Date | French National Ship (*Added to the Royal Navy) | Guns | Fate M Medals granted in 1849, in pursuance of *Gazette* notice of June 1st, 1847 M Flag-Officers' and Captain's gold medals |
|---|---|---|---|---|
| | ,, 13 | *Alcide* ........... | 74 | Struck to Ad. Hotham, but accidentally blew up, Medit. |
| | | *Echoué* .......... | 28 | Run ashore and destroyed on Rhé by *Phaeton,* 38, Capt. Hon. R. Stopford |
| | Aug. 16 | *Résolue* .......... | 10 | Taken by Commod. H. Nelson, Alassio Bay |
| | ,, ,, | *République,* g.b. ... | 6 | Taken by Commod. H. Nelson, Alassio Bay |
| | ,, ,, | *Constitution,* galley . | 5 | Taken by Commod. H. Nelson, Alassio Bay |
| | ,, ,, | *Vigilante,* galley .... | 5 | Taken by Commod. H. Nelson, Alassio Bay |
| | ,, 31 | *Suffisante** ........ | 14 | Taken by Ad. Duncan off the Texel |
| | ,, ,, | *Victorieuse** ....... | 14 | ,, ,, ,, ,, ,, |
| | Sept. 2 | *Assemblée Nationale* | 22 | Driven ashore by *Diamond,* 38, Capt. Sir W. S. Smith off Treguier |
| | ,, ,, | *Rude,* g.v. ......... | 12 | Burnt by *Pomone,* 44, Capt. Sir J. B. Warren, coast of France |
| | ,, 3 | *Vigilante,* cutter .... | 6 | Taken by *Childers,* 14, Com. Rich. Dacres, off St. Brieux |
| | ,, 22 | *Sans Culotte* ....... | 18 | Burnt by *Aimalle,* 32, Capt. Chas. Sydney Davers, W. Ind. |
| | Oct. 10 | *Superbe* .......... | 22 | Taken by *Vanguard,* 74, Capt. Simon Miller, W. Ind. |
| | ,, 10 | *Brutus* ........... | 10 | Taken by *Mermaid,* 32, and *Zebra,* 16, W. Ind. |
| | ,, 14 | *Républicain** ....... | 18 | Taken by *Mermaid,* 32, and *Zebra,* 16, W. Ind. |
| | ,, 15 | *Eveillé* ........... | 18 | Taken by Commod. Sir J. B. Warren, off Rochefort |
| | Nov. | *Droits du Peuple* ... | 36 | Wrecked off Trondhjem |
| | Dec. 1 | *Pandore* (**as *Pandour*) ...... | 14 | Taken by *Caroline,* 36, Capt. Wm. Luke, North Sea |
| 1796 | Mar. 9 | *Nemesis** .......... | 28 | Taken by *Egmond,* 74, Capt. John Sutton, and consorts, off Tunis |
| | ,, ,, | *Sardine** .......... | 22 | ,, ,, ,, ,, ,, ,, ,, |
| | ,, 10 | *Bonne Citoyenne** .. | 20 | Taken by *Phaeton,* 38, Capt. Hon. Robt. Stopford, Cape Finisterre |
| | ,, 10 | *Aspic,* cutter ....... | .. | Taken by the *Quebec,* St. George's Channel |
| | ,, 18 | *Etourdie* .......... | 16 | Burnt by *Diamond,* 38, Capt. Sir W. S. Smith, off Cape Fréhel. M (*Diamond, Liberty, Aristocrat*) |
| | ,, | *Favorite* .......... | 22 | Taken by *Alfred,* 74, Capt. Thos. Drury, off Cape Finisterre |
| | ,, | *Marsouin* ......... | 26 | Taken by *Beaulieu,* 44, Capt. Lancelot Skynner, W. Ind. |
| | ,, 20 | *Etoile,* armed storeship .... | 28 | Taken by Commod. Sir. J. B. Warren, coast of France |
| | | *Alerte,* ........... | 14 | Taken by *Cormorant,* 18, Com. Joseph Bingham, W. Ind. |
| | | *Mutine,* brig ....... | .. | Taken by frigates in the Bay |
| | Apr. 13 | *Unité** ........... | 36 | Taken by *Révolutionnaire,* 38, and consorts, coast of France |
| | ,, 15 | *Robuste* (**as *Scourge*) ...... | 22 | Taken by Commod. Sir. J. B. Warren, off the Saintes |
| | ,, 20 | *Unité* (**as *Surprise*) | 28 | Taken by *Inconstant,* 36, Capt. Thos. Fras. Fremantle, Medit. |

| Year | Date | French National Ship (*Added to the Royal Navy) | Guns | Fate — *M* Medals granted in 1849, in pursuance of *Gazette* notice of June 1st, 1847 — **M** Flag-Officers' and Captain's gold medals |
|------|------|--------------------------------------------------|------|------------------------------------------------------------------------------------------------------------------------------------------|
| | ,, 21 | *Perçante* (*as *Jamaica*) ...... | 26 | Taken by *Intrepid,* 64, Capt. Hon. Chas. Carpenter, W. Ind. |
| | ,, 22 | *Virginie** ......... | 40 | Taken by squadron of Sir E. Pellew, off the Lizard. *(Indefatigable)* **M** |
| | ,, | *Aurore* ........... | 10 | Taken by *Cleopatra,* 32, Capt. Chas. Rowley, America |
| | ,, 27 | *Ecureuil,* lugger .... | 18 | Burnt by boats of *Niger,* 32, Capt. E. J. Foote, off Penmarck |
| | May 2 | *Abeille,* cutter ...... | 14 | Taken by *Dryad,* 36, Com. John King Pulling (actg.), off Lizard |
| | ,, 4 | *Volcan* ........... | 12 | Taken by *Spencer,* 18, Com. And. Fitzherbert Evans, off Bermuda |
| | ,, 7 | *Cygne,* cutter ...... | 14 | Taken by *Doris,* 36, Capt. Hon. Chas. Jones, off Scilly |
| | ,, 8 | *Athénienne** ....... | 14 | Taken by *Albacore,* 16, Com. Robt. Winthrop, off Barbados |
| | ,, 31 | *Genie,* ketch ....... | 3 | Taken by Commod. H. Nelson, at Oneglia |
| | ,, ,, | *No. 12,* g.b. ........ | 1 | ,, ,, ,, ,, ,, ,, |
| | June 8 | *Tribune* ........... | 36 | Taken by *Unicorn,* 32, Capt. Thos. Williams (4), Ireland |
| | ,, 8 | *Tamise* (*as *Thames)* | 32 | (ex Brit. *Thames).* Retaken by *Sta. Margarita,* 36, Capt. T. Byam Martin, Ireland |
| | ,, 10 | *Utile* ............. | 24 | Taken by *Southampton,* 32, Capt. Jas. Macnamara (2), off Hyères **M** |
| | ,, 11 | *Truis Coulers,* brig .. | 10 | Taken by Commod. Sir E. Pellew, off Ushant |
| | ,, ,, | *Blonde,* brig ....... | 16 | Taken by Commod. Sir E. Pellew, off Ushant |
| | ,, 13 | *Proserpine* (*as *Amelia*) ....... | 40 | Taken by *Dryad,* 36, Capt. Lord Amelius Beauclerk, off C. Clear **M** |
| | ,, 22 | *Légère** .......... | 22 | Taken by *Apollo,* 36, and *Doris,* 36, off Scilly |
| | July 12 | *Renommée** ....... | 36 | Taken by *Alfred,* 74, Capt. Thos. Drury, off San Domingo |
| | Aug. 19 | *Alerte* ............. | 16 | Taken by *Carysfort,* 28, Capt. Thos. Alexander, E. Ind. |
| | ,, 22 | *Andromaque* ...... | 36 | Destroyed by Commod. Sir J. B. warren, near Arcachon |
| | ,, 28 | *Elisabeth* .......... | 36 | Taken by V.-Ad. Geo. Murray (2), N. Amer. |
| | Oct. 18 | *Eliza* ............. | 10 | Taken by *Fury,* 16, Com. Hy. Evans, W.I. |
| | Nov. 1 | *Cerf Volant* ........ | 18 | Taken by *Magicienne,* 32, Capt. Wm. Hy. Ricketts, off San Domingo |
| | ,, 13 | *Etonnant* .......... | 18 | Destroyed by *Minerva,* 44, and *Melampus,* 36, off Barfleur |
| | ,, ,, | *Etna* (*as *Cormorant*) .... | 18 | Taken by *Melampus,* 36, and *Childers,* 14, coast of France |
| | ,, 27 | *Décius* ........... | 28 | Taken by *Lapwing,* 28, Capt. Robt. Barton, W. Ind. (destroyed Nov. 28th) |
| | ,, ,, | *Vaillant,* brig ...... | 4 | Destroyed by *Lapwing,* 28, Capt. Robt. Barton, W. Ind. |
| | Dec. 3 | *Africaine* ......... | 18 | Taken by *Quebec,* 32, Capt. John Cooke (2), off San Domingo |
| | ,, 10 | *Général Leveau* .... | 16 | Taken by *Mermaid,* 32, and *Resource,* 28, off San Domingo |
| | ,, 13 | *Vestale* ........... | 36 | Taken by *Terpishore,* 32, Capt. Rich. Bowen |

| Year | Date | French National Ship (*Added to the Royal Navy) | Guns | Fate M Medals granted in 1849, in pursuance of *Gazette* notice of June 1st, 1847 M Flag-Officers' and Captain's gold medals | |
|---|---|---|---|---|---|
| | ,, 16 | *Séduisant* .......... | 74 | Wrecked near Brest | |
| | ,, 30 | *Scévola* ........... | 44 | Foundered off Ireland | |
| | ,, ,, | *Impatiente* ........ | 44 | Wrecked near Mizen Head | |
| | ,, 31 | *Amaranthe** ....... | 14 | Taken by *Diamond*, 38, Capt. Sir R. J. Strachan, off Alderney | |
| | ,, | *Justine*, st. ship, en flûte .......... | 44 | Lost off Irish Coast | |
| 1797 | Jan. 5 | *Tortue** later *Ariane)* ....... | 40 | Taken by *Polyphemus*, 64, Capt. Geo. Lumsdaine, off Ireland | |
| | ,, 7 | *Ville de Lorient*, en flûte .......... | 36 | Taken by *Doris*, 36, *Unicorn*, 32, and *Druid*, 32, off Ireland | |
| | ,, 8 | *Suffren*, st. ship .... | 44 | Sunk by *Majestic*, 74, *Daedalus*, 32, and *Incendiary*, 14, off Ushant | |
| | ,, 10 | *Atalante** ......... | 16 | Taken by *Phoebe*, 36, Capt. Robt. Barlow, off Scilly | |
| | ,, 12 | *Allègre*, st. ship .... | .. | Taken by *Spitfire*, 16, Com. Michael Seymour (1), off Ushant | |
| | ,, 13 | *Droits de l'Homme* . | 74 | Wrecked in action with *Indefatigable* and *Amazon*, off Penmarck **M** | |
| | ,, | *Surveillante* ........ | 36 | Scuttled in Bantry Bay | |
| | Feb. 13 | A schooner ........ | 2 | Taken by *Matilda*, 28, Capt. Hy. Mitford, off Barbados | |
| | Mar. 9 | *Résistance* (*as *Fishguard*) ..... | 40 | Taken by *San Fiorenzo*, 44, and *Nymphe*, 36, off Brest | |
| | ,, ,, | *Constance** ........ | 22 | Taken by *San Fiorenzo*, 44, and *Nymphe*, 36, off Brest | **M** |
| | | *Modeste* .......... | 20 | Taken by *Fox*, 32, Capt. Pulteney Malcolm, off Vizagapatam | |
| | Apr. 17 | *Hermione* ......... | 36 | Destroyed by *Thunderer*, 74, and *Valiant*, 74, off San Domingo | |
| | May 13 | *Jalouse** .......... | 18 | Taken by *Vestal*, 28, Capt. Chas. White, North Sea. | |
| | ,, 29 | *Mutine** ........... | 14 | Cut out by boats of *Minerve* and *Lively* (Lieut. T. M. Hardy), Santa Cruz **M** | |
| | June 12 | *Harriette* .......... | 6 | Taken by *Aigle*, 32, Capt. Chas. Tyler, off Lisbon | |
| | July 17 | *Calliope* .......... | 36 | Destroyed by Commod. Sir J. B. Warren, coast of France | |
| | ,, ,, | *Freedom*, en flûte ... | 8 | Taken and burnt by Commod. Sir J. B. Warren, coast of France | |
| | Aug. 11 | A ship corvette ..... | 22 | Taken and bilged ,, ,, ,, | |
| | ,, ,, | A brig, g.v. ........ | 12 | Taken and sunk ,, ,, ,, | |
| | ,, 20 | *Gaïeté** .......... | 20 | Taken by *Arethusa*, 38, Capt. Thos. Wolley, Atlantic | |
| | ,, 23 | *Egalité*, chasse-marée | 8 | Taken by Commod. Sir J. B. Warren, coast of France | |
| | ,, 27 | *Petit Diable*, cutter . | 18 | Taken and bilged by Commod. J. B. Warren, coast of France | |
| | Sept. 10 | *Espoir** .......... | 16 | Taken by *Thalia*, 36, Capt. Lord Hy. Paulet, Medit. | |
| | Oct. 9 | *Decouverte* ....... | 18 | Taken by *Unité*, 36, Capt. Chas. Rowley, Channel | |
| | ,, 14 | *Ranger** .......... | 14 | Taken by *Indefatigable*, 44, Capt. Sir Ed. Pellew, off Tenerife; retaken | |
| | Nov. 6 | *Venturier* (ex *Ranger*)* ....... | 14 | Retaken by *Galatea*, 32, Capt. Geo. Byng | |
| | ,, 12 | *Expervier* .......... | 16 | Taken by *Cerberus*, 32, Capt. John Drew (2), off Ireland | |
| | ,, | *Méduse* .......... | 40 | Foundered on passage from America | |

| Year | Date | French National Ship (*Added to the Royal Navy) | Guns | Fate M Medals granted in 1849, in pursuance of *Gazette* notice of June 1st, 1847 M Flag-Officers' and Captains' gold medals |
|---|---|---|---|---|
| | Dec. 22 | Néréide* .......... | 36 | Taken by *Phoebe*, 36, Capt. Robt. Barlow, off Scilly *M* |
| | ,,  28 | Daphné* as 20 ..... | 30 | Retaken by *Anson*, 44, Capt. P. C. Durham, B. of Biscay |
| | ,, | République Triomphante ....... | 14 | Taken by *Severn*, 44, and *Pelican*, 18, W. Ind. |
| 1798 | Jan.  5 | Chéri ............. | 26 | Taken by *Pomone*, 44, Capt. Robt. Carthew Reynolds, B. of Biscay, and foundered |
| | ,,  16 | Désirée ............ | 6 | Taken by pinnace (Lt. Saml. Pym) of *Babet*, 20, W. Ind. |
| | Feb. 16 | Scipion ........... | 20 | Taken by *Alfred*, 74, Capt. Thos. Totty, Guadeloupe |
| | ,,  26 | Souris, chasse-marée | 16 | Taken by *Badger*, 4, Lt. Chas. Papps Price, and consorts, St. Marcou |
| | Apr.  5 | Sainte Famille, chasse-marée ....... | .. | Taken by *Impéteux*, 78, and *Sylph*, 16 |
| | ,,  19 | Arrogante, g.v.* .... | 6 | Taken by *Jason*, 36, Capt. Chas. Stirling (1), off Brest |
| | ,,  21 | Hercule* .......... | 74 | Taken by *Mars*, 74, Capt. Alex. Hood, off Bec du Raz *M* |
| | May  1 | Quatorze Juillet .... | 74 | Accidentally burnt at Lorient |
| | ,,  7 | Flibustier .......... | .. | Taken during attack on St. Marcou. *(Badger, Sandfly)* *M* |
| | ,,  13 | Mondovi* ......... | 16 | Cut out by boats (Lt. Wm. Russell) of *Flora*, 36, at Cerigo |
| | ,,  31 | Confiante ......... | 36 | Run ashore and destroyed by *Hydra*, 36, Capt. Sir Fras. Laforey, near Le Hâvre |
| | June 22 | Corcyre ........... | 16 | Taken by *Flora*, 32, Capt. Robt. Gambier Middleton, off Sicily |
| | ,,  ,, | Egalité ............ | 20 | Destroyed by *Aurora*, 28, Capt. Hy. Digby, B. of Biscay |
| | ,,  27 | Sensible .......... | 36 | Taken by *Seahorse*, 36, Capt. E. J. Foote, Medit. |
| | ,,  30 | Seine* ............ | 40 | Taken by *Jason*, 36, Capt. Chas. Stirling (1), and *Pique*, 36, Capt. David Milne |
| | Aug.  1 | Orient ............ | 120 | Burnt in action with R.-Ad. Sir H. Nelson |
| | ,,  ,, | Franklin (*as Canopus) ...... | 80 | Taken in Aboukir Bay by R.-Ad. Sir. H. Nelson |
| | ,,  ,, | Tonnant* ......... | 80 | ,,  ,,  ,,  ,,  ,,  ,,  ,, |
| | ,,  ,, | Timoléon .......... | 74 | Destroyed by her crew after action with R.-Ad. Sir H. Nelson *MM* |
| | Aug.  1 | Guerrier .......... | 74 | Taken in Aboukir Bay by R.-Ad. Sir H. Nelson and burnt |
| | ,,  ,, | Spartiate* ......... | 74 | Taken in Aboukir Bay by R.-Ad. Sir H. Nelson |
| | ,,  ,, | Conquérant* ....... | 74 | ,,  ,,  ,, |
| | ,,  ,, | Aquilon (*as Aboukir) ...... | 74 | ,,  ,,  ,, |
| | ,,  ,, | Heureux .......... | 74 | ,,  ,,  ,,  and burnt |
| | ,,  ,, | Mercure .......... | 74 | ,,  ,,  ,,  ,,  ,, |
| | ,,  ,, | Souverain Peuple (*as Guerrier) ...... | 74 | ,,  ,,  ,, |
| | ,,  ,, | Artemise .......... | 36 | Burst after action with R.-Ad. Sir H. Nelson |
| | ,,  ,, | Sérieuse ........... | 36 | Sunk in action with R.-Ad. Sir H. Nelson |
| | ,,  3 | Aventurière ....... | 14 | Cut out by boats (Lt. Thos. Geo. Shortland) of *Melpomène* and *Childers*, Corigou |

| Year | Date | French National Ship (*Added to the Royal Navy) | Guns | Fate M Medals granted in 1849, in pursuance of *Gazette* notice of June 1st, 1847 M Flag-Officers' and Captain's gold medals |
|------|------|------|------|------|
| | '' 7 | *Vaillante* (*as *Danaë*) | 20 | Taken by *Indefatigable,* 44, Capt. Sir E. Pellew, B. of Biscay |
| | '' '' | *Liguria* (Genoese) ... | 26 | Taken by *Espoir,* 16, Com. Loftus Otway Bland, Medit. **M** |
| | '' 11 | *Fortune* (*as 10) .... | 18 | Taken by *Swiftsure,* 74, Capt. Benj. Hallowell, coast of Egypt; retaken May 8th, 1799 |
| | '' 12 | *Neptune* ........... | 20 | Taken by *Hazard,* 16, Com. Wm. Butterfield, coast of Ireland |
| | '' 22 | *Légère,* g.v. ........ | 6 | Taken by *Alcmene,* 32, Capt. Geo. Hope (1), off Alexandria |
| | '' 24 | *Décade** ........... | 36 | Taken by *Magnanime,* 44, and *Naiad,* 38, off Finisterre |
| | '' 25 | *Torride,** ketch ..... | 7 | Taken by boats (Lt. Wm. Debusk) of *Goliath,* off Aboukir; retaken Mar. 18th, 1799 |
| | Sept. 1 | *Réunion* ........... | 6 | Taken by *Oiseau,* 36, Capt. Chas. Brisbane, E. Ind. |
| | '' 2 | *Anémone,* g.v. ..... | 4 | Destroyed off Damietta by *Seahorse,* 38, and *Emerald,* 36 |
| | Oct. 12 | *Hoche* (*as *Donegal*) | 74 | Taken by Commod. Sir. J. B. Warren, coast of Ireland |
| | '' '' | *Embuscade* (*as *Ambuscade*) ... | 36 | '' '' '' '' |
| | '' '' | *Coquille* .......... | 36 | '' '' '' '' |
| | '' '' | *Bellone* (*as *Proserpine*) .... | 36 | '' '' '' '' |
| | '' 13 | *Résolue** ......... | 36 | Taken by *Melampus,* 36, Capt. Graham Moore, coast of Ireland |
| | '' 18 | *Loire** ........... | 40 | Taken by *Anson,* 44, Capt. P. C. Durham, and *Kangaroo,* 18, Com. Ed. Brace, Ireland |
| | '' 20 | *Immortalité* ....... | 40 | Taken by *Fishguard,* 38, Capt. Thos. Byam Martin, off Brest **M** |
| | '' 29 | *Fulminante,* cutter .. | 8 | Taken by *Espoir,* 16, Capt. Loftus Otway Bland, Medit. |
| | Nov.17 | *Fouine,* lugger ..... | 8 | Taken by *Sylph,* 16, Com. John Chambers White, off Brest |
| | '' 20 | *Hirondelle* ........ | 20 | Taken by *Phaeton, Ambuscade,* and *Stag,* Channel |
| | Dec. 28 | *Wilding,* armed transport ......... | 14 | Taken by *Spitfire,* 20, Com. Michael Seymour, B. of Biscay |
| 1799 | Feb. 9 | *Prudente* ......... | 36 | Taken by *Daedalus,* 32, Capt. Hy. Lidgbird Ball, Cape of Good Hope |
| | '' 28 | *Forte** ........... | 44 | Taken by *Sibylle,* 44, Capt. Edward Cooke, Bengal **M** |
| | Mar. 1 | *Marianne* ......... | 4 | Taken by Commod. Sir W. S. Smith, coast of Syria |
| | '' 3 | *Leander** ......... | 50 | Taken by Russians and Turks at Corfu; restored to Brit. |
| | '' '' | *Brune* ............ | 28 | Taken by Russians and Turks at Corfu |
| | '' 18 | *Hirondelle* ........ | 16 | Taken by *Telegraph,* 16, Lt. Jas. And. Worth, off Isle Bas **M** |
| | '' '' | *Négresse** ........ | 6 | Taken by Commod. Sir W. S. Smith, coast of Syria |
| | '' '' | *Foudre* ........... | 8 | '' '' '' '' |
| | '' '' | *Dangereuse** ...... | 6 | '' '' '' |
| | '' '' | *Marie Rose* ....... | 4 | '' '' '' |
| | '' '' | *Dame de Grâce** .... | 4 | '' '' '' '' |

(The Oct. 12–13 group of four ships — *Hoche, Embuscade, Coquille, Bellone* — are braced together with **M**)

| Year | Date | French National Ship (*Added to the Royal Navy) | Guns | Fate M Medals granted in 1849, in pursuance of Gazette notice of June 1st, 1847 M Flag-Officers' and Captain's gold medals |
|------|------|------|------|------|
| | ,, ,, | *Deux Frères* ........ | 4 | ,, ,, ,, ,, |
| | ,, ,, | *Torride* .......... | 2 | ,, ,, ,, ,, |
| | | *Courier* .......... | 16 | Taken by *Zealous,* 74, Capt. Saml. Hood (2), Medit. |
| | Apr. 4 | *Sans Quartier* ...... | 14 | Taken by *Danaë,* 20, Capt. Lord Proby, coast of France |
| | ,, 27 | *Rebecca,* chasse-marée ....... | 16 | Taken by *Black Joke,* 10, Lt. Jas, Nicholson, off Ushant |
| | ,, | A corvette ........ | 16 | Taken by *Lion,* 64, Capt. Manley Dixon, Medit. |
| | June 18 | *Junon* (*as *Princess Charlotte)* ......... | 38 | Taken by squadron under Capt. John Markham, Medit. |
| | ,, ,, | *Alceste** .......... | 36 | ,, ,, ,, ,, |
| | ,, ,, | *Courageuse** ....... | 36 | ,, ,, ,, ,, |
| | ,, ,, | *Salamine* (*as 16) ... | 18 | ,, ,, ,, |
| | ,, ,, | *Alerte* (*as *Minorca)* | 14 | ,, ,, ,, ,, |
| | Aug. 20 | *Vestale* ........... | 36 | Taken by *Clyde,* 36, Capt. Chas. Cunningham, mouth of Garonne |
| | ,, ,, | *Hussard* (*as *Surinam)* ...... | 18 | Taken by V.-Ad. Lord Hugh Seymour, Surinam |
| | ,, 26 | *Républicaine* ....... | 28 | Taken by *Tamer,* 32, Capt. Thos. Western, off Surinam |
| | Sept. 13 | *St. Jacques* ........ | 6 | Taken by *Triton,* 32, Capt. John Gore (2), off Lorient |
| | Oct. 10 | *Aréthuse* (*as *Raven)* | 18 | Taken by *Excellent,* 74, Capt. Hon. Robt. Stopford, off Lorient |
| | ,, 12 | *Iphigenie* .......... | 24 | Blown up in action with *Trincomale,* 16, Com. John Rowe, Red Sea |
| | Nov. 10 | *Charente* .......... | 36 | Wrecked off Lorient |
| | Nov. 22 | *Egyptienne,* en flûte, 44 ....... | 20 | Taken by *Solebay,* 32, Capt. Steph. Poyntz, off San Domingo |
| | ,, ,, | *Eole* (*as *Nimrod)* .. | 16 | ,, ,, ,, ,, |
| | ,, ,, | *Lévrier* ............ | 12 | ,, ,, ,, ,, |
| | ,, ,, | *Vengeur* (ex Brit. *Charlotte)* ......... | 8 | ,, ,, ,, ,, |
| | Dec. 11 | *Preneuse* .......... | 36 | Destroyed by boats (Lt. Ed. Grey) of *Tremendous* and *Adamant,* off Port Louis |
| 1800 | Jan. 7 | *Brule Gueule* ....... | 20 | Wrecked off Brest |
| | Feb. 6 | *Pallast* (*as *Pique)* .. | 38 | Taken by *Loire, Danaë,* and consorts, coast of France *(Fairy, Harpy)* M |
| | ,, 9 | A polacre (Genoese) | 14 | Driven ashore and destroyed by *Pearl,* 32, Capt. Sam. Jas. Ballard, Medit. |
| | ,, 10 | *Vedette* .......... | 14 | Taken by *Triton,* 32. Capt. John Gore (2), coast of France |
| | ,, 18 | *Généreux** ........ | 74 | Taken by R.-Ad. Lord Nelson, Medit. |
| | ,, ,, | *Ville de Marseille,* st. ship ............ | .. | ,, ,, ,, ,, |
| | ,, 19 | No. 57, g.v. ........ | 1 | Taken by *Aristocrat,* 18, Lt. Corbet Jas. d'Auvergne, C. Fréhel |
| | Mar. 21 | *Ligurienne* ......... | 16 | Taken by *Petrel,* 16, Com. Fras. Wm. Austen (1), near Marseilles M |
| | ,, 30 | *Guillaume Tell* (*as *Malta)* ........ | 80 | Taken by *Lion,* 64, *Foudroyant,* 80, and *Penelope,* 36, Medit. *(Penelope, Vincejo)* M |
| | Apr. 13 | *Diligente* .......... | 6 | Taken by cutter (Master Buckley) of *Calypso,* 16, W. Ind. |
| | ,, | *Neptune,* schooner .. | 4 | Taken by *Mayflower,* privateer, Jas. Le Blair, coast of France |
| | May 5 | *Dragon* ........... | 14 | Taken by *Cambrian,* 40, and *Fishguard,* 44, Channel |

| Year | Date | French National Ship (*Added to the Royal Navy) | Guns | Fate M Medals granted in 1849, in pursuance of *Gazette* notice of June 1st, 1847 M Flag-Officers' and Captain's gold medals |
|------|------|------|------|------|
| | ,, 20 | *Prima*, galley ...... | 2 | Taken by boats under Com. Philip Beaver, Genoa |
| | ,, 31 | *Légère*, lugger ...... | 3 | Taken by *Netley*, 16, Lt. Fras. Godolphin Bond, Medit. |
| | June 1 | *Cruelle** .......... | 16 | Taken by *Mermaid*, 32, Capt. Robt. Dudley Oliver, off Toulon |
| | ,, 6 | *Insolente* ......... | 18 | Burnt by boats (Lt. John Pilfold) of *Impétueux*, 78, B. of Biscay |
| | ,, 11 | *Nochette*, g.b. ..... | 2 | Taken by boats of squadron of Sir. J. B. Warren, off Penmarck |
| | ,, ,, | A chasse-marée ..... | 10 | ,, ,, ,, ,, |
| | ,, ,, | A chasse-marée ..... | 6 | ,, ,, ,, ,, |
| | ,, | *Diligente* .......... | 12 | Taken by *Crescent*, 36, Capt. Wm. Granville Lobb, W. Ind. |
| | ,, 17 | *Revanche* .......... | 4 | Taken by *Phoenix*, 36, Capt. Laurence Wm. Halsted, Medit. |
| | July 2 | *Thérèse* .......... | 20 | Taken and burnt by boats (Lt. Hy. Burke) of *Renown*, *Fishguard*, and *Defence*, Bourgneuf Bay |
| | ,, ,, | A lugger .......... | 12 | ,, ,, ,, ,, |
| | ,, ,, | A gunboat ......... | 6 | ,, ,, ,, ,, |
| | ,, ,, | A gunboat ......... | 6 | ,, ,, ,, ,, |
| | ,, ,, | A cutter .......... | 6 | ,, ,, ,, ,, |
| | ,, 8 | *Désirée* .......... | 38 | Taken by *Dart*, 30, Com. Pat. Campbell, Dunquerque road **M** |
| | ,, 29 | *Cerbère* .......... | 7 | Cut out by boat (Lt. Jeremiah Coghlan, act., of *Viper*), of *Impetueux*, Port Louis |
| | ,, | *Boudeuse* .......... | .. | Destroyed to provide fuel, Valetta |
| | Aug. 5 | *Concorde* ........ | 40 | Taken by *Belliqueux*, 64, Capt. Rowley Bulteel, and consorts, off Rio |
| | ,, ,, | *Médée* .......... | 36 | Taken by Indiamen *Bombay Castle* and *Exeter*, off Rio |
| | ,, 24 | *Diane* (*as *Niobe*) ... | 40 | Taken by *Northumberland*, *Généreux*, and *Success*, off Malta |
| | ,, 25 | *Vengeance* ......... | 40 | Taken by *Seine*, 38, Capt. David Milne, in Mona Passage **M** |
| | Sept. 1 | *Capricieuse* ........ | 6 | Taken by *Termagant*, 18, Com. Wm. Skipsey, off Corsica |
| | ,, 4 | *Athénien** (Maltese) | 64 | Taken at the surrender of Valetta |
| | ,, ,, | *Dégo* (Maltese) ..... | 64 | ,, ,, ,, |
| | ,, ,, | *Cartagénoise* ....... | 36 | ,, ,, ,, |
| | Oct. 8 | *Quid pro Quo* ...... | 8 | Taken by *Gipsy*, 10, Lt. Coryndon Boger, off Guadeloupe |
| | ,, 22 | *Vénus* .......... | 28 | Taken by *Indefatigable*, 44, and *Fishguard*, 44, off Portugal |
| | Nov. 17 | *Réolaise* .......... | 20 | Driven ashore by *Nile*, 16, Lt. Geo. Argles, and burnt by boats (Lt. Wm. Hennah) of squadron |
| 1801 | Jan. 3 | *Sénégal* .......... | 18 | Cut out and destroyed by boats (Lt. Thos. Dick), of *Melpomène*, 38, Sénégal. |
| | , 18 | *Aurore** .......... | 16 | Taken by *Thames*, 32, Capt. Wm. Lukin, Channel |
| | ,, ,, | *Eclair* (*as 12) ...... | 4 | Cut out by *Garland*, tender, Lt. Kenneth Mackenzie, Guadeloupe |
| | ,, 20 | *Sans Pareille* ....... | 20 | Taken by *Mercury*, 28, Capt. Thos. Rogers, off Sardinia |
| | ,, 28 | *Dédaigneuse** ...... | 36 | Taken by *Oiseau*, 36, *Sirius*, 36, and *Amethyst*, 36, off Portugal |
| | ,, 29 | *Curieuse* .......... | 18 | Taken by *Bordelais*, 24, Capt. Thos. Manby, off Barbados; foundered |

231

| Year | Date | French National Ship (*Added to the Royal Navy) | Guns | Fate — M Medals granted in 1849, in pursuance of *Gazette* notice of June 1st, 1847 — M Flag-Officers' and Captain's gold medals |
|---|---|---|---|---|
| | '' | *Bombarde*, g.v. .... | 1 | Taken by *Boadicea*, 38, Capt. Rich. Goodwin Keats, off Brest |
| | Feb. 16 | *Furieuse*, xebec ..... | 6 | Taken by *Minorca*, 16, Com. Geo. Miller, Medit. |
| | '' 19 | Africaine* ......... | 40 | Taken by *Phoebe*, 36, Capt. Robt. Barlow, Medit. M |
| | '' 29 | *Arc*, cutter ......... | .. | Taken by boats of *Excellent*, 74, Quiberon Bay |
| | Apr. 9 | *Général Brune* ..... | 14 | Taken by *Amethyst*, 36, Capt. John Cooke (1), Channel |
| | | *Laurette* .......... | 26 | Taken by *Arrogant*, 74, Capt. Edw. Oliver Osborne, E. Ind. |
| | May 27 | *Corvesse* (?) disp. vsl. | 1 | Taken by *Corso*, 18, Com. Wm. Ricketts, Medit. |
| | May 28 | *Egypte* ............ | 16 | Taken by *Heureux*, 24, Capt. Loftus Otway Bland, off Barbados |
| | June 23 | *Tigre* (suspected pirate) ... | 8 | Taken by boats of *Mercury*, 28, and *Corso*, 18, G. of Venice |
| | July 12 | *St. Antoine* ........ | 74 | Taken by R.-Ad. Sir James Saumarez, off Gibraltar |
| | '' 22 | *Chevette* .......... | 20 | Cut out by boats (Lt. Keith Maxwell) of *Beaulieu*, *Doris*, *Uranie*, and *Robust*, near Brest |
| | '' 25 | A corvette ......... | 10 | Taken by *Déterminée*, 24, Capt. John Clarke Searle, off Alexandria |
| | Aug. 3 | *Carrère* * .......... | 38 | Taken by *Pomone*, 40, Capt. Ed. Leveson Gower. etc., off Elba |
| | '' 10 | *Eveillé*, lugger ...... | 2 | Taken by cutter (Mid. Fras. Smith) of *Atalante*, 16, Quiberon Bay |
| | '' 19 | *Chiffone* * ......... | 36 | Taken by *Sibylle*, 38, Capt. Chas. Adam, off Seychelles |
| | '' 21 | 4 howitzer-boats each | 1 | Taken or destroyed by boats (Lt. James John Charles Agassiz) of Capt. Jonas Rose's squadron, near Etaples |
| | Sept. 2 | *Succès* (*as *Success*) | 32 | Retaken by *Pomone*, 44, *Phoenix*, 36, and *Minerve*, 44, off Vado |
| | '' '' | *Bravoure* .......... | 36 | Driven ashore     '',      '',      '' |
| | '' '' | *Causse* ............ | 64 | Taken at capitulation of Alexandria; delivered to Turkey |
| | '' '' | *Egyptienne* * ....... | 44 | Taken at capitulation of Alexandria; retained |
| | '' '' | *Justice* ............ | 40 | Taken at capitulation of Alexandria; delivered to Turkey |
| | '' '' | *Régénérée* * ........ | 36 | Taken at capitulation of Alexandria; retained |
| | '' '' | Unknown (Venetian) | 32 | Taken at capitulation of Alexandria; delivered to Turkey |
| | '' '' | Unknown (Venetian) | 32 | Taken at capitulation of Alexandria; retained |
| | '' 7 | *Flèche* ............ | 18 | Sank after capture by *Victor*, 18, Com. Geo. Ralph Collier, E. Ind. |
| | '' 16 | *Bulldog* * .......... | 18 | Retaken by *Champion*, 24, Capt. Lord Wm. Stuart, near Gallipoli |

| Year | Date | Ships of the Batavian Republic. (*Added to the Royal Navy) | Guns | Fate M Medals granted in 1849, in pursuance of *Gazette* notice of June 1st, 1847 M Flag-Officers' and Captains' gold medals |
|------|------|-----------|------|------|
| 1795 | Aug. 18 | *Willemstad* (*as *Princess*) ...... | 26 | Taken by V.-Ad. Sir G. K. Elphinstone, Simon's Bay |
| ,, | ,, | *Ster*, armed brig .... | 14 | ,,   ,,   ,,   ,, |
| ,, | 20 | *Brak* (*as *De Braak*) . | 14 | Detained by *Fortune*, 16, Com. Fras. Wooldridge, Falmouth |
| ,, | 22 | *Alliantie* (*as *Alliance*, 20) ... | 36 | Taken by *Stag*, *Réunion*, *Isis*, and *Vestal*, off Norway |
| ,, | 28 | *Komeet* (*as *Penguin*) ...... | 18 | Taken by *Unicorn*, 32, Capt. Thos. Williams (4), Irish station |
| | Oct. 22 | *Overijssel** ........ | 64 | Taken by *Polyphemus*, 64, Capt. Geo. Lumsdaine, Queenstown |
| | ,, | *Maria Louise* ...... | 14 | Taken by *Rattlesnake*, 16, Com. Edw. Ramage, C. of Good Hope |
| 1796 | Jan. | *Harlingen* (*as *Amboyna*) ..... | 10 | Taken by R.-Ad. Peter Rainier (1), E. Ind. |
| | Mar. | *Zefir* (*as *Eurus*) ... | 36 | Detained by *Andromeda*, *Ranger*, and *Kite*, Firth of Forth |
| | ,, 4 | *Zeeland* (*as *Zeeland*) ...... | 64 | Taken by V.-Ad. Rich Onslow, in Plymouth |
| ,, | ,, | *Brakel** .......... | 54 | ,,   ,,   ,,   ,, |
| ,, | ,, | *Tholen* (*as *Thulen*) . | 40 | ,,   ,,   ,,   ,, |
| ,, | ,, | *Meermin* (*as *Miermin*) ...... | 16 | ,,   ,,   ,,   ,, |
| ,, | ,, | *Pijl** ............. | 16 | ,,   ,,   ,,   ,, |
| ,, | ,, | *De Brak* .......... | .. | ,,   ,,   ,,   ,, |
| | Apr. 22 | *Vlugheid* .......... | 12 | Taken by Adm. Duncan, coast of Norway |
| | ,, 23 | *Thetis* ............ | 24 | Taken by Commod. Thos. Parr at Demerara |
| ,, | ,, | *Zeemeeuw* ........ | 12 | ,,   ,,   ,,   ,, |
| | May 12 | *Argo* (*as *Janus*) ... | 36 | Taken by *Phoenix*, 36, Capt. Lawrence Wm. Halsted, etc., N. Sea |
| ,, | ,, | *Echo* ............. | 12 | Driven ashore by *Pegasus*, 28, Capt. Ross Donnelly, Vriesland |
| ,, | ,, | *Gier* ............. | 12 | ,,   ,,   ,,   ,, |
| ,, | ,, | *Mercurius* (*as *Hermes*) ....... | 12 | Taken by *Sylph*, 16, Com. John Chambers White, off the Texel |
| | June 8 | *Jason* (*as *Proselyte*) | 36 | Brought into Greenock by mutinous crew |
| | July 6 | *Bataaf* ............ | 12 | Taken by *Roebuck*, 44, Com. Alex. Saunderson Burrowes, off Barbados |
| | Aug. 17 | *Dordrecht* (*as *Dordrecht*) .... | 64 | Surrendered to V.-Ad. Sir G. K. Elphinstone, Saldanha Bay |
| ,, | ,, | *Revolutie* (*as *Prince Frederick*) ......... | 64 | ,,   ,,   ,,   ,, |
| ,, | ,, | *Maarten Harpertzoon Tromp* (*as *Van Tromp*) .......... | 54 | ,,   ,,   ,,   ,, |
| ,, | ,, | *Castor* (*as *Saldanha*) | 44 | ,,   ,,   ,,   ,, |
| ,, | ,, | *Brave* (*as *Braave*) .. | 40 | ,,   ,,   ,,   ,, |
| ,, | ,, | *Bellona* (*as *Vindictive*) ..... | 24 | ,,   ,,   ,,   ,, |
| ,, | ,, | *Sirene* (*as *Laurel*) .. | 26 | ,,   ,,   ,,   ,, |
| ,, | ,, | *Havik* (*as *Havick*) | 18 | ,,   ,,   ,,   ,, |
| ,, | ,, | *Vrouw Maria* ...... | 16 | ,,   ,,   ,,   ,, |
| 1797 | Oct. 11 | *Vrijheid** ......... | 74 | Taken by Adm. Adam Duncan in the battle off Camperdown *M*M |

| Year | Date | Ships of the Batavian Republic. (*Added to the Royal Navy) | Guns | Fate — *M* Medals granted in 1849, in pursuance of *Gazette* notice of June 1st, 1847 **M** Flag-Officers' and Captains' gold medals | | | | |
|---|---|---|---|---|---|---|---|---|
| ,, | ,, | *Jupiter* (*as *Camperdown*) | 72 | ,, | ,, | ,, | ,, | } |
| ,, | ,, | *Haarlem** ......... | 68 | ,, | ,, | ,, | ,, | } |
| ,, | ,, | *Admiraal Tjerk Hiddes De Vries* (*as *Admiral Devries*) | 68 | ,, | ,, | ,, | ,, | } |
| ,, | ,, | *Gelijkheid** ........ | 68 | ,, | ,, | ,, | ,, | } |
| ,, | ,, | *Wassenaar* ........ | 64 | ,, | ,, | ,, | | } **MM** |
| ,, | ,, | *Hercules** (later *Delft*) ........ | 64 | ,, | ,, | ,, | | } |
| ,, | ,, | *Delft* ............. | 54 | ,, | ,, | ,, | sank | } |
| ,, | ,, | *Alkmaar** ......... | 56 | ,, | ,, | ,, | | } |
| ,, | ,, | *Monnikendam* ..... | 44 | ,, | ,, | ,, | lost | } |
| ,, | ,, | *Embuscade* ........ | 32 | ,, | ,, | ,, | retaken | } |
| ,, | ,, | *Galathèe* .......... | 18 | ,, | ,, | '' stranded and abandoned | | |
| | | *Yonge Frans* (?) .... | 10 | Taken by *Resistance,* 44, Capt. Edw. Pakenham, E. Ind. | | | | |
| | | *Yonge Lansier* (?) ... | 10 | ,, | ,, | ,, | ,, | |
| | | *Wakker* (?) ........ | 10 | ,, | ,, | ,, | ,, | |
| | | *Limbi* ............. | 8 | ,, | ,, | ,, | ,, | |
| | | *Ternate* .......... | 4 | ,, | ,, | ,, | ,, | |
| | | *Resource* (?) ....... | 6 | ,, | ,, | ,, | ,, | |
| | | *Juno* .............. | 4 | ,, | ,, | ,, | ,, | |
| 1798 | Oct. 24 | *Waakzaamheid** .... | 24 | Taken by *Sirius,* 36, Capt. Rich. King (2), North Sea | | | | |
| ,, | ,, | *Furie* (*as *Wilhelmina*) ... | 36 | ,, | ,, | ,, | ,, | |
| 1799 | Apr. 26 | *Helena* ............ | 8 | Taken by *Virginie,* 44, Capt. Geo. Astle, E. Ind. | | | | |
| ,, | ,, | *Helena* ............ | 12 | ,, | ,, | ,, | ,, | |
| ,, | ,, | *Brak* ............. | 12 | ,, | ,, | ,, | ,, | |
| | May 24 | A brig ............ | 6 | Taken by *Arrogant* and *Orpheus*, E. Ind. | | | | |
| | Aug.11 | *Crash** ............ | 12 | Retaken by *Pylades,* 16, Com. Adam Mackenzie, and consorts, off Groningen *M* | | | | |
| ,, | | A schuyt (*as *Undaunted*) .... | 2 | Taken by ,, ,, | | | | |
| ,, | 14 | *Weerwraak*, g.v. .... | 6 | Burnt by ,, ,, | | | | |
| ,, | 20 | *Kemphaan* (*as *Camphaan*) .... | 16 | Taken by V.-Ad. Lord Hugh Seymour, Surinam | | | | |
| ,, | 28 | *Verwachting* ....... | 64 | Taken by V.-Ad. Andrew Mitchell, Niewe Diep, Texel | | | | |
| ,, | ,, | *Broedershap* ....... | 54 | ,, | ,, | ,, | ,, | |
| ,, | ,, | *Hector* (*as *Pandour*) | 44 | ,, | ,, | ,, | ,, | |
| ,, | ,, | *Duif* .............. | 44 | ,, | ,, | ,, | ,, | |
| ,, | ,, | *Expeditie* ......... | 44 | ,, | ,, | ,, | ,, | |
| ,, | ,, | *Belle Antoinette* .... | 44 | ,, | ,, | ,, | ,, | |
| ,, | ,, | *Constitutie* ........ | 44 | ,, | ,, | ,, | ,, | |
| ,, | ,, | *Unie* .............. | 44 | ,, | ,, | ,, | ,, | |
| ,, | ,, | *Heldin** .......... | 28 | ,, | ,, | ,, | ,, | |
| ,, | ,, | *Minerva* (*as *Braak*) | 24 | ,, | ,, | ,, | ,, | |
| ,, | ,, | *Venus* (*as *Amaranthe*) .... | 24 | ,, | ,, | ,, | ,, | |
| ,, | ,, | *Valk* .............. | 24 | ,, | ,, | ,, | ,, | |
| ,, | ,, | *Alarm* ........... | 24 | ,, | ,, | ,, | ,, | |
| ,, | 30 | *Washington* (*as *Princess of Orange*) | 70 | Surrendered to V.-Ad. Andrew Mitchell, in the Vlieter, Texel | | | | |

| Year | Date | Ships of the Batavian Republic. (*Added to the Royal Navy) | Guns | Fate  *M* Medals granted in 1849, in pursuance of *Gazette* notice of June 1st, 1847  **M** Flag-Officers' and Captains' gold medals |
|---|---|---|---|---|
| " | " | *Gelderland* \* ....... | 64 | "         "         "         " |
| " | " | *Admiraal De Ruijter* (\*as *De Ruyter*) ..... | 64 | "         "         "         " |
| " | " | *Utrecht* .......... | 64 | "         "         "         " |
| " | " | *Cerberus* (\*as *Texel*) | 64 | "         "         "         " |
| " | " | *Leijden* \* ......... | 64 | "         "         "         " |
| " | " | *Beschermer* \* ....... | 56 | "         "         "         " |
| " | " | *Batavier* \* ......... | 56 | "         "         "         " |
| " | " | *Amphitrite* \* ....... | 44 | "         "         "         " |
| " | " | *Mars* (\*as *Vlicter*) rasée ............. | 44 | "         "         "         " |
| " | " | *Embuscade* \* ....... | 32 | "         "         "         " |
| " | " | *Galatie* \* .......... | 16 | "         "         "         " |
| | Sept. | *Valk* ............. | 20 | Taken by V.-Ad. Andrew Mitchell, Zuidjer Zee, but lost Nov. 10th, 1799 |
| | " 12 | *Draak* .......... | 24 | Taken by *Arrow*, 28, Com. Nath. Portlock, and *Wolverine*, 13, Com. Wm. Bolton (1), off Vlie. } *M* |
| | " " | *Gier* \* ............ | 14 | "         "         "         " |
| | " 15 | *Dolfijn* (\*as *Dolphin*) | 24 | Surrendered to |
| | Oct. 9 | *Lijnx* ............ | 12 | Taken by boats of *Circe*, 28, Capt. Robt. Winthrop, River Ems |
| | " " | *Perseus* .......... | 8 | "         "         "         " |
| | Oct. | 4 gunboats .... each | 4 | Cut out by boats of *Dart, Hasty, Defender, Cracker*, and *Isis*, coast of Holland |
| 1800 | Aug.23 | A brig (\*as *Admiral Rainier*) ... | 16 | Taken by *Daedalus, Centurion, Braave*, and *Sibylle*, E. Ind. |
| | Oct. 28 | 5 gunboats ......... | .. | Burnt by *Admiral Rainier*, 16, Lt. Wm. Hugh Dobbie (1), Carawang River |
| | " 30 | 3 gunboats ......... | .. | Taken "         "         "         " |

## D—SPANISH NAVY

| Year | Date | Ships of the Spanish Royal Navy. (*Added to the Royal Navy) | Guns | Fate  *M* Medals granted in 1849, in pursuance of *Gazette* notice of June 1st, 1847.  **M** Flag-Officers' and Captains' gold medals |
|---|---|---|---|---|
| 1796 | Sept.16 | *Princesa* .......... | 16 | Detained by *Seahorse*, 38, Capt. Geo. Oakes, off Corunna |
| | Oct. 13 | *Mahonesa* \* ........ | 34 | Taken by *Terpishore*, 32, Capt. Rich. Bowen, off Cape de Gata. *M* |
| | Nov. 2 | *San Pio* ........... | 18 | Taken by *Regulus*, 14, Capt. Wm. Carthew, Atlantic |
| | " 23 | *Galgo* ............ | 18 | Taken by *Alarm*, 32, Capt. Edw. Fellowes, off Grenada |
| | Dec. 2 | *Corso* \* ........... | 18 | Taken by *Southampton*, 32, Capt. Jas. Macnamara (2), off Monaco |
| | " 20 | *Santa Sabina* ....... | 40 | Taken by *Minerve*, 38, Capt. Geo.   *M* Cockburn, Medit.; retaken Dec. 21st, 1796 |
| 1797 | Feb. 14 | *Salvador del Mundo* \* | 112 | Taken by the fleet of Adm. Sir John Jervis, K.B., off C. St. Vincent   **M***M* |

| Year | Date | Ships of the Spanish Royal Navy. (*Added to the Royal Navy) | Guns | Fate. *M* Medals granted in 1849, in pursuance of *Gazette* notice of June 1st, 1847. **M** Flag-Officers' and Captains' gold medals |
|---|---|---|---|---|
| | ,, ,, | *San Josef** ......... | 112 | ,, ,, ,, ,, ⎫ |
| | ,, ,, | *San Nicolas** ....... | 80 | ,, ,, ,, ,, ⎬ **MM** |
| | " " | *San Ysidro** ....... | 80 | ,, ,, ,, ,, ⎭ |
| | ,, 17 | *San Vincente* ....... | 80 | Burnt to prevent capture by R.-Ad. Hy. Harvey (1), Trinidad |
| | ,, ,, | *Arrogante* ......... | 74 | ,, ,, ,, ,, |
| | ,, ,, | *Gallardo* .......... | 74 | ,, ,, ,, ,, |
| | ,, ,, | *Santa Cecilia* ....... | 34 | ,, ,, ,, ,, |
| | ,, ,, | *San Damaso** ...... | 74 | Taken by R.-Ad. Hy. Harvey (1), Trinidad |
| | Mar. 12 | *Los Magellanes* ..... | 4 | Taken by *Dover,* 44, Lt. Hy. Kent, coast of Portugal |
| | Apr. 26 | *Ninfa* (**as *Hamadryad*) ... | 34 | Taken by *Irresistible,* 74, Capt. Geo. Martin (2), Lisbon station |
| | ,, ,, | *Santa Elena* ........ | 34 | Destroyed by *Irresistible,* 74, Capt. Geo. Martin (2), near Cadiz |
| | May 24 | *Nuestra Senora del Rosario* (**as *Rosario*) | 20 | Taken by *Romulus,* 36, and *Mahonesa,* 34, off Cadiz |
| | June 21 | *San Francisco* ...... | 14 | Taken by *Santa Margarita,* 36, Capt. Geo. Parker, off Ireland |
| | Nov. 14 | *Bolador* .......... | 16 | Taken by *Majestic,* 74, Capt. Geo. Blagden Westcott, Lisbon station |
| 1798 | May | *San Antonio,* packet | 6 | Taken by *Endymion,* 44, Capt. Sir Thos. Williams (4), off Ireland |
| | ,, 8 | *Receviso* .......... | 6 | Taken by *Aurora,* 28, Capt. Hy. Digby, Lisbon station |
| | July 15 | *Santa Dorotea** .... | 34 | Taken by *Lion,* 64, Capt. Manley Dixon, off Cartagena *M* |
| | Sept. 16 | *Velosa Aragonesa,* en flûte .......... | 30 | Taken by *Aurora,* 28, Capt. Hy. Digby, off the Azores |
| | Nov. 13 | *Petrel* ............ | 16 | Retaken by *Argo,* 44, Capt. Jas. Bowen (1), Medit. |
| | ,, 15 | A brig on the stocks (**as *Port Mahon*) ... | .. | Taken at the capture of Minorca |
| | ,, ,, | 14 gunboats ........ | .. | ,, ,, ,, |
| | ,, 28 | *San Leon* .......... | 16 | Taken by *St. Dorotea, Stromboli, Perseus,* and *Bulldog,* Lisbon station |
| 1799 | Jan. 2 | *Valiente,* packet .... | 12 | Taken by *Cormorant,* 20, Capt. Lord Mark Robt. Kerr, off Malaga |
| | Feb. 6 | *Santa Teresa** ...... | 34 | Taken by *Argo,* 44, Capt. Jas. Bowen (1), off Majorca |
| | Feb. 22 | *Africa,* xebec ...... | 14 | Taken by *Espoir,* 16, Com. Jas. Sanders, Medit. |
| | Mar. 16 | *Guadalupe* ........ | 34 | Driven ashore by *Centaur,* 74, and *Cormorant,* 20, Medit. |
| | ,, | *Urca Cargadora* .... | 12 | Burnt by *Prompte,* 20, Capt. Thos. Dundas, W. Ind. |
| | ,, 19 | *Vincejo** .......... | 18 | Taken by *Cormorant,* 20, Capt. Lord Mark Robt. Kerr, Medit. |
| | ,, 24 | *Golondrina,* packet | 4 | Taken by *Mermaid,* 32, and *Sylph,* 14, off Corunna |
| | May | *Pájaro,* packet ..... | 4 | Taken by *Alarm,* 32, Capt. Robt. Rolles, G. of Florida |
| | June 23 | *San Antonio* ....... | 14 | Taken by *Terpishore,* 32, Capt. Wm. Hall Gage, Medit. |
| | July | *Feliz* ............. | 14 | Taken by *Alarm,* Capt. Robt. Rolles, W. Ind. |
| | ,, | *Sandoval* (?) ....... | 4 | Taken by *York,* 64, and consorts, W. Ind. |

| Year | Date | Ships of the Spanish Royal Navy. (*Added to the Royal Navy) | Guns | Fate M Medals granted in 1849, in pursuance of *Gazette* notice of June 1st, 1847. M Flag-Officers' and Captains' gold medals |
|---|---|---|---|---|
| | Aug. 6 | *Infanta Amalia* (*as *Porpoise)* | 12 | Taken by *Argo,* 44, Capt. Jas. Bowen (1), coast of Portugal |
| | Sept. | A gunboat | 2 | Taken by *Mayflower,* privateer, Medit. |
| | ,, | A packet | 8 | ,,    ,,    ,, |
| | Oct. 17 | *Thetis* | 34 | Taken by *Ethalion,* 38, Capt. Jas. Young (2), and consorts, off Ferrol |
| | ,, 18 | *Santa Brigida* | 34 | Taken by *Naiad,* 38, *Alcmene,* 32, and *Triton,* 32, off C. Finisterre |
| | Oct. 25 | *Hermione* (*as *Retribution,* 32) | 34 | Cut out of Puerto Cabello by boats of *Surprise,* 32, Capt. Edw. Hamilton **MM** |
| | Nov. 15 | *Galgo** | 16 | Taken by *Crescent,* 36, Capt. Wm. Granville Lobb, Atlantic |
| 1800 | Jan. 26 | *N.S. del Carmen* | 16 | Taken by *Penelope,* 36, Capt. Hon. Hy. Blackwood, Medit. |
| | Feb. | *Cuervo* | 4 | Taken by *Alarm,* 32, Capt. Robt. Rolles, W. Ind. |
| | Apr. 7 | *Carmen** (as 36) | 34 | Taken by R.-Ad. John Thos. Duckworth, off Cadiz |
| | ,, ,, | *Florentina** (as 36) | 34 | ,,    ,,    ,,    ,, |
| | June 22 | *Cortez* | 4 | Taken by *Flora,* 36, Capt. Robt. Gambier Middleton, Lisbon station |
| | | *N.S. del Carmen,* felucca | 2 | Destroyed by *Bonetta,* 18, Com. Hy. Vansittart, W. Ind. |
| | ,, 29 | *Gibraltar,* g.b. | 10 | Taken by *Anson,* 44, Capt. Phil. Calderwood Durham off Gibraltar |
| | ,, ,, | *Salvador,* g.b. | 10 | ,,    ,,    ,,    ,, |
| | | A gunboat | 2 | Taken by *Rattler,* 16, Com. John Mathias Spread, W. Ind. |
| | July 27 | *Cantabro* | 18 | Taken by *Apollo,* 36, Capt. Peter Halkett, off Havana |
| | Aug. 20 | *Veloz* | 4 | Taken by *Clyde,* 38, Capt. Chas. Cunningham, Channel |
| | Sept. 3 | *Concepción* (alias *Esmeralda)* | 22 | Cut out by boats (Com. Jas. Hillyar) of *Minotaur,* 74, and *Niger,* 32, Barcelona |
| | ,, ,, | *Paz* | 22 | ,,    ,,    ,,    ,, |
| | ,, 30 | *Vivo* | 14 | Taken by *Fishguard,* 41, Capt. Thos. Byam Martin, coast of Spain |
| | Oct. 27 | *San Josef,* polacca | 8 | Cut out by boats (Lt. Fras. Beaufort) of *Phaeton,* 38, near Malaga **M** |
| | Nov. 10 | *Resolución* | 18 | Taken and destroyed by *Apollo,* 36, Capt. Peter Halkett, G. of Mexico |
| 1801 | Jan. 6 | *Reina Luisa* | 2 | Taken by *Hind,* 28, Capt. Thos. Larcom, off Jamaica |
| | May 6 | *Gamo,* xebec | 30 | Taken by *Speedy,* 14, Com. Lord Cochrane, near Barcelona |
| | ,, 16 | *Alcudia* | .. | Cut out by boats of *Naiad,* 38, and *Phaeton,* 38, near Pontevedra |
| | ,, ,, | *Raposo* | .. | ,,    ,,    ,,    ,, |
| | June 8 | *Duides,* cutter | 8 | Taken by *Constance,* 24, Capt. Zachary Mudge, off Vigo |
| | ,, 9 | A xebec | 20 | Sunk in action by *Kangaroo,* 18, and *Speedy,* 14, under a battery, Oropesa |
| | ,, ,, | 2 gunboats | .. | ,,    ,,    ,,    ,, |
| | July 5 | 5 gunboats | .. | Sunk in action by R.-Ad. Sir Jas. Saumarez, Algeciras |
| | ,, 12 | *Real Carlos* | 112 | Burnt in action with R.-Ad. Sir Jas. Saumarez, S. of Gibraltar |

The last two entries are braced together with **M**.

| Year | Date | Ships of the Spanish Royal Navy. (*Added to the Royal Navy) | Guns | Fate **M** Medals granted in 1849, in pursuance of *Gazette* notice of June 1st, 1847. **M** Flag-Officers' and Captains' gold medals |
|------|------|------|------|------|
| ,, | ,, | *San Hermenegildo* .. | 112 | ,,  ,,  ,,  ,, ⎫ |
| ,, | ,, | *Perla* ............ | 24 | Sunk after action  ,,  ,, ⎬ **M** |
| | Aug.20 | *Neptuno* (pierced for 20) ........... | .. | Taken by boats of *Fishguard,* 44, *Diamond,* 38, and *Boadicea,* 38, Corunna ⎭ |
| ,, | ,, | A gunboat ........ | 1 | ,,  ,,  ,,  ,, |
| | Sept.24 | *Limeño* .......... | 18 | Taken by *Chance,* privateer, 16, coast of Peru |

## DANISH NAVY

| Year | Date | Ships of the Danish Royal Navy (*Added to the Royal Navy) | Guns | Fate **M** Medals granted in 1849, in pursuance of *Gazette* notice of June 1st, 1847 |
|------|------|------|------|------|
| 1801 | Apr. 2 | *Sjoelland* ......... | 74 | Taken and burnt by V.-Ad. Lord Nelson, Copenhagen  ,,  ,,  ,, ⎫ |
| ,, | ,, | *Holsteen* * ........ | 60 | Taken by  ,,  ,,  ,, |
| ,, | ,, | *Infoedstretten* ..... | 64 | Taken and burnt by  ,,  ,,  ,, |
| ,, | ,, | *Dannebrog* ....... | 62 | Blew up after action with  ,,  ,, |
| ,, | ,, | *Proevesteen* ....... | 56 | Taken and burnt by  ,,  ,,  ,, |
| ,, | ,, | *Valkyrien* ........ | 48 | Taken and burnt by  ,,  ,,  ,, |
| ,, | ,, | *Jylland* ........... | 48 | Taken and burnt by  ,,  ,,  ,, |
| ,, | ,, | *Charlotte Amalie* ... | 26 | Taken and burnt by  ,,  ,,  ,, ⎬ **M** |
| ,, | ,, | *Kronborg* ........ | 20 | Taken and burnt by  ,,  ,,  ,, |
| ,, | ,, | *Rendsborg* ........ | 20 | Driven ashore and burnt by  ,,  ,, |
| ,, | ,, | *Nyborg* .......... | 20 | Sank after action with ,,  ,,  ,, |
| ,, | ,, | *Svoerdfisken* ....... | 20 | Taken and burnt by  ,,  ,,  ,, |
| ,, | ,, | *Haien* ........... | 20 | Taken and burnt by  ,,  ,,  ,, |
| ,, | ,, | *Aggershuus* ........ | 20 | Sank after action with ,,  ,,  ,, |
| ,, | ,, | *Soehesten* ........ | 18 | Taken and burnt by  ,,  ,,  ,, ⎭ |

# Appendix 2:
# Ship Losses of the Major Navies 1803-15

ROYAL NAVY

| Year | Date | H.M. Ship | Guns | Fate |
|------|------|-----------|------|------|
| 1803 | Mar. 26 | *Déterminée* ........ | 22 | Wrecked near Jersey |
| | May 31 | *Resistance* ......... | 36 | Wrecked on Cape St. Vincent |
| | July 2 | *Minerve* .......... | 38 | Grounded and taken near Cherbourg |
| | " 21 | *Seine* ............ | 38 | Wrecked off the Texel |
| | | *Surinam* .......... | 18 | Detained by the Dutch at Curaçoa |
| | Aug. | *Calypso* .......... | 16 | Run down in the Atlantic |
| | " | *Redbridge*, sch ..... | 12 | Taken by French off Toulon |
| | " 17 | *Porpoise*, storeship . | .. | Wrecked in the S. Pacific |
| | Nov. 16 | *Circe* ............ | 28 | Wrecked on the Lemon and Ower |
| | " | *Garland* .......... | 22 | Wrecked off Cape François |
| | Dec. 10 | *Shannon* ......... | 36 | Wrecked and burnt near La Hougue |
| | " | *Avenger* .......... | 14 | Foundered off the Weser |
| | " 15 | *Suffisanté* ........ | 16 | Wrecked in Cork Harbour |
| | " 31 | *Grappler*, g.v. ...... | 12 | Grounded and burnt by French at Chausey |
| 1804 | Jan. 2 | *Créole* ........... | 38 | Foundered in the Atlantic |
| | " 6 | *Raven* ........... | 18 | Wrecked near Mazari, Sicily |
| | " | *York* ............ | 64 | Supposed foundered in N. Sea. All lost |
| | Feb. | *Fearless* .......... | 12 | Wrecked in Cawsand Bay |
| | " | *Hussar* ........... | 38 | Wrecked on the Saintes, B. of Biscay |
| | " 19 | *Cerbère* .......... | 10 | Wrecked on Berry Head |
| | Mar. 1 | *Weazel* ........... | 14 | Wrecked near Gibraltar |
| | " 24 | *Wolverine* ........ | 14 | Taken by french privateer *Blonde*, Atlantic |
| | " 25 | *Magnificent* ....... | 74 | Wrecked near the Pierres Noires, Brest |
| | Apr. 2 | *Apollo* ........... | 36 | Wrecked on coast of Portugal |
| | " " | *Hindostan*, storeship .......... | .. | Accidentally burnt, Rosas Bay |
| | " 3 | *Swift*, hired cutter .. | 8 | Taken by a French privateer, Medit. |
| | May 8 | *Vencejo* .......... | 16 | Taken by French gunboats, Quiberon Bay |
| | July 14 | *Demerara* ......... | 6 | Taken by priv. *Grand Décidé*, 22, W. Ind. |
| | " | *Lily* .............. | 16 | Taken by priv. *Dame Ambert*, 16, off Georgia |
| | Aug. 26 | *Constitution*, hired cutter ............ | 10 | Sunk in action, off Ambleteuse |
| | Sept. 3 | *De Ruyter*, storeship | 64 | Wrecked at Antigua |
| | " | *Drake* ............ | 14 | Wrecked off Nevis |
| | " 25 | *Georgiana*, hired cutter ............ | .. | Burnt to avoid capture, mouth of the Seine |
| | Oct. 24 | *Conflict* .......... | 12 | Wrecked off Newport, I.W. |
| | Nov. 12 | *Lord Eldon*, hired a.s. .......... | 16 | Taken by Spanish gunboats. Retaken later |
| | " 19 | *Romney* .......... | 50 | Wrecked near the Texel |
| | " 24 | *Venerable* ........ | 74 | Wrecked off Roundham Head, Torbay |
| | " | *Hannibal*, hired a.s. | 16 | Wrecked near Sandown Castle |
| | Dec. | *Duke of Clarence*, hired cutter ........ | 10 | Wrecked on coast of Portugal |
| | " 6 | *Morne Fortunée*, sch. | 6 | Wrecked on Atwood Key, W. Indies |
| | " | *Constance*, hired cutter ............ | 6 | Lost off the Irish coast |
| | " 15 | *Gertrude*, hired sch. | 16 | Run down by the *Aigle*, Channel |
| | " 18 | *Starling* .......... | 12 | Wrecked near Calais |
| | " 20 | *Tartarus*, bomb .... | 12 | Wrecked on Margate Sands |
| | " | *Mignonne* ........ | 18 | Driven ashore in the W. Indies |
| | " 21 | *Severn*, flûte ....... | 44 | Wrecked in Grouville Bay, Jersey |
| | " 25 | *Mallard* .......... | 12 | Grounded and taken near Calais |

| Year | Date | H.M. Ship | Guns | Fate |
|------|------|-----------|------|------|
| 1805 | Jan. 7 | *Sheerness* .......... | 44 | Wrecked near Trincomale |
| | " 21 | *Doris* ............ | 36 | Wrecked in Quiberon Bay |
| | " 29 | *Raven* ........... | 18 | Wrecked in Cadiz Bay |
| | Feb. 4 | *Arrow* ........... | 30 | Taken by the *Hortense* and *Incorruptible*, Medit. |
| | " " | *Acheron*, bomb .... | 8 | Taken by the *Hortense* and *Incorruptible*, Medit. |
| | " | *Arthur*, hired cutter | 6 | Taken by a French squadron, Medit. |
| | " 17 | *Cleopatra* ........ | 32 | Taken by the *Ville de Milan*, North America |
| | " | *Bouncer* .......... | 12 | Wrecked off Dieppe |
| | Mar. 1 | *Imogene* ......... | 18 | Foundered in the Atlantic |
| | " | *Redbridge*, sch. .... | 10 | Foundered near Jamaica |
| | ? May | *Hawk* ............ | 18 | Foundered in the Channel. All lost |
| | ? | *Seagull* ........... | 18 | Foundered, date unknown. All lost |
| | ? | *Mary*, hired ........ | 16 | Foundered, date unknown. All lost |
| | May | *Fly* .............. | 16 | Wrecked in the Gulf of Florida |
| | " 12 | *Cyane* ........... | 18 | Taken by the *Hortense* and *Hermione*. Retaken, 5 Oct. 1805 |
| | July 12 | *Orestes* ........... | 14 | Wrecked off Dunquerque |
| | " 16 | *Plumper* ......... | 12 | Taken by five gun-brigs, off St. Malo |
| | " " | *Teazer* ........... | 12 | Taken by five gun-brigs, off St. Malo |
| | " 17 | *Ranger* ........... | 16 | Taken and burnt by the Rochefort squadron |
| | " 19 | *Blanche* .......... | 36 | Taken and burnt by a French squadron, W. Indies |
| | Aug. 5 | *Dove*, cutter ....... | 6 | Taken by the Rochefort squadron |
| | " | *Pigmy*, sch. ........ | 14 | Wrecked in St. Aubin's Bay, Jersey |
| | .. | *Althorpe*, (hired cutter) ........... | 16 | Foundered in the Channel |
| | Sept.26 | *Calcutta* .......... | 54 | Taken by Allemand's squadron, off Scilly |
| | Oct. 2 | *Barracouta*, sch. .... | 4 | Wrecked on Jordan Key, Cuba |
| | " | *Orquijo* .......... | 18 | Foundered near Jamaica |
| | " 11 | *Squib*, hired ....... | 4 | Driven ashore and bilged, off Deal |
| | Nov.10 | *Biter* ............. | 12 | Wrecked near Calais |
| | " 18 | *Woodlark* ........ | 12 | Wrecked near St. Valery |
| | " | *Pigeon*, sch. ....... | 4 | Wrecked off the Texel |
| 1806 | Jan. | *Manly* ........... | 12 | Seized by the Dutch in the Ems |
| | " 6 | *Favourite* ......... | 18 | Taken by a French squadron, Atlantic |
| | .. | *Papillon* .......... | 10 | Foundered in the Atlantic. All lost |
| | .. | *Berbice* .......... | 4 | Foundered at Demerara. Date unknown |
| | Feb. | *Seaforth* ......... | 14 | Capsized, W. Indies. All lost save two |
| | " 23 | *Unique* ........... | 10 | Taken by a large French privateer, W. Ind. |
| | Mar. | *Agnes*, hired lugger | 6 | Lost off the Texel |
| | Apr. 12 | *Brave* ............ | 74 | Foundered off the Azores |
| | .. | *Dominica* ........ | 6 | Seized by mutineers. Retaken by *Wasp*, May 24 |
| | Aug. | *Dover*, prison ship, (in ord.) ........... | 44 | Accidentally burnt off Woolwich |
| | .. | *Heureux* ......... | 22 | Foundered in the Atlantic. All lost |
| | " 12 | *Belem*, sch. ........ | 6 | Taken at the recapture of Buenos Aires |
| | Sept. 5 | *Wolf* ............ | 16 | Wrecked among the Bahamas |
| | .. | *Serpent* .......... | 16 | Foundered on the Jamaica station. All lost |
| | .. | *Martin* ........... | 16 | Foundered in the Atlantic. All lost |
| | Oct. 12 | *Constance* ........ | 22 | Grounded and taken, near C. Fréhel |
| | " 18 | *Tobago*, sch. ....... | 10 | Taken by priv. *Général Ernouf;* W. Indies |
| | " 25 | *Hannah*, gunboat ... | .. | Taken by Spanish privateer, off Algeciras |
| | " 27 | *Athénien* ......... | 64 | Wrecked near Sicily; many lost |
| | .. | *Zenobia*, sch. ...... | 10 | Wrecked off Florida; date unknown |
| | Nov. 4 | *Redbridge*, sch. .... | 12 | Wrecked near Providence |
| | Dec. 9 | *Adder* ........... | 12 | Driven ashore and taken near Abreval |
| | " 17 | *Netley*, sch. ........ | 14 | Taken by two French cruisers, W. Ind. |

| Year | Date | H.M. Ship | Guns | Fate |
|------|------|-----------|------|------|
| | " | *Clinker* .......... | 12 | Foundered off Le Hâvre; all lost |
| 1807 | Jan. 4 | *Nautilus* .......... | 22 | Wrecked on Cerigotto, Mediterranean |
| | " 6 | *United Brothers,* hired tender ....... | 6 | Taken by a 12-gun priv., off the Lizard |
| | " | *Jackdaw* .......... | 4 | Taken by a Spanish row-boat. Retaken 15 Feb., 1807 |
| | " 22 | *Felix* ............. | 12 | Wrecked near Santander; all lost save three |
| | " 23 | *Orpheus* .......... | 32 | Wrecked on a coral reef, W. Indies |
| | .. | *St. Lucia* ......... | 14 | Taken by the French; W. Indies |
| | ? Feb.2 | *Blenheim* ......... | 74 | Foundered in Indian Ocean; all lost |
| | ? " 2 | *Java* ............. | 32 | Foundered in Indian Ocean; all lost |
| | Feb. 13 | *Woodcock* ........ | 4 | Wrecked at St. Michael's, Azores |
| | " 13 | *Wagtail* .......... | 4 | Wrecked at St. Michael's, Azores |
| | " 14 | *Ajax* ............. | 74 | Accidentally burnt, Mediterranean |
| | " 18 | *Prospero,* bomb .... | 8 | Foundered off Dieppe |
| | " 18 | *Inveterate* ......... | 12 | Wrecked off St. Valery en Caux |
| | " 18 | *Griper* ........... | 12 | Foundered off Ostend; all lost |
| | " 18 | *Speedwell* ........ | 14 | Foundered off Dieppe |
| | " 19 | *Ignition,* fire vessel | 8 | Wrecked off Dieppe |
| | " 19 | *Magpie* .......... | 4 | Driven into and taken at Perros |
| | .. | *Busy* ............. | 18 | Foundered, Halifax station; all lost |
| | " | *Atalante* ......... | 16 | Wrecked off Rochefort |
| | Mar. 2 | *Pigmy* ........... | 14 | Wrecked off Rochefort |
| | " 4 | *Blanche* .......... | 38 | Wrecked off Ushant |
| | " 9 | *Crafty* ........... | 10 | Taken by three privateers, south of Gibraltar |
| | " | *César* ............ | 16 | Wrecked off the Gironde |
| | " 31 | *Ferreter* .......... | 12 | Taken by seven Dutch gunboats, River Ems |
| | Apr. 20 | *Pike* ............. | 4 | Taken by a French priv. W. Indies |
| | May 26 | *Dauntless* ........ | 18 | Taken at the surrender of Danzig |
| | " 29 | *Jackal* ........... | 12 | Wrecked near Calais |
| | .. | *Cassandra* ........ | 10 | Foundered off Bordeaux |
| | Sept.10 | *Explosion* ........ | 12 | Wrecked near Helgoland |
| | " 17 | *Barbara* .......... | 10 | Taken by priv. *Général Ernouf,* 14, W. Indies. As *Pératy,* retaken, 17 July, 1808 |
| | .. | *Moucheron* ....... | 16 | Wrecked in the Mediterranean |
| | Oct. 16 | *Pert* ............. | 14 | Wrecked off Sta. Margarita |
| | " 26 | *Subtle* ........... | 8 | Wrecked off Bermuda |
| | Nov.10 | *Leveret* .......... | 18 | Wrecked on the Galloper |
| | " 11 | *William,* storeship .. | 12 | Wrecked in the Gut of Canso |
| | " 17 | *Firefly* ........... | 12 | Foundered off Curaçoa; nearly all lost |
| | Dec. 5 | *Boreas* ........... | 22 | Wrecked near Guernsey; many lost |
| | " 29 | *Anson* ........... | 44 | Wrecked off Mount's Bay |
| | .. | *Elizabeth* ......... | 12 | Foundered in the W. Indies; all lost |
| | .. | *Maria* ............ | 10 | Foundered in the W. Indies; all lost |
| 1808 | Jan. 12 | *Sparkler* .......... | 12 | Wrecked on the Dutch coast |
| | " 15 | *Lord Keith,* hired cutter ........... | 10 | Driven into, and seized at Cuxhaven |
| | .. | *Kingfish,* sch. ...... | 6 | Taken by a French priv., W. Indies. Retaken by *Pheasant* |
| | .. | *Bacchus,* cutter ..... | 10 | Taken by the French, Leeward Islands |
| | " 19 | *Flora* ............ | 36 | Wrecked and destroyed on Dutch coast |
| | " 31 | *Delight* ........... | 16 | Wrecked and burnt on Calabrian coast |
| | " 31 | *Leda* ............. | 38 | Wrecked at mouth of Milford Haven |
| | Feb. 15 | *Raposa* .......... | 10 | Destroyed to prevent capture, near Cartagena |
| | Mar. | *Hirondelle* ........ | 14 | Wrecked near Tunis; nearly all lost |
| | " 24 | *Muros* ........... | 20 | Wrecked in Honda Bay, Cuba |
| | " 25 | *Electra* ........... | 16 | Wrecked on coast of Sicily |
| | " 26 | *Milbrook* .......... | 12 | Wrecked on the Burlings |
| | Apr. 20 | *Widgeon* ......... | 8 | Wrecked on Scots coast |
| | " 22 | *Bermuda* .......... | 18 | Wrecked on Memory Rock, Little Bermuda |

| Year | Date | H.M. Ship | Guns | Fate |
|------|------|-----------|------|------|
| | May 18 | *Rapid* .............. | 12 | Sunk by batteries in the Tagus |
| | ,, 24 | *Astroea* ........... | 32 | Wrecked off Anegada, W. Indies |
| | June 4 | *Tickler* ........... | 12 | Taken by four Danish gunboats, Great Belt |
| | ,, 9 | *Turbulent* ........ | 12 | Taken by a Danish flotilla, Malmö Bay |
| | ,, 19 | *Seagull* ............ | 16 | Taken by a Danish flotilla, off the Naze |
| | ,, 30 | *Capelin* .......... | 8 | Wrecked off Brest Harbour |
| | July 10 | *Netley* ............ | 12 | Wrecked on Leeward Islands station |
| | ,, 27 | *Pickle* ............. | 10 | Wrecked off Cadiz |
| | ,, 30 | *Meleager* ........ | 36 | Wrecked on Barebush Key, Jamaica |
| | Aug. 2 | *Tigress* ........... | 12 | Taken by sixteen Danish gunboats, Great Belt |
| | ,, 4 | *Delphinen* ........ | 16 | Wrecked on the Dutch coast |
| | ,, 18 | *Rook* ............. | 4 | Taken by two French privs., off San Domingo |
| | Sept.15 | *Laurel* ........... | 22 | Taken by the *Cannonière*, 40, Indian Ocean |
| | ,, 29 | *Maria* ............. | 14 | Taken by *Dépt. des Landes*, 22, off Guadeloupe |
| | Oct. 3 | *Carnation* ........ | 18 | Taken by *Palinure*, 16, off Martinique |
| | ,, 4 | *Greyhound* ....... | 32 | Wrecked on coast of Luconia |
| | ,, 24 | *Volador* .......... | 16 | Wrecked in Gulf of Coro, W. Indies |
| | ,, 26 | *Crane* ............ | 8 | Wrecked off West Hoe |
| | Dec. 4 | *Banterer* ......... | 22 | Wrecked in the St. Lawrence |
| | ,, 6 | *Crescent* ........ | 36 | Wrecked on the coast of Jutland |
| | ,, 10 | *Jupiter* ........... | 50 | Wrecked in Vigo Bay |
| | ,, 15 | *Flying fish*, sch. .... | 4 | Wrecked off San Domingo |
| | ,, 23 | *Fama* ............. | 16 | Wrecked in the Baltic |
| | ,, 26 | *Bustler* ........... | 12 | Wrecked on coast of France |
| | .. | *Tang* ............ | 8 | Foundered in the Atlantic |
| 1809 | Jan. 9 | *Morne Fortunée* .... | 12 | Wrecked off Martinique |
| | ,, 11 | *Magnet* .......... | 18 | Wrecked in the ice, Baltic |
| | ,, 15 | *Pigeon* ........... | 4 | Wrecked near Margate |
| | ,, 20 | *Claudia* .......... | 10 | Wrecked off Norway |
| | ,, 22 | *Primrose* ......... | 18 | Wrecked on the Manacle, near Falmouth |
| | ,, | *Proselyte*, bomb .... | 4 | Wrecked in the Baltic |
| | ,, 30 | *Haddock* ......... | 4 | Taken by the *Génie*, 16, Channel |
| | Feb. 5 | *Carrier* ........... | 4 | Wrecked on the French coast |
| | ,, | *Viper*, sch. ........ | 8 | Supposed foundered off Gibraltar |
| | ,, 28 | *Proserpine* ........ | 32 | Taken by *Pénélope* and *Pauline*, off Toulon |
| | Mar. | *Harrier* ........... | 18 | Supposed foundered, Indian Ocean |
| | Apr. 11 | *Mediator*, t.s. as. f ship ............. | 36 | Expended in Basque Road |
| | ,, 29 | *Alcmene* ......... | 32 | Wrecked off Nantes |
| | May 31 | *Unique* ........... | 12 | Burnt at Basseterre, Guadeloupe |
| | June 18 | *Sealark* .......... | 4 | Wrecked in the North Sea |
| | ,, 20 | *Agamemnon* ....... | 64 | Wrecked in the River Plate |
| | July 11 | *Solebay* ........... | 32 | Wrecked on the coast of Africa |
| | Aug. 8 | *Lark* ............. | 18 | Foundered off San Domingo |
| | Aug.10 | *Alaart* ........... | 16 | Taken by a Danish flotilla |
| | ,, | *Lord Nelson*, cutter | 8 | Wrecked near Flushing |
| | ,, | *Hurd*, cutter ....... | 8 | Wrecked near Flushing |
| | ,, | *Dominica* ........ | 14 | Capsized off Tortola |
| | ,, 31 | *Foxhound* ........ | 18 | Foundered in the Atlantic; all lost |
| | Sept. 2 | *Minx* ............ | 12 | Taken by six Danish gunboats |
| | Nov. 2 | *Victor* ........... | 18 | Taken by the *Bellone*, 40, B. of Bengal |
| | ,, 3 | *Curieux* .......... | 16 | Wrecked in the W. Indies |
| | ,, | *Glommen* ........ | 16 | Wrecked in Carlisle Bay, Barbados |
| | Dec. 7 | *Harlequin* ........ | 16 | Wrecked near Seaford |
| | ,, 13 | *Junon* ............ | 38 | Taken by the *Renommée* and *Clorinde* |
| | ,, 14 | *Defender* ......... | 12 | Wrecked near Folkestone |
| | ,, 22 | *Salorman* ......... | 10 | Wrecked in the Baltic |

| Year | Date | H.M. Ship | Guns | Fate |
|------|------|-----------|------|------|
| | .. | *Contest* .......... | 12 | Supposed foundered in the Atlantic |
| | .. | *Shamrock,* sch. ..... | 8 | Lost in the Atlantic |
| | Dec. | *Pelter* .......... | 12 | Lost in the Atlantic |
| 1810 | Feb. | *Achates* .......... | 10 | Wrecked in the W. Indies |
| | ,, | *Wild Boar* ........ | 10 | Wrecked within the Scilly Isles |
| | Apr. 4 | *Cuckoo* .......... | 4 | Wrecked off the Dutch coast |
| | May 24 | *Flèche* .......... | 16 | Wrecked off the mouth of the Elbe |
| | ,, ,, | *Alban* .......... | 10 | Taken by a flotilla of Danish gunboats |
| | ,, ,, | *Racer,* cutter ....... | 12 | Wrecked on the coast of France |
| | Aug. 24 | *Néréide* .......... | 36 | Taken by a French squadron, off Grand Port |
| | ,, 25 | *Magicienne* ........ | 36 | Destroyed to avoid capture, off Grand Port |
| | ,, ,, | *Sirius* .......... | 36 | Destroyed to avoid capture, off Grand Port |
| | ,, 26 | *Lively* .......... | 38 | Wrecked near Malta |
| | 28 | *Iphigenia* .......... | 36 | Taken by a French squadron, near Grand Port |
| | Nov. 9 | *Conflict* .......... | 12 | Foundered in the B. of Biscay |
| | .. | *Mandarin* ........ | 12 | Wrecked on Red Island, Strait of Singapore |
| | ,, | *Plumper* .......... | 12 | Foundered in the St. Lawrence |
| | Dec. 18 | *Pallas* .......... | 32 | Wrecked off the Firth of Forth |
| | ,, 18 | *Nymphe* .......... | 36 | Wrecked off the Firth of Forth |
| | ,, 22 | *Minotaur* .......... | 74 | Wrecked on the Haak Sand, Texel |
| | ,, 25 | *Monkey* .......... | 12 | Wrecked near Belle Isle |
| 1811 | Jan. 8 | *Fleur de la Mer* ..... | 10 | Foundered in the Atlantic |
| | ,, 19 | *Satellite* .......... | 16 | Foundered in the Channel |
| | Feb. 13 | *Pandora* .......... | 18 | Wrecked in the Kattegat |
| | ,, 16 | *Amethyst* .......... | 36 | Wrecked in Plymouth Sound |
| | ,, 25 | *Shamrock* ........ | 10 | Wrecked on C. St. Mary |
| | Mar. 6 | *Thistle* .......... | 10 | Wrecked near New York |
| | ,, 12 | *Challenger* ........ | 16 | Taken by a French frigate, etc., off Ile Batz |
| | May 2 | *Dover* .......... | 38 | Wrecked in Madras Road |
| | ,, ,, | *Chichester,* storeship | 32 | Wrecked in Madras Road |
| | ,, 26 | *Alacrity* .......... | 18 | Taken by the *Abeille,* 20, off Corsica |
| | Mar. 2 | *Olympia* .......... | 10 | Taken by French privs., off Dieppe |
| | .. | *Black Jake,* hired cutter .......... | 4 | Taken by the French in the Channel |
| | June 28 | *Firm* .......... | 12 | Wrecked on the French coast |
| | ,, 29 | *Safeguard* ........ | 12 | Taken by the Danes in the Baltic |
| | .. | *Staunch* .......... | 14 | Wrecked off Madagascar; all lost |
| | July 15 | *Snapper* .......... | 4 | Taken by the *Rapace,* off Brest |
| | ,, 29 | *Guet-apens* (*"Guachapin"*) .... | 10 | Wrecked off Antigua |
| | Aug. 18 | *Tartar* .......... | 32 | Wrecked in the Baltic |
| | Sept. 2 | *Manly* .......... | 12 | Taken by three Danish brigs |
| | .. | *Swan,* cutter ....... | .. | Taken by Danish gunboats |
| | Oct. 14 | *Pomone* .......... | 38 | Wrecked on the Needles |
| | ,, 21 | *Grouper* .......... | 4 | Wrecked off Guadeloupe |
| | Dec. 4 | *Saldanha* .......... | 36 | Wrecked off Lough Swilly; nearly all lost |
| | .. | *Bloodhound* ....... | 12 | Wrecked near Trevose Head |
| | ,, 24 | *Fancy* .......... | 12 | Foundered in the Baltic; all lost |
| | ,, ,, | *St. George* ........ | 98 | Wrecked on the coast of Jutland; nearly all lost |
| | ,, ,, | *Defence* .......... | 74 | Wrecked on the coast of Jutland; nearly all lost |
| | Dec. 25 | *Hero* .......... | 74 | Wrecked on the Haak Sand; all lost |
| | ,, ,, | *Grasshopper* ....... | 18 | Taken in Nieuwe Diep, Texel |
| | ,, 26 | *Ephira* .......... | 10 | Wrecked near Cadiz |
| 1812 | Jan. 28 | *Manilla* .......... | 36 | Wrecked on the Haak Sand, Texel |
| | ,, 31 | *Laurel* .......... | 38 | Wrecked on the Govivas Rock, Teigneux Passage |

| Year | Date | H.M. Ship | Guns | Fate |
|------|------|-----------|------|------|
| | Feb. 29 | *Fly* .............. | 16 | Wrecked off Anholt |
| | May 3 | *Skylark* .......... | 16 | Grounded and was destroyed, near Boulogne |
| | '' '' | *Apelles* ........... | 14 | Grounded and was taken, near Boulogne. Retaken, 4 Mar., 1812 |
| | July 8 | *Exertion* .......... | 12 | Grounded and was destroyed in the Elbe |
| | '' 11 | *Encounter* ......... | 12 | Wrecked off San Lucar, Spain |
| | Aug. 3 | *Emulous* .......... | 18 | Wrecked on Sable Island |
| | '' 13 | *Alert* ............ | 16 | Taken by the U.S.S. *Essex,* 32 |
| | '' 14 | *Chubb* ........... | 4 | Capsized off Halifax; all lost |
| | '' 19 | *Attack* ........... | 12 | Taken by fourteen Danish gunboats, off Anholt |
| | '' '' | *Guerrière* ......... | 38 | Taken by U.S.S. *Constitution,* 44 |
| | '' 22 | *Whiting* .......... | 4 | Taken by the French priv. *Diligente* |
| | Sept. 8 | *Laura* ............ | 12 | Taken by the French priv, *Diligente* |
| | '' 28 | *Barbados* ......... | 28 | Wrecked on Sable Island |
| | Oct. 8 | *Avenger* .......... | 16 | Wrecked off St. John's, Newfoundland |
| | ? | *Magnet* .......... | 16 | Supposed foundered in the Atlantic; all lost |
| | '' 10 | *Sentinel* .......... | 12 | Wrecked off Rügen |
| | '' 18 | *Frolic* ............ | 18 | Taken by U.S.S. *Wasp,* 20 |
| | '' 25 | *Macedonian* ....... | 38 | Taken by U.S.S. *United States,* 44 |
| | Nov. 6 | *Nimble* ........... | 10 | Foundered in the Kattegat |
| | '' 24 | *Bellette* .......... | 18 | Wrecked in the Kattegat; nearly all lost |
| | '' 27 | *Southampton* ...... | 32 | Wrecked off Conception Island, Bahamas |
| | '' 30 | *Subtle,* sch. ........ | 10 | Foundered in the W. Indies; all lost |
| | Dec. 5 | *Plumper* ......... | 12 | Wrecked in the B. of Fundy |
| | '' 8 | *Fearless* .......... | 12 | Wrecked off the coast of Spain |
| | '' 18 | *Alban,* cutter ...... | 10 | Wrecked off Aldborough; nearly all lost |
| | 29 | *Java* .............. | 38 | Taken by U.S.S. *Constitution,* 44 |
| | ? | *Porgey* ........... | 4 | Foundered in the W. Indies |
| 1813 | Jan. 1 | *Sarpedon* ......... | 10 | Supposed foundered; all lost |
| | '' 7 | *Ferret* ............ | 18 | Wrecked near Leith |
| | '' 27 | *Daring* ........... | 12 | Destroyed to prevent capture by *Rubis* |
| | '' 21 | *Rhodian* .......... | 10 | Foundered in the Atlantic |
| | '' 24 | *Peacock* .......... | 18 | Taken by U.S.S. *Hornet.* Sank |
| | '' 25 | *Linnet* ............ | 14 | Taken by the *Gloire,* 40, off Madeira |
| | Mar. 22 | *Captain* .......... | 74 | Accidentally burnt in Hamoaze |
| | May 20 | *Algerine* .......... | 10 | Wrecked in the W. Indies |
| | June 16 | *Persian* .......... | 18 | Wrecked on Silver Keys, W. Indies |
| | July 2 | *Daedalus* ......... | 38 | Wrecked off Ceylon |
| | Aug. 5 | *Dominica* ........ | 14 | Taken by U.S. priv. *Decatur* |
| | '' 22 | *Colibri* ........... | 18 | Wrecked at Port Royal, Jamaica |
| | Sept. 5 | *Boxer* ............ | 12 | Taken by U.S.S. *Enterprise,* 16 |
| | '' 9 | *Highflyer* ......... | 8 | Taken by U.S.S. *President* |
| | '' 10 | *Alphea,* sch. ....... | 10 | Blew up in action with priv. *Renard;* all lost |
| | '' 21 | *Goshawk* ......... | 16 | Wrecked in the Mediterranean |
| | '' 27 | *Bold* ............. | 12 | Wrecked on P. Edward's Island |
| | Oct. 22 | *Laurestinus* ........ | 22 | Wrecked on the Silver Keys |
| | Nov. 5 | *Tweed* ............ | 18 | Wrecked on Shoal Bay, Newfoundland |
| | '' 6 | *Woolwich,* en flûte | 40 | Wrecked off Barbuda |
| | '' 10 | *Atalante* ......... | 18 | Wrecked off Halifax |
| | ? Dec. | *Dart* ............. | 10 | Foundered in the Atlantic |
| 1814 | Jan. 29 | *Holly,* sch. ........ | 10 | Wrecked off San Sebastian |
| | Feb. 14 | *Pictou* ............ | 16 | Taken by the U.S.S. *Constitution* |
| | Feb. 28 | *Anacreon* ........ | 18 | Foundered in the Channel |
| | Mar. 22 | *Decoy* ............ | 10 | Taken by French in the Channel |
| | .. | *Rapide,* tender ..... | 6 | Wrecked off the Saintes |
| | .. | *Vautour* .......... | 16 | Supposed foundered; all lost |
| | Apr. 29 | *Epervier* .......... | 18 | Taken by U.S.S. *Peacock* |
| | '' '' | *Ballahou* .......... | 4 | Taken by U.S. priv. *Perry* |
| | *May 19* | *Halcyon* .......... | 18 | Wrecked on a reef, W. Indies |

244

| Year | Date | H.M. Ship | Guns | Fate |
|---|---|---|---|---|
| | June 28 | *Reindeer* .......... | 18 | Taken by U.S.S. *Wasp,* Channel |
| | ,,    ,, | *Leopard,* troopship | 50 | Wrecked off Anticosti |
| | July 12 | *Landrail,* cutter .... | 4 | Taken by U.S. priv. *Siren,* Channel |
| | Aug. | *Peacock* .......... | 18 | Foundered off S. Carolina; all lost |
| | Sept. 1 | *Avon* ............ | 18 | Sank after action with U.S.S. *Wasp* |
| | ,,   15 | *Hermes* .......... | 20 | Destroyed in attacking batteries at Mobile |
| | ,,   30 | *Crane* ............ | 18 | Foundered in the W. Indies |
| | Oct. | *Elizabeth* ......... | 10 | Foundered in the W. Indies |
| | Oct. 10 | *Racer* ............ | 14 | Wrecked in the Gulf of Florida |
| | Nov.24 | *Fantôme* ......... | 18 | Wrecked on the Halifax station |
| | .. | *Cuttle* ............ | 4 | Foundered on the Halifax station |
| | .. | *Herring* .......... | 4 | Foundered on the Halifax station |
| 1815 | Jan. 17 | *Sylph* ............ | 18 | Wrecked on Southampton Bar, N. America |
| | Feb. 26 | *Statira* ........... | 38 | Wrecked off Cuba |
| | ,,   26 | *St. Lawrence*....... | 12 | Taken by U.S. priv. *Chasseur,* 24 |
| | Mar.20 | *Levant* ........... | 22 | Taken by U.S.S. *Constitution,* Retaken |
| | ,,   20 | *Cyane* ........... | 20 | Taken by U.S.S. *Constitution.* Retaken |
| | ,,   23 | *Penguin* .......... | 18 | Taken by U.S.S. *Hornet,* off Tristan d'Acunha |
| | May 1 | *Penelope,* troopship | 36 | Wrecked off Newfoundland |
| | Aug.15 | *Dominica* ......... | 14 | Wrecked off Bermuda |
| | ? | *Cygnet* ........... | 16 | Wrecked off the R. Courantyn |

FRENCH NAVY

| Year | Date | Name (*Added to the Royal Navy) | Guns | Fate<br>M Medals granted in 1849, in pursuance of *Gazette* notice of June 1st, 1847<br>**M** Flag-Officers' and Captains' gold medals |
|---|---|---|---|---|
| 1803 | May 18 | *Affronteur* (*as *Caroline,* hired) .... | 14 | Taken by *Doris,* 36, Capt. R. H. Pearson, off Ushant |
| | ,,   28 | *Franchise** ......... | 40 | Taken by *Minotaur, Thunderer,* and *Albion,* Channel |
| | ,,   ,, | *Embuscade* (*as *Ambuscade)* ....... | 32 | Retaken by *Victory,* 100, Capt. Sam. Sutton, Atlantic |
| | ,,   29 | *Impatiente* ........ | 10 | Taken by *Naiad,* 36, Capt. Jas. Wallis (1) |
| | June 3 | *Betsy* ............ | 4 | Taken and destroyed by *Russell,* 74 |
| | ,,   7 | *Vertu,* sch. ........ | 2 | Taken by *Racoon,* 18, Com. Austin Bissell, San Domingo |
| | ,,   ,, | *Ami de Colonnot* | 2 | ,,      ,,      ,,      ,, |
| | ,,   14 | *Inabordable,* sch. | 4 | Taken by boats of *Immortalité,* 36, etc., Cape Gris Nez |
| | ,,   ,, | *Commode* ........ | 4 | ,,      ,,      ,,      ,, |
| | ,,   ,, | *Arabe* ............ | 8 | Taken by *Maidstone,* 36, Capt. Rich. H. Moubray, Med. |
| | ,,   18 | *Colombe** ......... | 16 | Taken by *Dragon,* 74, and *Endymion,* 44, off Ushant |
| | ,,   24 | *Enfant Prodigue* (*as *Sta. Lucia)* ........ | 16 | Taken by *Emerald,* 36, Capt. Jas. O'Bryen, off St. Lucia |
| | ,,   25 | *Bacchante** ........ | 18 | Taken by *Endymion,* 44, Capt. Hon. Chas. Paget |
| | ,,   27 | *Venteux* .......... | 10 | Cut out by two boats of *Loire,* 36, Capt. Fred. L. Maitland (2),, Ile Batz. **M** |
| | ,,   28 | *Légère* .......... | 2 | Taken by priv. *Alarm,* Channel |
| | ,,   ,, | *Mignonne** ........ | 16 | Taken by *Goliath,* 74, off San Domingo |
| | ,,   29 | *Dart* ............. | 4 | Taken by *Apollo,* 36, Bay of Biscay |
| | June 30 | *Aiguille* .......... | .. | Taken by squadron of Capt. Hy. Wm. Bayntun, off San Domingo |

| Year | Date | Name (*Added to the Royal Navy) | Guns | Fate  M Medals granted in 1849, in pursuance of *Gazette* notice of June 1st, 1847  M Flag-Officers' and Captains' gold medals |
|---|---|---|---|---|
| ,, | ,, | *Vigilante* (as *Suffisante*) ........ | .. | ,,  ,,  ,,  ,, |
| ,, | ,, | *Supérieure** ........ | .. | ,,  ,,  ,,  ,, |
|  |  | *Poisson Volant* (*as *Flying Fish*) ........ |  | ,,  ,,  ,,  ,, |
| ,, | ,, | *Créole** .......... | 40 | ,,  ,,  ,,  ,, |
| July | 4 | *Providence,* sch. .... | 2 | Taken by boats of *Naiad,* 36, under Lieut. Wm. Dean, off Ile de Seins |
| ,, | 8 | *Alcion* (*as *Halycon*) | 16 | Taken by *Narcissus,* 36, Capt. Ross Donnelly, off Sardinia |
| ,, | 11 | *Lodi* .............. | 10 | Taken by *Racoon,* 18, Com. Austin Bissell, Léogane Road |
| ,, | 16 | *Adour* ............ | 20 | Taken by *Endymion,* 44, Capt. Hon. Chas. Paget, Atlantic |
| ,, | 25 | *Duquesne** ........ | 74 | Taken by *Bellerophon,* 74, *Vanguard,* 74, *Tartar,* 32, etc., San Domingo |
| ,, | ,, | *Oiseau,* sch. ....... | 16 | ,,  ,,  ,,  ,, |
| ,, | 27 | *Epervier** .......... | 16 | Taken by *Egyptienne,* 40, Capt. Hon. Chas. E. Fleeming, Atlantic |
| Aug. |  | *Deux Amis,* sch. .... | 3 | Taken by *Racoon,* 16, Com. Austin Bissell, off Cuba |
| ,, |  | *Trois Frères,* sch. ... | 3 | ,,  ,,  ,,  ,, |
| ,, |  | A schooner ........ | 2 | Destroyed by *Racoon,* 16, Com. Austin Bissell, off Cuba |
| ,, | 17 | *Mutine* ............ | 18 | ,,  ,,  ,,  ,, |
| Sept. | 4 | *Papillon** .......... | 6 | Taken by *Vanguard,* 74, St. Marc, San Domingo |
| ,, | 5 | *Courier de Nantes,* sch. ............. | 2 | ,,  ,,  ,, off San Domingo |
| ,, | 8 | *Sagesse* .......... | 28 | Taken by *Theseus,* 74, Port Dauphin, San Domingo |
| ,, | 9 | Two *chasse-marées* . | .. | Taken by boats of *Sheerness,* 8, Lieut. Henry Rowed, near Brest |
| ,, | 27 | A schooner ........ | 4 | Taken by *Jackal,* sch., Leiut. C. P. Leaver, off Nieuport |
| Oct. |  | *Goéland* (*as *Goelan*) | 18 | Taken by *Pique,* 36, and *Pelican,* 18, at Aux Cayes, San Domingo |
|  |  | A cutter .......... | 12 | ,,  ,,  ,,  ,, |
| ,, | 14 | *Petite Fille,* gun-brig | .. | Taken by *Racoon,* 16, Com. Austin Bissell, off Cuba |
| ,, | ,, | *Jeune Adèle* ....... | 6 | ,,  ,,  ,,  ,, |
| ,, | ,, | *Amélie* ........... | 4 | ,,  ,,  ,,  ,, |
| Nov. | 8 | No. 86 (gunboat) ... | 2 | Taken by *Conflict,* 14, Lieut. Dav. Chambers, off Calais |
| ,, | 10 | *Messager,* lugger ... | 6 | Taken by boats of *Ville de Paris,* 110, under Lieut. Watts, off Ushant |
| ,, | 16 | *Renard** ........... | 12 | Taken by Lord Nelson's squadron, Medit. |
| ,, | 25 | *Vautour* .......... | 12 | Taken by *Boadicea,* 38, Capt. Jno. Maitland (2), off Finisterre |
| ,, | 28 | *Bayonnaise* ........ | 28 | Destroyed to prevent capture by *Ardent,* 64, Capt. Robt. Winthrop |
| ,, | 30 | *Surveillante** ....... | 40 | Surrendered to Commod. John Loring at Cape François |
| ,, | ,, | *Clorinde** ......... | 40 | ,,  ,,  ,,  ,, |
| ,, | ,, | *Vertu** ............ | 40 | ,,  ,,  ,,  ,, |
| ,, | ,, | *Cerf* ............. | 12 | ,,  ,,  ,,  ,, |
| ,, | ,, | *Découverte* ........ | 6 | ,,  ,,  ,,  ,, |

| Year | Date | Name (*Added to the Royal Navy) | Guns | Fate<br>**M** Medals granted in 1849, in pursuance of *Gazette* notice of June 1st, 1847<br>**M** Flag-Officers' and Captains' gold medals |
|------|------|------|------|------|
| | Dec. 18 | No. 437 (gunboat) .. | 2 | Taken by *Basilisk*, 14, Lieut. Wm. Shepheard, Home station |
| 1804 | Jan. 3 | No. 432 (lugger) .... | 2 | Taken by *Archer*, 14, Lieut. Jno. Sherriff |
| | '' 14 | *Passe-Partout*, chasse marée ....... | 2 | Taken by boats of *St. Fiorenzo*, 40, E. Ind. |
| | '' 21 | *Chameau* ......... | 4 | Taken by *Cerberus*, 32, off La Hougue |
| | '' 30 | No. 43 (g.-brig) ..... | 3 | Taken by *Tribune*, 36 |
| | '' '' | No. 47 (g.-brig) ..... | 3 | '' '' |
| | '' '' | No. 51 (g.-brig) ..... | 3 | Taken by *Hydra*, 38 |
| | '' '' | No. 411 (lugger) .... | 1 | '' '' |
| | Feb. 4 | *Curieux\** ......... | 16 | Cut out by boats of *Centaur*, 74, under Lieut. Robt. Carthew Reynolds (2), Martinique **M** |
| | '' 24 | *Coquette*, sch. ..... | 2 | Taken by *Stork*, 18, Com. Geo. Le Geyt, Jamaica station |
| | Mar. 8 | *Colombe*, cutter .... | 4 | Cut out of Sluys by boats of *Cruiser* and *Rattler* and burnt |
| | '' 12 | *Penriche* ......... | 2 | Taken by *Harpy*, 18, Com. Edm. Heywood, near Calais |
| | '' 18 | *Terreur*, cutter ..... | 10 | Taken by *Pique*, 40, Jamaica station |
| | Apr. 28 | *Hirondelle\** ........ | 14 | Taken by *Bittern*, 18, Com. Robt. Corbett, Med. |
| | '' 29 | No. 360 (gunboat) | .. | Taken by boats of *Doris*, 36, Audierne Bay |
| | July 12 | *Charente* ......... | 20 | Driven ashore and burnt off the Gironde by *Aigle*, 36, Capt. Geo. Wolfe |
| | '' '' | *Joie* ............. | 8 | '' '' '' '' |
| | Aug. 23 | *Laurette*, sch. ...... | 5 | Taken by *Pelican*, 18, Com. Jno. Marshall (1), Jamaica station |
| | Oct. 1 | *Hasard* ........... | 16 | Taken by *Echo*, 16, Com. Edm. Boger, off Curaçoa |
| | '' 21 | *Gracieuse\** ........ | 14 | Taken by *Blanche*, 36, off Curaçoa |
| 1805 | Feb. 14 | *Psyché* (\*as *Psyche*) | 32 | Taken by *St. Fiorenzo*, 36, Com. Hy. Lambert (2) (actg. Capt.), E. Indies **M** |
| | '' 23 | *Ville de Milan\** ..... | 40 | Taken by Leander, 50, Capt. John Talbot, Halifax station |
| | '' '' | *Cleopatra* (\*formerly British) | 32 | Retaken by *Leander*, 50, Capt. John Talbot, Halifax station |
| | Apr. 9 | A schooner ........ | 7 | Sunk by *Gracieuse*, 12, Mids. John Bernhard Smith, Jamaica station. |
| | June 10 | *Amitié*, sch. ....... | 14 | Taken by *Blanche*, 36, Jamaica station |
| | '' 18 | *Colombe* ......... | 16 | Taken by *Endymion*, 44, Capt. Hon. Chas. Paget. |
| | Aug. 10 | *Didon\** ........... | 40 | Taken by *Phoenix*, 36, Capt. Thomas Baker, (1), off C. Finisterre **M** |
| | '' 15 | *Faune* ............. | 16 | Taken by *Goliath*, 74, and *Camilla*, 20, Channel |
| | '' 16 | *Torche\** .......... | 18 | Taken by *Goliath*, 74, Channel |
| | Sept. | *Hypolite* ......... | 4 | Driven ashore and destroyed by *Duncan*, 38, Lieut. Clem. Sneyd (actg. Capt.) |
| | Oct. 2 | *Actéon\** .......... | 16 | Taken by *Egyptienne*, 40, off Rochefort |
| | '' 5 | *Cyane* (\*formerly British) .......... | 31 | Taken by *Princèss Charlotte*, 38, Capt. Geo. Tobin, off Tobago |
| | '' 13 | *Naïade* (\*as *Melville*) | 22 | Taken by *Jason*, 32, Capt. Wm. Champain, Leeward Islands |
| | '' 21 | *Swiftsure\** ......... | 74 | Taken by the fleet of Lord Nelson at Trafalgar (formerly British) **MM** |

| Year | Date | Name (*Added to the Royal Navy) | Guns | Fate — M Medals granted in 1849, in pursuance of *Gazette* notice of June 1st, 1847 — M Flag-Officers' and Captains' gold medals |
|---|---|---|---|---|
| | ,, | ,, | *Achille* ........... | 74 | Taken by the fleet of Lord Nelson at Trafalgar, but blew up |
| | ,, | ,, | *Fougueux* ......... | 74 | Taken by the fleet of Lord Nelson at Trafalgar, but wrecked } MM |
| | ,, | ,, | *Aigle* ............ | 74 | Taken by the fleet of Lord Nelson at Trafalgar, but wrecked |
| | ,, | ,, | *Intrépide* ......... | 74 | Taken by the fleet of Lord Nelson at Trafalgar, and burnt |
| | ,, | ,, | *Redoutable* ....... | 74 | Taken by the fleet of Lord Nelson at Trafalgar, but sank |
| | ,, | ,, | *Berwick* .......... | 74 | Taken by the fleet of Lord Nelson at Trafalgar, but wrecked } MM |
| | ,, | ,, | *Bucentaure* ....... | 80 | Taken by the fleet of Lord Nelson at Trafalgar, retaken, and wrecked |
| | ,, | ,, | *Algésiras* ......... | 74 | Taken by the fleet of Lord Nelson at Trafalgar, but retaken |
| | ,, | 25 | *Indomptable* ....... | 80 | Wrecked off Rota, Cadiz |
| | Nov. 3 | *Formidable* (*as *Brave*) ........ | 80 | Taken by the squadron of Sir Richard John Strachan |
| | ,, | ,, | *Duguay Trouin* (*as *Implacable*) .... | 74 | ,, ,, ,, ,, } M |
| | ,, | ,, | *Mont Blanc** ....... | 74 | ,, ,, ,, ,, |
| | ,, | ,, | *Scipion** ......... | 74 | ,, ,, ,, ,, |
| | Dec. 24 | *Libre* ............ | 38 | Taken by the *Loire,* 40, and *Egyptienne,* 40, off Rochefort |
| | ,, | *Atalante* ......... | 40 | Wrecked off the Cape of Good Hope |
| 1806 | Feb. 6 | *Alexandre** (ex *Indivisible*) ..... | 80 | Taken by squadron of V.-Ad. Sir Jno. Thos. Duckworth, off San Domingo |
| | ,, | ,, | *Jupiter* (*as *Maida*) | 74 | ,, ,, ,, ,, |
| | ,, | ,, | *Brave** ........... | 74 | ,, ,, ,, ,, MM |
| | ,, | ,, | *Imperial* (ex *Vengeur*) ......... | 120 | Destroyed by squadron of V.-Ad. Sir Jno. |
| | ,, | ,, | *Diomède* ......... | 72 | Thos. Duckworth, off San Domingo |
| | ,, | 21 | *Rolla** ........... | 16 | Taken by squadron of Sir Home R. Popham, C. of Good Hope |
| | ,, | 27 | *Furet* ............ | 20 | Taken by *Hydra,* 38, Capt. Geo. Mundy, off Cadiz |
| | Mar. 4 | *Volontaire** ........ | 40 | Surrendered to squadron of Sir Home R. Popham, C. of Good Hope |
| | ,, | 12 | *Tremeuse,* sch. ..... | 3 | Taken by *Wolverine,* 18, Com. Fras. Aug. Collier, W. Indies |
| | ,, | 13 | *Marengo** ......... | 74 | Taken by squadron of V.-Ad. Sir. Jno. B. } M (London and Amazon) |
| | ,, | ,, | *Belle Poule** ....... | 40 | Warren, Atlantic |
| | ,, | 21 | *Lutine* (*as *Hawk*) | 18 | Taken by *Carysfort,* 28, and *Agamemnon,* 64, Leeward Islands |
| | ,, | 26 | *Phaëton* (*as *Mignonne*) ........ | 16 | Taken by the *Pique,* 36, Capt. Chas. B. H. Ross, Jamaica station } M |
| | ,, | ,, | *Voltigeur* (*as *Pelican*) .......... | 16 | ,, ,, ,, ,, |
| | ,, | 28 | *Néarque* .......... | 16 | Taken by *Niobe,* 38, Capt. Jno. Wentworth Loring, off Lorient |
| | Apr. 5 | *Tapageuse* ......... | 14 | Cut out of R. Garonne by boats of *Pallas,* Capt. Lord Cochrane |
| | ,, | 6 | *Malicieuse* ........ | 18 | Driven ashore in the Garonne by *Pallas,* 32, Capt. Lord Cochrane |
| | ,, | ,, | *Garonne* ......... | 24 | ,, ,, ,, ,, |

| Year | Date | Name (*Added to the Royal Navy) | Guns | Fate  M Medals granted in 1849, in pursuance of *Gazette* notice of June 1st, 1847  M Flag-Officers' and Captains' gold medals |
|------|------|---------------------------------|------|------|
| | ,, ,, | *Gloire* ........... | 22 | ,, ,, ,, ,, |
| | ,, 17 | *Bergère** .......... | 18 | Taken by *Sirius,* 36, Capt. Wm. Prowse (1), Medit. |
| | ,, 19 | Two *chasse-marées* | .. | Cut out by boats of *Colpoys* and *Attack,* Doëlan |
| | May 1 | *Pandour* .......... | 18 | Taken by squadron of R-Ad. Chas. Stirling (1), Irish station |
| | ,, 28 | *Diligent* (*as *Wolf*) | 16 | Taken by *Renard,* 18, Com. Jer. Coghlan, Jamaica station |
| | ,, 24 | *Impériale, sch.* ..... | 3 | Taken by *Cygnet,* 18, Com. Robt. Bell Campbell, off Dominica |
| | June 9 | *Observateur** ...... | 18 | Taken by *Tartar,* 32, Capt. Edw. Hawker, W. Indies. |
| | July 15 | *César* ............. | 18 | Taken by boats of squadron of Sir Sam. *M* Hood (2), under Lieut. Ed. Reynolds Sibly |
| | ,, ,, | *Charles, ketch* ...... | 3 | Taken by *Seaflower,* 14, off Rodriguez |
| | July 19 | *Guerrière** ........ | 40 | Taken by *Blanche,* 38, Capt. Thos. Lavie, off Faröe Isles  *M* |
| | ,, 27 | *Rhin** ............. | 40 | Surrendered to *Mars,* 74, Capt. Robt. Dudley Oliver, off Rochefort |
| | Sept. 14 | *Impétueux* ........ | 74 | Taken and burnt by *Belleisle,* 74, *Bellona,* 74, and *Melampus,* 36, off C. Henry |
| | ,, 25 | *Gloire** .......... | 40 | Taken by squadron of Commod. Sir Sam. Hood (2) off Rochefort |
| | ,, ,, | *Infatigable* ........ | 40 | ,, ,, ,, ,, |
| | ,, ,, | *Minerve* (*as *Alceste*) | 40 | ,, ,, ,, ,, |
| | ,, ,, | *Armide** .......... | 40 | ,, ,, ,, ,, |
| | ,, ,, | *Emilien* (ex Br. *Trincomale*) ....... | 18 | Taken by *Culloden,* Capt. Christ. Cole, E. Indies |
| | | *Napoléon, sch.* ..... | 1 | Taken by *Diligente,* 16, Jamaica station |
| | ,, 27 | *Présidente* (*as *Piémontaise,* 1815) | 40 | Struck to *Dispatch,* 18, Capt. Edw. Hawkins, with squadron of Sir Thos. Louis |
| | Oct. 2 | *Manette, slp.* ....... | .. | Cut out by boats of *Dominica,* 14, Lieut. Wm. Dean, St. Pierre, Martinique |
| | ,, ,, | *Dauphin, slp.* ...... | .. | ,, ,, ,, ,, |
| | ,, 4 | *Chiffonne, sch.* .... | .. | Taken by *Dominica,* Lieut. Wm. Dean |
| | ,, 12 | *Salamandre,* flûte ... | 26 | Taken and burnt at St. Malo by *Constance, Sheldrake, Strenuous,* and *Britannia* |
| | Nov. 12 | *Réunion, sch.* ...... | 10 | Taken by boats of *Galatea,* 32, Capt. Geo. Sayer (1), off Guadeloupe |
| 1807 | Jan. 2 | *Créole* ............ | 1 | Taken by a boat of the *Circe,* 32, under Lieut. Thomas, Leeward Islands |
| | ,, 21 | *Lynx* (*as *Heureux*) | 16 | Taken by boats of *Galatea,* 32, under Lieut. Wm. Coombe, off Caracas  *M* |
| | ,, 28 | *Favourite* (ex British) | 18 | Taken by *Jason,* 32, Capt. Thos. Jno. Cochrane, off Guiana |
| | Feb. 14 | *Dauphin, sch.* ...... | 3 | Taken by *Bacchante,* 20, Capt. Jas. Rich. Dacres (2), Jamaica station |
| | July 10 | *Jaseur* ............ | 12 | Taken by *Bombay,* 38, Capt. Wm. Jones Lye, E. Indies |
| | Aug. 23 | *Mosquito* .......... | 8 | Taken by *Lark,* 18, and *Ferret,* 18, Jamaica station |
| | Oct. 7 | *Safo* (Venetian) .... | 1 | Cut out by boats of *Porcupine,* 22, Guippana |
| | Nov. 6 | *Succès,* cutter ...... | 10 | Taken by *Volage,* 22, Capt. Phil. Lew. J. Rosenhagen, Medit. |

249

| Year | Date | Name (*Added to the Royal Navy) | Guns | Fate  *M* Medals granted in 1849, in pursuance of *Gazette* notice of June 1st, 1847  **M** Flag-Officers' and Captains' gold medals |
|------|------|------|------|------|
| 1808 | Feb. 13 | Gunboat No. 1 ..... | 3 | Cut out by boats of *Confiance,* 20, mouth of the Tagus. *M* |
| | Mar. 8 | *Piémontaise* ....... | 40 | Taken by *St. Fiorenzo,* 36, Capt. Geo. Nicholas Hardinge, E. Indies. *M* |
| | ,, 13 | *Apropos* ......... | 8 | Driven ashore and burnt by *Emerald,* 36, Capt. Fredk. Lewis Maitland (2), Vivero. *M* |
| | ,, 26 | *Friedland* (Italian) | 16 | Taken by *Standard,* 64, and *Active,* 38, off C. Blanco |
| | May 2 | *Ronco* (Italian) (*as *Tuscan)* ....... | 16 | Taken by *Unité,* 40, Capt. Pat. Campbell (1), off C. Promontoro |
| | ,, 11 | *Griffon** ......... | 16 | Taken by *Bacchante,* 20, Capt. Sam. Hood Inglefield, off C. Antonio |
| | June 1 | *Nettuno* (Italian) (*as *Cretan)* ....... | 16 | Taken by *Unité,* 40, Capt. Pat. Campbell, (1), Medit. |
| | ,, ,, | *Teulie* (*as *Roman)* | 16 | ,,     ,,     ,,     ,, |
| | ,, 14 | *Neptune* .......... | 80 | Surrendered to the Spanish patriots, Cadiz harbour |
| | ,, ,, | *Algésiras* ......... | 74 | ,,     ,,     ,,     ,, |
| | ,, ,, | *Pluton* ............ | 74 | ,,     ,,     ,,     ,, |
| | ,, ,, | *Héros* ............. | 74 | ,,     ,,     ,,     ,, |
| | ,, ,, | *Argonaute* ........ | 74 | ,,     ,,     ,,     ,, |
| | ,, ,, | *Cornélie* .......... | 40 | ,,     ,,     ,,     ,, |
| | ,, | *Atlas* ............ | 74 | Surrendered to the Spanish patriots, Vigo |
| | ,, 26 | *Volpe* (Neopolitan) | 1 | Taken by boats of *Standard,* 64, off Corfu |
| | ,, ,, | *Léger* ............. | .. | ,,     ,,     ,,     ,, |
| | July 16 | *Ortenzia* (Venetian) | 10 | Taken by *Minstrel,* 18, Com. Jno. Hollinworth, Medit. |
| | ,, 17 | *Serpent* (*as *Pert)* ... | 18 | Taken by *Acasta,* 40, Capt. Ph. Beaver, off La Guaira |
| | ,, 28 | *Requin* ........... | 16 | Taken by *Volage,* 22, Capt. Ph. Lew, J. Rosenhagen, Medit. |
| | Aug. 1 | *Vigilante* ......... | 2 | Taken by boats of *Kent,* 74, and *Wizard,* 16, Noli |
| | ,, 11 | *Sylphe* (*as *Seagull)* | 16 | Taken by *Comet,* 18, Com. Cuthbert Featherstone Daly, Channel. *M* |
| | | *Artémise* ......... | 40 | Driven ashore near Brest and burnt by blockading squadron |
| | | *Mouche,* sch. ...... | .. | Taken by *Cossack,* 22, Capt. Chas. Geo. Digby, Channel |
| | ,, 16 | *Espiègle* (*as *Electra)* | 16 | Taken by *Sibylle,* 38, Capt. Clotworthy Upton, Channel |
| | Oct. 8 | *Jéna* (*as *Victor)* ... | 18 | Taken by *Modeste,* 36, B. of Bengal |
| | ,, 20 | *Pilade* ............ | 16 | Taken by *Pompée,* 74, off Barbados |
| | ,, 31 | *Palinure* .......... | 16 | Taken by *Circe,* 32, off Diamond Rock |
| | Nov.11 | *Thétis* (*as *Brune)* .. | 40 | Taken by *Amethyst,* 36, Capt. Mich. Seymour (1), off Lorient. **MM** |
| | ,, 14 | *Colibri* ........... | 3 | Taken by boats of *Polyphemus,* 64, San Domingo |
| | Dec. 13 | *Cygne* ............ | 16 | Destroyed at St. Pierre by *Amaranthe,* 18, etc. |
| 1809 | Jan. 1 | *Gauloise,* cutter .... | 7 | Taken by *Imperieuse,* 38, Capt. Lord Cochrane, Medit. |
| | ,, ,, | *Julie,* lugger ....... | 5 | ,,     ,,     ,,     ,, |
| | ,, 2 | *Iris* (*as *Rainbow)* .. | 24 | Taken by *Aimable,* 32, Capt. Lord Geo. Stuart, N. Sea |
| | ,, 5 | *Hébé* (as *Ganymede)* ........ | 20 | Taken by *Loire,* 38, Capt. Alex. Wilmot Schomberg |

| Year | Date | Name (*Added to the Royal Navy) | Guns | Fate<br>*M* Medals granted in 1849, in pursuance of *Gazette* notice of June 1st, 1847<br>**M** Flag-Officers' and Captains' gold medals |
|------|------|------|------|------|
| | '' 16 | Colibri ............ | 16 | Taken by *Melampus,* 36, Capt. Edw. Hawker, Halifax station |
| | Jan. 22 | Topaze (*as *Jewel)* | 40 | Taken by *Cleopatra,* 32, *Jason,* 32, and *Hazard,* 18, off Guadeloupe |
| | Feb. 4 | Amphitrite ........ | 40 | Destroyed at the attack on Martinique |
| | '' 10 | Junon* ........... | 40 | Taken by *Horatio,* 38, (*M*) *Supériere,* 14, (*M*) *Latona,* 38, and *Driver,* 18, Halifax station |
| | '' 15 | Var (*as *Chichester)* | 26 | Taken by *Belle Poule,* 38, Capt. Jas. Brisbane, off Valona |
| | '' 24 | Italienne .......... | 40 | Driven ashore by squadron of R.-Ad. Hon. Robt. Stopford, Sables d'Olonne |
| | '' '' | Calypso .......... | 40 | ,,　　　,,　　　,,　　　,, |
| | '' '' | Cybèle ........... | 40 | ,,　　　,,　　　,,　　　,, |
| | '' | Rossollis ......... | 18 | Burnt to avoid capture at the taking of **M** Martinique |
| | '' | Carnation ........ | 18 | ,,　　　,,　　　,,　　　,, |
| | '' | Diligente (*as *St. Pierre)* ........... | 18 | Taken at the capture of Martinique |
| | Mar. 10 | Joseph, felucca ..... | 3 | Cut out by boats of *Argo,* 44, under Lieut. Chas. Fraser, San Domingo |
| | Apr. 1 | Léda ............. | 1 | Cut out by boats of *Mercury,* 28, Rovigno |
| | '' 6 | Niémen* .......... | 40 | Taken by *Amethyst,* 36, Capt. Mich. Seymour (1), coast of France. **M** |
| | '' 12 | Ville de Varsovie ... | 80 | Destroyed by fleet of Ad. Lord Gambier, Basque Road |
| | '' '' | Tonnerre .......... | 74 | ,,　　　,,　　　,,　　　,, |
| | '' '' | Aquilon .......... | 74 | ,,　　　,,　　　,,　　　,, |
| | '' '' | Calcutta, en flûte ... | 50 | ,,　　　,,　　　,,　　　,, |
| | '' '' | Indienne .......... | 40 | ,,　　　,,　　　,,　　　,, |
| | '' 17 | d'Hautpoult (*as *Abercrombie)* .. | 74 | Taken by *Pompée,* 74, *Castor,* 32, and *Recruit,* 18, off Puerto Rico. **M** |
| | May 4 | Champenoite ...... | 12 | Taken by *Renown,* 74, Capt. Phil. Chas. Durham, off Toulon |
| | '' 28 | Beau Narcisse ..... | 8 | Taken by *Moselle,* 18, Com. Henry Boys (1), W. Indies |
| | June 10 | Mouche .......... | 16 | Taken by the *Amelia,* 38, and *Statira,* 38, off Santander |
| | '' 18 | Félicité,* en flûte ... | 36 | Taken by *Latona,* 38, Capt. Hugh Pigot (3), W. Indies |
| | '' | Réjouie .......... | 14 | Taken by the *Amelia,* 38, and *Statira,* 38, off Santander |
| | '' | No. 7, sch. ........ | 4 | ,,　　　,,　　　,,　　　,, |
| | '' | Légère ........... | 2 | ,,　　　,,　　　,,　　　,, |
| | '' | Notre Dame ....... | 2 | ,,　　　,,　　　,,　　　,, |
| | July 6 | Furieuse (*as 36) .... | 20 | Taken by *Bonne Citoyenne,* 20, Com. Wm. Mounsey, Atlantic. **M** |
| | '' 28 | Six Italian gunboats (2 guns each) ....... | .. | Cut out by boats of squadron, Duino |
| | Aug. 16 | Fidèle (*as *Bourbon-naise* .............. | 40 | Taken at the surrender of Flushing |
| | '' 27 | Four gunboats (Venetian, ea. 1 gun) | .. | Cut out by boats of *Amphion,* 32, Cortellazzo |
| | '' '' | Two gunboats (Venetian, ea. 2 guns) | .. | ,,　　　,,　　　,,　　　,, |
| | Sept. 1 | Jason ............. | 10 | Taken by *Helena,* 18, Com. Jas. And. Worth, coast of Ireland |

| Year | Date | Name (*Added to the Royal Navy) | Guns | Fate — *M* Medals granted in 1849, in pursuance of *Gazette* notice of June 1st, 1847 — **M** Flag-Officers' and Captains' gold medals |
|---|---|---|---|---|
| | ,,    ,, | *Jean Bart* .......... | 4 | Taken by *Nassau*, 64, off the Start |
| | ,,  7 | *Pugliese* .......... | 7 | Cut out by boats of *Mercury*, 28, Barletta |
| | ,, 18 | *Aurore* ........... | 16 | Taken by *Plover*, 18, Com. Philip Browne (2), off Beachy Head |
| | ,, 21 | *Caroline* .......... | 40 | Taken by a military and naval force, Réunion |
| | Oct. | *Zéphyr* ........... | 18 | Taken by *Seine*, 36, Capt. Dav. Atkins, Channel |
| | ,, | *Améthyste* ........ | 14 | Taken by *Minerva*, 32, Capt. Rich. Hawkins |
| | ,, | *Incomparable*, brig | 8 | Taken by *Emerald*, 36, Capt. Fredk. Lewis Maitland (2), off Ireland |
| | ,, 22 | *Hirondelle*, sch. .... | 16 | Taken by *Plover*, 18, Com. Philip Browne (2), off Falmouth |
| | ,, 26 | *Robuste* .......... | 80 | Destroyed to avoid capture by Brit. fleet, off Frontignan |
| | ,,  ,, | *Lion* ............. | 74 | ,,       ,,       ,,       ,, |
| | ,, 30 | *Milan* ........... | 18 | Taken by *Surveillante*, 38, Sir Geo. Ralph Collier, off Ushant |
| | Nov. | *Etoile* ........... | 14 | Taken by *Euryalus*, 36, Capt. Hon. Geo. H. L. Dundas, off Cherbourg |
| | ,,  6 | *Fanfaron* ......... | 16 | Taken by *Emerald*, 36, Capt. Fredk. Lewis Maitland, off Guadeloupe |
| | ,, 13 | *Basque* ........... | 16 | Taken by *Druid*, 32, Capt. Sir Wm. Bolton (2) |
| | ,,  ,, | *Revanche* ......... | 16 | Taken by *Helena*, 18, Com. Jas. And. Worth |
| | ,, 17 | *Grand Napoléon* ... | 18 | Taken by *Royalist*, 18, Com. Jno. Maxwell, off Dungeness |
| | ,, 19 | *Intrépide* ......... | 20 | Taken by *Vestal*, 28, Capt. Edwards Lloyd Graham, off Newfoundland |
| | Dec.  3 | *Comtesse Laure* .... | 16 | Taken by *Surveillante*, 38, Capt. Sir Geo. Ralph Collier |
| | ,,  6 | *Heureuse Etoile* .... | 2 | Taken by *Royalist*, 18, Com. Jno. Maxwell |
| | ,, 10 | *Grand Rodeur* ..... | 16 | Taken by *Redpole*, 16, Com. Colin M'Donald |
| | ,,  ,, | *Beau Marseille* ..... | 14 | Taken by *Royalist*, 18, Com. Jno. Maxwell, Downs station |
| | ,, 12 | *Nisus* (*as *Guadeloupe* ....... | 16 | Taken by boats of *Thetis*, 38, Capt. Geo. Miller, etc., at Guadeloupe. **M** |
| | ,, 14 | *Béarnais* (*as *Curieux*) .......... | 16 | Taken by *Melampus*, 36, Capt. Edw. Hawker, W. Indies |
| | ,,  ,, | *Aigle* ............. | 14 | Taken by *Pylades*, 18, Com. Geo. Ferguson |
| | Dec. 18 | *Loire*, en flûte ...... | 40 | Destroyed by a squadron at Anse La Barque, Guadeloupe |
| | ,,  ,, | *Seine*, en flûte ...... | 40 | ,,       ,,       ,,       ,, |
| | ,, 19 | *Papillon** .......... | 16 | Taken by *Rosamund*, 18, Com. Benj. Walker, off Guadeloupe |
| | ,, 31 | *François* .......... | 14 | Taken by *Royalist*, 18, Com. Jno. Maxwell |
| | | *Joubert* .......... | 8 | Taken by *Topaze*, 36, Capt. Hy. Hope, Mediterranean |
| | | *Mentor* .......... | 6 | ,,       ,,       ,,       ,, |
| | | *Espérance* ........ | 3 | ,,       ,,       ,,       ,, |
| 1810 | Jan. 12 | *Oreste* (*as *Wellington*) ........ | 14 | Taken by *Scorpion*, 18, Com. Francis Stanfell, off Guadeloupe. **M** |

| Year | Date | Name (*Added to the Royal Navy) | Guns | Fate<br>M Medals granted in 1849, in pursuance of *Gazette* notice of June 1st, 1847<br>M Flag-Officers' and Captains' gold medals |
|---|---|---|---|---|
| | Feb. 3 | *Confiance* (ex *Canonnière)*, en flûte | 40 | Taken by *Valiant*, 74, off Belle Isle |
| | Mar. 21 | *Nécessité* .......... | 28 | Taken by *Horatio*, 38, Capt. Geo. Scott (1), Atlantic |
| | Apr. 12 | *Espérance* (ex Brit. *Laurel)* (*as *Laurestinus)* ....... | 22 | Retaken by *Unicorn*, 32, Capt. Alex. Robt. Kerr |
| | May 1 | *Estafette* .......... | 4 | Taken at Jacolet by *Néréide*, 36 |
| | 3 | *Sparviero* (Neapolitan) ....... | 8 | Retaken by *Spartan*, 38, Capt. Jahleel Brenton (2), G. of Naples. *M* |
| | '' 10 | *Canonnière* ....... | 3 | Taken by *Nonpareil*, 14, Lieut. Jas. Dickinson (3) off the Vilaine |
| | '' 17 | *Minerve* .......... | 18 | Taken by *Bustard*, 16, Com. Jno. Duff Markland |
| | July 25 | Six gunboats (Neapolitan) ....... | .. | Taken by squad. of Capt. Hon. G. G. Waldegrave, Amantea |
| | Sept. 18 | *Vénus* (*as *Néréide)* | 40 | Taken by *Boadicea*, 38, Capt. Josias Rowley, off Réunion *(Boadicea, Otter* and *Staunch)*. |
| | Dec. 6 | *Astrée* (*as *Pomone)* | 40 | Taken by squadron of V.-Ad. Albemarle Bertie at capture of Mauritius |
| | '' '' | *Bellone* (*as *Junon)* | 40 | '' '' '' '' |
| | '' '' | *Minerve* .......... | 40 | '' '' '' '' |
| | '' '' | *Manche* .......... | 40 | '' '' '' '' |
| | '' '' | *Iphigénie** (ex Brit.) | 36 | '' '' '' '' |
| | '' '' | *Néréide* (ex Brit.) | 36 | '' '' '' '' |
| | '' '' | *Victor* ........... | 14 | '' '' '' '' |
| | '' '' | *Entreprenante* ...... | 14 | '' '' '' '' |
| | '' '' | A brig ........... | 14 | '' '' '' '' |
| | '' '' | 5 gunboats ......... | .. | '' '' '' '' |
| | '' '' | *Ceylon*, pris. ship | 30 | '' '' '' '' |
| | '' '' | *Charlton*, pris. ship | 30 | '' '' '' '' |
| | '' '' | *United Kingdom*, pris. ship .......... | 30 | '' '' '' '' |
| | '' 23 | *Eliza* ............. | 40 | Destroyed by boats of *Diana*, 38, Capt. Chas. Grant, near La Hougue. *M* |
| 1811 | Feb. 12 | A trabacolo (Venetian) ......... | 6 | Taken by boats of *Cerberus* and *Active*, Ortona |
| | Mar. 13 | *Favorite* .......... | 40 | Destroyed by squadron *(Amphion, Active, Cerberus,* and *Volage)* of Capt. Wm. Hoste, off Lissa |
| | '' '' | *Corona* (Venetian) (*as *Daedalus)* .... | 40 | Taken '' '' '' |
| | '' '' | *Bellona* (Venetian) (*as *Dover)* ........ | 32 | '' '' '' '' |
| | '' 14 | *Etourdie* .......... | 18 | Burnt to avoid capture by *Pomone*, 38, Capt. Robt. Barrie, Monte Cristo |
| | '' 25 | *Amazone* .......... | 40 | Burnt to avoid capture by *Berwick*, 74, Capt. Jas Macnamara (2), near Barfleur |
| | '' 31 | *Dromadaire*, en flûte | .. | Taken by *Ajax*, 74, and *Unité*, 36, off Elba |
| | May 1 | *Girafe*, en flûte ..... | 20 | Blew up in action with boats of *Pomone, Unité* and *Scout*, off Corsica |
| | '' '' | *Nourrice*, en flûte ... | 20 | '' '' '' '' |
| | '' 5 | A gun-brig ........ | 18 | Destroyed by *Belle Poule* and *Alceste*, Parenzo |
| | '' 8 | *Canonnier* ........ | 11 | Taken by *Scylla*, 18, Com. Arthur Atchison, off Isle Batz |

The *Favorite* / *Corona* / *Bellona* entries are bracketed together with the mark **MM**.

20 May 1811: a British squadron with the frigates *Astrea, Phoebe* and *Galathe*
and the sloop *Racehorse* under Captain Charles Marsh Schomberg in action with
3 French frigates, each with 44 guns, under Commodore Roquebert off Madagascar.
Although inferior in men and guns (126 against 132 guns and 934 men against 1,410)
the British won the day and captured *Renomée* and *Néréide*, only *Clorinde* escaping
(*National Maritime Museum*)

| Year | Date | Name (*Added to the Royal Navy) | Guns | Fate **M** Medals granted in 1849, in pursuance of *Gazette* notice of June 1st, 1847 **M** Flag-Officers' and Captains' gold medals |
|------|------|-------|------|------|
| | " 20 | *Renommée* ........ | 40 | Taken by squadron of Capt. Chas. Marsh Schomberg, off Madagascar |
| | " 26 | *Néréide* .......... | 40 | Taken by squadron of Capt. Chas. Marsh Schomberg, at Tamatave |
| | July 21 | Eleven gunboats .... | .. | Taken by *Thames and Cephalus,* Porto del Infreschi |
| | " 27 | Three gunboats ..... | .. | Taken by boats of *Active,* 38, Capt. Jas. Alex. Gordon (1), Ragoznica |
| | Aug. 2 | Gunboats 22, 28, 31 and 71 (each) ...... | 3 | Taken off Norderney by boats under Lieut. Sam. Blyth |
| | " 19 | *Héron* ........... | 10 | Taken by *Hawk,* 16, Com. Henry Bouchier, Channel. **M** |
| | " 25 | *Teazer* (ex British) | 14 | Re-taken by *Diana,* 38, and *Semiramis,* 36, mouth of Gironde |
| | " " | *Pluvier* ........... | 16 | Burnt by *Diana,* 38, and *Semiramis,* 36, mouth of Gironde |
| | Sept.21 | *Ville de Lyon,* praam | 12 | Taken by squadron of Capt. Phil. Carteret (3) |

*(Astraea, Phoebe, Galatea, and Racehorse* **M**

| Year | Date | Name (*Added to the Royal Navy) | Guns | Fate |
|------|------|------|------|------|
| | Oct. 11 | Two gunboats (each of) .......... | 1 | Taken by boats of *Impérieuse*, 38, Positano |
| | ,,  ,, | One gunboat ....... | 1 | Sunk by *Impérieuse*, 38, Capt. Hon. Hy. Duncan (3) |
| | Nov. 2 | Four gunboats (Neapolitan) ....... | .. | Destroyed by *Impérieuse* and *Thames*, Palinuro |
| | ,,  ,, | Six gunboats (Neapolitan) ....... | .. | Taken by *Impérieuse* and *Thames*, Palinuro |
| | Nov. 27 | *Corcyre* .......... | 28 | Taken by *Eagle*, 74, Capt. Chas. Rowley, Adriatic |
| | ,,  29 | *Pomone* .......... | 40 | Taken by *Alceste*, *Unité*, and *Active*, Adriatic. *M* |
| | Nov. 29 | *Persanne*, storeship . | 29 | Taken by *Alceste*, *Unité*, and Active, Adriatic *(Alceste, Unité,* and *Active) M* |
| | Dec. 4 | A settee .......... | 8 | Taken off Bastia by boats of *Sultan*, 74, Capt. Jno. West } **M** |
| | ,,  ,, | A brig ........... | 6 | ,,  ,,  ,,  ,, |
| | | *Victoire* .......... | 16 | Taken by *Zephyr*, 16, Com. Fras. Geo. Dickins, off Dieppe |
| | | *Flore* ............ | 40 | Wrecked in the Adriatic, date unknown |
| 1812 | Feb. 13 | *Mérinos*, en flûte ... | 20 | Taken by *Apollo*, 38, Capt. Bridges W. Taylor, off Corsica |
| | ,,  22 | *Rivoli** ........... | 74 | Taken by *Victorious*, 74, Capt. Jno. Talbot, and *Weazel* 18, Com. Jno. Wm. Andrew. *M***M** |
| | ,,  ,, | *Mercure* .......... | 18 | Blown up by  ,,  ,,  ,, |
| | ,,  29 | *St. Joseph* (pierced for 16) ...... | .. | Taken by boats of *Menelaus*, 38, under Lieut. Rowland Mainwaring, off Fréjus |
| | Mar. 27 | Three brigs (each) ... | 4 | Taken by *Rosario*, 10, and *Griffin*, 16, off Dieppe. *M* |
| | Apr. 29 | A schooner ....... | 4 | Burnt by boats of *Undaunted*, etc., mouth of the Rhône |
| | May 22 | *Ariane* ........... | 40 | Destroyed by *Northumberland*, 74, Capt. Hon. Hy. Hotham, and *Growler*, 12, Lieut. Jno. Weeks } **M** |
| | ,,  ,, | *Andromaque* ...... | 40 | ,,  ,,  ,,  ,, |
| | ,,  ,, | *Mamelouck* ........ | 16 | ,,  ,,  ,,  ,, |
| | June 4 | *Dorade*, storeship ... | 14 | Taken by boats of *Medusa*, 32, under Lieut. Josiah Thompson, at Arcachon. Burnt |
| | Aug. 31 | *Tisiphone*, xebec ... | 3 | Cut out by boats of *Bacchante*, 38, under Lieut. Donat Henchy O'Brien, Canale di Leme } **M** |
| | ,,  ,, | A gunboat ......... | 3 | ,,  ,,  ,,  ,, |
| | ,,  ,, | A gunboat ......... | 1 | ,,  ,,  ,,  ,, |
| | Sept. 9 | *Danaé* ........... | 40 | Accidentally burnt at Venice |
| | ,,  17 | Two gunboats (each of) .......... | 1 | Taken by boats of *Eagle*, 74, under Lieut. Aug Cannon |
| | ,,  20 | *Ulysse*, xebec ...... | 6 | Taken by *Apollo*, 38, Capt. Bridges W. Taylor, off Corfu |
| | Dec. 23 | A brig ........... | 22 | Driven ashore by *Dryad*, 36, Capt. Edw. Galwey, Isle d'Yeu |
| 1813 | Jan. 6 | *Imdomptable* ...... | 2 | Taken by boats of *Bacchante*, 38, and *Weazel*, 18, off C. Otranto } **M** *(Bacchante.)* |
| | "  " | *Diligente* .......... | 2 | ,,  ,,  ,, |
| | ,,  ,, | *Arrogante* ......... | 2 | ,,  ,,  ,, |

| Year | Date | Name (*Added to the Royal Navy) | Guns | Fate — M Medals granted in 1849, in pursuance of *Gazette* notice of June 1st, 1847 — M Flag-Officers' and Captains' gold medals |
|---|---|---|---|---|
| ,, | ,, | *Salamine* ......... | 2 | ,,     ,,     ,, |
| ,, | ,, | *Calypso* .......... | 1 | ,,     ,,     ,,     **M** |
| ,, | 6 | No. 8 (gunboat) .... | 1 | Cut out by boats of *Havannah*, 36, under, Lt. Wm. Hamley |
| ,, | 29 | *Véloce* .......... | 1 | Taken by *Cerberus*, 32, Capt. Thos. Garth |
| Feb. | 5 | *Rubis* ........... | 40 | Wrecked off Los Islands |
| ,, | 7 | Four gunboats ..... | .. | Destroyed by boats of *Havannah*, 36, under Lieut. Wm. Hamley, off Manfredonia |
| ,, | 14 | *Alcinoüs* ......... | 2 | Taken by barge of *Bacchante*, 38, under Lieut. Silas Thos. Hood, off Otranto |
| ,, | ,, | *Vigilante*, desp. boat | .. | Taken by *Bacchante*, 38, Capt. Wm. Hoste |
| Apr. | 22 | Six gunboats ....... | .. | Destroyed by *Weazel*, 18, Com. Jas. Black, Bassoglina bay |
| May | 16 | *Fortune*, xebec ..... | 10 | Taken by boats of *Perwick*, 74, and *Euryalus*, 36 |
| ,, | 27 | Two gunboats (each) | 3 | Taken by boats of *Apollo*, 38, and *Cerberus*, 32 |
| June | 8 | *Agile* ............ | 8 | Taken by *Alcmene*, 38, Capt. Edwards Ll. Graham |
| ,, | 12 | Ten gunboats (Neapolitan) (each) | 1 | Taken by boats of *Bacchante*, 38, under Lieut. Silas Thomson Hood, Giulianova |
| July | 18 | Two gunboats (each) | 1 | Taken by *Havannah*, 36, and *Partridge*, 16 |
| Aug. | 18 | Three gunboats ..... | .. | Taken or destroyed at Cassis by boats of squadron |
| ,, | 24 | *Tonnante* ......... | 2 | Taken by *Weazel*, 18, Capt. Jas. Black |
| ,, | ,, | *Auguste* ......... | 2 | ,,     ,,     ,,     ,, |
| Oct. | 7 | No. 961 (lugger) .... | 6 | Taken by *Wolverine*, 16, Com. Charles Julius Kerr |
| ,, | 13 | *Flibustier* ......... | 22 | Destroyed by *Telegraph*, 12, Com. Tim. Scriven |
| ,, | ,, | A gunboat ........ | 2 | Taken by boats of *Bacchante*, 38, etc., under Com. Jno. Harper, of *Saracen*, 18 |
| ,, | ,, | A gunboat ........ | 2 | ,,     ,,     ,,     ,, |
| ,, | ,, | A gunboat ........ | 1 | ,,     ,,     ,,     ,, |
| ,, | ,, | A gunboat ........ | 1 | ,,     ,,     ,,     ,, |
| ,, | 21 | *Weser** ........... | 40 | Taken by *Scylla*, 18, Com. Colin M'Donald, and *Royalist*, 18, Com. Jas. Jno. Gordon Bremer |
| ,, | 23 | *Trave** ........... | 40 | Taken by *Andromache*, 36, Capt. Geo. Tobin |
| ,, | 31 | Two corvettes, building .......... | .. | Taken by boats, etc., under Com. Jno. M'Kerlie, in the Weser |
| ,, | ,, | Two gun brigs ...... | .. | ,,     ,,     ,,     ,, |
| Dec. | 20 | *Prospère*, sch. ...... | 2 | Taken by *Andromache*, 36, Capt. Geo. Tobin, coast of France |
| ,, | 23 | *Baleine*, storeship ... | 22 | Driven ashore near Calvi by *Euryalus*, 36, Capt. Chas. Napier (2) |
| ,, | ,, | *Flèche*, sch. ........ | 12 | Taken by *Alcmene*, 38, Capt. Jerem. Coghlan |
| 1814 | Jan. 6 | *Cerès* (*as *Seine*) .... | 40 | Taken by *Niger*, 38, and *Tagus*, 36, off Cape Verde |
| ,, | 16 | *Iphigénie* (*as *Gloire*) | 40 | Taken by the *Venerable*, 74, and *Cyane*, 22, off Madeira  **M** |
| | Jan. 20 | *Alcmène* (*as (a) *Dunira*, (b) *Immortalité*) .............. | 40 | Taken by the *Venerable*, 74, and *Cyane*, 22, off Madeira  **M** |

| Year | Date | Name (*Added to the Royal Navy) | Guns | Fate<br>*M* Medals granted in 1849, in pursuance of *Gazette* notice of June 1st, 1847<br>*M* Flag-Officers' and Captains' gold medals |
|---|---|---|---|---|
| | Feb. 3 | *Uranie* . . . . . . . . . . . | 40 | Destroyed to avoid capture at Brindisi |
| | ” ” | *Terpsichore* . . . . . . . . | 40 | Taken by *Majestic*, 56, Capt. Jno. Hayes (1) |
| | ” 26 | *Clorinde* (*as *Aurora*) . . . . . . . . . . | 40 | Taken by *Eurotas*, 38, Capt. Jno. Phillimore, and *Dryad*, 36, Capt. Edw. Galwey. *M* (*Eurotas*) |
| | Mar. 17 | *Alcion* . . . . . . . . . . . | 16 | Taken by *Ajax*, 74, Capt. Robt. Waller Otway (1) |
| | ” 26 | *Sultane** . . . . . . . . . | 40 | Taken by *Hannibal*, 74, Capt. Sir. Mich. Seymour (1), off Cherbourg |
| | ” 27 | *Etoile* (*as *Topaze*) | 40 | Taken by *Hebrus*, 36, Capt. Edm. Palmer, off La Hougue. *M* |
| | Apr. 2 | A gun brig . . . . . . . . . | .. | Taken by boats under Lieut. Robt. Graham Dunlop, in the Gironde |
| | ” ” | A schooner . . . . . . . . | .. | ” ” ” ” |
| | ” ” | Six gunboats . . . . . . . | .. | ” ” ” ” |
| | ” ” | Three chasse-marées | .. | ” ” ” ” |
| | ” ” | An imperial barge . . | .. | ” ” ” ” |
| | ” ” | A gun brig . . . . . . . . . | .. | Burnt by ” ” ” ” |
| | ” ” | Two gunboats . . . . . . | .. | ” ” ” ” |
| | ” ” | A chasse-marée . . . . . | .. | ” ” ” ” |
| | ” 6 | *Regulus* (and other vessels) . . . . . . . . . . . | 74 | Burnt to avoid capture in the Gironde |
| | ” 18 | *Brillant* (*as *Genoa*) | 74 | Taken at the surrender of Genoa |
| | ” ” | Four brigs . . . . . . . . | .. | ” ” ” ” |
| | May 25 | *Aigle*, xebec . . . . . . . | 6 | Taken by boats of *Elizabeth*, 74, under Lieut. Mitchell Roberts, off Corfu. *M* |
| 1815 | Apr. 30 | *Melpomène* . . . . . . . . | 40 | Taken by *Rivoli*, 74, Capt. Edw. Stirling Dickson, off Ischia |

SPANISH NAVY

| Year | Date | Name (*Added to the Royal Navy) | Guns | Fate |
|---|---|---|---|---|
| 1804 | Oct. 5 | *Medea* (*as *Impérieuse*) . . . . . . . . | 40 | Taken by *Indefatigable*, 40, Capt. Graham Moore, *Medusa*, 38, Capt. Jno. Gore, (2), |
| | ” ” | *Fama** . . . . . . . . . . . | 34 | (*Lively*, 38, Capt. Graham Eden Hamond, |
| | ” ” | *Clara*, (*as *Leocadia*) | 34 | and *Amphion*, 32, Capt. Sam. Sutton |
| | ” ” | *Mercedes* . . . . . . . . . | 34 | Blown up in action with *Amphion*, 32, Capt. Sam. Sutton |
| | Nov. 25 | *Matilda* (*as *Hamadryad*) . . . . . . . | 34 | Taken by *Medusa*, 38, Capt. Jno. Gore (2), and *Donegal*, 80 |
| | ” ” | *Amfitrite* (*as *Blanche*) . . . . . . . . . | 40 | Taken by *Donegal*, 80, Capt. Sir Rich. Jno. Strachan |
| | Dec. 7 | *Sta. Gertrudis* . . . . . . | 36 | Taken by *Polyphemus*, 64, and *Lively*, 38, off C. St. Mary |
| | ” ” | *Infanta Don Carlos** | 16 | Taken by *Diamond*, 38, Capt. Thos. Elphinstone |
| | ” ” | *Diligencia* (*as *Ligaera*) . . . . . . . . . | 28 | Taken by *Diana*, 38, and *Pique*, 40, off Altavela |
| 1805 | Feb. 4 | *Fuerte de Gibraltar* | 4 | Taken by *Mercury*, 28, Capt. Duncombe Pleydell Bouverie |
| | “ & | *Orquijo** . . . . . . . . . | 18 | Taken by *Pique*, 40, Capt. Chas. Bayne Hodgson Ross |
| | Apr. 3 | *Elizabeth* . . . . . . . . . | 10 | Taken by *Bacchante*, 20, Capt. Chas. |

| Year | Date | Name (*Added to the Royal Navy) | Guns | Fate — M Medals granted in 1849, in pursuance of Gazette notice of June 1st, 1847. M Flag-Officers' and Captains' gold medals |
|---|---|---|---|---|
| | | | | Dashwood, off Havana |
| | May | *Asunción* .......... | 36 | Wrecked in the River Plate |
| | July 22 | *San Rafael\** ....... | 80 | Taken by squadron of V.-Ad. Sir Robt. Calder |
| | " " | *Firme\** ............ | 74 | " " " " |
| | Aug.13 | *Caridad Perfecta,* sch | 12 | Taken by *Mariamne,* sch., Lieut. Jas. Smith (3), at Truxillo |
| | Sept.30 | *Galgo* (pierced for) | 14 | Taken by *Port Mahon,* 18, Com. Sam. Chambers |
| | Oct. 11 | No. 4 (gunboat) .... | 1 | Taken by *Dexterous,* 14, Lieut. Robt. Tomlinson, (2), off Gibraltar |
| | " 21 | *Bahama\** .......... | 74 | Taken by the fleet of Lord Nelson, at Trafalgar |
| | " " | *San Juan Nepomuceno* (\*as *Berwick*) ... | 74 | " " " " |
| | " " | *San Ildefonso\** ..... | 74 | " " " " |
| | " " | *Santisima Trinidad* . | 130 | " " " and destroyed |
| | " " | *San Agustin* ....... | 74 | " " " and burnt |
| | " " | *Argonauta* ......... | 74 | " " " but sank |
| | " " | *Monarca* .......... | 74 | " " " but was wrecked |
| | " " | *Neptuno* .......... | 74 | " " " but was retaken |
| | " " | *Santa Ana* ........ | 112 | " " " " |
| | " 24 | *Rayo* ............. | 100 | Taken by the fleet after Trafalgar, but was wrecked |
| | Nov.29 | *San Cristovil Pano* | 7 | Taken by boats of *Serpent,* 16, Com. Jno. Waler (1), Jamaica station |
| 1806 | Jan. 7 | *Raposa\** (pierced for) | 16 | Taken by boats of *Franchise,* 36, Capt. Chas. Dashwood, off Campeche |
| | Jan. 29 | *Carmen* (pierced for) | 14 | Taken by *Magicienne,* 32, Capt. Adam. Mackenzie, Mona Passage |
| | Feb. | Two gunboats, ea. of | 2 | Taken by priv. *Felicity,* M. Novella, Medit. |
| | " 11 | No. 4 (gun-brig) .... | 5 | Taken by priv. *Envy,* off Cape de Gata |
| | Apr. 4 | *Vigilante* (\*as *Spider*) | 18 | Taken by *Renommée,* 38, Capt. Sir Thos. Livingstone, Medit. |
| | " 12 | *Argonauta* ......... | 12 | Taken by *Hydra,* 38, Capt. Geo. Mundy, coast of Spain |
| | May 2 | *Virgen del Carmen,* sch. .............. | 4 | Taken by *Niger,* 32, Capt. Jas. Hillyar, coast of Spain |
| | " 4 | *Giganta* .......... | 9 | Cut out by boats of *Renommée,* 38, and *Nautilus,* 18, under Lieut. Sir Wm. Geo. Parker |
| | June 27 | *Belem\** ............ | 4 | Taken by Commod. Sir Home Riggs Popham, at Buenos Aires |
| | " " | *Dolores* .......... | 4 | " " " " |
| | " " | Six gunboats ....... | .. | " " " " |
| | July 30 | *Arrogante* ........ | 2 | Taken by *Diadem,* 64, off Montevideo |
| | Aug.23 | *Pomona* (\*as *Cuba*) | 34 | Taken by *Arethusa,* 38, Capt. Chas. Brisbane, and *Anson,* 41, Capt. Chas. Lydiard, off Cuba. *M* |
| | " " | Twelve gunboats ... | .. | Destroyed by *Arethusa,* 38, Capt. Chas. Brisbane, and *Anson,* 44, Capt. Chas. Lydiard, off Cuba |
| | " 30 | A schooner ........ | 10 | Taken by *Pike,* 4, Lieut. Chas. Spence, Jamaica station |
| | Sept. 3 | A felucca .......... | 14 | Taken by *Supérieure,* 14, *Flying Fish,* 12, and *Pike,* 4, off Batabano |
| | " " | A schooner ........ | 10 | " " " " |

| Year | Date | Name (*Added to the Royal Navy) | Guns | Fate M Medals granted in 1849, in pursuance of *Gazette* notice of June 1st, 1847 M Flag-Officers' and Captains' gold medals |
|---|---|---|---|---|
| | ,,  ,, | Three vessels, each of | 1 | ,,        ,,        ,,        ,, |
| | Oct. 3 | No. 2 (gunboat) .... | 3 | Taken by barge of *Minerva,* 32, Capt. Geo. Ralph Collier, Arosa Bay |
| | ,,  9 | A schooner ........ | 4 | Cut out by boats of *Galatea,* 32, under Lieut. Rich. Gittins, Barcelona |
| | ,,  21 | A tartan .......... | 4 | Taken by boats of *Renommée,* 38, under Leiut. Sir Wm. Geo. Parker, Port Colon |
| | ,,  ,, | Two settees, each of | 3 | ,,        ,,        ,,        ,, |
| | ,,  22 | A settee .......... | 2 | ,,        ,, off tower of Falconara |
| | Nov. 20 | Velox ............. | 10 | Taken by *Néréide,* 36, Capt. Robt. Corbett, Atlantic |
| | ,,  ,, | Dolores .......... | 3 | Taken by boats of *Orpheus,* 32, Capt. Thos. Briggs, off Campeche |
| 1807 | Jan. 1 | A schooner ........ | .. | Capsized while chased by *Lark,* 18, Com. Robt. Nicholas |
| | ,,  27 | Postillón ......... | 3 | Taken by *Lark,* 18, Com. Robt. Nicholas, Subsequently destroyed |
| | ,,  ,, | Carmen .......... | 5 | ,,        ,,        ,, |
| | Feb. 1 | A schooner ........ | 3 | Cut out by *Lark,* 18, Com. Robt. Nicholas, Cispata Bay |
| | ,,  3 | Paula ............ | 22 | Taken in Rattones Harbour by R.-Ad. Chas. Stirling (1), and Brig.-Genl. Auchmuty |
| | ,,  ,, | Fuerte* .......... | 22 | ,,        ,,        ,,        ,, |
| | ,,  ,, | Héroe ............ | 20 | ,,        ,,        ,,        ,, |
| | ,,  ,, | Dolores .......... | 10 | ,,        ,,        ,,        ,, |
| | ,,  ,, | Paz* ............. | 10 | ,,        ,,        ,,        ,, |
| | ,,  ,, | Reina Luisa ....... | 26 | ,,        ,,        ,,        ,, |
| | ,,  ,, | A frigate ......... | 28 | Destroyed to prevent capture by |
| | ,,  ,, | Three gunboats ..... | .. | ,,        ,,        ,,        ,, |
| | Aug. 7 | Principe Eugenio ... | 16 | Taken by *Hydra,* Capt. Geo. Mundy, from under forts of Bagur, Catalonia M |
| | ,,  ,, | Bella Carolina ..... | 10 | ,,        ,,        ,,        ,, M |
| | ,,  ,, | Carmen del Rosario | 4 | |
| | ,,  14 | No. 5, No. 9 (gunboats) ......... | .. | Taken off Majorca |
| | ,,  18 | Cautela (pierced for 12) ........... | 6 | Taken by *Narcissus,* 32, Capt. Chas. Malcolm, Atlantic |
| | Dec. 11 | San Josef ......... | 12 | Taken by *Grasshopper,* 18, Com. Thos. Searle, off Cape Palos |
| 1808 | Feb. 19 | Two gunboats ...... | .. | Sunk by *Impérieuse,* 38, Capt. Lord Cochrane, near Cartagena |
| | ,,  ,, | One gunboat ....... | 4 | Taken by *Impérieuse,* 38, Capt. Lord Cochrane, near Cartagena |
| | Apr. 4 | Two gunboats ...... | .. | Destroyed by squadron of Capt. Murray Maxwell, off Cadiz |
| | ,,  23 | Two gunboats ...... | .. | Taken by *Grasshopper,* 18, Com. Thos. Searle, and *Rapid,* 14, Lieut. Hy. Baugh |
| | ,,  ,, | Two gunboats ...... | .. | Driven ashore by *Grasshopper,* 18, Com. Thomas Searle, and *Rapid,* 14, Lieut. Hy. Baugh |
| | May 7 | A mistico .......... | 4 | Taken by the *Redwing,* 18, Com. Thos. Ussher, near Trafalgar |
| | ,,  ,, | Four gunboats ..... | .. | Destroyed by the *Redwing,* 18, Com. Thos. Ussher, near Trafalgar |

## DUTCH LOSSES

| Year | Date | Name (*Added to the Royal Navy) | Guns | Fate |
|---|---|---|---|---|
| 1803 | Aug. 2 | Haasje | 6 | Taken by *Caroline,* 36, Capt. Benj. Wm. Page, off C. of Good Hope |
| | Sept. 20 | Hippomenes* | 18 | Taken by Commod. Sam. Hood (2) at surrender of Demerara |
| | ,, 26 | Serpent, sch. | .. | Taken by *Heureux,* 24, Capt. Loftus Otway Bland, at surrender of Berbice |
| 1804 | Mar. 1 | Draak, sch. | 5 | Taken by *Lily,* 18, Lieut. Wm. Lyall, off Bermuda |
| | ,, 23 | Antilope | 5 | Taken by boats of *Stork,* 18, Com. Geo. Le Geyt, W. Indies |
| | ,, 31 | Athalante | 16 | Taken in the Vlie by *Scorpion,* 18, and *Beaver,* 18. **M** |
| | May 4 | Proserpine (*as Amsterdam) | 32 | Taken by Commod. Sam. Hood (2), at surrender of Surinam |
| | ,, ,, | Pylades (*as Surinam) | 18 | ,,  ,,  ,,  ,, |
| | ,, ,, | George, sch. | .. | ,,  ,,  ,,  ,, |
| | ,, ,, | Seven gunboats | .. | ,,  ,,  ,,  ,, |
| | ,, 16 | No. 98 (a schuit) | .. | Taken by squadron of Commod. Sir Wm. Sidney Smith, N. Sea |
| | ,, ,, | Five schuits | .. | Sunk |
| 1805 | Apr. 24 | Seven schuits | .. | Taken by squadron of Capt. Robt. Honyman, off C. Gris Nez |
| | ,, 25 | Two gunboats | .. | Taken by *Archer,* 14, Lieut. Wm. Price, off C. Gris Nez |
| 1806 | Jan. 9 | Bato | 68 | Destroyed by Dutch at surrender of C. of Good Hope to Commod. Sir Home Riggs Popham |
| | May 28 | Schrikverwekker | 68 | Wrecked in the E. Indies |
| | July 6 | Belgica | 12 | Taken by *Greyhound,* 32, Capt. Chas. Elphinstone, and *Harrier,* 16, Com. Edw. Thos. Troubridge |
| | ,, 26 | Pallas (*as Celebes) | 36 | ,,  ,,  ,, |
| | Oct. 18 | Zeerob | 14 | Taken by *Caroline,* 36, Capt. Pet. Rainier (2), E. Indies |
| | | Maria Reijgersbergen (*as Java) | 36 | Taken by *Caroline,* 36, Capt. Pet. Rainier (2), off Batavia |
| | Nov. 27 | Phoenix | 36 | Taken or destroyed at Batavia by squadron of R.-Ad. Sir Edw. Pellew |
| | ,, ,, | Avonturier | 18 | ,,  ,,  ,,  ,, |
| | ,, ,, | Zeeploeg | 14 | ,,  ,,  ,,  ,, |
| | ,, ,, | William | 14 | ,,  ,,  ,,  ,, |
| | ,, ,, | Maria Wilhelmina | 14 | ,,  ,,  ,,  ,, |
| 1807 | Jan. 1 | Kenau Hasselaar (*as Halstaar) | 36 | Taken at capture of Curaçoa by squadron of Capt. Chas. Brisband    } **MM** |
| | ,, ,, | Suriname (*as Surinam) | 22 | ,,  ,,  ,,  ,, |
| | ,, ,, | Vliegende Visch | 14 | ,,  ,,  ,,  ,, |
| | ,, ,, | A schooner | .. | ,,  ,,  ,,  ,, |
| | Feb. 25 | Utrecht | 32 | Wrecked among the Orkneys |
| | Aug. 31 | A schooner | 8 | Taken by *Psyche,* 36, Lieut. Fleetwood, B. R. Pellew (actg. Capt.), at Samarang |
| | Sept. 1 | Scipio | 24 | Taken by *Psyche,* 36, Lieut. F. B. R. |

| Year | Date | Name (*Added to the Royal Navy) | Guns | Fate<br>*M* Medals granted in 1849, in pursuance of *Gazette* notice of June 1st, 1847<br>**M** Flag-Officers' and Captains' gold medals |
|---|---|---|---|---|
| | Dec. | *Revolutie* | 68 | Pellew (actg. Capt.), off Java<br>Burnt by squadron of R.-Ad. Sir Edw. Pellew, at Griessee |
| | ,, | *Pluto* | 68 | ,, ,, ,, ,, |
| | ,, | *Kortenaar* | 68 | ,, ,, ,, ,, |
| 1808 | May 19 | *Gelderland* (*as *Helder*) | 36 | Taken by *Virginie*, 38, Capt. Edw. Brace, N. Sea. *M* |
| | \ug. 6 | *Vlieg* | 6 | Taken by *Diana*, 14, Lieut. Wm. Kempthorne, off Java |
| | Oct. 8 | *Hoop*, armed transport | .. | Taken by *Lightning*, 16, Com. Bentinck Cavendish Doyle |
| 1809 | Jan. 1 | *Manly** (ex-British) | 16 | Retaken by *Onyx*, 10, Com. Chas. Gill, N. Sea. *M* |
| | May 20 | *Piet Hein*, sch. | 7 | Taken in the Vlie by boats of *Princess Caroline*, 74 |
| | June | *Calais*, g-boat | .. | Taken in the Jade |
| | July 15 | *Tuijncelaar* | 8 | Cut out by boats of *Modeste* and *Barracouta*, under Lieut. Wm. Payne, St. of Sunda |
| | Sept.11 | *Zefir* | 14 | Taken by *Diana*, 10, Lieut. Wm. Kempthorne, off Celebes. *M* |
| 1810 | Jan. | *Mandarin* | 12 | Sunk by Dutch at capture of Amboyna (*Mandarin* later weighed) |
| | ,, | *San Pan*, cutter | 10 | Sunk by Dutch at capture of Amboyna |
| | ,, | A cutter | 12 | ,, ,, ,, ,, |
| | Feb. 6 | *Rembang* | 18 | Taken by *Dover*, 38, Capt. Edw. Tucker, E. Indies |
| | ,, ,, | *Hoop* | 10 | ,, ,, ,, ,, |
| | ,, 10 | *Havik* | 10 | Taken by *Thistle*, 10, Lieut. Pet. Proctor. *M* |
| | Mar. 1 | *Margaretta* (pierced for 14) | 8 | Taken at Amblaw by boats of *Cornwallis* under Lieut. Hy. Jno. Peachey |
| | Apr. 26 | *Echo* | 8 | Taken by *Sylvia*, 10, Lieut. Aug. Vere Drury, off Batavia. *M* |
| | Aug. | *Claudius Seurlis* | 16 | Taken at the reduction of Java by R.-Ad. Hon Robt. Stopford |
| | ,, | Twelve gunboats | .. | ,, ,, ,, ,, |

## DANISH LOSSES

| Year | Date | Name (*Added to the Royal Navy) | Guns | Fate |
|---|---|---|---|---|
| 1807 | Aug. 16 | *Frederikscoarn** | 32 | Taken by *Comus*, 22, Capt. Edm. Heywood, off Marstrand. *M* |
| | Sept. 7 | *Christian VII** | 84 | Taken by British Navy (Lord Gambier) and Army at surrender of Copenhagen |
| | | *Neptunos* | 84 | ,, ,, ,, |
| | | *Waldemaar** | 84 | ,, ,, ,, |
| | | *Prindsesse Sophie Frederike* (*as *Princess Sophia*) | 74 | ,, ,, ,, |
| | | *Justitia** | 74 | ,, ,, ,, |
| | | *Arveprinds Frederik* (*as *Heir Apparent*) | 74 | ,, ,, ,, |
| | | *Kronprindsesse Marie* (*as *Kron Prinsessen*) | 74 | ,, ,, ,, |

261

| Year | Date | Name (*Added to the Royal Navy) | Guns | Fate. M Medals granted in 1849, in pursuance of *Gazette* notice of June 1st, 1847. **M** Flag-Officers' and Captains' gold medals | | |
|------|------|------|------|---|---|---|
| | | Fyen* . . . . . . . . . . . . | 74 | ,, | ,, | ,, |
| | | Odin* . . . . . . . . . . . . | 74 | ,, | ,, | ,, |
| | | Trekroner (*as *Tre Kronen*) . . . . . . . . . . | 74 | ,, | ,, | ,, |
| | | Skjold (*as *Skiold*) | 74 | ,, | ,, | ,, |
| | | Kronprinds Frederik (*as *Kron Princen*) | 74 | ,, | ,, | ,, |
| | | Danmark (*as *Dannemark*) . . . . . . . | 74 | ,, | ,, | ,, |
| | | Norge* . . . . . . . . . . . . | 74 | ,, | ,, | ,, |
| | | Prindsesse Caroline (*as *Princess Caroline*) . . . . . . . . . | 74 | ,, | ,, | ,, |
| | | Dithmarschen . . . . . . | 64 | ,, | ,, | ,, and destroyed |
| | | Mars . . . . . . . . . . . . . | 64 | ,, | ,, | ,, ,, |
| | | Seierherre (*as *Syeren*) | 64 | ,, | ,, | ,, |
| | | Perlen (*as *Pearlen*) | 38 | ,, | ,, | ,, |
| | | Harfrue (*as *Har-Fruen*) . . . . . . . . . . | 36 | ,, | ,, | ,, |
| | | Freija (*as *Freya*) . . . | 36 | ,, | ,, | ,, |
| | | Iris* . . . . . . . . . . . . | 36 | ,, | ,, | ,, |
| | | Rota* . . . . . . . . . . . . | 38 | ,, | ,, | ,, |
| | | Venus* . . . . . . . . . . . . | 36 | ,, | ,, | ,, |
| | | Nayaden (*as *Nyaden*) . . . . . . . . . . | 36 | ,, | ,, | ,, |
| | | Nympfen (*as *Nymphen*) . . . . . . . . | 36 | ,, | ,, | ,, |
| | | Triton . . . . . . . . . . . . | 28 | ,, | ,, | ,, |
| | | Frederiksteen (*as *Frederickstein*) . . . . . | 28 | ,, | ,, | ,, |
| | | Lille Belt (*Little Belt) . . . . . . . . . . . . | 24 | ,, | ,, | ,, |
| | | St. Thomas . . . . . . . . | 24 | ,, | ,, | ,, ,, |
| | | Fylla* . . . . . . . . . . . . | 24 | ,, | ,, | ,, |
| | | Elven* . . . . . . . . . . . . | 20 | ,, | ,, | ,, |
| | | Eyderen* . . . . . . . . . . | 20 | ,, | ,, | ,, |
| | | Gluckstad (*as *Gluckstadt*) . . . . . . . | 20 | ,, | ,, | ,, |
| | | Sarpen* . . . . . . . . . . . | 18 | ,, | ,, | ,, |
| | | Glommen . . . . . . . . . | 18 | ,, | ,, | ,, |
| | | Nid Elven* . . . . . . . . | 18 | ,, | ,, | ,, |
| | | Delphinen . . . . . . . . | 18 | ,, | ,, | ,, |
| | | Flyvendefiske (*as *Flewende Fisk*) . . . . . | 14 | ,, | ,, | ,, |
| | | Allart . . . . . . . . . . . . | 18 | ,, | ,, | ,, |
| | | Mercurius* . . . . . . . . | 18 | ,, | ,, | ,, |
| | | Coureer (*as *Q. Mab* and *Courier*) . . . . . . . | 18 | ,, | ,, | ,, |
| | | Ornen, sch.* . . . . . . . | 12 | ,, | ,, | ,, |
| | | Brevdrageren . . . . . . | 14 | ,, | ,, | ,, |
| | | Three gunboats, each of . . . . . . . . . . . | 2 | ,, | ,, | ,, |
| | | Twenty-two gunboats each of . . . . . . . . . . | 2 | ,, | ,, | ,, and destroyed |
| 1808 | Mar. 2 | Admiral Jawl . . . . . . | 28 | Taken by *Sappho*, 18, Com. Geo. Langford, off Flamborough Head. **M** | | |
| | ,, 23 | Prinds Christian | | Burnt by *Stately*, 64, Capt. Geo. Parker, | | |

| Year | Date | Name (*Added to the Royal Navy) | Guns | Fate<br>M Medals granted in 1849, in pursuance of *Gazette* notice of June 1st, 1847<br>**M** Flag-Officers' and Captains' gold medals |
|---|---|---|---|---|
| | | *Frederik* ........... | 74 | and *Nassau,* 64, Capt. Robt. Campbell (1). *M* |
| | May 15 | A gunboat ......... | 2 | Sunk off Bergen by *Tartar,* 32, Capt. G. E. B. Bettesworth |
| | ,,   24 | A cutter ........... | 8 | Blown up in action with *Swan,* 10, Lieut. M. R. Lucas |
| | June 16 | A gun-vessel ....... | 2 | Taken by boats of *Euryalus,* 36, and *Cruiser,* 18, under Lieut. Michael Head, Great Belt |
| | Aug. 11 | *Fama* ............. | 18 | Taken off Nyborg by boats under Capt. Jas. Macnamara (2) |
| | ,,   ,, | *Salorman\** ........ | 12 | ,,         ,,         ,, |
| | ,,   ,, | *Acertif* (pierced for 12) ........... | 8 | Taken by *Daphne,* 22, Capt. Fras. Mason, Baltic |
| | Oct.   1 | A schuyt ......... | 10 | Taken by *Cruiser,* 18, Lieut. Thos. Wells (2), off Göteborg |
| 1809 | Mar.   2 | *Aalborg* .......... | 6 | Taken by *Egeria,* 18, Com. Lewis Hole |
| | May | *Coureer* .......... | 1 | Taken by boats of *Briseis,* 10, and *Bruiser,* 14, N. Sea |
| | ,, | *Edderkop* ........ | 2 | Taken by boats of *Majestic,* 74, Baltic |
| | ,,   29 | *Snap* ............. | 3 | Taken by *Patriot,* 10, Lieut. E— W— Mansell, N. Sea |
| | May 31 | *Christianborg* ...... | 6 | Taken by *Cruiser,* 18, Com. Thos. Rich. Toker, off Bornholm |
| | | A cutter .......... | 6 | Destroyed by boats of *Melpomene,* 38, Capt. Pet. Parker (2), off Jutland |
| | ,, | *Fire Bredre* (? priv.) | 4 | Taken by *Earnest,* 14, Lieut. Rich. Templar, Wingö Sound |
| | ,, | *Makrel* ........... | 2 | ,,         ,,         ,,         ,, |
| | June 13 | *Loven* (? priv.) ..... | 2 | Taken by *Talbot,* 18, Com. Hon. Alex. Jones, N. Sea |
| | Sept. | *Dorethea Catherine* (? priv.) .......... | 6 | Taken by *Strenuous,* 14, Lieut. Jno. Nugent, off the Naze |
| | Oct. | *Christiania* ....... | 8 | Taken by *Snake,* 18, Com. Thos. Young, off Bergen |
| | Nov.   6 | *Réciprocité* (? priv.) | 4 | Taken by *Briseis,* 18, Com. Jno. Miller Adye, off Helgoland |
| 1810 | July 23 | *Balder* ........... | 8 | Taken by boats of *Belvidera* and *Nemesis,* Studland |
| | ,,   ,, | *Thor* ............. | 8 | ,,         ,,         ,,         ,, |
| | ,,   ,, | A gunboat (No. 5) | 7 | Burnt ,,         ,,         ,,         ,, |
| 1811 | Mar. 27 | Two gunboats ...... | .. | Taken by *Sheldrake,* 16, Com. Jas. Pattison Stewart |
| | May 11 | *Alban,* cutter ...... | .. | Taken by *Rifleman,* 18, Com. Jos. Pearce. Retaken |
| | July   5 | Four gun-vessels, each of ........... | 5 | Taken by *Sheldrake,* 16, Com. Jas. Pattison Stewart, and consorts |
| | Aug.   2 | Three gun-brigs .... | .. | Taken by boats under Lieut. Sam. Blyth, Jade. *M* |
| | Sept. 20 | Two gun-vessels .... | .. | Taken by boats of *Victory,* 100, under Leiut. Edw. Purcell, Wingo Sound. *M* |
| 1812 | July   6 | *Nayaden* .......... | 40 | Destroyed by a squadron on coast of Norway |
| | ,,   ,, | *Laaland* .......... | 20 | Taken by a squadron on coast of Norway, |
| | ,,   ,, | *Samsö* ............ | 18 | but abandoned |
| | ,,   ,, | *Kiel* .............. | 18 | ,,         ,,         ,, |
| | Aug.   2 | No. 114 (schooner) | 6 | Taken by boats of *Horatio,* 38, under |

The 1812 group is braced with **M** and the note *(Dictator, Podargus, Calypso, and Flamer.)*

| Year | Date | Name (*Added to the Royal Navy) | Guns | Fate<br>_M_ Medals granted in 1849, in pursuance of _Gazette_ notice of June 1st, 1847<br>_M_ Flag-Officers' and Captains' gold medals |
|---|---|---|---|---|
| | ,,    ,, | No. 97 (cutter) ..... | 4 | Lieut. Abr. Mills Hawkins<br>,,      ,,      ,, |
| | | No. 28 (lugger) ..... | .. | Taken by a boat of the _Dictator,_ 74, under Lieut. Thos Duell |
| | Dec. 12 | _Abigail_ ........... | 3 | Taken by _Hamadryad,_ 36, Capt. Edw. Chetham |
| 1813 | Mar. 21 | _Unge Troutman_ .... | 5 | Taken by two boats of _Blazer,_ 14, and _Brevdrageren,_ 14, under Lieut. Thos. Barker Devon |
| | ,,    ,, | _Liebe_ ............ | 5 | ,,      ,,      ,, |

### RUSSIAN NAVY

| Year | Date | Name (*Added to the Royal Navy) | Guns | Fate |
|---|---|---|---|---|
| 1808 | June 24 | _Apith_ ............ | 14 | Taken by _Salsette,_ 38, Capt. Walt. Bathurst, off Nargen |
| | Aug. 26 | _Sewolod_ .......... | 74 | Taken and burnt by _Centaur,_ 74, and _Implacable,_ 74. _M_ |
| 1809 | | _Speshnoi_ ......... | 44 | Detained at Plymouth, but not proceeded against |
| | | _Wilhemia_ ......... | 30 | ,,    ,,    ,,    ,, |
| | July 7 | Six gunboats (2 guns each) ............ | .. | Taken by boats of squadron, Barö Sound |
| | ,,    ,, | One gunboat ....... | 2 | Sunk    ,,    ,,    ,, |
| | ,,   25 | Gunboats No. 62, 65 and 66 (2 guns each) | .. | Taken by boats of squadron, Frederikshamn |

### TURKISH NAVY

| Year | Date | Name (*Added to the Royal Navy) | Guns | Fate |
|---|---|---|---|---|
| 1807 | Feb. 19 | A corvette ........ | 18 | Taken off Point Pesquies by fleet of V.-Ad. Sir Jno. Thos. Duckworth |
| | ,,    ,, | A gunboat ........ | 2 | ,,    ,,    ,,    ,, |
| | ,,    ,, | A ship of the line | 64 | Destroyed    ,,    ,,    ,, |
| | ,,    ,, | A frigate ......... | 40 | ,,    ,,    ,,    ,, |
| | ,,    ,, | A frigate ......... | 36 | ,,    ,,    ,,    ,, |
| | ,,    ,, | A frigate ......... | 36 | ,,    ,,    ,,    ,, |
| | ,,    ,, | Three corvettes, in all | 42 | ,,    ,,    ,,    ,, |
| | ,,    ,, | A brig ........... | 10 | ,,    ,,    ,,    ,, |
| | ,,    ,, | Two gunboats, each | 2 | ,,    ,,    ,,    ,, |
| | 27 | A gunboat ........ | 2 | Taken off Prota by fleet of V.-Ad. Sir Jno. Thos. Duckworth |
| | Mar. 1 | A brig ........... | 10 | Taken by boats of _Glatton,_ 50, and _Hirondelle,_ under Lieut. Edward Watson, at Sigri |
| | ,,   21 | A frigate ........ | 40 | Taken by squadron of Capt. Benj. Hallowell, at surrender of Alexandria |
| | ,,    ,, | A frigate ......... | 34 | ,,    ,,    ,,    ,, |
| | ,,    ,, | A corvette ........ | 16 | ,,    ,,    ,,    ,, |
| 1808 | July 6 | _Badere-i-Zaffér_ .... | 44 | Taken by _Seahorse,_ 38, Capt. Jno. Stewart, Archipelago. _M_ |

| Year | Date | Name (*Added to the Royal Navy) | Guns | Fate<br>**M** Medals granted in 1849, in pursuance of *Gazette* notice of June 1st, 1847<br>**M** Flag-Officers' and Captains' gold medals |
|---|---|---|---|---|

## UNITED STATES NAVY

| | | | | |
|---|---|---|---|---|
| 1812 | July 16 | *Nautilus* (*as *Emulous*) . . . . . . . . . | 14 | Taken by squadron of Capt. Phil. Bowes Vere Broke |
| | Aug. 22 | *James Madison* (rev. sch.) . . . . . . . . | 10 | Taken by *Barbados,* 28, Capt. Thos. Huskisson |
| | Oct. 18 | *Wasp* (*as *Peacock*) | 18 | Taken by *Poictiers,* 74, Capt. Sir Jno. Poo Beresford |
| | Nov. 22 | *Vixen* . . . . . . . . . . . . | 14 | Taken by *Southampton,* 32, but lost off the Bahamas |
| 1813 | Jan. 17 | *Viper* . . . . . . . . . . . . | 12 | Taken by *Narcissus,* 32, Capt. Jno. Rich. Lumley |
| | June 1 | *Chesapeake** . . . . . . . | 38 | Taken by *Shannon,* 38, Capt. Phil. Bowes Vere Broke. **M** |
| | July 14 | *Asp* . . . . . . . . . . . . . | 3 | Taken by boats of *Contest* and *Mohawk* |
| | '' 29 | *No.* 121 (gunboat) | 1 | Taken by boats of *Junon,* 38, under Lieut. Phil. Wesphal |
| | Aug. 14 | *Argus** . . . . . . . . . . . | 16 | Taken by *Pelican,* 18, Com. Jno. Fordyce Maples. **M** |
| 1814 | Feb. 28 | *Essex** . . . . . . . . . . . | 32 | Taken by *Phoebe,* 36, Capt. Jas. Hillyar, and *Cherub,* 20, Capt. Thos. Tudor Tucker. **M** |
| | Apr. 20 | *Frolic* . . . . . . . . . . . . | 22 | Taken by *Orpheus,* 36, Capt. Hugh Pigot (3) |
| | June 22 | *Rattlesnake* . . . . . . . . | 16 | Taken by *Leander,* 50, Capt. Sir Geo. Ralph Collier |
| | July 12 | *Siren* . . . . . . . . . . . . | 16 | Taken by *Medway,* 74, Capt. Aug. Brine |
| 1815 | Jan. 15 | *President** . . . . . . . . | 44 | Taken by *Endymion,* 40. Capt. Hy. Hope, and consorts **M** *(Endymion.)* |

British vessels bombarding the French coast near Genoa in June 1812. Note that the righthand vessel is being propelled in the dead calm by means of sweeps through the gunports (*National Maritime Museum*)

# Appendix 3:
# Glossary of British Naval Terminology in the Napoleonic Wars

| | |
|---|---|
| Aback | – the state of the sail of a ship when its forward surface is pressed upon by the wind |
| Abaft | – the rear part of a ship or the term applied to indicate something towards the rear of a ship |
| Abeam | – on a line at right angles with the ship's length |
| Aboard | – the inside of a ship; to fall aboard is to strike against another ship; to haul aboard is to bring the clew of the mainsail down to the chess-tree |
| About | – the situation of a ship immediately after she has tacked |
| Abreast | – side by side facing the same way |
| Adrift | – the state of a ship moving without control |
| Afore | – all that part of a ship which lies forward or near the stem |
| Aft, After | – behind, or near the stern of a ship |
| Aloft | – up at the masthead or in the higher yards and rigging |
| Alongside | – close to the side of a ship |
| Amidships | – the middle of a ship |
| Anchor | – 'best bower' and 'small bower'; the largest and main anchors stored furthest forward or near to the bows, the 'best' on the starboard bow, the 'small' on the larboard bow. The sheet anchor is the same size and weight as either of the bowers; the stream anchor is smaller and the kedge anchor is the smallest of all |
| An-end | – any spar or mast placed perpendicularly |
| Astern | – behind the ship |
| Athwart hawse | – the situation of a ship when she lies across the stem of an anchored ship (whether or not they touch) |
| Athwart the fore-foot | – a cannon shot fired across another ship's bows as a signal to her to stop |
| Aviso | – fast, small ships used for patrol and communication work, about the size of a brig (see Brig) |
| Ballast | – heavy material placed in a ship's hold to add to her stability |
| Bar | – a shoal running across a harbour or river mouth |
| Bare poles | – having no sail up |
| Barque | – a three-masted ship with square-rigged sails on fore- and mainmast and a lugsail on the mizzenmast |
| Barricade (Bulwark) | – the wooden parapet on each side of the open decks |
| Beam, on the | – the direction to either side of the ship at right angles to her keel line |
| Bear up or bear away | – to change the ship's course in order to make her run before the wind after she has sailed for some time into the wind or close-hauled |
| Bearing | – the point of the compass at which any object appears relative to one's own ship |
| Beating | – making progress at sea, in a zig-zag line, against the direction of the wind by tacking |
| Belay | – to make fast or tie |
| Bend the sails | – fix them to the yards |
| Bends | – the strongest planks on a ship's sides |
| Berth | – place of anchorage; cabin or apartment |
| Bight | – a collar or eye formed with a rope |

| | |
|---|---|
| Binnacle | – the frame or box which contains the compass |
| Bits | – large, upright pins of timber, with a cross piece over which the bight of the cable is put; also smaller pins to belay ropes |
| Board | – the distance covered in one tack between any two places where the ship changes her course by tacking or the line over which she runs between tack and tack |
| Boarding netting | – network strung up around a ship to prevent boarders from entering |
| Boom | – the spar holding the foot of the fore-and-aft sail |
| Bow | – the rounded part of the ship's side forward; on the bow – an arc of the horizon not exceeding 45° to either side of the direction in which the ship's bow points |
| Bowlines | – ropes made fast to the leeches or edges of the sails, to pull them forward |
| Bowsprit | – small spar extending horizontally forward of the bow and to which the jib boom is fixed |
| Box off | – a situation when a ship, having got up in the wind or been taken with the wind ahead, the head yards are braced round to counteract its effects and prevent the ship turning in an unwanted fashion |
| Box haul | – to veer round on keel for lack of space |
| Braces | – ropes attached to the ends of the yardarms to swing the yards around the mast in accordance with the direction of the wind |
| Brails | – ropes attached to the after leeches of the driver and to some of the staysails to draw them up |
| Break ground | – to weigh anchor and move off |
| Breeching | – a strong rope fixed to the cascabel of a gun and fastened to the ship's side to prevent the gun running in too far |
| Brig | – a two-masted ship with square-rigged sails on both masts and a lugsail additionally on the mizzenmast |
| Bring to (or come to) | – to bring a ship's bows up into the wind and check her speed by arranging the sails in such a manner that they counteract one another and keep her nearly stationary. A ship in this condition is said to 'lie by' or 'lie to' |
| Bring up | – to cast anchor |
| Broach to | – when a ship is forced by the elements to windward of her desired course in defiance of the helm |
| Bulkheads | – partitions in a ship |
| Bumkin | – a short boom or beam of timber projecting from each side of the bow to extend the clew or lower edge of the foresail to windward |
| Cable | – a heavy rope by which the ship is attached to her anchor or mooring |
| Cable's length | – 120 fathoms or 240 yards (219.46m) |
| Cap | – a thick block of elm with a round hole in the forepart for the topmast and a square one abaft into which the head of the lower mast fits |
| Capstan | – a machine for weighing the anchor or warping |
| Careening | – the process of beaching a ship and turning it on its side to scrape off barnacles and seaweed which slow its progress |
| Carronade | – a short-barrelled, large calibre gun designed for close-range work, invented in 1779 by the Carron Company, Scotland |
| Cat-head | – a strong projection from the forecastle on each bow, fitted with sheaves or strong pulleys to which the anchor is lifted after it has been raised to the bow by the capstan |
| Cat's paw | – a light breeze of short duration |

267

| | |
|---|---|
| Chains or channels | – strong projections from the sides of a ship below the quarterdeck and forecastle ports in large ships but above the guns in small ones to which the shrouds or rigging of each lower mast are secured by means of wooden blocks or dead eyes |
| Chess-tree | – a perpendicular piece of wood on each side of the ship near the gangway to confine the clew of the mainsail; it has a hole near the top through which the tack passes that extends the clew of the sail to windward |
| Clew garnet | – fore or main, a rope running double from nearly the centre of the fore- or mainyard to the clews or corners of the sail, where the tack and sheet are affixed; it is the principal means of clewing up or taking in the sail |
| Close-hauled | – the arrangement of a ship's sails when she tries to make progress in the closest direction possible into the wind towards that point of the compass from which the wind is blowing |
| Club-hauling | – tacking by means of an anchor |
| Coamings | – the edges of a hatchway which extend above the deck |
| Conning the ship | – the act of a senior officer (captain, master, pilot or quarter-master) giving directions to the helmsman |
| Corvette | – a flush-decked ship, smaller than a frigate with one gundeck |
| Courses | – the name by which the fore, main and driver sails are distinguished |
| Crank | – a ship with so little ballast that she cannot carry much sail for fear of being upset |
| Cutter | – a single-masted, 'fore and aft' rigged vessel of about 18 tons; sometimes called a sloop |
| Cutwater | – the knee of the head or the forward edge of the ship's prow |
| Davit | – a piece of timber used as a crane to hoist the flukes of the anchor to the top of the bow, an operation called 'fishing' the anchor |
| Driver | – a large sail suspended from the mizzen gaff; also called a spanker |
| Edge away | – when a ship changes her course by sailing 'larger', or more before the wind, than she had done previously |
| En flute | – the state of a warship having some or all of its guns removed from the gundecks and stored either in the hold or ashore |
| Espingar | – a large rowing boat |
| Fill | – to distend the sail that has been shivered (fluttering) or hove aback; bring the ship to |
| Fleet | – ten or more ships of war |
| Flotilla | – a fleet of small ships of war |
| Flukes | – the broad plates or palms of an anchor |
| Fore and aft | – along the ship from stem to stern |
| Forging ahead | – to be forced ahead by the wind |
| Founder | – to sink |
| Frigate | – warship, smaller than a ship of the line but larger than a corvette |
| Furl | – to wrap or roll a sail close to the yard, stay or mast to which it belongs and to bind it there with a gasket or cord |
| Gaff | – the top yard of the lugsail on the mizzenmast |
| Galley | – a vessel propelled by oars, usually also equipped with a lateen sail and having a single deck |
| Galliot | – a small galley |
| Gasket | -- a piece of plait to fasten sails to yards |
| Grain | – to be 'in the grain' of a ship is immediately to precede her in the same direction |

| | |
|---|---|
| Gripe | – a condition in which a ship carries too great a quantity of after sail, inclines too much to windward and requires her helm to be kept a-weather or to windward |
| Gunboat | – a small vessel carrying one or more large guns |
| Gunshot | – the maximum range of a missile – about 1¼ miles (2.2km) |
| Halyard | – a rope for raising and lowering sails |
| Haul the wind | – to steer the ship as near as possible into the wind |
| Hawse | – the situation of the cables when a ship is moored by two bower anchors; also a small distance ahead of a ship or the distance between her head and the anchors by which she rides |
| Hawse holes | – holes through which a cable passes |
| Hawser | – a small cable |
| Heave to (or bring to or lie to) | – when all the cable is taken up until the ship is directly over the anchor prior to it being weighed out of the ground; to bring a vessel to a standstill with head into wind |
| Hemmema | – a Baltic ship the size of a frigate which could also be propelled by oars |
| Jib | – a triangular staysail from the far end of the jib boom to fore-topmast-head or from bowsprit to mast-head |
| Knot | – one nautical mile; 6,080 feet (1.85km) |
| Labour | – to pitch and roll heavily |
| Larboard (or port) | – the left side of a ship when looking forward from the stern |
| Large | – a term applied to the wind when it crosses the line of a ship's course in a favourable direction |
| Lasking | – when a ship steers an oblique course towards another |
| Lateen (sail) | – a triangular sail |
| Lie to | – (see Bring to and Heave to) |
| Line, ship of the | – man of war, 1st–4th raters (see Rating), large enough to take up position in the line of battle |
| Luff | – to put the tiller towards the lee side of the ship in order to make the ship sail nearer to the direction of the wind |
| Lug (sail) | – a four-sided sail with unequal vertical dimensions on the sides |
| Mainsheet | – a large rope fixed to the lower corner or clew of the main-sail, by which, when set, it is hauled aft into its place |
| Main tack | – another large rope, fixed to the same corner of the sail as the mainsheet but designed to haul it on board, or down to the chess-tree on the forepart of the gangway; when set upon a wind, or close-hauled, the foresail is fitted with a similar rope |
| Masts | – vertical poles used to support yards and sails on a ship, from front to rear of a ship called foremast, mainmast and mizzenmast; to the basic mast further, lighter masts could be added to increase its height—in ascending order these additional masts were called topmast, topgallant mast and royal mast |
| Messenger | – an endless rope loop laid in the centre of the gundeck, moved by means of the capstan and used to weigh the anchor by having the cable bound to it by 'nippers' |
| Mizzenmast | – the aftmost mast on a ship |
| Nippers | – short lengths of rope used to tie the anchor cable to the messenger when it is being weighed; also the name given to ship's boys who tied and removed these ropes as the cable was drawn in by the messenger |
| Offing | – a long way from shore |
| Overhaul | – to examine; to overtake a ship in a chase |

| | |
|---|---|
| Ply round off | – when near the wind, to fall off from it against the helm despite all efforts to prevent it |
| Plying | – turning to windward |
| Pojama | – a two-masted Swedish vessel with square-rigged mainsail, lug mizzensail, single-decked with large calibre guns at bow and stern; also propelled by oars |
| Polacca | – a small, three-masted Mediterranean vessel with lateen sails |
| Port (or larboard) | – the left side of a ship seen from the stern looking forward |
| Port the helm | – the order to put the helm over to the larboard side of the ship |
| Quarter | – the upper part of a ship's side which lies towards the stern – between the aftmost end of the main chains and the quarter-pieces (at the sides of the stern) |
| Rake | – a broadside which sweeps another ship fore and aft; also the inclination of masts, stern, sternpost or bowsprit |
| Ratlines | – the horizontal ropes fastened across the shrouds to form ladders leading up to the mast tops |
| Rating | – rating of ships of the Royal Navy was introduced in 1626 under King Charles I; there were six rates of ships of the line, divided according to the number of battery (gun) decks and not just according to the number of guns. *1st Rate* – 3 gundecks, and guns on forecastle, quarterdeck and poop; *2nd* 3 gundecks and quarterdeck; *3rd* 2 gundecks, forecastle, quarterdeck and poop; *4th* 2 gundecks and quarterdeck; *5th* 1 full gundeck, 1 partial gundeck and quarterdeck; *6th* 1 gundeck and possibly a quarterdeck |
| Reef | – to reduce the area of sail by tying part of it to the yards with plaits |
| Ride | – to be held by the cable |
| Rigging, running | – the ropes used to alter the amount or attitude of area of sail carried by a ship |
| Rigging, standing | – the ropes used to give permanent support and staying to the masts and yards of a ship, consisting of stays and shrouds |
| Round to | – to come round towards the wind by use of the helm when going large (or before the wind) |
| Sail | – a piece of canvas attached to the masts or spars of a ship to propel it by offering resistance to the wind |
| Schebeck | – a two- or three-masted lateen-rigged Mediterranean craft also propelled by oars |
| Schooner | – a two-masted ship with square-rigged sails on the foremast and a lugsail on the mizzenmast |
| Scuttle | – a hole with a lid or closing device in the side or on the deck of a ship; also to sink a ship by making holes in the bottom |
| Sheets | – ropes attached to the lower corners of sails for changing the position of the sail |
| Ship, to | – to set or fix in a prepared place, such as oars, masts or rudders |
| Shrouds | – part of the standing rigging supporting the masts laterally and housing cross ropes forming ladders (the ratlines) |
| Slings | – heavy ropes holding the main weight of the yards (at the central point) to the mast; frequently reinforced by chains before going into action |
| Slipping the cable | – unsplicing it from the ship, a buoy having previously been attached to it to aid relocation of the anchor |
| Spar | – a stout pole slung across a ship's mast from which the sails were hung; also called a yard or yardarm |
| Splicing | – the method by which the broken ends of a rope are united |

| | |
|---|---|
| Spring, to anchor with a | – before letting go the anchor, a small cable or hawser was passed out of a stern or quarter port and taken forward outside the ship, in order to be bent or fastened to the ring of the anchor so that the ship could be brought to bear broadside in any desired direction when the anchor was lowered |
| Spring, to | – refers to a mast or yard and the action of it being split or rent by an overpress of sail, a heavy pitch, a jerk of the ship in rough seas, or by the rigging being too slack |
| Squadron | – a group of less than ten ships of war |
| Stay | – to stay a ship is to arrange sails and rudder so as to bring her head to the direction of the wind, in order to get her on to the other tack |
| Stays | – ropes running forward from the masts to give support in a fore-and-aft direction; part of the standing rigging |
| Steer | – to guide a ship by helm, wheel or other means |
| Studding sails (stunsails) | – small lugsails attached at the extremities of the mainsails by means of small yards fixed to the existing yards |
| Tack | – change of course from one board to another; alternate movements to port or starboard to take advantage of a contrary wind |
| Tant, or tan-rigged | – when a ship has very high masts; 'all-o-tanto' is when a ship, having had some of her masts struck, has rehoisted them. |
| Tartan | – a small coastal craft, lateen-rigged, propelled by oars |
| Taut | – tight |
| Thrum, a sail | – to insert into it, through small holes made by a bolt, rope needle or marlinspike, a number of short pieces of rope-yarn or spun yarn so that by drawing the sail over a hole in the ship's bottom it assists in stopping a leak |
| Tow | – to draw a ship or boat through the water by means of a rope attached to another vessel |
| Truck | – wooden disc at the top of the mast with holes and pulleys for halyards |
| Turuma | – a three-masted, square-rigged Swedish vessel of corvette size with a lug mizzensail; also propelled by oars |
| Turning to windward | – (see Beating) |
| Udema | – a Swedish three-masted, single-decked, lateen-rigged vessel with a single row of cannon along the keel line; also propelled by oars |
| Unmoor | – to reduce a ship to the state of riding by a single anchor and cable after she has been moored (or fastened) by two or more cables |
| Unship | – to remove an article from a fixed position on board a ship |
| Wake | – to be immediately behind or in track of a ship; also when a ship is hidden from view by another ship |
| Warp, to | – to change the position of a ship by hauling on warps (ropes or hawsers) attached to buoys, other ships, anchors or stable objects ashore; motion is achieved by pulling on these ropes by hand or by application of some purchase such as tackle, windlass or capstan |
| Watch | – the crew of a ship was divided into two watches (port and starboard) each of which worked and rested alternately in four-hour stretches except between 4pm and 8pm when the stretches were only of two hours' duration |
| Way | – a ship is 'under way' when she is free to answer pressures of the wind, tide or current |

| | |
|---|---|
| Wear, to (veer) | – to change a ship's course from one board to another by turning her stern to windward |
| Weather, to | – to sail to windward of a ship, headland, etc; the weather gauge implies the situation of one ship to windward of another when in action |
| Weigh | – to lift up a ship's anchor from the water |
| Work a ship | – to direct her movements by adapting the sails to the force and direction of the wind; 'to work to windward' means to beat, tack, turn to windward |
| Yard | – (see Spar) |

# Select Bibliography

Anderson, R. C. *Oared Fighting Ships* (Kings Langley 1962)

Clowes, Sir W. L. *The Royal Navy, a History* six volumes Vols 4 & 5 (London 1899)

Daly, Lt-Cdr R. W. 'Operations of the Russian Navy during the Reign of Napoleon I' (extract from *The Mariners' Mirror* – 1948)

James, W. *The Naval History of Great Britain From the Declaration of War by France in 1793 to the Accession of George IV* six volumes (London 1860)

Jurien de la Graviere, Captain J. P. E. *Sketches of the Last Naval War (The French Navy)* two volumes (1848)

Lehnert *Geschichte der Österreichischen-venetianischen Kreigsmarine während der Jahre 1797 bis 1802*

Longridge, C. N. *The Anatomy of Nelson's Ships* (1961)

Pemsel, Helmut *Atlas of Naval Warfare* (London & Melbourne 1975)

Steel, D. *Steel's Original & Correct List of the Royal Navy* published monthly 1792–1815

Stenzel, Alfred *Seekreigsgeschichte* five volumes (Hannover & Leipzig 1911)

Teuber & Ottenfeld *Die Osterreichische Armee* two volumes (Vienna)

*Zeitschrift für Heereskunde* (Deutsche Gesellschaft für Heereskunde)